SI/

Capt. G.R. Gopinath is the founder a... chairman and managing director of Deccan 360. Prior to starting Deccan 360, Capt. Gopinath had setup Air Deccan, India's first low-cost airline, in 2003.

Born in 1951, in a remote village of Karnataka's Hassan district, Capt. Gopinath studied in a Kannada-medium village school till class VII. He later studied at the prestigious National Defence Academy (NDA) and in 1971 he was commissioned as an officer in the Indian Army and served in the Bangladesh Liberation War. He resigned from the army after eight years of service and decided to chart a new path for himself. In May 2006 he was knighted with 'Chevalier de la Legion d'Honneur', the highest civilian award conferred by the French government. Among other awards and honours he has also been conferred the 'Laureate Award' in the Outstanding Global CEO category by *Aviation Week*, New York.

Praise for the Book

'*Simply Fly* is a riveting story of a serial Indian entrepreneur. It is inspiring. We can all learn practical lessons.'

—**Ram Charan**, author, teacher, business consultant,
'Economic Times Global Indian of the Year, 2008-2009'

'The Common Man has spoken. And it is as inspirational as the very best of the best, overwhelming with generosity and a keenness of spirit that is as deeply Indian as it is universal. This is a remarkable story of a remarkable life, which reminds the reader that beyond achievement lies fulfillment, beyond material goods a greater good.'

—**Kunal Basu**, University Reader in Marketing,
Said Business School at University of Oxford, and acclaimed novelist

'After reading this book, I feel it is an eminently suitable guide for entrepreneurs and could be prescribed as a textbook in all management and entrepreneurial development institutions in the country, since it is an Indian experience. It is my hope that this book will help inspire readers to take challenges as they come and explore new vistas in life.'

—**Dr A.P.J. Abdul Kalam**, former President of India

'*Simply Fly* is an inspirational account of an entrepreneur's journey. Here is a story full of "heart, gut, energy and enterprise". Lucidly written, this is a must read for those who want to understand the entrepreneurial revolution in India.'

—**Prof C.K. Prahlad**

From the reviews of *Simply Fly*

'If there was a statue of Captain Gopinath anywhere, thousands of Indians would be lining up to offer garlands of gratitude.'

—*India Today*

'*Simply Fly* should be made compulsory reading in Indian business schools, and by anyone who has ever thought of striking out on his/her own.'

—*Man's World*

'Not all autobiographies written by famous men necessarily have literary merit—but Captain Gopinath is a brilliant writer and he has a fascinating story to tell.'

—*Indian Express*

'When you flip the last page of *Simply Fly*, you come away with the image of a man who is a maverick, but who also enjoys the simple pleasures of life— until the next big idea strikes him.'

—*Deccan Herald*

'*Simply Fly* teaches some good lessons for management students and others as well.'

—*Outlook Money*

'*Simply Fly* is an entertaining and lucid account of how the retired army officer built one of India's great brands.'

—*Open*

'*Simply Fly* is a story of triumph over adversity.'

—*The Pioneer*

'*Simply Fly* is a competent piece of work—racy and engaging.'

—*Business Standard*

'Capt. Gopi's autobiography answers key questions.'

—*Mint*

'A searingly honest account of an overachiever—a warts and all book.'

—*Mail Today*

'There are plenty of takeaways from the book but the most important of them is the hope it gives to several entrepreneurs who are struggling to see their dreams come true.'

—*Business Line*

SIMPLY FLY
A Deccan Odyssey

CAPT G.R. GOPINATH

*With a Foreword by A.P.J. Abdul Kalam
and
a special story by Henry Mintzberg*

Collins

An Imprint of HarperCollins Publishers

First published in hardback in India in 2009 by Collins Business
An imprint of HarperCollins *Publishers* India
a joint venture with
The India Today Group

First published in paperback in 2011

ISBN: 978-93-5029-155-9

2 4 6 8 10 9 7 5 3 1

Capt. G.R. Gopinath asserts the moral right
to be identified as the author of this work

The views and opinions expressed in this book are the author's own
and the facts are as reported by him, and the publishers are not in
any way liable for the same.

HarperCollins *Publishers*
A-53, Sector 57, Noida 201301, India
77-85 Fulham Palace Road, London W6 8JB, United Kingdom
Hazelton Lanes, 55 Avenue Road, Suite 2900, Toronto, Ontario M5R 3L2
and 1995 Markham Road, Scarborough, Ontario M1B 5M8, Canada
25 Ryde Road, Pymble, Sydney, NSW 2073, Australia
31 View Road, Glenfield, Auckland 10, New Zealand
10 East 53rd Street, New York NY 10022, USA

Typeset in 10/13.2 Sabon
Jojy Philip New Delhi 110015

Printed and bound at
Thomson Press (India) Ltd.

To my father:
Who taught me that
I must dream but not envy.
I must lose myself in action but not in despair.

To my wife:
Who sacrificed everything and stuck with me and my 'madness'
and displayed stoic courage.

To my buddies Capt. Sam, Capt. Jayanth and Capt. Vishnu who are
really the 'unsung heroes'. Without whom the story of Deccan
would not have happened.

And most significantly all the colleagues, close to 4000 of them,
who gave their heart and might to Deccan and gave wings
to the Common Man.

CONTENTS

FOREWORD

I am happy to write the foreword for the book *Simply Fly—A Deccan Odyssey*, the autobiography of Captain G. R. Gopinath, the father of Indian low-cost airlines. Inspired by the story of Vietnamese orphan girl who takes to flying helicopters to help her country rebuild after the 1969–75 Vietnam war, Capt. Gopinath takes up flying low-cost airlines as his venture. This also demonstrated the spirit of true entrepreneurship as defined by Peter Drucker who says, 'Entrepreneur is one who creates wealth where it did not exist earlier by creating a new market and a new customer. They create something new, something different, they change and transmute values; and on a size and scale that will impact society.' The low-cost airline created by Capt. Gopinath became a pace-setter for the entire aviation business in India and brought about healthy competitiveness in the Indian aviation sector. In each and every task undertaken by Capt. Gopinath right from his army days, he has shown his indomitable spirit. The book is an inspiring story of a young man whose courage to take risks in life results in providing a new dimension to the air-transportation sector. Deccan Airlines emerged out of his vision and passion for flying high in life. Every chapter of the book gives a feeling of his determination to get things done inspite of all the challenges.

I liked particularly liked the chapter on the foundations of a new venture, where he describes about his first encounter with politics and the ordeal he had to undergo in election campaigning and ultimately losing the election by a huge margin. Though he had no money to fight an election on his own, he had the inner confidence that he could create something out of nothing. Another interesting chapter is the one which describes his preparation for the helicopter launch, where he describes his risk taking capabilities. Without any formal approval from the DGCA for flying a helicopter, he went ahead with the inauguration of the first helicopter service with the then chief minister presiding over the function and flying him in the helicopter.

After reading *Simply Fly*, I felt that this book containing invaluable entrepreneurial and leadership experience should be an eminently suitable guide for entrepreneurs and could be prescribed as a text book in all the management and entrepreneurial development institutions in the country, since it is an Indian experience. It is my hope that this book will help inspire readers to take challenges as they come and explore new vistas in life. I wish Capt. Gopinath success in all his future endeavours.

APJ Abdul Kalam

INTRODUCTION

This is not a 'How to Book'. It's everything but that. This is just a simple story of a poor village boy who after doing myriad things in life built India's largest airline. It is a very personal journey capturing my early years in a village, my days with the Indian Army, my eventual return to the village as almost a refugee in a literal and metaphorical sense, and my subsequent ventures in life.

This is my story.

I set off on a voyage of 'discovery' and pitched a tent in a remote, barren grazing land—allotted to my family as compensation for land taken away by the government for building the dam across the river Hemavathy. I lived in a tent and then a mud-thatch hut for many years, and took to taming and farming the land. For the next fifteen years my life was entwined with the land, with its ebb and flow, its seasons, its rhythms, its sighs, moods, its very breath, its gentle rains and the mystic magic of monsoons, its playful truant teasing ways. It almost echoed something I had read by my favourite poet, Tagore:

> … like the atmosphere round the earth where lights and shadows play hide-and-seek, and the wind like a shepherd boy plays upon its reeds among flocks of clouds. It never undertakes to lead anybody anywhere to any solid conclusion or any definiteness of an answer; yet it reveals endless spheres of light, … it has only the music that teases us out of thought as it fills our being.

And oh, the monsoon rains! Its fury and its fickleness, its indifference and absence which wreaked havoc on our lives, yet in the end taught me a stoic resignation without bitterness or despair. I possessed little but was suffused with ineffable, inexplicable joy.

But, in the end, we all have to live and work for a living and find our meaning and salvation through good meaningful work. My life in rural India enriched and ennobled me—farming, poverty, debt, and often when it all seemed the very end with my back to the wall, I tapped into an unknown inexhaustible well of optimism and energy to get up each time after falling, summon strength and courage and start all over again!

I was forever seeking and forever striving. I lived two lives, like a palimpsest—one imposed over the other—while life in the country intoxicated me and I roamed like a 'musk deer mad with mirth and drunk on its own perfume', I was also repeatedly brought back to earth, to try to earn a living, and feed a family and constantly, instinctively unbeknown to myself, found myself in venture after venture.

I reared cattle to sell milk, got in poultry farming, silkworm farming, then turned a motor cycle dealer, an Udupi hotel owner, a stock broker, irrigation equipment dealer, an agriculture consultant, a politician and finally an aviation entrepreneur—struggling, falling, rising, falling, rising again and taking off.

In a sense my story is the story of the new India. The India of possibilities in spite of all her problems of poverty, ignorance, corruption, bureaucratic apathy. The turmoil, and unrest, mindless violence. Crazy, insane, gross, and grotesque politics. And yet I feel enveloped in a great magnificence, a refulgence, a kind of luminous morning light which bathes my body and fills my soul.

When I was running Deccan Helicopters and later Air Deccan and my earlier ventures, I was like a man possessed. The competition did not know how to deal with me, my colleagues and my family did not know what to do with me; and even I did not know how to deal with myself. I needed to be 'exorcized! I was inconsiderate, sometimes ruthless, and brutally pushed people almost to the edge. As one colleague in an interview to the media when asked to describe me said—'He's always angry, is always very impatient ....'

I have not been an ideal leader, husband or father. While young I was arrogant, dogmatic, argumentative, delinquent, intolerant towards others' failings but tolerant of my own; selfish, short tempered and would fly into a rage and may have appeared a 'pompous fool' to elders and even my contemporaries. I was probably a tyrant also with my wife and children and made them suffer needlessly and helplessly while I was obsessed with whatever venture I had embarked upon. It troubles me still that I could have been a better boss, friend, son, husband and father. Like Somerset Maugham said in his *A Writer's Note Book*:

> I have done various things I regret, but I make an effort not to let them fret me; I say to myself that it is not I who did them, but a different I that I was then. I injured some, but since I could not repair the injuries I had done I have tried to make amends by benefitting others.

Many strangers and some friends who all have not been named here came into my life like 'angels' and helped me and saved me from many disasters and perilous circumstances. And a few of those glorious friendships in the rough and tumble of life and business, because of incompatibilities, intolerance, ego, pettiness or want of magnanimity got swept away in the rush and vortex of the tide of business and life. It is a haunting regret that I did not do enough to save those friendships.

After the success of Air Deccan, whenever I went on speaking engagements both here and abroad, one question was invariably flung at me. How could I, the son of a poor school teacher, with nothing but a paltry sum of Rs 6000 as my settlement money from the army build an airline, which is the most capital intensive business? When they heard what I did, many came and urged me to write my story.

So, here it is. If you detect 'hubris' here or arrogance, I need your indulgence. If you are young, with dreams of making a difference—but struggling, getting beaten, feeling cheated, frustrated and trying to surmount the odds, and about to throw in your towel, don't emulate everything that is here—try to beat your own path, your own trail. If you are older and wiser, have been there and done that, and seen it all, just read it for the lark and enjoy the story.

1

Heaven lies about us in our infancy!
—William Wordsworth

Growing up by the River

Snuggled somewhere deep within the Western Ghats, beyond Mudigere, lies the source of a pretty river called Hemavathy. This is the south-western corner of Karnataka. Meandering through the lower ranges, the river flows past hundreds of small hamlets before joining the Kaveri as its principal tributary. Gorur, of which I have vivid and pleasant childhood memories of my parents and my home, is one such village situated along the banks of the Hemavathy. It is not surprising that people in these parts consider the river sacred, for Hemavathy is Gorur's lifeline, watering its fields and sustaining the settlements along its banks. Looking back with fondness, there is a realization that quaint old Gorur, attractive in its own way, holds a special place in my heart.

A few words may not be appropriate to describe the lush countryside and the alluring landscape of Gorur and its neighbourhood, where I spent my early years. Located 23 km to the south of Hassan, the district headquarters, the settlement has an abundance of coconut groves, areca plantations, betel-leaf creepers, paddy fields, and mango orchards. The village, like many others in this region, has been a beneficiary of the water management technology evolved over centuries by local chieftains and the maharajas of Mysore, who built check-dams further upstream to facilitate irrigation of thousands of acres of farmland. These stonework barriers were constructed employing simple, eco-friendly technology that caused no deforestation or displacement of local residents, allowing the river to flow perennially, supporting human, animal, and plant life all along its course.

Gorur lies on the fringes of Malnad, which means the 'land of hills' and also the 'land of rains' in Kannada. It refers specifically to the southern ranges of the Western Ghats of Karnataka and their foothills. Malnad features some well-known towns such as Mudigere, Chikmaglur, Shringeri, Madikeri, and Tirthahalli. The hillside is awash with coffee estates and dense pristine rainforests.

Like most other Indian villages, Gorur had its clearly defined social hierarchy. The village was a composite one, with separate quarters marked out for Brahmins, fishermen, shopkeepers, carpenters and other tradesmen. There was tacit power play between the various communities and castes. When there were disputes or important settlements, the village gowda or patel had the final say, and the Brahmins were still generally considered superior to all the other residents though they wielded no real power. Exchange of articles and services between communities was not exactly taboo. However, the Dalit colony was set apart from the rest of the village, outside the main boundary, an unfortunate tradition inherited from the past.

My father, like his father before him, was a school teacher and a farmer by profession. He taught in a neighbouring village, and though poorly paid he continued in this profession, for him a labour of love. There were many like my father, teachers who were paid a pittance—worked hard, and lived frugally. Father remained a teacher for forty years, each day waking up at daybreak, walking miles to his school and walking back at the end of the day to reach home at sundown.

I was born not in Gorur but at my mother's parental home in Melkote, an ancient temple town near Mysore. It is famous as a centre for the followers of scholar—saint Ramanuja.

My maternal grandfather was a Sanskrit scholar who also performed priestly duties. My mother often visited her native town and I accompanied her. Indeed, for us children, vacation was when our mothers went visiting their native villages. I roamed the beautiful countryside with my grandfather and my cousins. We explored water tanks, temple ruins, and the rugged hillsides, where from a distance, were visible layers upon layers of brownish-yellow rocks, balanced one on top of another like loaves of bread. My grandfather was a member of a group of Sanskrit scholars, and I was privy to what they discussed and debated. I saw and touched palm leaf manuscripts secured in folios; I watched as scholars sat at a low desk and wrote on palm leaves using special writing equipment.

In Gorur, distinctions of caste and profession were once considered crucial to sustain the social hierarchy. As a Brahmin boy, I was aware of an unwritten code of conduct, which compelled artisans and Dalits to live at a distance from us in separate colonies. The Brahmins were not particularly well-off, but assumed they were different and maintained the social distinction.

As a boy, I was also conscious of the difference in status between the exploiters and the exploited. This was largely because my father was not a typical Brahmin and spoke disapprovingly of the system that encouraged and justified the 'superiority' of many upper castes and their exploitation of the artisan class and the Dalits.

My father did not enrol me in school till the fifth standard. He believed, like Gandhi, Tagore, and our own Shivaram Karanth that schools are systems of regimentation and that children are better off at open-air schools, free from the burden of examinations. He said, quoting Tagore, 'Real education is in life's experiences; school is like a jail,' and told me, 'Look, Gopi, I'll teach you at home!'

Each morning my father woke me up at dawn and took me for a dip in the river Hemavathy. This became an unchanging ritual. Even in pouring rain we went to the river. After the swim we returned home for breakfast. He then took me to the coconut and areca-nut plantations that stood like islands in an ocean of paddy-fields. Being different, he never performed sandhya vandana, the tribute to the Sun god, but the act of bathing in the river at daybreak was for him a gesture of reverence.

As we walked to the small family areca garden, father showed me the Dalit men and women in the paddy-fields, soaking wet to the bone, transplanting saplings. He would draw examples from their lives for my benefit. 'You are a Brahmin,' he would say. 'You are supposed to be sophisticated and cultured in the arts. But look at these people. Their women sing while working; these poor farmers sing because there is joy in their hearts.'

These people came to work with two bags. Into one bag they threw tiny crabs that hopped around in the slush and into the other they stuffed wild greens growing all around. Father identified the local greens for me. He explained how the 'lowly' greens were in fact full of nutrition. Most people at the time were vegetarian. It was considered demeaning to eat crabs. Even hardcore non-vegetarians did not eat crab or beef. Dalits ate both and belonged to the lowest rung of the social hierarchy. Only many years later, while travelling in Europe did I learn that crabs are considered among the most expensive seafood delicacies. In India, in urban areas, mushrooms were until recently available only at five star hotels. In the countryside the Indian farmer has picked and eaten mushrooms free for centuries, when weeding and planting the fields. My father would often point to the Dalits and say, 'Take a look! Their bodies are like steel.'

He often read to me the books he most loved. These influenced me greatly in those formative years, and even later in my life. He taught me arithmetic and the sciences for an hour or so every morning after our swim, and also on most evenings. He also read out from the classics, which included the writings of Gandhi, Tagore, Socrates through Plato's works, Emerson, and Oliver Goldsmith.

My mother was a devout lady, generous, hospitable, and a culinary expert who spent a lot of time in the kitchen. Many still recall her warm hospitality during their stay with our family. Once in the US, after I had delivered a speech, someone from the audience came up to me and said, 'Capt. Gopi, I was part of a World Bank team that visited Gorur twenty years ago. I remember your mother. We had been invited to your home and your mother served us the most delicious meal.' In later life, I met quite a number of people who had vivid memories of my mother, long after she had passed away. People close to the family would often say to me, 'You know, Gopi, your mother's grace is guarding you!'

In sharp contrast to my mother's generosity, my father tended to be frugal. My mother went out of her way to shower hospitality while my father refused to entertain freeloaders and was austere in his dealings. Mother was religious while father was an agnostic of sorts and had no faith in rituals. He, however, never interfered with my mother's ways. He was more of a mystic, and when my mother went to the temple, he took me on his lap and read out passages from Gandhi's and Tagore's writings. He usually read out a couple of his favourite Tagore poems:

This is my prayer to thee, my lord—strike, strike at the root of penury in my heart.
Give me the strength lightly to bear my joys and sorrows.
Give me the strength to make my love fruitful in service.
Give me the strength never to disown the poor or bend my knees before insolent might.
Give me the strength to raise my mind high above daily trifles.
And give me the strength to surrender my strength to thy will with love.

I have always admired my parents' quiet strength. For forty years of his life as a schoolteacher, he rose morning at six, went to the river, gave me lessons, and then taught a large number of restless children, returned in the evening and again sat with me for the last lesson of the day before dinner. He never showed any sign of weariness, depression, or frustration. He did not know what boredom was and was able to remain happy and relaxed without external forms of 'entertainment'. He reminded me of the great Bertrand Russel.

Perhaps some element of boredom is a necessary ingredient in life. Wars, pogroms and persecutions have all been part of the flight from boredom. Even quarrels with neighbours have been found better than nothing. A life too full of excitement is an exhausting life, in which continually stronger stimuli are needed to give the thrill that has come to be thought of as an essential part of pleasure and too much excitement not only undermines the health, but dulls the palate for every kind of pleasure, substituting titillations for profound organic satisfactions, cleverness for wisdom, and jagged surprises for beauty. A certain power of enduring boredom is therefore essential to a happy life, and is one of the things that ought to be taught to the young. No great achievement is possible without persistent work ... that certain good things are not possible except where there is a certain degree of monotony.

I was the second of eight children. We had little money in those days but my father's only concern was to give his children the best education possible and teach them good values. Though he never showed it, he was often hard-pressed for money, but he dealt with life with great cheer. And though we were always stretched, life was full of sunshine as there was no envy. As Albert Camus said, 'Poverty, first of all was never a misfortune for me: it was radiant with sunlight' .... I owe it to my family, first of all, who lacked everything and who envied practically nothing.

This was how I learnt to cope with life, thanks to my parents. The lesson came in handy in later life, after I had resigned from the army, when I had no steady source of income for a long time and there were times when I went penniless. I, however, sought sustenance from my wealth of spirits and from the little joys offered by my farm.

My father drew a small monthly salary of Rs 40 in 1951, the year I was born. With that salary and the little income he made from his farm, father met his household expenses, which included the meals of a few children of poorer relatives or close acquaintances who lived with us. He put into practice an age-old tradition that worked in many parts of Karnataka. Poor Brahmins were keen to give their children a good education but could not afford the expense. They sent their children to Gorur, the only village in the neighbourhood with a school. As there were no hostels in those days, the children stayed alternately with various relatives to ease the pressure on a single household, following a cyclical pattern of hospitality called 'vaara' or 'vaaranna'. My father had decided to educate and bring up as many children of poor relatives as he could afford. We often, therefore, had more than five or six children staying with us and sleeping in the attic. The vaara system catered to boys only, as young girls could not be sent out to live with strangers and in consequence were denied access to basic education. My mother was unselectively generous and hospitable with the vaara boys, and therefore our house was forever bustling with activity.

Father did not appreciate freeloaders but he was even more generous than my mother in times of need, and offered shelter, food and education to anybody who was in genuine need. I used to believe that one needed to be rich to be able to afford charity. Over the years I realized that my father was far from being rich; indeed was forever short of money. I however recognized my father's wisdom, learning that one can share in poverty too, and this is a lesson that has remained with me.

My Schooldays Begin

My father got me admitted to school quite late and I straightaway joined the fifth standard. There was no uniform and I went barefoot. My first recollection of school is that it was large and I often sat on the floor. It was the only middle-school in the area, teaching children from twenty villages in the cluster. Though I was now formally in school my father continued to teach me.

In the 1950s there was one middle-school for about forty villages and one primary school for twenty villages. Children had to walk miles to reach school. I remember how many of my schoolmates came to class soaked to the skin. They could not afford an umbrella and instead wore a goraga, a triangular reed raincoat. They also wore a peak cap made from areca-nut palm leaf to protect their heads from the rain.

Apart from the Hemavathy, there was a river called Yagachi, upstream. The two rivers flowed into each other at the sangam, the confluence of rivers. I have vivid images of the confluence, of the large sand dunes that formed along the banks when the rivers were not in flood, and of how the waters swirled around the village temple and flowed right into the first house in the village when heavy rains caused floods. Children who came from far away crossed the river in a ferry, fashioned from buffalo hide. When the river was swollen, the ferry took a long time to cross and children arrived at closing time.

The medium of instruction in school was Kannada and we were taught maths, science, and social studies. English was just another subject. School life was also great fun. We went on picnics and learnt how to cook and light a campfire, stole fruits from orchards, and also filled our pockets with wild varieties from the fields. Sometimes, after school hours, I played marbles and chinni kolu (a simple and popular village game played with two sticks, called gilli-danda in Hindi) with other boys. I, however, have my own special reasons for remembering school and particularly our headmaster, who was a very enterprising individual.

As a young village boy, I had no clue about my future career. I nurtured a desire to move out and explore the world outside: 'Beyond the temple, beyond the woods, beyond the borders let us go to new lands yonder!', in the words of Kannada poet Pu Thi Narasimhachar. One day, our headmaster spoke to us about a competitive admission exam for a novel military training school called Sainik School and asked whether anyone was interested in taking the test. Without a thought I raised my hand.

I began to dream of stepping out into the unknown. Meanwhile, our headmaster had filled in my application and sent it. I would have to travel to Hassan on a particular Sunday and take the written test. I did not know what 'military' meant, associating the word with a kind of restaurant called Military Hotel, which served non-vegetarian food I assumed 'Military' must mean non-vegetarian food. In rural Karnataka, a vegetarian would never visit a hotel. Travellers ate at the homes of relatives along their way and most temples offered a meal, often portions of the food offered to the deity. My father explained the actual meaning and helped me form a basic idea of the army.

I was very excited and so was the entire village, as if taking the exam was itself a great event. My father was away on invigilation duty when I received the notice. I approached my father's elder brother, told him I had to go to Hassan, and borrowed twenty rupees from him. Packing a small gunny-bag with a change of clothes, I walked to the bus stop on the day before the examination, to catch the 6 a.m. bus to Hassan. It was well past dusk when I got off at Hassan and walked to my uncle's house.

I had many uncles. The one who lived in Hassan was a Sanskrit and Kannada pundit and particularly religious. The family woke early in the morning to chant prayers and shlokas. Post prayers, I walked to the government school to take the military exam. There were about twenty students taking the examination from Hassan district. I opened the question paper and after a glance went totally blank. The questions were in English. With my little English, I could not answer a single question and whiled away the time doodling on the answer sheet. Later, I frankly told my headmaster that I had not understood a word because the question paper was set in English.

The headmaster, B.S. Nanjundiah, was a very imposing figure. He wrote strongly to the ministry of defence in Delhi from our remote village in Karnataka, challenging the examination and suggesting that the exam, as it was an all-India one, be conducted in regional languages. He said that conducting this examination in English was shameful because by doing so the authorities were equating capability and intelligence with knowledge of English. My headmaster's action was largely intuitive but the lesson I learnt at the time was an important one. One has to be proactive and steer the course to make things happen.

After a few weeks had passed, the headmaster called for me and announced that the defence ministry had decided to conduct fresh examinations in Kannada. He asked me whether I was still interested. I gave it another try and realized that enterprise pays. This was 1962 and I was in the seventh standard. I answered the exam in Kannada and knew I had done well. My mother was anxious. She did not want me to take the exam, much less pass it. People provoked her. 'What's wrong with you, Jayalakshmi?' they asked. 'Your son is only eleven and he's going off to join the military?' Mother prayed fervently night and day for God's intervention. She would have been delighted if I had failed the exam.

My father waited to meet me after the exam and took me to an Udupi hotel, the south Indian fast food restaurants that serve clean, tasty, and hot vegetarian food in a no-frills atmosphere. About a month later, the headmaster told me that I had been selected. There was much rejoicing and the headmaster made a formal announcement in school. I was looked upon as a hero because I was the only student to get selected from Hassan. There were speeches at the send-off. Everybody congratulated my father and I was an instant celebrity.

A day after the examination I received an interview call. I was told that it would be held at the district deputy commissioner's office in Hassan and that Lt. Col. R.N. Mullick would interview me. Someone had advised me to salute the officer. On the day of the interview, I took special care with my clothes and hair, which was well combed and glistened with coconut oil. I wore a new pair of shorts, specially tailored for the occasion, and a pair of earrings that my mother forced me to wear. The *haute* icing on my *couture* were my bare feet that stuck out in all their gaunt nakedness. The colonel was imposing in stature—tall, fair, and severe. I clacked my bare feet together, raised my hand in an awkward salute, and said, 'Good Morning Sir' in a booming tone. If he was amused, the colonel did not show it. He asked me a few questions and let me go.

Soon after the interview I received the offer letter for admission to Sainik School. Appended was a long list of things a boarder needed to carry. It included items like shoes, socks, shoe polish, shoe brush, toothbrush, toothpaste, necktie, nail clipper, and soap. I had not seen a single one of these things before. My mother gave us Nanjangud Ayurvedic Tooth Powder for brushing our teeth, while farmers and other villagers chewed on a neem twig. My mother wrote to her brother who lived and worked in Mysore, asking if he could help me with the shopping. My uncle readily agreed, accompanied me to the shops in Mysore, and bought me all the items listed. I was excited about my new possessions and could barely wait for the journey to my new school.

Jayachamarajendra Wodeyar, the maharaja of Mysore, was at the time the governor of Karnataka. He had offered land and one of his palaces in Mysore to establish the school but this had been refused. The education minister, S.R. Kanthi was from Bijapur, a backward district town, and he wanted the school to be set up there.

Bijapur was a full twenty-four-hour train journey from my village. The entire village gathered to see me off. When I saw my mother crying, I felt a lump rise in my throat. She was very upset and blamed my father for sending me away. My father too looked dangerously close to tears but he managed to maintain a tough exterior. I was to catch the train to Bijapur from Hassan and the entire experience was incredible, as it would be the first time I saw a train! I was, however, already homesick!

At Hassan, a horse-drawn tonga took us to the railway station to catch the train at 11 p.m. The tonga ride remains fresh in my memory. I can almost hear the rhythmic clip-clop-clip-clop of the horse's hooves and the clang of wheels on the rough surface of the road. Wordsworth aptly describes the emotion I experienced on seeing the steam-engine-drawn, train chugging in, as I waited with my father on the platform: 'My heart leaps up when I behold a rainbow in the sky/ So was it when I was a child / So is it now that I am a man'. I still feel the same emotion whenever I see a train about to depart for some distant destination.

The other recollection I have of that journey is of my father reading out passages from essays by Gandhi, Nehru, Tilak and Gokhale. The authors discussed their lives, ideals, and the struggles they negotiated to achieve their goals. Father also read to me excerpts from western authors like Thoreau, Goldsmith and Emerson, and poems by Tennyson and Wordsworth. I remember my journey that day as a medley of images, the principal one is of my father reading to me the most interesting and inspiring works of great leaders and philosophers.

It was mid-September when I enrolled as a student in Sainik School, Bijapur. The school did not have a building of its own and was housed in a temporary civil structure rented from a local college called Vijaya College. There were only eight of us in my class. I was twelve years old at the time and was admitted in the eighth standard. A huge campus was on the anvil but what we actually had were makeshift premises that included tents, where we also had our classes. I readily took to life in a tent; the tent became a recurring motif in my later life and I kept going back to tents.

I was in a trauma of sorts during my first days in school. The boys came from two different kinds of background. One group came with a private school or Christian missionary-run convent background, and they did not mix with boys like me who came from a village school. The boys from rural areas formed a majority. They did not know a word of English and lacked city polish. I remember there was an uneasy undercurrent of bullying and of tension between the city slickers and the village bumpkins.

A positive factor in our lives was the presence of excellent teachers who were also extremely sensitive. They sensed the divide and gently ironed out the differences to help us settle down. The faculty represented a cross-section of independent India. The principal and the headmaster were Sikhs while the registrar was a Bengali. There were teachers from Haryana, Gujarat, Andhra Pradesh, Tamil Nadu, Uttar Pradesh, and Karnataka. Among the students there were Sikhs, Hindus, Christians, Muslims and at least one Jain boy. A majority of the students were from Karnataka.

K.D. Singh, the principal, was an inspiring figure, a strict disciplinarian, and commanded the respect of students and teachers alike. He was a wing commander in the Education Corps of the Indian Air Force.

I was extremely homesick, full of self-pity, and cried into my pillow each night. My father wrote to me very frequently. In his letters he asked me to be courageous, to take hold of my life and make something of it. I bemoaned my fate each night and regretted the sudden end to my carefree life in the village. I missed the freedom of running wild, the frequent raids on neighbours' jamun orchards, and detested my new life with all my heart. I longed to break free and run away.

I deeply resented the regimented life in school. A bugle, sharp at 5 a.m., was our wake up call. I felt like a tethered creature. Once out of bed, we ran rounds of the field, did Physical Training (PT), and one hour of prep from 7–8 a.m. We scrambled back for a wash, changed our clothes, and headed to the tent where breakfast was served. We rushed to class after this and continued with classes, till lunch was served at 1p.m. A short break followed, after which we were herded into another hour of prep. Tea and games followed; dinner was served at 8 p.m. A lull followed dinner, when I acutely felt the distance from my home and village. Lights were switched off at 9 p.m.

I cried a lot, but through my tears I would sense a steely determination take shape within me. I would not return empty-handed, I told myself. My friends in Gorur looked upon me as a hero. Running away from school would amount to letting them down, and it would also be a great disappointment for my father.

The teachers were very friendly. Among them, John Mathias in particular took me under his wing. He groomed us in city manners and social etiquette.

He did not spare us if we were badly turned out. 'Stand straight, with your chest out,' he would command. He showed us how to sit at a table, taught each of us table manners and the use of knives and forks at the dining table without inconveniencing the persons seated beside us with sideways thrusts of the elbows. He taught us to say grace before a meal. I was aware only of the Vedic graces before a formal community meal back in my village.

John Mathias also taught me how to dress formally, the norms of social etiquette as well as using a public utility service, like a western-style toilet. His personal tastes were impeccable and he set a great example for us. He demonstrated how one polished a shoe and put a gloss on it. This whole exercise in grooming continued throughout our schooldays, training us to become responsible citizens. I also remember G.D. Kale, our Hindi and Sanskrit teacher who also supervised our NCC drills and occasionally PT. Kale was a strict taskmaster and he wanted us to develop a robustness of character.

One day, most unexpectedly, Mr Mathias recommended my name for house captain. It was a great day. Still raw and rustic, I felt on top of the world. I was being given the opportunity to prove myself. I loved the outdoors and sports, though I did not excel in any. Mr Mathias inspired me to pursue sports and extra-curricular activities. I led an active life under his guidance and my confidence touched new heights.

Like all the other young boys, I was curious about life and keen for some adventure. However, the fear of rustication and being sent home always stopped me from engaging in misadventure. School was very strict about personal conduct and language etiquette. Our principal K.D. Singh reacted sharply to the use of the word 'bloody', warning us of dire consequences if he ever heard anyone using it. On another occasion someone stole something from the tuckshop. His identity was uncovered and he was given a stern warning. Wing Commander Singh came down heavily on the guilty boy and demoted him from a senior school position he was then holding. These were major scandals in school and I remember how terrified I was. I did rather well in extra-curricular activities like theatre. The special parade was another. I was fortunate to attract the attention of the school authorities and was selected for the Republic Day parade in New Delhi. I looked upon that as an important landmark during my Sainik School days.

Trekking was another activity close to my heart. I was sent to a cadets' camp in Bhubaneshwar and to the Himalayan Mountaineering Institute (HMI) in Darjeeling for an adventure course. School opened my eyes to an entirely new world of adventures. These trips revealed the different faces of India and the diversity of its culture. On my way to the camps, the train passed through many states of India where I observed different ways of life hitherto totally unknown to me in my insulated life as a village boy.

Four years flew by in study, sports, theatre, and camps. I was ready for the next phase in my life. By the time I was fourteen, having spent just two years at school, I was cast into a new mould but was totally unaware of it. One of the curricular objectives of Sainik Schools is to prepare boys to join the National Defence Academy (NDA) in Khadakvasla, Pune. One becomes eligible to join the NDA only after passing a tough exam and facing an interview. There is also a test of the physical, mental and emotional strength of the candidates. The Union Public Service Commission (UPSC) conducts these exams and thousands of candidates appear for it every year. In those days there was a good deal of glamour and prestige attached to the army, and it was also considered a great career option, the armed forces a genuine alternative to the IAS and the IPS. The NDA, the principle training ground for the armed forces had—and continues to have a world famous training curriculum and has created within its expansive confines an awe-inspiring world of its own. Other boys in my school too were preparing to compete for the NDA. We were painfully aware that not being selected would bring ignominy; sound a death knell for our careers. It did at the time seem a question of life and death.

Life in the village was still something I cherished, but didn't want to return without having accomplished my task. I did not wish to become a doctor or an engineer, so it seemed quite natural for me to think of the army as my immediate goal. I was obsessed with the idea and studied hard.

I was visiting the home of one of my uncles when the NDA entrance exam results were announced. I walked 5 km to the next village to make a telephone call from the office of the electricity board. After a long wait I learnt that I had cleared the exam. Excited, I returned to my village the next day and quickly prepared to join the NDA.

My NDA Days

The NDA was the second most critical stage in my life after Sainik School, but this time I was much better prepared. The NDA campus is one of the most spectacular military school campuses in the world. The sprawling 7000 acres of lush green had horse-riding tracks, several swimming pools, squash courts, a gliding course, yoga club, nature club, photography club, gyms, sailing school, shooting ranges, and several kinds of intricate obstacle courses to test the mental and physical agility of cadets. At the end of the rigorous three-year academic course at the NDA, in order to be commissioned as an officer in the Indian Army, one needs to spend a year at the Indian Military Academy (IMA) in Dehradun. The navy and the air force have other centres of specialized training. I chose the army and looked forward to the next four years before I became an officer.

The NDA offered the most advanced, exemplary, and well-rounded training. It offered the best in academics, among the best libraries, and a fine movie hall where they screened the latest and best selection of international films every week. There were of course practises at the NDA that normal civil decorum would not approve of. The campus idiom, for example, was freely peppered with four-letter words. Gradually, I grew accustomed to it and began using it myself!

The practise of ragging at the NDA too would not be looked upon positively by normal civilian society. In plain terms, it was excruciatingly painful. I was as much a victim of ragging as were the other cadets. Once I wore a shirt with one button missing. That was cause enough for a senior cadet to leap up and rip the remaining buttons off my shirt. I obviously could not go to class button-less, so I rushed back to my room and put on a new shirt, ensuring it had all its buttons intact. As I headed for class I realized that the shirt I was wearing had not been ironed. Nobody attends class in NDA in a wrinkled shirt. I was, therefore, late for class and was punished a second time. My tormentor had more in store for me. He asked me to take out a handkerchief and stitch buttons on it so that there was not a single spot left. I counted 500 buttons that I bought and stitched on to a handkerchief. My persecutor got time for some more creativity when I was busy embroidering the hanky with buttons. He asked me to appear outside his cabin at 11 p.m. wearing my swimming trunks. I had to obey him. He emerged and ordered me to knock every hour on his door till five in the morning—the hour when cadets get ready for the day's curricular activity. The punishment that day, therefore, spilled over to the next. I passed the night sleepless, standing out in the cold in my swimming trunks. My oppressor had a change of heart by five in the morning. He asked me simply to 'disperse'. I ran back to my room, shaved, got ready for class, and carried on. That was just another day!

During those three years, cadets went through a series of physical and mental rigours that steeled them to face extreme conditions in the future as servicemen. The day I was forced to stitch 500 buttons on the handkerchief, I knew I would never again wear a shirt that had a button missing.

Our early mornings were packed with activity. There was physical training or horse riding, or weapons training, or games, or swimming. We barely had twenty minutes to gulp down breakfast. We rushed back to our rooms, changed and readied ourselves for classes. Lunch was at 2 p.m. That done, we headed out to the grounds for more sports. We had just half an hour after sports to bathe. Sharp at seven the bugle sounded. By then you had to be ready, dressed formally for dinner, and seated at the desk in your room. The rooms were on either side of a long corridor. Windows opened out into the corridor and the tables faced the windows. And on each table was kept a copy of the poem *If* by Rudyard Kipling.

You had your books spread out on the table. The reading lamp would be on, shade turned inward. The windows and doors were opened ajar. Between seven and eight in the evening, you could study or dream or stare vacantly into space. Whatever that might be, there at the table you must sit in silent and obedient observance of NDA rules. One of the divisional officers would be walking the corridor to check on us. By eight that evening we would receive some punishment. The probability was high and the hit rate considerable. It would be a long action-packed day and the chance of a goof-up was immense. Any trifling mess-up, from a sloppy salute to a gaffe at the dinner table, was sufficient for another round of punishment. Some seniors made us roll down the stairs on our backs before the day was over. Our backs ached all night.

The first term was the most challenging. It was an ordeal to stay awake in class, but the vast curriculum had to be mastered. We had to make superhuman effort not to fail. One or two cadets did not make it. Some gave up and went home and some got injured during training or ragging. Sometimes ragging events became downright degrading. On those occasions first-term students were made to eat socks or do vulgar things like masturbate in public. Some senior guys were demented and took pleasure in harming juniors. The authorities handed out severe punishment to the tormentors and even expelled some of them. I was fortunate not to suffer such humiliation.

There was another aspect to life at the NDA. There were frequent night raids by the cadets on the orchards just outside the campus. As these raids entailed a closely coordinated effort, they helped generate bonding and camaraderie. I took part in one of these expeditions for the thrill it provided. The raids formed part of a strict honour code among cadets. A cadet who passed out from the NDA without having ever taken part in a raid was not considered by his peers to have passed with 'honours'.

Farmers lay in wait to protect their farmland and capture cadets plundering their orchards. They caught anybody they could lay their hands on and took them to the police station. A cadet who got caught on two or more occasions faced the prospect of expulsion from the academy. Nothing however deterred the boys. They gathered in bands of twenty-five or thirty and planned the raid. The sweet-lime orchards adjoining the campus were the most frequently raided. The orchards were 7–8 kms away so one had to run cross-country to the 'battleground' in the middle of the night, in battle fatigues and military boots. It was besides far from a mock military attack, where you knew that the whole thing was a fake drill and your 'enemies' were your own batchmates.

On my first expedition, all the raiders returned unscathed in the first round, but the farmers had been alerted and were ready for us. They nabbed a few cadets the second time and tied them up. There was a scuffle and a brief but intense battle. A couple of raiders were beaten up along with some farmers who were also roughed up. The farmers took their captives to the police station. I was fortunate to return safely from all the raids in which I participated. Adventure lurked in every corner. On another occasion, the cadets plotted a campaign against the canteen contractor, who they believed was exploiting them. One night a senior decided to ransack the canteen. The raiding party turned everything upside down, emptied the contents of soft drink bottles, and created havoc. They took away sweetmeats and distributed them in my squadron!

The three years at the NDA were filled with fun and frolic, and I learnt a great deal during my stay. I was, however, beginning to hate the regimentation and my mind rebelled against army straightjacketing. I found solace in literature; in the writings of great thinkers and in poetry. I spent hours in the library reading; I had also begun to entertain a secret disdain for conventional education. However, I passed out of the NDA without losing a term and went on to pursue my military training at the IMA in Dehradun.

On graduating from the IMA, I was asked to choose one of the three wings of the army: the infantry, the artillery, or the engineering corps. I was certain I didn't want to be in the engineering corps; infantry beckoned with the promise of adventure in the mountains; but the guns and the armoury proved the most attractive and I joined the artillery as a twenty-year old officer. It was the realization of a dream that had taken shape in Gorur many years earlier.

The passing out parade at the IMA is a great ceremonial event; an impressive parade of military pomp and regalia. When I took part in the ceremony, I became aware of the one single emotion that had become deeply ingrained in all of us, drilled into us from the very first day at the NDA. That piece of motivation has stayed with me even after I left the army. It has given me abiding strength and support. This was the credo emblazoned on the main auditorium:

> The safety, honour and welfare of your country comes first, always, and every time
> The safety, honour and welfare of the men you command comes next always and every time
> Your own safety, honour, and welfare come last, always and every time.

The second lesson in leadership came from Capt. J.S. Verma of the armoured corps, who was my instructor and divisional officer. He later retired as a general. Capt. Verma told me:

> In everything that you do, if you want to earn the respect of your men, you have to be professionally better than them. You have to work harder than them. You have to stretch yourself more than them. You cannot spare yourself. Do not spare your men but more importantly do not spare yourself. If you ask them to work six hours you must work eight hours. If you ask them to walk ten miles you must walk twenty. If you tell them to go without food, you must go without food and water. Whatever you do, you must ensure that you are better than them in the quantum of your effort and competence. Whatever you do, you must put them before you. Putting them before you will always show you the way. Whether you are in the army or in civilian life, putting your men before you—will always lead the way for you.

As an officer cadet, I went to the Artillery School in Devlali, near Nashik. I was proud of being an officer but there was a deja vu of village life with its social hierarchy. The army is hierarchical, with a three-tier hierarchy. Officers occupy the top rung. Junior commissioned officers belong to the second, and jawans occupy the lowest. At twenty, I had people with twenty to thirty years' experience reporting to me. I was conscious of occupying a position of formal superiority, yet I knew I was in no way superior to them. I did not know how to resolve this conundrum either. Officers took their meals in a separate officers' mess. The jawans ate in the langar. I was proud of my training and upbringing, I held aloft the values of honour, service, and welfare, yet I could not help noticing the unfair advantage an officer enjoyed.

2

The courage of a soldier is found to be the cheapest and the most common quality of human nature.

—Edward Gibbon

My Stint in the Indian Army

The life of the army jawan is the toughest in comparison to the lives of people in other professions. It is very difficult to imagine the hardships he faces. During long and difficult postings jawans do not have their families with them. There is no accommodation provided to them on the front. When they return to a peace station, less than half of them get housing. I was aware of the hardships 'my men' faced and a sense of guilt preyed on my mind. I did not however know how to resolve it. Even as this dilemma troubled me, I continued to live the life of a regular young officer, following the traditional army lifestyle of working hard, drinking and playing hard.

During September–October 1971, I was training at the School of Artillery when the Bangladesh Liberation War broke out. The training was cut short and I was dispatched to my unit stationed in Sikkim. I had no idea at the time that my close buddies at the School of Artillery, Capt. Sam, Capt. Jayanth Poovaiah, and Capt. Vishnu Rawal, would play such a major role in my future career and life.

From Devlali I travelled to Bagdogra by train, and from there by jeep to Gangtok. My unit was stationed in the field area on the China border, and from there it had been moved to Gangtok. Orders had been given to mobilize troops for war. There was palpable tension in the air. When a country is about to go to war, there is excitement and tension among the troops. When war is in the air there is excitement because war is what you have been preparing for; there is tension because there is adventure in the offing and the possibility that you might not come back alive. Everybody feels it but nobody talks about it.

While preparations were afoot for the impending war, the daily newspapers were full of rumours. The Pakistan government had sent troops to occupy East Pakistan, which is now Bangladesh. The reason for the troop movement was to quell the dissent that was brewing among the people of East Pakistan against the Pakistani establishment. The Pakistan army had begun a violent campaign to crush the opposition, its principle target a rebel organization called the Mukti Bahini, which was fighting for independence from Pakistani rule and had the support of the local people in East Pakistan.

There was a state of civil war in East Pakistan. The violence unleashed by the Pakistan Army had resulted in a massive exodus of refugees from the east to India, over ten million people having crossed over. Meanwhile, the Indian Army was training the Mukti Bahini to overthrow the Pakistan Army and to ensure that the refugees from East Pakistan (formerly East Bengal in undivided India) were able to return safely to their country.

My unit had guns, medical and signal resources. When you move for war, you leave non-essentials behind at the base. The movement of a division entails a massive exercise in logistics, planning. First, surface transport such as trains and trucks move the men and materials of the unit. The unit carries only the bare essentials to fight the war. The officers need to know how much a railway wagon or truck can carry, and having calculated that, decide how many trains will be required to transport the unit; in some kinds of terrain, mules are used for transportation, and again a calculation has to be made of the number of mules required to carry the mountain guns and other supplies.

When mobilization is ordered, all army leave is cancelled and soldiers' families are sent home. A unit on move order, begins an operational drill that works with clockwork precision. I realized that effective management and administration of resources and people are the principle criteria of a good army. When I reached my unit in Sikkim it was night. I had been told at the base station that I would be attached to the commanding officer, Lt. Col. K.L.K. Singh. The commanding officer wanted an 'intelligence' officer to be attached to his staff.

As intelligence officer, I shadowed my commanding officer (CO) and closely observed the entire planning process. Lt. Col. Singh was part of an infantry brigade commanded by a brigadier. He was a great soldier. Honest and courageous, he had a razor-sharp mind in conceiving a sound strategy and taking instant decisions. Decisions had to be taken in a split second because they concerned men whose lives were under threat. I couldn't but realize that we were no longer engaging in mock battles.

The unit began moving at five in the morning. It consisted of a convoy of over 100 trucks carrying all that was needed to fight a war, including engineers and doctors. On the first day the unit halted at Siliguri, close to the border where the 33 Corps had its headquarters. I accompanied the CO wherever he went and began getting an insider's view of a major war from the perspective of the top brass.

In a war the artillery supports the fighting arms—the infantry and the armour. A brigade has all the wherewithal to support the soldier who goes out to face the enemy. Artillery support allows the foot soldier of the infantry to physically engage the enemy in hand-to-hand combat.

Arrangements were made swiftly every day. These included administering the unit and checking whether supply lines were open and the troops were well provided for. Napoleon is known to have said that an army marches on its stomach. What this implied was that an army needs to ensure that the soldier has everything he needs to fight a war: food, boots, guns, and vehicles on time.

At Siliguri, I accompanied my CO to the brigade commander for a briefing. Until then I had only read about war and military strategy. I now found myself at an actual meeting being held in the large underground command headquarters where the general officer commanding the division, a major general, and the brigade commander planned their strategy of invading and liberating East Pakistan. I listened in awe as their grand plan unfolded. In the bunker, I stood next to the brigade commander and the major general as they laid out their battle plans. I made notes, kept records, and passed on instructions issued by my CO.

In the course of the next three or four days our unit would move into East Pakistan. We were to move under cover of darkness and penetrate deep into enemy territory. It would be an infantry-led attack, supported by the artillery and armour. I encountered many of my batchmates from the academy, meeting in the makeshift mess at night. We were told that guns would be placed just behind the infantry lines, and that an officer from each of the nine artillery regiments stationed in Siliguri would be accompanying the infantry in the attack.

The artillery also had air observation posts known as Air OPs, comprising small helicopters and aeroplanes. That was when the foundation of Deccan Aviation was laid. When the situation demanded, a helicopter or aeroplane circled above the attacking infantry, the pilots observing and directing the artillery fire. However, in all attacks there is an artillery officer, called the forward observation officer (FOO), who moves along with the attacking forces to direct the artillery fire. This fire is provided by the gun position officer (GPO).

The orders for the advance were issued and I returned from the mess, privy to the battle plan. Nobody else in the unit knew about it. They would learn about it only when the CO briefed the unit later in the day. Lt. Col. Singh drew the battle plan for the unit and said that the infantry would move in and mount an attack in four days. Guns were also to advance and deploy to provide the necessary back-up support. One officer from each of the battery units would accompany the infantry during the attack and there were to be nine to twelve such units. We, therefore, knew that we would part with one another the following morning. We were asked not to indicate our locations or plans in the letters we wrote, and these were read and censored whenever necessary by army intelligence.

I was careful about what I wrote in the letters to my mother. Mother poured her heart out in her letters and told me she was undertaking pilgrimages and praying for my safe return. I wrote back asking her not to worry and that I wasn't anywhere near the front. On a personal level, each of us knew that these were defining moments; that we might not see each other again and that some of us might never return from the engagement.

Armed with the battle plan, we gathered for a drink in the officer's mess. Just before we left, General Manekshaw visited our camp in Siliguri, and I had the good fortune to catch a glimpse of him for a few fleeting moments at the headquarters. He shook hands with me and I was struck by his charisma.

I vividly remember the eve of our move into East Pakistan territory. It was a sultry October night. The local civilian authorities had organized a farewell dinner for the armed forces, attended by the heads of police and the civil services, my CO, people from the intelligence services.

Then the campaign began. We moved in and prepared our gun positions. The first attack was launched on a small village in Dinajpur district called Bhurangmari, which the Pakistani army unit had made its headquarters. The attack began at about ten at night. The infantry attack was led by Maj. M.C. Nanjappa. I was with my CO during the attack, speaking with Maj. Nanjappa (who later became a general), on my CO's behalf while he was coordinating the artillery support for the entire brigade. We were talking to another officer, Lt. Manjunath, in Kannada to avoid interception. At one point, Manjunath reported that he had become isolated by heavy gun-fire and needed urgent support. He was grievously wounded in the battle and succumbed to his injuries after two days of fighting. The Pakistanis fought desperately to hold on to their positions and it took us two days and two nights to overrun their headquarters in the village. Once the crust was cracked, the Indian Army made good progress.

Loss of close associates is a bitter reality in army life. Before he died,

Manjunath and I had had a drink together. I discovered that he was from Shimoga, a neighbouring district of Hassan. There was another officer from my unit to whom I was very close. He was hit by shrapnel from an exploding shell which pierced his helmet and opened up his skull. Fortunately he survived. Maj. Nanjappa was decorated for his role in the war and received the Vir Chakra for his gallantry. In the same battle, another colleague Capt. Tirath Singh of my unit, who was the FOO, took over command of the attacking infantry when their company commander was injured. He successfully led the attack with a small band of infantry soldiers and, along with Maj. Nanjappa, captured the Pakistani headquarters at Bhurangmari. He too was awarded the Vir Chakra.

Along our march, we saw that entire villages had been abandoned. Thousands of people crossed over to India as refugees to escape persecution. The Pakistan army had occupied Bangla territory for over a year and a half. It was technically not an occupation but amounted to that because of the repression and torture of Mukti Bahini cadres and leadership. The Pakistan army had captured many women who were held as hostages and human shields in village houses and were regularly raped. The Pakistan army authorities supported these heinous acts and to avoid pregnancy, liberally supplied condoms to its men. I saw with my own eyes that the women were in a terrible and pathetic condition. They were pathologically fearful of everything and everyone around them, as they had been dishonoured, exploited, and physically abused for months.

We rescued the women, sent them to rehabilitation camps and moved on. The war was far from over. As the strength of our officers was depleted due to injuries, my CO called me and announced that he could no longer afford the luxury of an intelligence officer. I, therefore, became a gun position officer (GPO), and this move sent me right into the thick of battle.

The GPO is required to respond promptly and accurately to the call for fire from the OP officer. He has to deploy the guns at the right place at the right time and ensure that they are ready to provide supporting fire. His efficiency has a direct bearing on the success of an attack. The responsibilities shouldered by a GPO are immense. A regiment has three batteries, each with six guns. In any war, the artillery can wreak great devastation upon the enemy. Artillery gun positions are sometimes isolated and are vulnerable to enemy attacks. During war, there is round-the-clock activity. Even eating and sleeping are activities undertaken in a state of high alert. During prolonged periods of engagement with the enemy and notwithstanding the lack of proper meals or sound sleep, there is an inexplicable kind of adrenaline rush.

However, even in the midst of pitched battles, shelling, and air raids, we would not hesitate to grab a drink with buddies and fellow soldiers during a brief lull. During these times, the uncertainty of life became more pronounced and constantly played on one's mind. After the initial phase, our troops moved with lightning speed. The aim was not to allow the enemy time to regroup. This was especially so in the Dinajpur and Chittagong zones. Whilst Capt. K.J. Samuel and I were in the eastern sector, many of my course-mates like Jayanth Poovaiah were fighting in the west.

The Indian Army's strategy was based on the riparian geography of East Pakistan. The idea was to cut off supplies by demolishing bridges that spanned a number of rivers. The campaign ensured isolation of Pakistani divisions. The Pakistanis initially fought fierce battles but were soon on the run. One important reason for their defeat was their moral degradation. The Pakistani soldiers were degenerate and misbehaved with the local people, so they did not receive any local support. Our army received ample help from the local people, Mukti Bahini cadres, and from our own officers disguised as members of the Mukti Bahini. History is replete with instances where occupying armies which had become morally degraded eventually lost the will to fight and suffered defeat at the hands of those who occupied a higher moral plane. The contrast was obvious. While on the western front the Pakistani Army was highly motivated, and fought bravely and well, on the eastern front it was a dispirited force.

The rapidity of the retreat of the Pakistan Army was also manifested by how quickly we moved from place to place. In fact, we often received orders to move while getting the guns in position for attack. During three battles I was at the guns. We kept firing all day and night. There was one occasion when I encountered the enemy at close quarters. My battery commander Maj. Balkar Singh called me to say that Pakistani commandos had infiltrated our lines. They would be targeting my unit's artillery gun positions because they are easily identifiable sitting targets. Sometime earlier Pakistani soldiers had placed grenades in the barrels and killed some artillery men and destroyed the guns.

﹌

I received a call late that night, that radio communication had been intercepted between Pakistani commandos. When decoded, the communication indicated that they were planning an ambush close to where I was. We therefore dug trenches in front of the guns and my gunners got ready to defend their positions from the impending raid. I commanded 100 men and had six artillery guns to protect. It was a critical moment. I remembered what my instructor Capt. J.S. Verma had said: 'to command the loyalty and confidence of your men, you have to work harder and put your men before yourself ....'

I did not know from which direction the Pakistani commandos would come. My orders were to repel them and prevent casualties and damage on our side. I spent the night walking from trench to trench under cover of darkness. It is not that we were not scared. Courage is the counterpoint of fear. Courage appears when in war or business, one is indeed scared. It was something akin to what the actor John Wayne had once said: 'It is not that you are not scared. You are scared but you saddle up anyway.' I was watchful all the time. I kept talking to my men and inspired them to stay awake. Thankfully, the Pakistani commandos sprang no surprise on us. Soon thereafter the entire Pakistani army had been surrounded and asked to surrender. I was listening to the radio at the time. It was one of the most inspiring moments of my life.

Our unit and brigade moved into Bangladesh in October and entrenched itself. We fought a series of battles. However, full-scale war lasted only about two weeks. General Manekshaw addressed the Pakistani troops over radio. He asked them to lay down arms and surrender. 'Brothers from the Pakistan Army,' he said. 'You are surrounded. You have no way out. Lay down your arms. We will not harm you. You have one last chance. So I urge you: Surrender, surrender, surrender!'

His words must have sent shivers down the spine of the Pakistan Army. To us it was wonderfully inspiring. The Pakistan Army had been surrounded on all sides. They were completely cornered and their spirit broken. Had we attacked them we would have perpetrated the biggest bloodbath in modern history. The surrender came. It was like a scene from a movie. The commander of the armed forces of Pakistan in East Pakistan was made to surrender along with the troops at a public ceremony. They were disarmed and the surrendered soldiers were sent to POW camps located at various locations in India. It was the largest surrender in history: over 100,000 fighting troops surrendered to the Indian Army.

We then moved out of what is now Bangladesh. My unit was moved to Sikkim. People cheered us all along the road from Dinajpur to Rangpur to Sikkim. They were celebrating on the streets, and raised a victory cry, 'Indira Gandhi zindabad,' 'Indian Army zindabad', 'Manekshaw zindabad'. In the towns and villages, even in the smallest of hamlets, people had woken to a sense of freedom and of being citizens of a newly independent Bangladesh. Peasants, common people, college girls and children welcomed us with garlands and flowers; they gave us sweets as a token of friendship.

After the war, I was posted in Sikkim for a year and a half. This was the beginning of a period of deep spiritual awakening within me. Sikkim was a kingdom and not yet a part of India. It was however an Indian protectorate, with India looking after its economic and foreign affairs, its army, and its infrastructural needs.

After Sikkim I was posted at a picket called 4752 on the Sino-Indian border. This picket adjoins the famous Nathu La pass where some fierce battles were fought during the India–China war of 1962. India had lost the war on account of lack of anticipation and failure of leadership. Picket 4752 is the highest picket in the region: it translates to 4,752 metres (15,586 feet) above mean sea level (MSL). I was posted as observation post officer, with the responsibility to observe the Chinese border and give a daily report. This posting was with the infantry and was my first engagement with the Himalayan terrain. I had accessed the lower ranges of the Himalaya as a cadet at the HMI, Darjeeling, but this was a forbidding height. We had to move up to the altitude in stages allowing the body to acclimatize. One of the first camps was before the famous Changu Lake at a height of over 3,000 metres. It was breathtakingly beautiful, its water a turquoise blue and crystal clear. I had heard that it froze completely in winter and one could drive a jeep across the ice. From there on, you moved further up along the road for about three or four kilometres and set up another transit camp. The road ended there and you had to trek for about four hours up the steep mountain slopes to reach 4752. Some stretches were perennially snowbound. My picket was attached to the Jammu and Kashmir Rifles. I was the only officer in the bunker and the rest of the unit was about 60 metres feet below me. I had the support of two jawans from the artillery who also billeted in a bunker a little below.

Those were amongst the finest days of my life. I rose each morning to the sight of the majestic range of Kanchenjunga bathed in pre-dawn sunlight. We enjoyed clear weather from six to about nine in the morning most of the year. Visibility fell to zero after that. Below my picket and down the slope, there was a lake that froze in winter. It was my first experience of a frozen lake. The frozen surface was sufficiently hard to permit animals to walk across it. It had however no formal name, an unnamed lake on the map lying between the Indian picket and the Chinese border. Every day the Chinese blared Chinese music at us for two to three hours. They followed this up with lectures on the greatness of the communist way of life. In turn, the Indian army played two or three hours of Hindi music, and followed this up with an account in Hindi, English, and Chinese of the wonders of life in India.

I closely observed the Chinese soldier on the opposite side and he reciprocated in kind. There was a cold war between us. I had to send a daily situation report (SITREP). On some days I heard blasts on the other side and reckoned that they were part of road-building, bunker-construction, or embankment-erection projects to facilitate gun positions. I often saw packs of mules on the move. Sometimes I saw mountain yaks. The yak is the kamadhenu, or the multipurpose miracle cow of Hindu mythical lore, for the local tribals of the Himalaya. It is used for its milk, meat, and hide, and also for transportation.

It was painfully cold out there and we felt numb to the bone in the chill. The sights are heavenly but the acute climate is inhospitable, to say the least, accompanied by oxygen deficiency. The maximum day temperature in summer would touch a 'high' of minus two or three degrees Celsius. Night temperatures dropped to minus twenty degrees Celsius.

The assignment was really challenging. There was no fresh water and Sherpas had to drill a hole through the ice cover to reach the underground water level, scoop up water in ladlefuls, and carry it up to the picket in jerry-cans. I lived on canned food. The army supply line to Gangtok was two to three days away. Sometimes I was cut off altogether because of the snow. Food rations were airdropped during such emergencies. It is extremely difficult for troops, even when they are not engaged in war, to spend prolonged periods in this hostile environment. Soldiers are completely deprived of the comforting visions and experiences of mundane existence: that of women and children going about their daily chores, of running water, greenery, and of the humdrum of normal human life elsewhere, which we take for granted. There is nothing to comfort starved eyes and the parched mind in this barren, icy wilderness, except the occasional mountain goat that strays into those heights or the snow leopard poised for a possible kill. The sound of running water and the sight of greenery after four months of camp life in these desolate reaches of the Himalayas, seemed to me like rebirth.

The relative isolation of the picket had its merits too. I had plenty of time to read my favourite authors and spent hours devouring Tolstoy, Dostoevsky, Camus, Maupassant, Somerset Maugham, Pushkin, Sartre, and Sholokhov. The second good thing that came my way was the wonderful experience of enjoying rare mountain sights. I volunteered for long range patrols (LRP) in the mountains which involved long treks along the Indo–Tibetan border and lasted fifteen to twenty days, when we scaled such forbidding heights of 6000 metres above the MSL. These patrols were designed to monitor possible infiltration by Chinese troops and identify for us suitable gun positions. On my first patrol, I was awestricken by the sights the mountains offered. I saw the most spectacular scenes, of gushing waterfalls, snow-capped mountain peaks, and winding rivers. I was immersed in Tagore's poetry at the time and the entire experience was deeply spiritual. As a bonus, I visited remote places in Sikkim where the residents had never seen a motor-vehicle before. We distributed medicines in these high-altitude settlements, drank yak milk and survived on yak meat on those mountain forays.

Sikkimese women are extraordinarily pretty. It was not uncommon to find the women doing all the work while the men sat drinking thumba, home-brewed alcohol made from millets. From Sikkim we moved to Bhutan. The king had suddenly passed away and the seventeen-year-old crown prince was to be crowned. The army sent me with my unit on two missions. One was a reconnaissance of the China–Bhutan border, the other to attend the coronation. Bhutan was a Shangri La, an unexposed virgin land of sorts, hidden from the rest of the world, its people and culture pure in their ethnicity. There were no newspapers or any communication channel with the outside world, the people wore their traditional national attire and practised their own customs. They had a benign king and loved him much more than they feared him. The more I saw of Bhutan the more I was convinced that it deserved to be called a Buddhist haven. I spent a wonderful month and a half in Bhutan, took part in the coronation, and witnessed the gun salute. I also travelled and explored the interior regions of Bhutan.

After the war, a strange restlessness gnawed within me. My father had introduced me to Gandhi, and at the time I saw everything through Gandhi's eyes. I poured over all his writings and wondered what Gandhi would have done had he been in my position. I was undergoing the turmoil of an emotional–spiritual crisis and transition. I wrote to my father to say that the army and its mission had ceased to be my driving force. In fact, they meant nothing to me. In the letter, I expressed the desire to do something with a social–spiritual orientation, and didn't believe I could achieve that in the army. However, if I left the army to work for the poor, I would end up being a burden on society because I would have no job to pay for my living. My father wrote long letters advising me to continue with my chosen path. He said I had become a coward. He sent me quotations from the Gita: 'Do thou thy allotted task; for action is superior to inaction; with inaction even life's normal course is not possible.' He reminded me that the fruits of one's actions would inexorably visit me in later life.

Army life had been wonderful. It was secular, comfortable, and it taught me many things but was too regimented and predictable for my liking. I engaged in a long dialogue on these lines with my father. He said with some finality: 'Gopi, your karma and your dharma are in your actions.' Not being able to offer an alternative viewpoint at the time, I stayed on. It was in this state of ferment that I went on a posting to Kashmir. There I had a very definitive experience. On one of my climbing expeditions, I lost my balance and hurtled twelve metres down to a glacier. This was a miraculous escape from almost certain death and my men carried me a distance of 25 kilometres from the Machui Glacier into which I fell to our base camp in Sonamarg. My arm had been crushed in the fall, and I was unsure whether I would ever be able to use it again. As those four men carried me on their backs, I realized and I remembered Einstein's words that our lives depended on the labour of others—past and living, in significant measure. Our lives and actions are mutually dependant, as in a symbiotic web.

I faced a dilemma as I no longer wished to remain in the army but was uncertain what I should do instead? I wanted to cut loose all bonds and set myself free to become a monk, but that would be expecting the world to feed me and add to its existing burdens. I expected a solution to evolve through my work and experience. The pain was virtually unbearable. I had been given morphine and I lay helpless and supine on the stretcher, gazing up at the vacant sky above, seeking an answer to my spiritual quest. The accident, the pain, and the terrifying prospect of losing a limb calmed me. The trauma helped me resolve my dilemma. From Sonamarg I was taken to the base hospital in Srinagar. The treatment took four months and included an operation. I eventually recovered, and when I felt physically better, I headed out on a voyage of self-discovery.

I stayed for a year in Bengaluru on medical posting. I was medically unfit because my arm was severely damaged. Then an interesting thing happened. After I had recuperated, I was posted in Thiruvananthapuram as commandant of a small unit under a brigade headed by Brigadier N.S.I. Narahari (he later became a general and much later, chairman of Deccan Aviation). He was my commander, an outstanding soldier, engineer, paratrooper, deep-sea diver and sportsman. He had also taught at the infantry school. I got an insight into his philosophy of life when he made a speech at the officers' brigade on the day he took over and concluded with these remarks: 'I work very hard. I play harder than I work. I party harder than I play. On work and play there will be no compromise.'

I looked up to the brigadier for sound advice. He went a notch up in my esteem after a few memorable incidents. I was mess secretary in Thiruvananthapuram. Emotionally I often swayed between extremes. An army dinner had been arranged, which a general was supposed to attend. I was told in private that the general drank only Scotch. It was a tradition in the army that if a general drank Scotch, the mess secretary was bound to make a special effort to provide it while the rest of the officers at the station would pay for it. According to army traditions, a general is never presented a food and beverages bill.

Being the kind of person I was, I decided against carrying out this 'unfair' tradition. If the general wanted to have Scotch, he could have it but he must be given a bill. I went to Brig. Narahari and told him of the message from the general's ADC. Brig. Narahari said, 'Nothing doing. We will not give him a bill but we will serve him what we have.' He then inquired, 'What do we have?' 'We have Indian whisky and rum,' I replied. 'Serve him what we have,' Brig. Narahari commanded.

The general arrived in due course but we were very tense. Departing from army traditions and the set pattern of dealing with the top brass would certainly irritate the general and one could expect a bad report. By evening the officers' mess was abuzz with the tinkle of glasses and the hushed conversation of officers, marked by an occasional guffaw. The general strode in and took his seat. Whisky was brought in and the general raised his glass. He was an accomplished Scotch drinker and connoisseurs like him can tell in millionth of a second whether the drink is genuine Scotch or not! The general swirled the liquid in his glass and got a whiff not of Scotch but Indian whisky. He spoke in a booming voice and made no effort to conceal his displeasure, saying he would have soup instead. By this time one tradition had already been broken. Another was in the pipeline. Traditionally, if the general did not drink, nobody drank. Brig. Narahari however ordered his drink and said in a measured tone, 'I'll have my rum'. The general left in a huff.

Brig. Narahari drank hard but remained straight. Although a very senior officer, he played all the outdoor and indoor games, partied hard, and occasionally danced in the officers' mess till the wee hours of the morning. It was great fun to have him as your commandant. Very pleasant in demeanour, fair in his dealings, and balanced, he was also very firm and outspoken. In the IAS, promotions are time-bound. Narayana Murthy of Infosys once commented that an IAS officer takes an exam only once during his administrative career: when he joins the service. The army officer, on the other hand, is tested at every critical stage of his career. One in a hundred servicemen is promoted to the rank of a colonel. The ratio for the brigadier's post is even higher. A general is selected from among thousands. It is generally believed that in many organizations, and especially the army, if one is outspoken one doesn't make it to the top. Brig. Narahari was however a singular example of an officer who was both upright and forthright, and whom nothing could stop from reaching the top.

My unresolved dilemmas did not prevent me from seeking new adventures. I went trekking and swimming. I headed out to nowhere land on my motorcycle, inspired by Gandhi who had spent a year touring the country before involving himself seriously with the freedom movement, I had long cherished the idea of travelling the length and breadth of India. I, therefore, headed for Rajasthan on my Java bike, armed with my tent, sleeping bag, and other personal effects. I started from Bikaner and travelled 4000 km in three months. I wanted to acquaint myself with my land and its people, and form my own idea of real India. I avoided hotels and spent the nights at ashrams or by a riverside. In exchange for a small sum of money, I stayed at the homes of farmers or in one corner of their paddy-fields or in an empty cottage. For Rs 15–20, farmers cooked khichdi for my dinner and let me spend the night in their homes. From Bikaner I travelled to Jaipur, Jaisalmer, Ajmer, Delhi, Lucknow, Kanpur, Khajuraho, Sanchi, Bhopal, Ujjain, Mandu and Ahmedabad. I saw temples, palaces, forts, and encountered different kinds of people. The glimpses of India in its vibrant palette of colours were hugely fascinating.

While on the road, riding past the rich countryside, I decided I had to leave the army. I had discussed my plans to leave the army with Brig. Narahari. 'Perhaps you should,' he had said. 'I see that your heart is not in this job. It's also better for the army that you leave. But what will you do?' It was indeed a conundrum. I only had a soldier's skills and knew no other. I, therefore, said I would venture out and discover my calling. In the meantime, I planned to do some farming. I also had romantic notions of going abroad and working as an apprentice at the National Geographical Society for a couple of years to travel the world. I would travel to Egypt, Greece, and Italy. Perhaps I would gradually learn the ropes and be able to apply and qualify for a correspondent's job at the National Geographic. I was clear in my mind, however, that I did not want to continue in the army and nor wanted a government job.

I had not considered the prospect of being financially insecure, having thus far led a very sheltered life. My first salary as an officer in the army was Rs 400 plus Rs 223 as allowances. I sent home Rs 200 every month to assist my father in bringing up my siblings. My monthly mess bill would amount to Rs 100. There were very few other expenses, so I saved some money and enjoyed a good life. I however felt the need to go 'beyond the woods and beyond borders'; longed for adventure. The safest place for a ship is in the harbour, but ships are built for sailing. I, therefore, decided to cut my ropes, abandon the sheltered life, and set sail to discover myself and my true passion. It was indeed a crazy idea; but it had taken hold of me. It was at this uncertain juncture that I met a certain girl and had a strange experience.

We were a bunch of youngsters in Thiruvananthapuram. She stayed in a hostel and we became good friends. I used to take her out on my bike.

She had two friends who two of mine, Capt. E.J. Kochekan (now major general) and Capt. Suresh Rao, were seeing. Her parents lived abroad. Although we were very good friends, the intensity of our feelings towards each other differed. She was in love with me; I did not entirely reciprocate. I had however made this quite clear right at the outset. My only aim in life at that time was to get out of the army, and therefore had no wish at that juncture to embark on a serious relationship or marry. We often went out together. Somehow her parents learnt that she was seeing me. I was cool and almost clinical about this aspect of my life. In no time her parents flew down from the Middle East. They had found a boy for her and she would have to marry him.

She called me one day while I was playing tennis with Brig. Narahari. Sobbing hysterically, she said her wedding was to take place in fifteen days. Her parents had locked her up and she asked me to help her. I had been honest all the while and not made false promises. She knew perfectly well that I was reluctant to settle down but wanted me to free her and send her away from her parents with some money till she found a job. 'I'm not in a condition to get married. So please, can you help me?' she pleaded. I thought the matter over and agreed to rescue her from her first-floor bedroom at midnight and send her off to Bengaluru. I felt it was only fair to help her. I asked her once again not to be under the illusion of any promise of marriage as I planned to resign from the army. Asking her to dress light and pack bare necessities, I also reminded her to wear canvas shoes.

My NDA training had helped me to organize such a raid. I called Kochekan, who was dating the other girl, and shared the plan with him. We arranged a second motorcycle with the help of another friend. I had planned to 'rescue' her, drive her in an army jeep to Quilon, from where Kochekan would take her to Cochin and put her on a train to Bengaluru where my friends would receive her and provide her shelter for a few days till she found a job. Meanwhile, I would return to camp.

The rescue was planned like a typical army raid. We did a daytime survey and figured out the approach pathways. On reaching her house around 10 p.m., we stole up to the wall. Kochekan stood with his back to the wall, facing me. I placed one foot on his arm, climbed up the pipe, and finally the fire escape ladder. She was packed and ready to leave. I led her out and helped her climb down, put her on the second bike and we rode straight to my friend's house.

I happened to be the commandant of military police, responsible for the discipline of the brigade. I was aware that my act was wrong but, curiously, succumbed to uncontrollable emotions as I had little control over my personal life and had lost my sense of direction at that point of time. I paid for the military vehicle and drove her all the way to Quilon. From there Kochekan took her to Cochin and put her on a train to Bengaluru as planned.

On the following day I reported for duty as usual. My girlfriend's parents had discovered her absence and the needle of suspicion pointed in my direction. There was a call from the police but I denied everything. Later, Brig. Narahari summoned me and informed me that the chief minister and the local MLA had called him and threatened to raise the issue in the assembly. It would be a major embarrassment for the army. Brig. Narahari looked me in the eye and asked curtly, 'Do you know something about it? If you tell me the truth I'll defend you.'

Brig. Narahari was also a father of two daughters of the same age. I decided it was time to speak the truth and told him how and why I had done it. 'I've given her Rs 5000. She is looking for a job. There is nothing to worry about,' I said. 'But her parents will worry,' the Brigadier reminded me. I was instrumental in getting her back home later, promising her that her parents would not force her to get married. A fortnight later Brig. Narahari called me home and said with a smile, 'Fellow, have your cake and eat it too. The girl's parents have sent the 5000 bucks you gave her, along with a "thank you" note.'

I took the money and saluted. Any other commander could have seen it in very poor light, had me arrested and court-martialled. Brig. Narahari had however taught me an important lesson in life in the process: of looking beyond the obvious 'black' and 'white' of life and judge people and situations in the fair light of reason and tolerance. I was somewhat ruthless in punishing corrupt people but this incident helped me realize that one need not always punish an erring person in order to drive home a message. It helped me see the need to give people a second chance.

After reading *Travels with Charlie* by John Steinbeck, where the author decides to travel within his country in a custom-built caravan with dog Charlie for two years in a bid to properly acquaint himself with America, I decided to visit my elder sister Bhagya and my brother-in-law for a few days in Washington DC. My brother-in-law worked for the World Bank. I had begun to settle down to a routine of listless ambles when someone asked me, 'Gopi, have you come all the way from India to meet Ramaswamy and Kuppuswamy and eat idli and sambhar in the USA?' That shook me up. I went straight to a shop selling camping gear, bought myself a pair of jeans, a tent, a sleeping bag, assorted camping gear, and a Grey Hound bus pass and set out on a 10,000 km hitch-hiking trip. I started from Washington DC, the trip taking me to upstate New York. I had $500 in my pocket. My journey took me to Ohio, Illinois, South Dakota, North Dakota, Montana, Utah, across the Yellowstone National Park and Grand Teton National Park, Sequoia National Park, Colorado, Grand Canyon, Las Vegas, Nevada, Nebraska, Los Angeles, San Francisco, and back. I hoped to get deep into interior America. I followed one basic economy travel rule: of spending less and seeing more. I could not afford to stay in hotels and hitched rides wherever I could. I made friends on the way, shared meals, exchanged life stories with total strangers, and also keepsakes, before moving on. I had my camping gear: a stove, cooking pots, and a tent. I met a Danish army major who travelled in a custom-made bunk caravan equipped with a microwave oven, a TV, and a dining table. We were fellow-travellers for a few days before we parted.

I usually set up camp outside a city. In New York I met a man I thought was Indian. I spoke to him in Hindi. He replied in Hindi and Punjabi. I was pleasantly surprised to discover he was from Pakistan and learnt that he was a veterinary doctor now working as a waiter in a restaurant while he searched for a more appropriate job and the proverbial green card. When he realized that I was hitch-hiking he said he would show me around New York and invited me to share his one-room tenement in Brooklyn. He treated me to dinner and took me out after that. His large-hearted legendary Punjabi hospitality overwhelmed me. He gave me a guided tour of Big Apple's nightlife, taking me to the 42nd Street, the centre of New York's night life in the 1970s. There we encountered middle-aged Indian couples, officials of the Indian government, and people from various walks of life. We saw proselytizers of the Hare Krishna movement, volunteers of the Save Jesus movement, pimps, blue bars and sex shops. Some movie halls continually screened one-dollar porn movies. There was live sex on stage. It was much more than a culture shock for me.

I also visited the Grand Canyon, where I took a camping permit from the authorities at the top of the rim to camp in Bright Angel National Park at the bottom of the Colorado gorge. I was well-equipped for the night with my stove and camping gear. It's a 51-km walk to and from the nearest settlement to the bottom of the Grand Canyon. People walked in groups while I trekked alone. After a while I realized that someone was trailing me. I stopped and when the trailing figure caught up with me, I saw that it was a girl. She was nice company. We walked on and my trekking companion told me she was a nurse and part-time student from Nebraska. I said I planned to camp that night at the Canyon. She asked if she could join me.

Descending the gorge is tough business. It gets very hot and temperatures can reach 41–42 degrees celsius in summer. However, the parking amenities were excellent, and there were toilets for public use. People were spread out all over the canyon and had lit little fires. I found a good spot to camp. The Colorado, the lifeline of the local American Indian tribes, flowed a hundred yards away. The water was icy cold but it was extremely hot outside. I therefore stripped and jumped into the water. Sometime later I turned around to see my trekking companion also swimming in the river, naked!

Finally, we returned to the campsite, pitched our tent, cooked our meal of tinned food on campfire and turned in for the night. I still remember the night vividly. I woke up in the middle of the moonlit night to find hundreds of deer huddled close to the camping area. Couples were also lying naked all over the campus because of the impossible heat, their bodies bathed in the moonlight. The following day we walked back the entire stretch of 29 kilometres. She had a Volkswagen in which we travelled together for the next few days and then we bade each other goodbye. It was time for me to return to India.

Return to India

When I returned, I went up straight to Brig. Narahari and said I had made up my mind to leave the army. I was still unsure about what I would do after I left. I would return to my village and figure things out. He gave me his clearance and I put in my resignation papers and returned home to Gorur. On paper I said I wanted to leave the army to take care of my ageing parents and to bring up my siblings. It crossed my mind that the possibility of my becoming chief of the army staff in the future was equally good or bad. My friends and senior officers joked about this. They said, 'Capt. Gopinath, you will either become a general or receive a court-martial, in all probability the latter!'

I had not put in pensionable service in the army and so, when my dues were finally settled, I received the princely sum of Rs 6350, my accrued provident fund and gratuity. A captured Pakistani rifle, allotted to me during my tenure in the army, came to me as a bonus. There was exultation in my heart. I felt free. The future was unknown but I was at peace with myself. I was confident I could shape my future and soon discover my new calling.

When I returned home to Gorur I found my family and the entire village bewildered and amazed at my decision. My father was particularly shell-shocked and devastated. My other relatives, including my own siblings, were headed for America or to one of India's metropolitan cities. I was homing in instead, to nest and roost. One person was delighted: my mother. Though she was stoic and showed no outward emotion, she was certainly extremely happy and relieved that I was no longer in the army.

The government had in the meanwhile decided to build a dam at the confluence of the rivers Hemavathy and Yagachi, which had been planned almost twenty years earlier. Government machinery is slow to move but it was now time for the construction to begin. Our village was spared as the site was a kilometre, upstream but sixty villages in the neighbourhood were to be submerged. The family's jointly-owned farmland would also be lost to the swirling backwaters of the dam.

A large portion of the land owned by our family were under tenancy, tillers receiving a part of the produce, we the balance. The dam was close to completion and the imminent submersion of villages and plots of ancestral land was the talk of the town. The dam development project would physically uproot the local people and their livestock overnight. These lands had been the source of the villagers' livelihood for centuries and they were naturally gripped by a sense of fathomless despair and anger. The government compensation was not a match for what they would be losing and the emotional turmoil they would be experiencing as refugees with an uncertain future.

Our entire extended family was in a state of shock. We however consoled ourselves by reminding one another that we would still have our house, and being an educated family in a village where most of the poor villagers, who would be losing their homes to the dam, had never received even basic school education, we would be in a far less vulnerable position than they.

My father and his three brothers had received ten acres each in a dry tract of land situated beyond the Belur and Halebid temples. These were many kilometres away from the village and no one in the family had ever set their eyes on the land. My family did not however wish to move from Gorur and the ancestral home, aware that it would be difficult to make ends meet on the new land. Father had planned to sell the land received as compensation, because the allotted land was largely barren, with patches of jungle and scrub forest, without even proper access or an approach route. The place lacked basic civic amenities such as roads, electricity, a ready source of water, hospital, or school. The lack of social and physical infrastructure is a major deterrent and no one was inclined to move to the new land. The prospect of working on it from scratch did not seem to be lucrative or viable proposition to my father. Meanwhile, I did not rush into a project but spent time walking and running across the fields and swimming in the river. These physical activities helped me keep a distance from the problem and view things from a different perspective.

During the reign of the maharajas of Mysore, the rulers allotted large tracts of pasture land where the state royal cattle were allowed to graze. The cattle migrated from season to season, searching for the best pasture within the boundaries of these lands. In Karnataka they were called Amrit Mahal kaawal (grazing) lands, named after a legendary breed of oxen belonging to the old Mysore state. The cattle were traditionally used by the king's army to carry loads and provide milk. They would graze peacefully on these lands, free to wander where they wished, without fear or hindrance. The maharaja appointed a sevadar (caretaker) to look after this land, and the land we were given in compensation formed part of these pastures.

I hopped on to a bus one morning in order to have a look at the land and dropped in at the office of the village headquarters closest to this and met the village accountant. He graciously walked with me, accompanying me with a guide map to the spot, eight kms from Javagal, the nearest village. After a while, we came to a shallow stream. We waded across quite easily but the other bank was covered by impenetrable undergrowth. We therefore walked down the numerous, narrow foot-tracks of local herdsmen, soon reaching a hillock rising from the embankment. We climbed the hillock and stood looking down at what my guide referred to as our land, stretching out to the distance alongside the stream. At that moment, I was overcome by a very strong emotion, which gave birth to my dream and obsession.

It was quite a quick decision I took, to live there and work on the land. I wanted to set up a farm and the idea gradually grew and took root in me. I literally had visions of cows grazing in verdant meadows, bullocks drawing carts, crops standing in the field, and coconut fronds swaying in the breeze. I saw myself taking walks morning and evening. I gazed longingly at the vast stretch of undulating land skirting the scrub forest, with its patches of greenery. I realized this land was centuries-old and formed part of a forgotten royal tradition. I longed to share the mystery of the past with my present and future!

I was agog with new enterprise and excitement. The earthy odours were a heady mix of the smell wafting out of moist soil and thick flora, reminding me of the first summer rains. I was bewitched, to say the least, and could not resist bending down and scooping out a lump of sod in my fist, pressing it, and feeling it gently crumble against my palm. I walked back completely possessed. When I returned home, I declared that I had found the land to be a beautiful stretch of virgin, fertile land where I had decided to build my farm and live. My father was speechless. He finally exclaimed, 'Ningenu huccha?' ('Are you mad?').

We talked all night, and father tried to dissuade me from becoming a farmer. He listed a farmer's travails in getting the right seeds, finding good people to work on the fields, and coping with the vagaries of the monsoon.

Above all, a farmer struggled all his life to make ends meet. He did not want me to end up disillusioned, once the initial excitement wore off. He warned that the enthusiasm might not last. The image of a farmer was romantic, he agreed, but for most romantics it was often a passing fancy and the dropout rate was extremely high.

For my part, I said it was important in life to do what one wanted to. 'Why should I live to impress others?' I retorted. The army had made a man out of me; had taught me skills to overcome physical challenges. It had steeled me and given me mental strength. The farm was already taking shape in my mind and I was ready to take on the challenges. I saw endless possibilities.

Before he had realized it, my father had begun to look at my side of the perspective and had begun giving me positive advice on how to be a good farmer. It was close to six in the morning. The cock crowed with the rising sun and the birds were astir. It was comforting to know that my father was with me. I finally fell asleep, quite exhausted, basking in the glow of a strange, new-found tranquility and self-confidence, delighted with father's change of outlook and priorities. He actually ended up advising me what to grow, when to grow, and how to manage the farm!

I remembered Sarvagna, the great Kannada poet, who wrote glowingly about farming. He said, 'Koti vidyegalu; koti vidyeyalli meti vidyeye melu' ('There are innumerable professions; among them the profession of the plough is the best'). Again, as Emerson said, 'Farming is man's first calling. It is the original calling of his race. The food which was not, he causes to be. All trade rests at last on his primitive activity. The first farmer was the first man.'

I acted quickly after the decision had been taken and walked over to my uncle. I had calculated that three shares of 10 acres each would amount to 30 acres, sufficiently large for viable farming. My uncles, like father, were not keen about using the new land. I knew I had to strike a deal with my uncles who wanted to sell their plots and keep the money in the bank. Money was my only problem. I had only Rs 6000. I would pay them from the crops I grew on the land. I never doubted my ability to generate funds from the land but not sufficient to buy the land. I made my first entrepreneurial deal with my uncles. I offered to pay them a much higher amount than they would get by selling the land; I would also pay them interest at a higher rate than that which the banks offered. There was only one condition: I would pay them from the crops I grew on the land so the payment would come much later. I never doubted my ability to generate funds from farming. The plan worked like magic. My uncles agreed to my proposal and before I knew it, I had already solved the first problem of an entrepreneur: raising funds for a project.

I drove to Bengaluru, bought a second-hand Enfield Bullet motorcycle and a tent. I also bought a Doberman to keep me company on the farm. I had my army rifle. In Hassan, I picked up camping and farming equipment, and a month's rations. It was an exciting idea: to till the land and live on my own. My mother set an auspicious date for my departure. At last it seemed that things were falling into place.

Bonded labour had been abolished on paper after Independence and its practise was punishable by imprisonment, but much to my shock and disbelief, I found that the practice was still a part of the reality of rural society. With most of my youth having been spent away from home in the relative isolation of the school and academy, I was unaware of its existence. It was a social contract and nobody spoke out against it. Anyone who did became a social outcaste.

A fifteen-year-old Dalit boy Raju, worked in my house and also our neighbour's houses. There was a tacit agreement that he would work in our houses probably because his father had borrowed money from a few households of the village. He took the cattle to graze in the village commons and did odd jobs. One day I laid out my plans to Raju and asked him if he would accompany me and help prepare the land, till it, and raise a crop. The deal between us was that when I worked on the farm, he would cook; when he worked I would cook. Raju perceived his own freedom in this new plan and readily agreed.

On the day of departure, a hired truck arrived from Hassan. I loaded the truck with provisions, the camp equipment, and my one-month-old pup who I fondly called Tipoo. People of the village had once again gathered to witness an unusual expedition and departure. I noticed when I was taking my parents' blessings that my mother's expression was identical to that she had on the day when I left for the army. I was again off to a remote part to live in a tent in the wilderness. I was embarking on yet another adventure and seeking a new life in the unknown. Who knew what misadventures awaited me? All prospects of danger were equal in my mother's eyes.

⤴

It was afternoon when we drove off in the direction of a new beginning. Dusk had fallen when we reached the land. The road-head terminated at the stream and our truck had to stop there. We unloaded and carried our luggage across the stream, trudging four to five furlongs to reach our site just before it got pitch dark. I selected the highest point as a suitable camping

site because it offered a strategic view of the entire land. We brought out
the sickle and spade, and Raju and I set about clearing the camping ground
of undergrowth. We cleaned it up, levelled it, and dug a foot-deep trench
all around to ensure safety from snakes and rainwater seeping into the
tent. Pitching the tent right at the centre, we gathered some firewood and
brush, and lit our campfire. On it we cooked our first meal. My mother had
given me some sambhar masala and I tossed in some vegetables. We boiled
some rice and enjoyed a simple yet delicious meal. I unrolled a reed mat
in front of the tent and then spread a cotton durree (the thick, home-spun
ethnic Indian mat) across it. I lay there in silence that evening, observing
the stars in the sky, satisfied that I had at last found my true calling in life.
I was exhausted from the travel and the toils of the evening, but at peace
with myself. I sensed a bonding with the earth, the surrounding vegetation,
and the stream, the local fauna, the sky and the stars. I seemed part of the
enigma, and was relieved of the burden of solving the riddle of life. We slept
soundly in the open, under the stars and rose next day to a glorious morning
and the cacophony of nameless birds.

3

All that matters is Love and Work.
—Sigmund Freud

Days on the Farm

I lay no claim to being an ornithologist. That I was unable to identify the birds that sang in concert did not trouble me in the least. As the physicist Richard Feynman said: 'I learned very early the difference between knowing the name of something and knowing something.' The music filled my soul with joy and what I beheld, was with delight. The beauty and mysticism of the experience was all that mattered. Earlier, on army treks, I had experienced the same mystic touch at dawn and dusk; it had relieved me of all fatigue.

As Wordsworth said:

> Earth has not anything to show more fair
> Dull would he be of soul who could pass by
> A sight so touching in its majesty...
> Never did sun more beautifully steep
> In his first splendour, valley, rock, or hill;
> Ne'er saw I, never felt, a calm so deep!

I began my tryst with my karmabhoomi with an energetic walk. Amazed at the variety of the innumerable birds, bees, and insects on view, the beauty of the wildflowers and the undergrowth, I made a mental note that I should consult someone who knew about the farm's flora and fauna. Raja and I led a simple life on the new land and shared the work. We adhered to a single menu for our meals throughout the year. Vegetable upma for breakfast, tasty, nutritious (I had learnt that from my grandmother), easy and quick to cook. Lunch and dinner were always a combination of rice, vegetable sambhar, and curd. The campfire every evening was time to treat myself to rum and tender coconut water. On an occasional weekend, we allowed ourselves the luxury of chicken or lamb curry.

Right from the very first day I was conscious that time flowed quickly and that there was so much to do. I explored the farm, looking at the topology, each time with fresh eyes.

In his *Seven Pillars of Wisdom: A Triumph* (1926), T. E. Lawrence of *Lawrence of Arabia* says:

> All men dream: but not equally. Those who dream by night in the dusty recesses of their minds wake in the day to find that it was vanity: but the dreamers of the day are dangerous men, for they may act their dreams with open eyes, to make it possible.

I was dreaming with my eyes open. My mind teemed with ideas for the farm. The gobar (dung) gas plant topped my agenda. I think it is a very useful and innovative creation of modern science . It has a simple operating principle. You fill a pit with cow dung slurry and cover it with a floating lid. When the dung ferments it produces methane which is as effective as LPG. It lights up with a beautiful blue flame and you can cook by placing a burner on it. It burns with an incandescent warm yellow glow which can be used to light up homes. Subsequently, the dung dries up to produce good manure. The gobar gas plant is ideal for rural ecology.

I dreamt of rearing cows and grazing them on the grassy land. They would supply the milk for my tea. I would set curd, churn it for whey, and make butter from the milk. As I would be cooking on a kerosene stove, I would need alternative fuel; milk for myself, manure for the farm, draught for ploughing and drawing the bullock-cart. Cattle offered the best solution. I spent almost every waking moment strolling across the semi-wilderness of the countryside, dreaming of my farm, bathing in the stream skirting the land, and breathing in the heady fragrance of wildflowers. I felt I could conquer the world.

I decided to undertake physical work during the day; work on my plans and read after sundown. Such images flashed in and out of my mind, prodding me to plan and act. A dairy would generate a daily income, I thought, while a poultry and silkworm rearing would bring in a monthly income. I would grow seasonal crops and could get three yields a year. Bananas would be a good annual crop, I reckoned, and coconuts, miraculous trees that they were, would keep me going for a hundred years if I nursed the saplings for about seven or eight years. In the scriptures, the coconut tree is called kalpavriksha, the tree that lives a long, long time and grants all wishes. As the success or failure of my farm would be decided by the end of the time-span I needed to grow my coconut palms, I decided to dedicate myself entirely for ten years to build an integrated farm.

I was blessed with a natural farming instinct, I would like to believe. I had been exposed to the ways of the farmer as a child. My father was my guide and mentor. Farming was our family profession and I guessed that my natural willingness to work amidst nature would more than make up for the initial mistakes I made.

I began by clearing the brush and bramble undergrowth. My work routine also included a daily splash in the stream. While I was in the process of growing familiar with the land I found saplings and shoots, curiously beneath wild clumps of thorns not where the land was barren. I asked an old farmer about it. Birds perched on the branches of the thorn-bushes and dropped a seed after eating the fruit or sometimes the seed would drop into the soil beneath the thorny thickets wrapped in its own dung. And with the onset of monsoon, a sapling would sprout. He identified the saplings as neem, sandal, honge, tamarind, fig, jamun, and the likes.

Along the periphery of my farm ran a meandering perennial stream. In the rains, it was in spate and in the hot season it ran in a trickle. The alternating wet and dry phases made it capable of sustaining a variety of vegetation. The foliage formed a natural habitat for throngs of bugs, beetles, rodents, and snakes as well as wild cats, leopards, wild dogs, wolves, rabbits, and jackals. My father said it formed a natural barrier, putting a brake on wind speed, while the wadi would also help keep the soil moist.

Typical new-age farmers brought in heavy farm equipment to clear the existing vegetation. They dug up the earth with heavy bulldozers and clean-shaved the undergrowth. When it became known that the government would be compensating the loss of land in the submersion area with land that once supported the grazing of royal cattle, neighbouring farmers moved in quickly and felled the trees standing on it for timber and firewood. What now remained was thick undergrowth.

I could not explain why, but I was uncomfortable with this approach. Later I discovered how, from the fruit seeds in bird droppings amidst the vegetation, nature produced its own best conditions for the seeds to sprout with the first rains, grow into saplings, and eventually, trees. Subsequently I discovered the first rule of farming: *Do not clear up the land.*

I pondered about which trees I should grow on the farm. It was not a cause of concern for me as I was confident that the birds would bring in the right seeds from fruit-bearing trees. What was good for the birds would be good for the farm. The trees would provide a mixture of habitats and nurture a wide variety of bird species.

There is a saying: *Less government is good government.* I recognized a parallel saying that was true for farming: *Less farming is good farming.* I set a diktat—nobody should touch anything that grew on the land, the rule extending right up to the periphery. I gradually learnt to recognize local tree and plant species and worked towards ensuring that they were allowed to thrive, selectively clearing the undergrowth to expose the soil.

I also needed to arrange for funds in order to ensure the best returns from my investments. My financial resources were limited: a total of approximately Rs 40,000 including my army settlement money and about Rs 35,000 borrowed from friends with the promise that I would return the amount once the bank loan came through.

The monsoons were a good six months away and I urgently needed to raise a loan before the onset of the farming season. I paid daily visits to Hassan on my motorcycle, peddling my dream to local banks, where the managers asked me for a business plan. I submitted an elaborate handwritten plan of my intended investments but I was unable to specify the time-frame within which I would be able to repay the loan.

I completed a round of all the eight or ten public sector banks in Hassan, including nationalized ones like Canara Bank, Syndicate Bank, and Vijaya Bank. I routinely returned empty-handed, the managers promising to get back to me. One day, a manager sent word that he was busy and would not be able to meet me. I lost my temper, stormed into his room, and charged him of harassing me, using a double expletive of which my school principal would certainly not have approved.

The authorities also have their prerogatives. The shell-shocked manager handed back my file and said: 'Please take this. There is nothing I can do.' That was the end of all transactions with him. I was, however, determined not to give up and was prepared to appeal to higher authorities.

Those were the days of Janardhan Pujari at the helm of the finance ministry. He had taken a staunch pro-borrower position and was notorious for his public humiliation of bank managers who did not lend money to farmers. The government had cried itself hoarse with policy announcements favouring the farmer. Government functionaries proclaimed agriculture to be the number one priority sector. Farmers must be given loans and every support, they said. I, however, discovered the ground reality to be very different.

Bankers were rude, apathetic, and indifferent. I occasionally lost my temper but not my patience. I realized that bank managers, as custodians of public funds, would not be easily inclined to lend money to poor farmers whose prospects of paying back dues in time were generally low. I was however persistent in my efforts and could never imagine going home empty-handed. The government's pro-farmer policy gave me confidence. I had sustenance for the present and was content but I lived in the future and tried to generate new ideas about the ways and means of approaching the banks.

There were five or six other farmers who had been rehabilitated and had settled on their new plots of land. They however did not have any formal education or much exposure. There was only one who had come over with the idea of doing something with his new land. He was my neighbour, and lived in a thatched hut. One night I heard a commotion in the neighbourhood. It transpired that villagers who had traditionally grazed their cattle on the grazing land—since no one objected—had come to attack the new settlers. They had ransacked huts, scattered pots and pans, and attacked the cattle. In one sense the villagers' anger was justified, though they had no legal claim to the land given to the new settlers—who now had to face their wrath.

People have this strange tendency of not sharing space. While travelling on a train they do not want new passengers to join them midway. All of us share similar emotions and subconsciously label the new claimant of the seat next to us as an intruder. The local farmers felt the same way about us, the new colonizers. They were loath to give up their 'right' over their grazing land. The situation was tense.

I was sleeping in my tent and woke up to the sound of rumbling earth just before daybreak. I scrambled out and was shocked to find a large number of farmers working on my land, digging furrows in the earth with the help of cattle, uprooting saplings and young plants which had just about taken root. They ransacked all they could. I guessed the reason and decided in a split-second what should be done.

I came out, looked the leader in the eye, and thundered, 'Look here, I will not take an inch of land that does not belong to me. But at the same time I will also not forego an inch of land that belongs to me. This land is mine by law.' I had realized that these people would be sharing the same neighbourhood and local resources with me. We would in the future occasionally require one another's help. These farmers were good people and they were resentful simply because the government had drawn-up faulty plans and had used these natural pastures to rehabilitate displaced farmers and landowners after building dams that had submerged their villages and agricultural land.

I reasoned with the marauders, promising to try persuading the government to allot them the remaining land and bring over the government surveyor to clearly define the extent of my land. Till then, I promised to do no tilling, not dabble in village politics or interfere in other people's affairs. My neighbours took me at my word and we shook hands.

The surveyor came and marked the boundaries of my farm. He also declared the remaining land, ranging over hundreds of acres, to be unclaimed. Local farmers could send a petition to the government with a request that the unclaimed land be allocated to them. It was a time when the government was awarding ownership rights to tenants and sharecroppers, i.e., the people who cultivated but did not own the land. My neighbours were thrilled with the news. The government subsequently legalized their ownership.

This was my first encounter with a village mob. I learnt my first lesson and developed the art of working with the local people and finding mutually acceptable solutions. I had an ingrained skill of looking at things from other people's perspectives, which my father had helped me to develop. This guided me in resolving many conflicts. I would have been a fool to pick up a fight with the local people, making the environment hostile. I knew they would see my point of view if I was patient and discussed their problem with empathy. They did and they are all friends now. They come to work for me, and I also promised to work towards the improvement of the infrastructure, particularly the roads, and bring electricity to the villages. They accepted the barter offer and withdrew.

The stream marked a kind of boundary between the new arrivals and the traditional dwellers. The new settlers had been given land (2000 acres of unclaimed grazing land) to the west and north of the stream. Land to the south and east was the property of the old inhabitants. I, in a sense, held centre ground. The grazing land was a testimony to the maharaja's foresight. His government had planned economic development, keeping the future generations in mind. General economic infrastructure development included roads and highways, tanks and check-dams, state-managed orchards, and common grazing land. The trees selected for lining the roads and the borders of tanks were either fruit-bearing or produced timber. They provided shade and shelter against the occasional harsh winds that swept the open countryside. The maharajas of old have a lesson for our modern maharajas in the appreciation of ecology and a holistic approach to development.

One of the things that I observed with much curiosity during the first days on my land was what the visiting relatives and guests did on a neighbour's farm. I watched, with a sense of wonder and a twinge of shame, how they busied themselves with farm chores right from dawn. The guests helped milk the cows, gather the dung, and plaster the walls with cowdung patties. They cleaned the courtyard, helped in the kitchen, picked vegetables, and helped cook breakfast. Later in the day they took part in whatever farming activity the host had planned during that part of the season. The relatives and guests were well looked after but they shared the work. I found it a very humbling experience, unlike guests who come to our houses who are wined and dined and never joined in the farm work.

One day, as I was clearing the field, I saw a very dark, handsome man in his mid-forties approaching me. Features exquisitely chiselled, he was solid of build, clad in a pure white dhoti, and had a firm and confident bearing. The visitor introduced himself as Manje Gowda, my neighbour. I did a 'namaste' and we shook hands, I felt the reassuring hand of a farmer, rough and calloused with years of work on the land. I had only heard of Manje Gowda, a very capable and helpful farmer, who had settled south and east of the stream. I had also heard that he was a recluse. His family property had come up for division about thirty years ago. Manje Gowda had taken the larger piece of land that was untamed. He had come away with his bride, set up camp and (now) lived in a thatched hut across the stream. There were many legends about the man; about his fearlessness, his indomitable courage, and about how he had tamed the wild and raised a coconut plantation. He had fought off brigands and dacoits, staved off the attacks of wild animals. He must have had his share of other irritants too, but he had remained absolutely aloof from village politics (and had prospered through sheer willpower).

As we shook hands I saw how strong the man was and I had no doubt that most of the legends about him must be true. I also felt my conceit peg down a notch because till then I had entertained the implicit belief that my adventure had been quite unique. On the positive side, I felt a greater confidence that I would succeed in my farming project.

Manje Gowda was a farmer in the widest sense of the term. He had five children—all grown up. Like other farmers in Karnataka who traditionally worked on the land with their families providing support by performing complementary farm chores—weeding, ploughing and sowing, protecting the crop from grazing cattle, harvesting, carrying, threshing, winnowing, and the rest—Manje Gowda worked alone on his land.

He had observed my labours on the farm and knew that I cooked myself. For some strange reason he had taken a liking for me. Then, as days passed, we became friends. This was a true friendship. I would often receive a meal of ragi roti and chutney from the Manje Gowda household. His wife would carry a small basket of rotis wrapped in a banana leaf on her head, walk two kilometres to my farm, wade through a stream, and deliver the meal. Manje Gowda persuaded his wife to volunteer. 'This young fellow lives in a tent. He works on the field all by himself. He is not married. His family is not with him. So why don't you give him some food,' he would say. The pure affection I received touched me profoundly. Manje Gowda and his wife were like parents to me. Whenever there was a village festival (habba) they called me over for a meal. Those were some of the best parties I attended. The Gowdas hardly had any wealth of their own but their generosity was unmatched. People like them and my father show how you need not possess a lot to be able to give and share.

People dropped by to give me farming tips. I was aware of the hardships and problems of rural life. Nonetheless, I derived inspiration from the inexhaustible enthusiasm, and zest for life of farmers and the near-landless workers on my farm. They had mastered the art of living with meagre resources. Rather than despairing and brooding over their misfortune or the uncertainty ahead, they remained firmly rooted to the present and stoically went about their daily business. They would often quote a Kannada proverb: 'If He has created you, won't He feed you?' And on a festival day, they would abandon everything else, prepare the traditional festival sweet dish (payasa), and celebrate. People offered help with labour, bullocks, and new ideas. My money was running out but I never worried because I was so completely involved with the life around me.

One afternoon I was completely immersed in my work, when my sixth sense alerted me to the presence of a stranger. I turned around and saw a gentleman in formal western clothes.

'Hello!' I said.

The visitor introduced himself as Chandrashekhar, manager at Vijaya Bank's Javagal branch. I wondered what the manager was doing on my farm. How had he got there in the first place? Had he waded across the stream? One could wade through if the water was sufficiently shallow.

Chandrashekhar said he had heard about a crazy army officer who lived all by himself in a tent. He wanted to see this maverick with his own eyes. I was not aware that people were calling me a huccha (Kannada for crazy)! The bank manager said he admired my pioneering spirit and courage. The village was apparently under the impression that as I had been unable to secure a bank loan, I would pack up and leave. He had come over to see if he could prevent it.

I asked the manager to stay for lunch. It was a meal I had prepared with my own hands. The menu was the invariable vegetable-dunked sambhar and rice. The only addition was a kosambhari. Kosambhari is a raw salad that is made with softened daal and grated cucumber, carrot, or any other vegetable that can be eaten raw. Curd rice (mosaranna) completed the simple but tasty meal. It was particularly memorable, because at last I had a glimmer of hope. A little sluice of light had opened up somewhere in the dark tunnel. The manager asked me over to his house for a first-hand discussion about the merits of my case.

That evening I reached the manager's house at the appointed hour. The latter had his living quarters on the floor above the bank. I wrote out my plan in simple longhand on a foolscap paper and Chandrashekhar created the blueprint of all my dreams on an ancient manual typewriter.

I spelt out my plan. I wanted to fence the farm and dig a borewell, buy and commission a gobar gas plant, buy cattle and build a dairy farm. I hoped to establish a silkworm-rearing house and raise mulberry. In addition I wanted to cultivate plantation crops like banana and coconuts.

I decided to keep my requirements to the bare minimum as I was wary of borrowing a great deal of money and resolved to initially allot a limited amount of money to each project and manage. Cost-cutting has been my passion. Years later, while working to launch Air Deccan, I sought to cut costs in every possible way. Indeed, the seed of my low-cost airline was sown on my farm!

I ruthlessly imposed cost-cutting regulations on myself too. The logic was very simple: whatever was not going to bring me returns was wasteful expenditure. By that logic, the house was last on the list as it would not generate any income. I loved nature, my needs were simple, and I was happy living in my tent. However, as I realized that the tent might not last more than two years, I set aside Rs 5000, the cost of mud, thatch, and labour, for a thatched hut to live in to enable me to move out of the tent in the future.

Meanwhile, the manager translated the blueprint into a seven-year business plan. He estimated a cash flow and evolved a virtual repayment plan. Thanks to him, I learnt what capital expenditure meant; what cash-flow and amortization implied. In short, I learnt a rudimentary banking vocabulary.

On the following day, Chandrashekhar took my proposal to his regional manager, hoping to persuade his seniors to approve the loan. I do not tire of repeating what becomes for me a formula, a driving inspiration, a truism. It is the golden rule of the entrepreneur:

> Your energy, your passion, your ability to lose yourself in the entirety and the nitty-gritty of your venture to the exclusion of everything else is more important than capital. Thinking is the capital; enterprise is the way; hard work is the solution.　　　　　　　　　　　　　—A.P.J. Abdul Kalam

From the day I set foot on my farm till the day I left it ten years later, the farm and its success were my only obsession. I worked to make the farm a flourishing enterprise with a missionary zeal. The Hindu scriptures say: 'If you want to achieve liberation or moksha, you have to dissolve yourself in the ocean of transcendent reality.' My farming experience was almost vedantic. For me the entrepreneur becomes the idea, dissolves in it; does not exist outside of it. The entrepreneur and the idea becomes one. Mystics perceive God in all that they see. I saw my venture in everything I saw and did; I gave it my heart and soul. It was a spiritual journey of sorts. Leonard Bernstein the great composer once said: 'If you are an artist you don't ask, "Shall I be a violinist?" You simply start playing.' Such was my experience with the farm.

A week later the bank manager came once more to my farm. I received him with great expectations, and trepidation too. The good news was broadcast first. A loan amount of Rs 1,47,000 had been sanctioned. The bad news followed and my joy was short-lived. The bank had a condition; I must provide a guarantor for the loan. This was a new word for me. It meant that someone with sound financial standing would have to vouch for me. The bank had valued my farm at Rs 90,000. The loan amount they were ready to sanction was of greater value and therefore the bank wanted a guarantor, as farmers were forever in debt and were usually unable to repay.

I did not despair, and the very next day I set off on my motorcycle expecting to visit all my friends and relatives and request them to stand as my guarantor. I had a good estimate of my self-worth. However, as I moved from door to door with my application, I began to realize that they were more than a little dubious about my performance credentials in business. However, I had no doubts about my earning handsome returns from the farm and paying back the loan with no difficulty.

My relatives and friends were polite. Nobody denied me help and all promised to get back to me but nobody actually did. I was running out of time and realized that I lacked understanding of the real world. My father had once defined a good friend as one who stands by you when you are in need of money. I did the rounds of Bengaluru, Mysore, and Hassan but in the end nobody actually volunteered.

One day, after returning from one of my frustrating motorcycle trips in search of a guarantor, I found my neighbour and good friend Manje Gowda at the gate. He approached me with a sense of apprehension and said, in Kannada, 'Captain Sahib! I have heard that you may be going back because you could not get a loan. And you are not getting a loan because you don't have a guarantor. Is it true?' I said, 'Yes, it's true.' 'Captain, do not worry,' my neighbour replied solemnly. 'I will stand guarantee. I will mortgage my fields. You are a great inspiration to my children. I don't want you to go. We stand to benefit from your being here.' I was stunned and speechless. Here was a farmer whom I had known only for three months, and he of all the people in the world was willing to pledge his land for me. It was as though Manje Gowda had been sent by God to lend me a hand and see me through my worst crisis. Most battles are fought in the mind. Had I abandoned the farm project and gone back, I would have felt dejected, defeated, and bitter. Manje Gowda's timely offer of help however renewed my faith in people.

Receiving unexpected succour from my neighbour reminded me of a story about P.G. Wodehouse. A friend went to see him. He sat and watched as Wodehouse wrote a letter. The author completed his missive, placed it in an envelope, sealed it, and wrote an address on it. Then, walking to the window of his third-floor apartment, Wodehouse threw the letter out on to the street below. The friend expressed surprise at what he had seen.

Wodehouse told the visitor: 'You will be surprised by how much goodness there is in this world. Anybody who will pick it up will place it in the post box. They will assume somebody has dropped it by accident!' In a similar vein, 'Men are cruel but man is kind', in the words of Tagore.

I was hesitant about accepting Manje Gowda's offer, but he led me by hand and took me to the bank. There he deposited documents of ownership of his ten acres of coconut plantation. I received a loan of Rs 1,47,000 to invest in the various projects on my farm.

I more than once enjoyed the hospitality of Manje Gowda and his wife, Jayamma. One such occasion was a festival day during Dussehra, which is observed as a commemorative day for the ancestral spirits with an offering of prayers and feasting. Senior members of Manje Gowda's clan took turns to invite one another; Manje Gowda invited me.

Traditionally, a sacrificial lamb is fattened for the feast day. The meat is marinated and cooked with strong spices over a wood fire as the main dish of the multi-course meal; the heady odour hangs heavy in the air for a long time.

On the eve of the feast there was a light drizzle. The rain became heavier overnight and the stream overflowed its banks. Manje Gowda had become a close friend by now and there was no way I could give the feast a miss. It was late evening when I decided to swim across. The stream in full spate spanned approximately twenty metres, shore to shore. On either side, there was shallow ground, while the maximum depth of the stream was five–six metres. Being an experienced swimmer, I wore shorts and a t-shirt, waded through shallow ground, and swam across. As I waded through the remaining stretch of slush, I found myself soaked to the bone and shivered in the cold wind.

I walked another kilometre to reach the house of my hosts and called out. Manje Gowda and Jayamma could not believe their eyes when they saw me standing, looking virtually like an apparition. Overjoyed, Manje Gowda brought me a towel and a change of clothes, followed by rum and coconut water.

The Gowda family showered me with hospitality. Dinner was served. The meal featured a variety of dishes and plenty of well-cooked mutton. The rich food, the rum, and the nippy weather made me feel intoxicated and euphoric. I stayed over that night and slept like a log. I still consider that evening's meal the best I have ever had.

Thanks to Manje Gowda's offer of help, I now had the money and set about putting my plan into action. First on the agenda was the dairy. I scouted around among the neighbouring villages for milch cows and built a gobar gas plant. (The gobar gas plant is working to this day, thirty years after it was set up.) I built a rearing house for sericulture using mud bricks and mud plastering. I bought a bullock-cart and gave Rs 3000 to a local contractor to build me a house.

My younger brother Sampath had recently completed a master's degree in industrial chemistry with a very high first class. He had seen me living on the farm and felt sufficiently inspired to resist the temptation of a well-paid nine-to-five job and joined me on the farm.

I invested the money gradually, but I had grossly underestimated the costs. Every project had a cost overrun. The dairy farm needed Rs 12,000 rather than the budgeted Rs 8000. The sericulture project too required more. I put back the money I earned into the projects and I did not have any left to repay the loan. I might have tasted success sooner had I borrowed a larger amount or taken up fewer projects.

Marriage and Farming

Things got busy on the farm; days passed rapidly. One day, out of the blue, father asked me to come over to Gorur. There was a marriage proposal for me. 'I am aware that you don't have a steady source of income to support a wife, but you are twenty-seven years old. You should look into the proposal,' he said. I did not pause to think and quickly shot back to my father. 'Please tell them that I am not one of those well-to-do farmers who are owners of flourishing farms with a bungalow,' I replied. 'I am not an officer in the army any longer. They might be under that impression and you must explain the actual situation to them.' I asked my father also to let them know about the infancy of the farm, the huge loan I had taken from the bank, and that I was nowhere close to breaking-even. That, I thought, would surely put them off because no girl or family would want a prospective bridegroom in such straitened circumstances. I myself was not considering marriage; I would not have been able to support a family at the time.

I met my father a month later. He said the girl knew my story and because of it, and notwithstanding its somewhat outlandish contours, she seemed even more eager to meet me. I was amused, but my practical side saw how impossible the idea was. I asked father to write to them again, impressing upon them the fact that I had no job. There was a second round of letters between my father and the girl's father, but the girl was insistent, even a little adamant.

The meeting took place at my parents' home in Gorur. On the appointed day, the guests came over. The party was made up of the girl, her sister, her parents, and the village matchmaker. This composition of visitors is common in the case of arranged marriages in villages. The matchmaker is the one who performs all the due diligence on the prospective bride and groom. It is customary among some Iyengar families for the boy to visit the girl's home. In others it is the other way round. A groom is eventually selected on the basis of his educational and professional achievements. Lacking these, a poorly qualified candidate might find inheritance of property and wealth weighing in his favour! If a girl is able to sing, play the sitar or veena, cook, or do embroidery, these qualities add to her suitability as a prospective bride. Special emphasis is laid on the girl's accomplishments in the fine arts. Social graces and homemaking skills are regarded as an additional asset. Where these social graces are in short measure, the belief is that an offer of dowry will fill the void!

The girl who came to meet me sang a song for us. She had a beautiful voice and was very charming. She was demure and had a pleasing, radiant smile. I was smitten. I was however conscious that marriage could be a recipe for disaster. I was torn between the two equally strong emotions. I had to figure a way out of this. I, therefore, asked whether I could speak with her. Our village house had a balcony, and we went up there. I described my material circumstances without embellishment. I told her candidly that I had neither a proper house to live in nor a steady income. She listened attentively and asked me a sensible question. What my source of income would be in future, she asked. I told her in all honesty that I was investing funds raised through a bank loan in plantation crops; in a cattle dairy, and in sericulture. These would be my sources of income. She said she was okay with that and admitted she would like to marry me. For my part, I realized I would have company in my lonely life on the farm and a wife who would cook my meals. I was favourably inclined to the marriage but I suggested that both of us gave some time and thought to the prospect. I thought she might care to visit my farm before making up her mind. The girl's name was Bhargavi. She did not want to come and was convinced that everything was fine. I however wanted her to see for herself the situation she was getting into. It was important because it could very well have been a strange, exotic dream image that she had woven around the concept of life on a farm. A date was therefore set for her family to come and visit my farm.

Bhargavi's father, like mine, was a teacher but he was also a government functionary: deputy director of education for a district in Karnataka. Their family lived in Shimoga, a more northerly town in Malnad and the district headquarters. She came from a simple family like mine with a rural background. They too were middle-class in their value system. She had lived all over the state and had a steady head on her shoulders. I was confident she would be able to get along well with my family and my relatives who were very ordinary middle-class people. I did not want a wife with stars in her eyes and to have to continually stretch my limits to meet her expectations. In that, and in every other sense, Bhargavi was well suited for me. I knew we would hit it off.

We chose a date for Bhargavi and her family to visit the farm, which was eight kilometres from the nearest bus stop. There was no convenient transport. My friend Manje Gowda offered me his bullock-cart. He hitched a great old pair of oxen called Rama and Bhima to the cart, choosing them for their docility of temperament. He gave them a good wash, swept the cart, and spread a clean carpet inside it. Manje Gowda's son Sheena drove the cart, I hopped on to my bike and we headed for the bus stand. Bhargavi and her family got into the bullock-cart while I rode on ahead to ensure a proper reception at Manje Gowda's home. We then expectantly awaited the cart's arrival.

The typical bullock-cart in Karnataka is unsurpassed in its design for rural roads. The wheels are made of teak and come with a standard diameter of five feet. The rim is lined with steel. Thanks to the traditional design, the bullocks can effortlessly pull the cart through the most testing slush and bog.

We could hear the cart a mile down the village road. Sounds of the snorting and heaving were borne by the wind. We could also hear the grinding of the wheels on the firm bottom of the rut. The cart bells made a sound between a tinkle and a thud and I wondered what Bhargavi thought of all this. Her parents were probably not particularly enthused by all this adventure. Even as I fell in to reverie listening to the approaching bullock-cart, I was suddenly alerted when Manje Gowda sprang to his feet and rushed out to the bullock-cart, yelling expletives at his son Shrinivas (Sheena). '*Aeye* Sheena, *aeye Munde Magne*, where is the axle pin?' he thundered. Shrinivas, in his excitement at bringing the bride home had forgotten to put on the buttress pins that fastened axle to wheel. It was a miracle how the cart had safely made the eight-kilometres journey with such precious cargo, on those impossibly rutted roads. The wheel could easily have come off. Had that occurred; it would have been a disaster and a very bad omen for the marriage.

I do sometimes think that marriages are probably made in heaven. Perhaps marriages *are* made in heaven! The party disembarked from the cart. Manje Gowda was anxious whether my prospective father-in-law would be comfortable eating in his house, but Bhargavi and her parents gladly accepted his hospitality. Lunch served, the party walked to my farm, a kilometre away. Visitors to my farm had to negotiate a small stream. I had placed boulders in the bed of the stream as stepping stones to help them cross without having to wade through.

On seeing the farm, my future mother-in-law could not repress her disappointment at what she found there. She could not hold herself back from blurting out, 'There is nothing but thorn here.' That was like a slap in my face. She seemed to be cautioning her daughter, in an oblique manner, to think again. This would be her last chance before committing herself to this desolate destiny. Her daughter could still say a polite no!

I quickly recovered and set out to explain. It was because the land I had chosen to come to and work on was in absolutely untrammelled wilderness that I had taken it up as a challenge. I would make something out of it. I could have gone on living with my father at the family home in Gorur, but didn't want to. My future mother-in-law was very pleasant about the whole thing. She said she understood my adventurous spirit and was glad for me. She wished me success.

They stayed overnight. It was like having family over. They cooked dinner for us all. It was quite easy to like them. I showed Bhargavi around the farm. We chatted for a long time, about three or four hours, beneath a banyan tree, which still stands on the farm. I told her about my past, my passions, and my dreams. I told her I wanted to be on the farm for at least ten years. I had no plans about what I would do thereafter. I however was determined to create a really good farm. I said, 'If you like farming or living in a remote area, we could have a good life here. You might even come to enjoy it.' In my heart I hoped she would agree, but I did not hide the hardship that comes with living on a farm. She said she had made her decision; she would not back off from it. She wanted to marry me. The Buddha had made a crucial decision beneath the Bodhi tree, and walked away from his family. The two of us made our decision about life beneath the banyan tree, to come together!

Bhargavi and her parents took leave the next day. Manje Gowda personally ensured that the bullock-cart had been made secure this time and that the buttressing pin held fast to the axle! It was decided that the marriage would take place on 26 October. It was April–May, the late spring season of the year. I still had time to put things in place.

Over the next six months, I saw the farm slowly take shape. I heeded many pieces of advice given to me in passing. One person gave me a gem. He said, 'Be careful not to erode even an ounce of precious topsoil. It is the topsoil which is holding this world together.' I was fortunate to receive advice from people who knew good farming techniques. I met all kinds of farmers, some good, some bad; some used ancient practices, some modern.

I observed there existed a disconnect between low-expense, low-yield methods and high-expense, high-yield methods. I had reservations about the use of fertilizers. The use of machinery such as tillers, tractors, and combine harvesters seemed too heavy-handed whereas the traditional approach was gentler and more in tune with nature.

The old-fashioned farmers seemed to be inspired in their farming methods by a sense of 'beregu'. In traditional practice, farming is all about being in harmony with nature. That means the right season, right day, right time, right temperature, right humidity, and right soil conditions to plant the seed and harvest the crop. Farming was second nature to these farmers; they did it almost by instinct.

Modern agriculture is about the conquest of nature. I was not in a position to decide between the two approaches. Both modern science and ancient wisdom tell us that topsoil is the most precious element in agriculture. I, therefore, opened up the topsoil very gently and cautiously, like a surgeon would a patient's skin. I put in place ridges and bunds to capture rainwater and to protect topsoil erosion. I planted a wide variety of crops, ranging from coriander and ragi to jowar and Bengal gram. Traditional farmers intuitively understood the nature of the soil, the nature of the weeds, which system of irrigation will work best, how much rainwater the plants absorb, and on the like. I continually observed them, talked to them, and learnt from them.

I employed the products of modern technology too, by building a gobar gas plant, setting up dairy, poultry, and silkworm-rearing sheds. Soon, much like the other farmers, I got into debt. No matter what I did, I was unable to repay the loan. I knew something was going wrong somewhere. I had my share of problems with farming. If the seed was right, the sprouting wasn't; if the saplings rose fine, the water wasn't sufficient. There was too much rain or too little. One way or other, the vagaries of nature, or rather, not understanding nature or not being able to tune in perfectly, hit me hard. Beyond nature were the market forces; they too conspired to harm me. I got a good crop but did not get a good price. I was getting deeper and deeper into debt. I did everything recommended by the government, agriculture and horticulture departments but things simply didn't seem to work.

My struggle with farming lent my life a spiritual dimension. I sensed within me a sense of oneness with the environment. In one breath I took in the mystic aura of the early morning sunrise; the sweet fragrance rising from freshly churned earth as I walked across the fields. I was in search of a natural method of understanding the crops, the seasons, and the soil. On the one hand, I was trying to be a conventional farmer. I sought to cultivate crops, sell the produce in the market, and get paid in order to repeat the cycle. I had the bank loan in mind, too. However, this quotidian aspect of life did not keep me from being sensitive to the deep symbiosis of the forces of nature: the soil, the crops, and the cultivator. It was a great beginning, and all I knew was that I didn't know much about farming.

There were problems. There were viral attacks, pests, and weeds. I planted bananas, an evergreen crop. I got the first crop but the second was attacked and destroyed by virus. I learnt it the hard way that there is no medicine in the world to combat the banana virus.

I was also able to get an insight into the debt cycle of farmers. It was a triple jackpot for the local money-lender. He gave farmers seeds on credit and made money on the exchange value of seeds and also on the interest on the loan. He gave farmers fertilizers and pesticides on credit and made money on their worth plus the interest he charged the farmers. He bought the farmers crop on mortgage, cheap and below the market price, and made money on that too. The money-lender made profits on all counts even before a farmer brought his produce to the market. Conversely, the farmer got beaten at all the four points of sale: seeds, fertilizers, pesticides, and crops. As there was no market reference for their produce, they undersold a crop before it was due for the market. Most farmers therefore found themselves in debt. The money-lender deducted principle and a usurious interest, often leaving the farmer with nothing to take home. There was no way the farmer could get out of the vicious cycle of debt and usury.

In addition to the cycle of usury, I also grew to realize one curious lesser-known little fact: *the modern farmer inputs more than the output.*

The farm offered me lessons in natural history, and I imbibed them voraciously. There were millions of insects on the farm. I saw that when they died, their remains returned to the topsoil and replenished soil fertility. While the intensive use of fertilizer and pest-control chemicals brought in relatively high yields in a short time-frame, the techniques were double-edged. Aggressive, intensive, deep-trench tilling exposed soil to the elements of nature, resulting in erosion. The use of fertilizers and chemicals acted on the biotic activity of the topsoil; they too stripped the soil of its natural layer of nutrients. Artificial fertilizers also altered soil chemistry and rendered it sterile.

I began realizing that farming was not just about phosphorous and nitrogen compounds or chemical pest and weed killers. These were the agents of interference that we had brought into play in our limited understanding. Farming was wholly about building and nurturing natural relationships. Modern science asked farmers to aggressively use chemicals at all stages of food crop production. It did not realize that by doing so, the soil was stripped of all its nutrients. The first crop might benefit from the artificially introduced nutrient, but after one crop, the soil did not sustain the yield unless greater quantities of chemicals were used.

I saw that farmers were being asked to replenish the soil with artificial fungi and earthworms (vermiculture). What this overlooked was that earthworms are a part of the natural life of the soil. They don't need to be cultivated. It is like generating some oxygen for yourself at home; like polluting the city and then visiting an oxygen bar to get a whiff of life.

We have taken it upon ourselves to regulate natural agents. Who, or which agency, prevented termite attack in the forests, for example? Forests sported the most luxuriant and wildest of growth and undergrowth but one did not hear of disease afflicting a prime forest. A queen termite lays 15,000 to 20,000 eggs every day for more than ten years. There is therefore no way their propagation can be prevented; termites like ants are a force of nature. And why indeed should it be prevented? The termite is a part of the balance established by nature and effectively returns hardwood to the earth.

These experiences gave me insight into the logic and method of scientific discovery. One experience I can describe as a kind of eureka moment! On a visit to the wildlife sanctuary of Bandipur, something caught my eye. This came in handy in evolving useful farming practices. I saw that only dead trees were attacked by termite; the healthy ones were untouched. Could it be, I thought, that termites did not attack healthy trees because there was plenty of food for them below the trees? Food was present in the form of tree-droppings such as twigs and branches, leaves, flowers, ripened fruit, seed, bird-droppings, and the carcasses of insects and animals. The termites ate their fill and left the trees alone.

When termites attacked the coconut trees on the farm we had used benzene hexachloride to get rid of them. When it rained, the spray was washed down into the soil and the stream nearby, carrying the residual chemicals along with it, polluting the soil, the stream, the ponds, and the groundwater. The chemical pesticide killed all the organisms in the soil and also affected the ecosystem of the stream. I quickly realized that termites were attacking the coconut trees because the soil was like a clean concrete floor, offered them no nourishment. In our obsession to keep the soil clean we had been removing all twigs, branches, dead organisms, thereby disturbing soil ecology.

I was trying to understand how to farm naturally and yet get a high yield. Nothing worked to my advantage at the time, I was sore about the way the market worked. Prices of all products were on the rise, except for farm produce. I was annoyed that businessmen took a salary over and above expenditure and still ensured profits for themselves at the end of the working year. However, my acutest and most intense cause of chagrin was that a farmer never took a salary and was never able to gauge whether or not the year had been profitable. A farmer worked from dawn to dusk. There is no farmer in this country who has an ounce of unwanted fat. My city friends spoke of gyms and exercise. A farmer would think you were crazy if you suggested to him that he should take 'exercise'. Exercise was futile labour for him. He walked several kilometres a day: to and from his fields and around them. He worked all day in season, sowing, ploughing, weeding, shooing birds off the crop, harvesting, winnowing, and storing the grain. He personally carried the produce to the market, stretching each sinew of his body. There is sweat and blood, and many a tear, in the life of the farmer.

The wedding day drew near! As I wanted to put most of the money in the productive areas of the farm, I grudgingly built a room 20 ft by 30 ft. One corner served as the bath partition, one was devised as the kitchen, a third was the bedroom where my wife and I would sleep. Raju would sleep in the tent which would continue to remain where it was earlier.

I travelled to Hassan and picked up six cane chairs and other furniture for the house. I spent Rs 1200 extra on the house which had been budgeted for Rs 3000 and felt that I had spent a fortune on it. Looking back however I feel truly sorry for what I put my wife through. I could have built a slightly more comfortable hut. At the time however I was so obsessed with the farm that an extra rupee spent on the house would have been considered an unjustified indulgence.

Dowry was as much a social reality in those days as it is now. If it was not explicit in the abstract form of cash, it existed in tacit forms. It made me proud that my father had taken nothing from mother's parents. I had nothing to do with dowry and bluntly told the bride's mother not to send anything, not even the traditional saris that accompanied the bridal trousseau. I wanted a simple wedding and wanted no gifts to be given to my mother or sisters or brothers. I said I would buy them saris.

Indian weddings are contexts for one-upmanship. People like to show that they are a notch higher in social status than they actually are. The pressure is immense on the girl's father. I have seen it in my own family. When my sister got married, my mother put tremendous pressure on my father and he was forced to borrow money. I had witnessed the difficulties my father faced and decided I would not allow needless grandeur and pomp. I was severely critical of this lavish extravagance but little did I realize that some of these very practices would help my helicopter business in the future. One day, a rich businessman would use the helicopter for dropping rose petals on the wedding couple at the time of the wedding ceremony. Another would bring the groom's baraat to the bride's residence in the helicopter rather than on a horse!

I held a feast at my village temple in Gorur. The Yoganarasimha Swamy temple is right on the banks of the river in Gorur and we couldn't have asked for a more picturesque venue for it. The entire village was invited. There were relatives, friends from the village and from the army. My army friends teased me about my having become a total farmer, and took me out on one last bachelors' drinking binge.

The wedding took place in Hassan. This town is sometimes referred to as the poor man's Ooty because it enjoys a salubrious climate throughout the year and its cost of living is reasonably low. It was a typical Iyengar Brahmin wedding and the ceremonies lasted three days. We had chosen the simplest of ceremonies for observance. Sanskrit shlokas on marriage were chanted.

Uncle Gorur Ramaswamy Iyengar attended the wedding. We sat around a bonfire after the wedding, chatting, exchanging stories and anecdotes, and sharing jokes. My wife looked beautiful in a traditional Iyengar silk sari. She looked petite (not that I am toweringly tall). My uncle observed everything keenly and said to me, 'Today is your day in the sun. Make the most of it.'

He then related a raunchy story, the import of which I understood much later. He narrated an event that had taken place in Sabarmati Ashram. He said there was a man who was an ethnic Baluch or Pakhtun. Was he referring to Khan Abdul Ghaffar Khan, who was later called Frontier Gandhi? I am not certain. The Khan was an extremely tall man. This particular man in uncle's story had a wife who was very short in stature. The inmates of the Ashram had a standing joke about the Pathan. They had given him a nickname bhoochumbi, which, loosely translated, means 'earth kisser'. The reference was very physical and the humour lay in the image of this man bending almost as low as the earth to kiss his bride. His bride was so painfully short in stature that the act of kissing his bride, his friends at the ashram imagined, would almost certainly be like kissing the earth. It was a joke, of course, and the audience laughed. Uncle however kept a straight face. I wondered for quite a while what the joke was about, but later when it flashed on me, I walked away, laughing.

I invited thirty-five people to my farm on the day following our wedding and told them that as I had just one room to spare they would have to squeeze in and make themselves comfortable. I lighted a roaring campfire and arranged for rum. The guests sat around the fire in the open and partied late into the night. It was about two in the morning when it began raining.

We therefore went in and huddled together. We slept end to end, shoulder to shoulder. The room looked like an avalanche of bodies and it accommodated exactly thirty-five people, wall to wall. The following morning, when the guests began to leave, I could see that the finality of marriage was overwhelming my new bride. She looked at her mother, tearfully. Marriages are a mixture of joy and tears. It must have been a worrying thought for her parents that they were leaving their daughter behind to live in a thatched hut at the back of beyond in the wilderness, with just me as company. On the other hand, they must also have been consoled by the other side of reality that it was the beginning of a new life for their daughter. In a sombre tone that was carried through only by the strength of her dignity, my mother-in-law said, 'Take care of my daughter'. Her eyes welled up with tears but she bravely held herself back from breaking down altogether. I too was overwhelmed by the awareness that a new life was beginning for me and felt also a deep concern: would she be able to take the rigours of such a life? There was no running water, no electricity, everything had to be devised from scratch, and I possessed none of the interesting distractions or modern gadgets of urban life apart from a simple radio, a few kitchen utensils and a slew of cane chairs. That was the material world in which Bhargavi now found herself.

Each day there was one moment of magic at the farm: that single moment at the fall of dusk when the entire stretch of the farm was bathed by the setting sun in a pale golden glow. It triggered a strange feeling in those who happened to witness it: a nostalgic mix of joy and vague longings. This golden moment conveyed to me in a mysterious way that a new life was about to begin, not only for me and my new bride, but for the farm as a whole.

The next few years were the most wonderful in my life. My new bride and I had a lot of time with each other. We did not speak very much but silence is a golden link and conveyed more than words. We had friends visiting us once in a while. It was however mostly Bhargavi and I alone on the farm. We took long walks every morning and evening. She was, and is, an excellent cook. We ate our meals together and enjoyed a drink each, in the evenings. I would sometimes see her from a distance. She looked beautiful and delicate as the flowers on the farm. She became part of the landscape—and of my life!

The farm however needed tending and I found it increasingly hard to repay the bank loan and ploughed all my earnings back into the farm. We led an absolutely frugal life, in material terms, but spiritually there was so much wealth and so much depth in the little lineaments of our life!

I devoted my entire self in the search of alternative ways of income-generation. The way out of difficulty is not frustration, not fear nor despair.

I had sensitized myself sufficiently closely to be able to listen to nature's subtle and nuanced ways of being. I also read authors who had spent their lives observing and understanding how nature works. I read Rachel Carson, David Orr, Henry David Thoreau, Ralph Waldo Emerson, David Attenborough, Albert Einstein, Richard Feynman, Masanobu Fukuoka, Edwin Schrodinger and Lewis Thomas. Thomas was a great biologist and pathologist. He served as president of the Memorial Sloan-Kettering Cancer Center in New York City. Among his great works are *Lives of a Cell* (1975) and *The Medusa and the Snail* (1986). Lewis Thomas describes the intricate relationships and symbiosis between the creations of nature. There is mystery to the ways of nature but there is also an underlying science. Scientists who explored the limits often did not see a difference between nature and the mystical, seeing rather a common thread running through the universe of life and matter. I gleaned insights into agriculture from their writings although they do not directly speak of farming as an activity.

Cloud-Watcher: More Incidents on the Farm

During the early days on the farm people often asked me what I did. I told them in a matter of fact way, 'I am a cloud-watcher.' I was indeed one. All farmers are cloud-watchers. Farmers have a deep psychological relationship with the idea of timely rain, because their life depends on it. That was the case with me too. Each day I would gaze intently into the western sky hoping to see signs of rain-bearing clouds. I did not have electricity on the farm and was hoping that my recent representation to the electricity department would bear fruit quite soon. I did not therefore invest in a diesel pump-set. In the olden days farmers used various versions of the Persian wheel to raise water from a stream or waterbody. I had seen many in operation as a child. The yeta leverages a weight on one side and allows an operator to scoop water from a well and pour into a trough from which it flows into a channel. This is a regular fixture in every areca-nut plantation in Karnataka. A man stands astride a wooden plank at the edge of a pond. Above him is a see-saw contraption that leverages a fulcrum. The back end of the see-saw is weighted by a heavy stone while at the front end is a trough that dangles by a rope. The man who stands astride on the plank pulls down the trough to the bottom of the pond, fills it with water, and raises it up. When the trough comes up to ground level he tips it into the half-sawed section of wooden channel and the water flows out to the field.

The yeta is now seen only in the remote interiors. In the distant past every farm had a pond with a yeta and every house had a deep well for drawing potable drinking water.

I was on a shoestring budget. Buying a diesel pump-set would now be useless, I thought, because when the electricity came, I would have to sell it. I was an incurable optimist. In my solipsistic optimism, I refused to see that things had a way of their own. I did not see that I was confusing foolhardiness with a positive outlook. This predilection of mine often saw me through the worst of crises, but it got me into deep trouble as well. I could not decide whether it was a good or bad thing.

I went to the horticulture department and to growers and bought about a 1000 coconut saplings. My farm was in a zone that did not have high rainfall. Most agriculture in India is rain dependant. This explains why prudent agricultural techniques and rain management techniques have evolved on Indian soil over the centuries. These methods are suited to specific sub-geographical conditions and cover the entire subcontinent. Farmers in low-rainfall areas had access to rain-water harvesting technologies. They knew how best to conserve and use water to the last drop. This knowledge has passed from generation to generation in the form of farm lore.

My farmer friends and acquaintances told me that things were now changing. Perhaps because of climate change, there were unmistakable changes in rainfall patterns. Farmers remarked that, barring the odd famine, the rains followed the pattern of the cloud-sky map, the rhythm of the seasons, the movements of the planets. They simply followed the map and knew when to plant seed, when to sow, and when to reap the harvest. I had complete faith in the farmers' wisdom and never thought things could go awry. So it became a routine for me to watch the sky, the clouds, every morning and evening. I eagerly looked out for the rain-bearing clouds. And so became a self-professed cloud-watcher.

On the one hand I was suffused by the lyrical, mystical magic of the monsoon: watching with fascination as the sky changed colour, wondering at the emergence of life in the seed, observing plants as they grew inch by inch, gazing in amazement at the renewed vigour of animals, birds, and bees. On the other I observed my own human endeavour as a farmer. Those rare moments when I was able to suspend the hubris of being me, and became part of nature that was transforming itself all around me.

The first rains marked the onset of spring. If you live on a farm and are in tune with the elements, you sense that your breathing, sighing and emotions are synchronized with the breathing, sighing of the earth.

The sky changes colour when the first rains are about to fall. There is a lull, a sudden silence and warmth, thunder rumbles, and lightning flashes. You long for the rain to soak you to your bones. With the first drops of rain, the fragrance of the earth blends with your being. I remember the thrill that coursed through me when the rains arrived.

This was before my marriage. We had formed a band of eight to ten workers ahead of the rain. As soon as the rains came, we dug up the earth, placed precious coconut saplings in deep pits, covered them with earth and manure, and thrust stakes in the ground and secured the saplings. At the end of day two, we had covered twenty acres of land and planted some 800 coconut saplings. I stood on high ground in the farm and looked at the first crop we had planted. I imagined the two-feet high saplings growing-up inch by inch and becoming tall trees.

After a long day's work, I returned home, overcome with exhaustion, yet felt a sense of elation and fulfilment. A fine drizzle had begun. I slept in my tent and woke up in the morning to find myself dripping wet: it had been raining all night. There is a saying in Kannada that the evening rain and the evening guest are here to stay. The rains did not cease all morning, water seeping into the tent.

I had never imagined that rains could be so heavy; otherwise I might have built a concrete platform on the floor of the tent. I huddled in a corner. The first rains are always a sign of good fortune. Soon I heard voices. Raju was trying to call out to me and so were some farmers and cattle-herders. Raju cried, 'Sir, come and take a look at what has happened!' I rushed out and saw that the stream was in spate, having overflowed its banks. The entire twenty-acre stretch on which I had planted coconut saplings was under water. Water flooded the fields. The stream had risen fifteen to twenty feet above its normal level. I climbed up to an elevated spot to survey the damage and saw a sea of destruction. All my efforts, Raju's efforts, and the efforts of my farm workers had simply been washed away. Not a trace of vegetation remained.

It was a great shock. The water did not recede for three days, and when it finally did, it left my land exactly as it had been on the day I had set foot there. The stream had left in its wake an extremely fertile residue of silt. Without brooding over what I had lost I straightaway began thinking about how to put the silt to good use. On one hand it was a huge setback; on the other I rejoiced that the stream had left behind such golden soil. I had long known, and it was discussed in the textbooks of my schooldays, that it was the silt of the receding rivers that had sustained the flourishing civilizations of the past: in the Indus Valley, in the Gangetic Plains, and in the Nile Delta. I now began thinking how I would in future protect my coconut saplings from being washed away when I planted them again, and if this was an annual occurrence, to devise a method of capturing the fertile silt each year.

My father had always advised me never to cut plants growing alongside the stream to prevent soil erosion. I marked off a band of about twenty to forty feet alongside it to enable the natural flora to establish itself without human interference. I planted a wide variety of trees that were ecologically adapted to the area wherever the heavy rains had washed off the bank of the stream and created gullies. I cordoned off the area and asked my people to strictly keep off that swathe. I also constructed a high ridge alongside the stream to allow the receding waters to deposit their silt. I wanted that patch alongside the stream and ditch to become an area of dense foliage. We resolved that next time we would tie the saplings to stone pillars, deeply entrenched. Wooden stakes would be of no help if it rained heavily, we thought, and would also be prone to termite attacks.

Coconut palms love water. The flood should work to our advantage, rather than the reverse, we decided. The trenches we dug in that season helped keep the farm flood free. They captured the silt and acted as rain-water harvest sinks, and also encouraged a wide range of undergrowth to flourish. The stream and the trenches were already in the process of forming a mutually advantageous ecosystem.

The coconut saplings were planted a second time and faced the prospect of several dry winter months as there would be no precipitation until the next rainy season. They would therefore need water so I decided that I must now vigorously pursue the electricity department.

In pursuit of electricity I knocked at several doors. I was frequently in government offices asking them for a connection. The stock reply was, 'Don't worry sir, we are looking into it.' They said they would have to bring electricity from a distribution node that was fifteen kms away. The electricity board needed a minimum utilization of 300 horsepower for it to be viable to them because they had to make a huge investment to bring electricity over such a distance. My farm could use a maximum of 20 HP; what would I do with the remaining 280 HP?

I hit upon an idea to solve the problem. I spoke to like-minded farmers in the neighbourhood. Manje Gowda signed up for 10 HP. I trekked the route along which the electricity would come and got committed users for 300 HP. I found that people would always wait for someone else to take the initiative. Several farms were irrigating with rainwater and would jump at the prospect of electricity for irrigation. I took signed applications from them and presented a solid case to the electricity department.

The department did not however initiate the project. The system had its own inertia, with some prevailing on those willing to undertake the work, to do nothing unless a bribe was offered. They thought they were doing us a favour. The idea of giving bribes revolted me. I could have had them over to dinner; could have given them a few bottles of rum, but the mere suggestion of a bribe made me see red.

I went to Bengaluru to meet the secretary to the department of electricity.

I had no calling card so I sent in my request for an appointment with him on a slip of paper with my name and title written by hand. The slip of paper read, 'Capt. Gopinath'. The secretary called me in. I introduced myself and said to him, 'Sir, I am an army officer and live in a tent on my farm. Your government has spoken a great deal about supporting farming. I have applied for electricity for my farm. For the past year I have been going from pillar to post and nothing has moved. Your department said that they cannot give me less than 300 HP when I need only 20 HP. On my own initiative I have collected a group of farmers to make up the required amount 300 HP. But I still see no sign of any action. My coconut saplings are dying. I planted them in anticipation that electricity will power the irrigation pump-set. This has not happened. I work all day from five in the morning to six in the evening irrigating my fields by hand. Can you please intervene and help me?'

God truly helps those who help themselves. You can't just sit back and complain that officials take bribes; you have to go and fight for your rights. You have to demand what you want. I believe in another principle and this could prove to be another law: If faced with something unfair don't sit back and moan and wallow in melancholy; revolt and fight against it!

Not everyone is corrupt. The secretary gave me a patient hearing and asked me where my farm was located. He then spoke directly to the executive engineer of the district electricity board. He told him, as I listened, that if electricity did not reach Capt. Gopinath's farm in thirty days, he was not fit to hold that position and that he would be dismissed. He turned to me and said, 'If this does not happen in the next thirty days, please come to see me.' I took a bus from Bengaluru and headed back to the farm. The very next day, just after sunrise, there was a flurry of activity on my farm. There were about twenty people milling around the farm from the local, the taluq, and district electricity boards. This I reckoned was the result of the secretary's tongue-lashing. It had electrified them into action; I saw light at the end of the tunnel!

In those days I travelled frequently to Hassan. On days when my bike was sent to the mechanic for repairs, I had to walk back a good five kms from the nearest bus-stop, through picturesque countryside. One day, I found myself in the middle of a group of donkeys. Herding the animals was an agasa, the local washerman. He was leading a caravan of several donkeys. The draught animals carried large bundles. The beasts of burden were small, the loads they carried were huge, their bellies almost touching the ground. Sometimes the washerman walked alongside the animals. I picked up a desultory conversation. The washerman said he was an agasa by birth; that was on his way to the local pond. I was curious about the lives they led, and kept up the conversation. Despite the hard work, there was much cheer and sunlight in the washermen's lives. They took pleasure in little things. A festival for instance was a great occasion for the entire community.

Farm workers were also used to enjoyment of festivities. Unmindful of their trials and travails, farm workers did not work on festive occasions, taking a day off on either side of the festival and spending their meagre earnings on new clothes, sweets, and flowers. On festive occasions when eating meat is permitted, they bought and cooked chicken and shared a meal with family and friends. Their celebration included music and dance, and a visit to the local deity.

During my conversation with the washerman it struck me that the donkeys were an economical proposition for washermen, which a tractor or a jeep would not have been . The washerman informed me that a donkey cost him between Rs 65–75. A flash of inspiration passed through my mind at that moment. Eventually, however, the thought proved more asinine than inspirational. Electricity was still a distant dream. Why not employ donkeys to fetch water from the stream? I was at the time hiring workers to physically fill and carry pitchers. It would save my expenses on labour, which was expensive. Labour was also difficult to get as those who had small landholdings tilled their own land and did not offer services as farm workers. The numbers of farm workers were rapidly dwindling. I decided to buy donkeys and gave Raju Rs 700, instructing him to buy ten to twelve animals, and that was how I became a donkey owner.

One day Raju piloted a posse of seven to eight donkeys in a procession. Word got around and it soon became known in the neighbouring villages that we had donkeys on the farm. People were curious. Was I planning to become a washerman? Was there a new business venture afoot? They came over to the farm to see for themselves. I asked the agasa what he fed the donkeys. He said he let them free to roam the village. The donkeys ate whatever they could lay their muzzle on. They ate kitchen leftover, hay, and they grazed on freehold. I realized that the much ridiculed donkey was a very intelligent animal. Every morning, there was evidence of this: the donkey's ability to learn and its ability to teach us a lesson in good turn. Nobody on the farm knew how to deal with a donkey. On the first day we tied two pitchers dangling on either side of each donkey.

From ancient times, animal management had become the job of specialists. Mahouts tamed and goaded elephants to work. Cowherds herded cattle. Swineherds best understood pigs. Ranchers knew their horses, poulterers their birds, and shepherds their flocks. Riders elicited varying responses from the horses they rode because each emoted differently with their riders. It was clear from the very first day that dealing with donkeys was no easy task and the washermen alone knew how to. Our ignorance of donkey psychology led to some hilarious moments. When urged to carry the pitchers back to the farm from the stream, some animals stuck their hooves into the ground and refused to move. Some raised and kicked their hind legs in air, some sprinted. Some emitted a loud shriek. The donkey's bray is a raucous concatenation of singular notes. On a scale of five it produced the least euphony. Some simply stood still, some kicked, some brayed, some ran amok. For the curious onlookers it was a moment of great hilarity, for us a great frustration.

When buying animals, I remember attending spectacular village fairs, or jatres, where domestic animals were bought and sold. Farmers came from all over the state and camped on open ground with their animals in tow. My relatives also came to these camps with their cattle. People camped there, cooked their meals over a bonfire, and slept beneath the bullock-cart. For those who knew what this meant, it was like going to Woodstock! At these fairs, farmers and traders inspected each animal for particular traits: the lakshanas. If you are buying cattle you check their teeth for age. You need to check if a cow is good for milk and if an ox is fit for draught. Donkeys too must be recognized by some traits; the dhobis or washernmen know them, we don't. Raju at least was blind to them when he bought the donkeys. We were able to work out a minimal taxonomy of donkeys based on the way they behaved on the farm. There are different kinds of donkeys. Those who were reluctant to work were the *equus truantus*. The michievous ones could be classified as *equus naughticus*, those not used to being team players could be called *equus singularis*! Many animals that we harnessed refused to take the load. They began prancing and dancing; nobody could get them to stay still. Horses have reins; cattle are amenable to halters or nose strings, a donkey simply refuses a harness. The workers on the farm were at their wit's end, so was I.

Our donkeys not only kicked but also bit the hand that fed them. Just one or two behaved well and were useful, the balance seemed to enjoy our frustration. If they did stay still to take a load of water, they soon spilt all of it by their measured shakes and wriggles. People had a great laugh at my expense, but that did not bother me because I was able to get some help from the donkeys.

Two factors finally decided whether the donkeys stayed on the farm or not. Their early morning truancy was one. There is something very dogged about the early morning donkey, something very dogged about the donkey in the afternoon, and also something very dogged about the donkey at night. When they arrived at the farm they looked innocent enough, and I even thought somewhat lovable. Gradually however these positive feelings had given way to misgivings, leading to frustration and despondency. Here was a species that challenged all my ingenuity, and by the time I had begun to pride myself as being innovative and capable of surmounting any challenge, but I was proved wrong by these creatures who made me eat humble pie, or so it seemed. It was an important chore for all of us on the farm to catch the donkeys as they grazed freely on the grass on the farm. If we caught them we could harness them to other farm tasks. The donkeys were far smarter than I gave them credit for. They knew we were going to hitch them to a harness. The moment any one of us approached them, they ran hither and thither, as though for dear life. They evaded capture and delayed getting caught and made to work.

The last straw was what happened one summer night as Bhargavi and I slept in the open yard under the stars. We had spent the day harvesting Bengal gram. The harvest had been plenty and we had packed the crop in gunny-bags and stacked them in the threshing yard in piles for transport to the market the following day.

In summers when it was extremely hot we slept under the open sky. That night we slept in the threshing yard. We were fast asleep when Bhargavi woke me up. She said she had heard a sound. Sure there was. It was the sound of something going 'chomp, chomp, chomp'. I raised my head and saw the entire herd of donkeys tucking their teeth into the harvest. I rose and chased them away. We went back to sleep. We were woken up a second time. It was the same story. I again had to chase the beasts away. Then again it happened a third time. That was when I decided we would not have them on the farm any longer. I would miss them for certain, and some still looked innocent, but there was certainly more to farm life than looking after donkeys!

Water-divining and Other Matters

One year there was severe drought in the region. There had been no rains and the stream had run dry. With no water on the farm, digging a bore-well was the only solution. Friends suggested that I hire a geologist to locate the right spot for a well. I found a trained geologist at the department of mines and geology and brought him over to the farm. The geologist consulted his map and marked it with little flags to identify the local plateaus, outcrop, gullies, and valleys.

He did a physical survey of the farm and he pointed out several spots. 'Dig here and you will find water,' he said. We brought the bore well rig and dug at the spots indicated but found no water even at a depth of sixty metres!

The geologist having failed miserably, I decided to get a geophysicist. He brought along an ultrasonic device and sent pulses into the earth and took measurements. He marked a spot for drilling. When we dug there we hit an underground massif of rock. Further drilling became impossible and we stopped.

I was now a desperate man. If we did not have water soon enough, our efforts over the past months would have proved futile. Worse, my waterless coconut plants would wilt. Science had not come in handy. Someone recommended a water-diviner. On the particular evening the water-diviner was to come to the farm, it had been pouring. The stream had risen and could not be easily forded. The small bridge of stone slabs that we had laid across it was of no use because water was overflowing it. The water-diviner could not swim so we had to devise a way to bring him across.

We decided to a tie a rope to the other end so that the man could hold it and pull himself across. It was a heavy coir rope. The strongest among us tried to throw it to the other side but each time it fell into the water getting wet and heavier. I swam across and tied the rope to a stout tree. The others stayed back to help the water-diviner. They tied a rope to the man's waist and held the other end of the tether. With great difficulty and much encouragement from all of us, the diviner eventually managed to cross the stream.

There are different kinds of water-diviners. One kind uses a metallic pendulum tied to a metal bar. The diviner holds the bar horizontal and goes about the job. He acts as the medium for the passage of energy to the pendulum. Where there is water, the pendulum experiences a strong force and begins oscillate in a circular direction. The oscillation suggests that the source of water is somewhere below that point.

Our water-diviner was not of this kind. He used a twig he tore off from one of the wild trees on the farm. He chose a twig that was shaped loosely like a Y, a much larger piece than one would use for making a catapult. He pruned off the leaves and made himself a serviceable divining tool. With both hands he held the twig at an arm's distance from his stomach, in such a way that the protuberance that made it look like a Y rather than a U or a V, distended. He slowly toured the farm, walking steadily but as if in a trance.

The water diviner had decided, from the sceptical expression on my face, that I was a non-believer. Therefore, in order to convince me that he could really help me find water and to justify the rather high fee of Rs 1000, the diviner held out a guarantee. He said he would definitely locate the water source. He was sure of that. However, on the slim prospect of failure, he said he would return the money. It was a proper money-back guarantee!

Twig-using water-diviners were supposed to look for sudden, energetic backward and forward swings of the twig; the greater the impulse on the twig, the larger and closer the water deposits.

I followed him closely, with hope in my heart, but all the while chiding myself for being so gullible as to trust someone whose logic made no sense to me. The man stopped suddenly. Whether it was a sleight of hand, made to appear plausible through years of practice, or because it was indeed the action of a new kind of force that physicists are yet to unravel, a miracle occurred: the twig did a vertical twirl. The diviner bent down in a state of half reverie and half reverence and examined the spot. Then, drawing in a deep breath, he said with cocky finality, 'Dig here and you shall find water'.

He went around for a little while longer and showed me one or two other spots as well. We dug at one spot but nothing came of it, we dug at another and were disappointed, at the third place we found a thin jet of a little spring at sixty metres. It yielded a few gallons an hour, sufficient for cooking and bathing. We installed a small pump. The water diviner had proved to be more successful than the others, but that was just by chance. Strangely, however, as the days passed, the bore-well began to yield more and more water. After a year it was yielding 2000 gallons of water an hour! I desist from comment but I still think that all the three were playing blind man's bluff. A few years later, judging that it was a game of chance, I asked Raju to dig at ten places: our hit rate was 40 per cent!

We worked on a shoestring budget. Economy was the necessity which spawned the idea of the donkey draft. What sees us through difficult situations in life is not resources but the ability to be resourceful. As Steve Jobs of Apple said, 'sometimes when you innovate, you make mistakes. It is best to admit them quickly and get on with improving your other innovations'. All of us, my workers included, constantly came up with ideas. Some were good; some outrageous. We tried to experiment with cattle, harvesting, and planting. Thinking up new ideas had become a way of life on the farm. Subsequently, the electricity supply reached the farm, and when the pump-set became operational I decided to sell the donkeys.

On the periphery, the patch along the dry bed of the stream which I had left undisturbed, a small clump of 'rainforest' sprang up in five years. Owls came to nest in the trees, a leopard found its way to the thick brushwood, then came bees and wasps. One day hundreds of bats came and colonized the trees along the stream. Birds of various hues homed in. A whole new mysterious world had sprung up in the farm.

An important lesson I learnt from nature was that a successful harvest is directly related to the presence of an optimum number of insects in the cultivated field. As students we were told that 80 per cent of our food crops were cross-pollinated. Insects are the inadvertent pollinators. They visit millions of flowers for nectar and pollen, which is their food, and in so doing, deposit grains of pollen between individual plants and thus cross-fertilize them. There are millions of insects and millions of varieties of flowers. Each insect has evolved to relate to a particular species of flower. The balance in nature thus created is quite delicate and it is absolutely essential for farmers not to upset the local ecology. The crop that a farmer grows gets pollinated only incidentally; the insect's principle goal is to locate its specific flower and savour its nectar. Therefore, by indiscriminate destruction of existing flora, the ignorant farmer actually lessens the prospect of a good yield at the outset. Scientists are still researching the relationship between particular insect varieties and particular flora.

One example of the unforeseen consequence of the blanket use of chemical pesticides is that of the spider. The spider can become the unintended victim of chemical spray. Spiders perform various roles on the farm. By laying their webs at various levels, they act as physical barriers to a variety of insect predators. There are many species of spider and harming them actually removes a friendly species from the farm environment.

An insect is a cross-pollinator and a useful natural assistant to the farmer. While acknowledging the insect's positive role, the farmer must also be willing to allow the insect to eat and not go hungry. It will eat what is readily available: the leaf of the crop the farmer is growing. This is a trade-off. A caterpillar eats leaf. There are a thousand varieties of caterpillars, that become moths or butterflies. The butterfly is a pollen courier, so if you get rid of the leaf-eating caterpillar, you also lose the butterfly. We cannot therefore eliminate insects and have a great crop.

The people of Gorur once ate fish caught from the river. Today, there are no fish. There were little ponds in every village where fish were reared for local consumption, the fish pond serving as a common village resource. Now we have commercially operated fisheries and the poor have no fish to eat. The use of weedicide, pesticide, and other chemical agents on farms has had a deleterious effect on riverine fauna. There are frequent media reports of fish coming out of the water and dying on riverbanks in thousands. Every piece of the earth is home to many varieties of plant and animal life. Forests, wildernesses, grasslands, the open plains, the water marshes, and cultivated land with its natural and artificial hedges are habitats for life of all species. The same applies to the fringes of human habitation and human habitats themselves, including villages, towns, and urban outskirts. The human habitat is slowly eating into the natural habitat of plant and animal life. Species become extinct as this pincer movement colonizes more land from the wild.

The newly 'captured' land, flatteringly described as 'development', is subject to the creation of new urban habitats and new farming. The methods used to reserve more land for agriculture, horticulture, and animal husbandry are predominantly chemical-driven. Overall, there is an alarmingly massive use of chemicals everywhere, which leach into the soil, ruin natural water reserves, and run into surface waterbodies such as lakes and rivers, and eventually the sea. The result is a slow poisoning of the earth.

In 1984, Rotary International invited nominations of people from four different fields to attend a scholarship programme in the US. They chose a doctor, a banker, a lawyer, and a farmer. I was the farmer selected for this group. The programme comprised visits to American farms. The scholar would be enabled to experience at first-hand, farming techniques in vogue in that country. I stayed for six weeks in the US and visited Vermont and New Hampshire. I did gather some useful farming practices but also came across a phenomenon at one American farm that shocked me. That experience reaffirmed my faith in natural farming and I became a dyed-in-the-wool convert overnight.

I belong to a generation that has always held rivers in awe and reverence. I have looked upon them as sacred, which have sustained life and cleansed people of their material and moral trespasses. I have looked upon the river as the embodiment of all that is pure. A single dip in one was sufficient for me to emerge clean and spiritually energized. In my childhood the river in Gorur was a constant draw: it was the undercurrent of my life. For us boys, it was the most natural thing to rush off to the river at the slightest pretext. When thirsty, we simply cupped our palms, scooped up water, and drank the sweet-tasting, crystal-clear water. My father was not a 'believer' in the normal sense of the word, but even he seemed to me to have had an implicit, unspoken, spiritual bond with the river. My mother and the other ladies of the village also deified the river, but they related to it on a more day-to-day basis. They walked in a group to the bank of the river, unfailingly, every morning and every evening of their lives. They filled their copper pitchers and pots, did their washing, chatted about each other's lives, and brought back the same, delicious water for cooking and drinking.

Two recent personal experiences have made me realize the irredeemable extent to which we have polluted our water sources. On a visit to Delhi a few years ago, a friend of mine took me to what he called a riverside farm house. We sat on the patio of the farmhouse chatting. I was eager to see the river because a river gave me a spiritual high. We walked perhaps a hundred steps to the river. I expected to see a river flowing majestically, with trees along the banks. I believed I would see bends in the river, little ripples of water lapping the banks, birds, insects, and a myriad of plants and aquatic life. The sun was setting and I should have seen, framed against the crimson of the horizon, the silhouette of birds swooping down on the river for a catch. I certainly did not expect what I actually saw. It was an appalling spectacle of a black, slushy, marshy, viscous mass of fluid meandering and losing its way among an archipelago of half-dried up beds of part-silt, part-plastic, and what looked like rotting semi-processed fabric and other solid urban wastes. The nondescript mass had nothing life-giving about it. It looked like a purveyor of death and disease. I asked my friend which river it was. He said without emotion, 'Oh! It is the Yamuna!' My heart sank, my soul imploded. It was the greatest blow to the image of a river that I had deified as a boy. I asked myself how human civilization could even hope to sustain itself into the future if this was how we treated our ancient, sacred rivers.

The other experience was in the US. On one of my visits, a farmer told me he did not drink water dug from his farm or from the stream running alongside. I found it impossible to believe that anyone could be so distrustful about water from a well or river. I found it impossible to believe that water could be poisoned. This visit took place over twenty years ago. India had a very little concept of packaged water. My host informed me that chemical analysis of water samples from depths of 100–150 metres had shown that they were completely polluted, and contained harmful compounds far above the permissible levels. The cause of this pollution, as I was to discover, was the 'no till' farming ideology that farmers had been practising.

In 'no till' agriculture the farmer applied a thick blanket of weedicide over the field after every crop. This approach stemmed from ignorance of the meaning of the term 'weed'. What's a weed? One definition, ascribed to Ralph Waldo Emerson, is: 'A weed is a plant whose useful properties have not been discovered yet'. A weed is therefore an integral part of the eco-system and to maintain the balance, you have to recycle the weed back to nature.

US agricultural scientists had discovered this technique of completely destroying weeds. A 'no till' planter sowed seeds for the next crop of maize or wheat. The new agricultural cycle began with the weedicide. It was followed by chemical manure and chemical pesticide. Chemicals in their most virulent forms were getting into the soil. They were then being washed into waterbodies. The water as it flowed in channels, streams, and rivers gathered more of this chemical and became completely undrinkable. It was true, however, that American farmers managed very high crop yields, but at what cost? That surely is not sustainable farming.

Not only for modern-day farmers but for all of us as stakeholders of this planet, I would like to take the liberty of quoting, at length, Lewis Thomas. Thomas says:

> It is not a new thing for man to invent an existence that he imagines to be above the rest of life; this has been his most consistent intellectual exertion down the millennia. As illusion, it has never worked to his satisfaction in the past, any more than it does today. Man is embedded in nature. The biological science of recent years has been making this a more urgent fact of life. The new, hard problem will be to cope with the dawning, intensifying realization of just how interlocked we are …. A good case can be made for our non-existence as entities. We are not made up, as we had always supposed, of successively enriched packets of our own parts. We are shared, rented, occupied … by little separate creatures, the colonial posterity of migrant prokaryocytes, probably primitive bacteria that swam into ancestral precursors of our eukaryotic cells and stayed there. Ever since, embedded inside us they have maintained themselves and their ways replicating in their own fashion, privately with their own DNA and RNA, quite different from ours. They are as much symbionts as the rhizobial bacteria in the roots of beans. Without them, we would not move a muscle, drum a finger, think a thought …. I am consoled, somewhat, by the thought that the green plants are in the same fix …. The viruses, instead of being single-minded agents of disease and death, are now beginning to look more like mobile genes. We live in a dancing matrix of viruses; they dart rather like bees from organism to organism, from plant to insect, to mammal to me, and back again and into the sea ….

By observing the primeval forest, talking to older farmers, and reading people like Lewis Thomas I realized that we as modern-day farmers approached insects in isolation as pests and tried to eliminate them with all the tools and pesticides at our command. The ants are the biggest foragers of the soil. They create the soil even as they look for food. As they work, and they work incessantly, they loosen the soil, they process and sift dead insects in the soil, and enrich it by the juices of the dead and the living.

I learnt more about ants from experience. One day I returned home with thirty bags full of seeds. These bags contained insects that were steadily boring into the seed sheath and eating the food from within. Many of the insect-bored seeds were hollow and crumbled easily. I opened the bags and spread the seeds on the floor to air them. When I returned I found as many insects as there were grains. I saw a line of ants heading to and from the seed mass. I was a little dismayed that an ant attack was in progress, but on closer observation I saw that the ants were carrying away not seeds but the insects that had infested the seeds. The ants were preying on the insects and nature had provided me with the best possible pesticide! I sensed immediately and intuitively that this must hold the key to making farming natural yet productive and viable.

I made it a point to visit farms in the neighbourhood as well as villages some way off to observe farming practices. Kolar, Chamarajanagar, and Kunigal are silkworm-rearing areas. During my trips to hundreds of farms, there was one common denominator: all the farms, notwithstanding very heavy doses of chemical manure, were unable to get good quality and abundant quantity of mulberry leaves. The result was that they were repeatedly losing silkworm crops because of the poor nutritional quality of the leaf. The breed of silkworm which has made Karnataka famous for its silk over the centuries fed on mulberry leaves, a perennial crop. However, the use of heavy chemical manure in recent years had completely rendered the soil sterile and toxic, resulting in a point of no return and pushing thousands of farmers into poverty.

Farmers are advised to put in nitrogen through urea, potassium through potash, and phosphorous through phosphates. These are the three principle ingredients used along with other micronutrients. The soil has to be in a particular condition, which the traditional farmers know by intuition. They know that the tree is its own food. The tree cannibalizes its post-mortem. However, this is a law of nature, and there is nothing morbid about it. Therefore, if you have a coconut tree, you actually have the tree stem, the frond, the flowers (inflorescence), and the fruit, including the husk, the shell, and the copra. All that the farmer needs to do is to take the copra and give everything else back to the tree. This wisdom is not even about science. It simply enjoins you not to sell or burn what you consider to be the waste of the coconut tree. Instead, it suggests, that you put all of it back as happens in the forest where the rotting fallen trunk, frond, and nut continually enrich the soil.

We had been, on the one hand, selling off both coconut husk and leaves, and on the other, were paying to buy manure for the coconut trees. Therefore, in the light of all the new knowledge I had acquired, one day I told my workers not to remove anything from the coconut grove. I asked them to leave all the fallen remains of the trees where they were. Miraculously, we found that termites had stopped attacking the coconut trees and were now feeding on the waste material around them.

Rodents are the bane of every coconut farmer because they feed on coconuts. If you use rodent poison, the rodents die, but their carcasses are eaten by other animals. An owl or eagle or other raptor bird that eats a poisoned rat, dies eventually. Over a period of time, the rats become resistant to the poison. They resume their old rate of multiplying. The owls on the other hand do not reproduce as quickly and there is eventually an imbalance in the proportion of rodents to birds. There will be more rodents and fewer owls. It is therefore prudent to accept that while you may lose a part of the crop to rodents and insects, in the larger scheme of things they maintain the ecological balance and give you a better yield in the longer run.

I decided to gradually increase the number of coconut trees and mulberry plants on the farm. The journal like *Science, Nature, National Geographic,* featured articles written by biologists, botanists and scientists of various natural sciences, and using their insight I evolved package of practices for the farm. The farm was slowly but surely being transformed. My input costs began falling, the yields began increasing. At this point I really wanted to quickly scale up silkworm-rearing. I experimented a great deal with mulberry and innovated new methods of growing it. The different kinds of practices I attempted included integrating rain-water harvesting and impounding water in ponds, managing weeds, moisture retention in the soil, discreet ploughing, and selective biological pest control.

I took advice and learnt from traditional sericulture practitioners. Their native sense and their intuitive ways greatly impressed me. The older farmers had been farming silkworms for the past sixty to seventy years and knew how to enlist nature as an ally in farming. Based on my observations of them I made radical changes in my farming methodology. This helped me scale up my sericulture project.

I began to grasp an idea for which I may not have had researched empirical data but one that was born out of my experience and observation, and more importantly because my farm was becoming more and more viable. I realized that whatever 'was not ecologically sound, was not economically viable in the long run.'

I introduced new measures at the cocoon-harvesting stage. Farmers used bamboo stems and branches as the cocooning sites for the silk worms. The general preference for bamboo translated into a demand for thousands of bamboos. Cocoons were harvested on bamboo montages, and these required storage space and had to be kept free of infection. Farmers used disinfectants that harmed both workers in the vicinity and eventually the soil into which the chemical drained.

I decided to harvest silkworm cocoons in paddy straw which could be recycled as mulch enriched by the droppings of the worm back to the farm. This is a forgotten age-old practice. I revived it and improvised on the basic technique. The financial return was too less but my input costs had become negligible. It became profitable and my balance-sheet looked respectable. The method consistently proved its worth, and I did not lose a single crop. Also, the yields were higher and the rates better than they would have been had I followed the chemical route. A corollary emerged to the central idea of linking economy and ecology, initially vaguely and later coalesced as: 'What is low-cost is eco-friendly and conversely many eco-friendly practices are low-cost.'

Besides harvesting cocoons in friendly paddy-straw beds, I did away with bamboo montages. I realized that if this was adopted across the state it would save millions of bamboos from felling, and simultaneously eliminate the repeated use of disinfectant on the generally reused bamboo montages. I also used a large thatched hut to house the project rather than a concrete building. By doing so I managed to eke out four times the built-up area in the thatched building for the same capital cost. In addition to the extra space, there was automatic and better temperature regulation: the interior was warm for the cocoons in winter and cool in summer. It lowered costs while improving the climate for the silkworm.

The cattle-feed I bought in the market was nothing other than grain repackaged by cattle-feed companies. The companies bought grain from the farmers and sold it back to them as cattle-feed. The value they added was perceived in the packaging and the brand name which dazzled the farmers. This was a redundant cycle, and the farmers were just paying for their own grain. It got me thinking. It occurred to me that instead of buying cattle-feed from the companies I could buy the grain directly from surrounding farmers and grow some of it myself to feed my cattle. I also kept some country chicken and allowed the chicks to forage in the cattle shed to control the ticks on the cattle. The cattle egret and the mynah are assiduous tick-pickers. In modern dairying, milch cattle are kept in enclosures, where the population of ticks multiplies quickly because egrets and mynahs do not get access to the cattle. The farmers for their part resort to the use of chemicals to get rid of the ticks.

These creative ways of farming with nature helped introduce many useful practices on the farm and opened up an entirely new life for me. Fairly soon I became financially solvent and repaid all my bank loans. I was not rich but reasonably well-off in four or five years.

People came to visit my farm. They came in buses, on motorcycles, in cars. Farmers came in droves: from Karnataka, Andhra Pradesh, Tamil Nadu, and many other parts of India. They were curious to see how I had transformed silkworm farming.

Local newspapers and magazines wrote about the sericulture experiment. Local radio stations aired programmes and discussed the new ideas. More and more people got to know my name. The Rolex committee recognizes people in three different categories through an award plus cash, identifying people who have done pioneering, and groundbreaking work. The three areas are: technological innovation that has changed the lives of people, adventure and discovery that has furthered our knowledge of the world, and work done to preserve local ecology that has led to improvements in living standards for people. The award, given once in three years, is called the Rolex Laureate Award. Someone asked me whether he could send my name as a nominee, describing the work I had done in support of the nomination. I agreed. I gave lectures at agricultural universities and was invited to sericulture seminars. I had also begun writing articles for magazines. These were not serious in nature but in them I described my experiences as a farmer. My work was sent to Rolex and the committee sent a team to my farm. The team met and discussed the merits of my work with various people in the state. They met Dr Udupi Shrinivasa, professor at the Indian Institute of Science, who is known for his many environment-related innovations and research. They also met people from the department of silkworm-rearing. The team then visited my farm. They said they had shortlisted 100 candidates from thousands of nominations from around the world. They also told me they would eventually choose the best projects and work from across the world for the award comprising a cash component and a steel-and-gold Rolex watch. I was awarded the Rolex Award for Enterprise in 1996. More than the money, it gladdened me that my work would help spread environmental awareness and eco-friendly ways of farming. There is always the danger of being dubbed a Luddite if one strikes a posture that seems to oppose modern farming and technology.

I seriously believed that farmers must not get blindly carried away; that they must think like prudent businessmen and realize that the existing methods will not only not enable them repay their debts but will gradually become a vicious cycle of debt, environmental damage, poor yield, more fertilizer and chemicals leading to further damage to the environment. Through their current practices they are destroying the very foundation of the environment: the soil and the mixture of habitats. They must realize that agriculture is not a factory and appreciate that everything in agriculture is a community of living organisms.

The insights into nature, and intuitions and instincts, proved to be the foundation of my future businesses. *If something is not ecologically sound, it is not economically viable.* This is a simple law that I think applies to every aspect of life. For a business to be viable, entrepreneurs need to create the right ecology for business and for the interactions that it entails. That seed of my future low-cost airline and other businesses was sowed here.

⟨⟩

After the farm became self-sustaining, I shifted to Hassan, shuttling between Hassan and the farm. There was a particular reason for moving to Hassan, my daughter. Two years after our marriage our daughter Pallavi was born. She grew up like any other child on a farm. Village children quite routinely see cows giving birth or a bull mating a cow. They gain an understanding of nature's ways all quite naturally and freely. Now I needed to attend to her education.

I must not forget to mention the kind of dilemma I got into with dairy farming. Dairy farmers were impressed by the achievements of the White Revolution in milk led by the legendary visionary, Dr Verghese Kurien. There was however a flip side to it when, across India, large-scale artificial insemination was undertaken. Cattle that are indigenous to India are highly adapted to conditions here, but they are not prolific producers of milk. They are nonetheless hardy, low on maintenance, and also good draught animals. Most farmers do not need to spend a rupee on the Indian cow. The irony was that many farmers who went in for dairy farming ended up bankrupt. Any farmer will tell you that very high-yielding milch cows bred through intensive artificial insemination led to unviable business models. The cattle are injected with calcium on a regular basis to replace the calcium lost through heavy milk production. Their maintenance costs also proved to be high. At the end of the day, the dairy farmer's income generally doesn't meet his expenditure. This was the story of most farmers who got into dairying. However, the genius of Kurien lay in getting the farmers to organize under a cooperative society and derive the benefits of production and distribution of milk and milk products without the intervention of middlemen. It also led to the creation of a mechanism of harnessing the entire milk potential of the country. Kurien has no parallel in this achievement, but independently of Kurien, the National Dairy Development Board (NDDB) and similar state-level bodies took up a massive artificial insemination programme across the country which led to the loss of the country's genetic pool of cattle.

While the local variety of cattle delivered only two or three litres of milk against the 25–30 litres of the hybrid/imported cow, the farmer had to spend nothing on the upkeep of the former. They grazed in the fields and ate household leftovers. The two or three litres of milk they brought in gave the farmer a net income as he had no expenditure whatsoever. Though the initiatives of NDDB and other state-level bodies have made India the largest milk producer in the world today, it is not known what catastrophic outcome this may have.

Thanks to Verghese Kurien of Anand, whom I met later, the lives of farmers across the country have been transformed. The Anand cooperative movement has succeeded in creating a brand and a smooth distribution mechanism for the dairy farmers and also empowered them. It is however unfortunate that in the blind rush for artificial insemination, farmers have routinely begun inseminating every cow in the village. This craze for the imported variety has led to neglect of local breeds. We are in danger of losing native breeds of cattle such as Amritmahal, Halikar, and Ongole.

A New Enterprise Begins

I also dabbled in enterprise. I rode an Enfield motorcycle in those days in my travel from farm to farm. One day I went to Hassan to get my bike repaired. The shop was closed and the mechanics said the dealership had been terminated; the owner had closed shop. There were two very popular motorcycles. One was JAVA manufactured by Ideal Java in Mysore, one of the great enterprises of that time. It no longer exists but used to be a favourite with youngsters. The other was the Royal Enfield made in Chennai, its manufacturers later becoming Enfield India. When I heard the dealership had been closed, the first question that arose in my mind was, who would now service the hundreds of motorcycles on the road in the region and who would provide the spare parts? Whatever the reason for the dealer being removed, services would still be required in Hassan. At the time I was also thinking of taking up residence in Hassan and enrolling my daughter Pallavi in a school. Hassan had a Central School—Kendriya Vidyalaya. I also needed to get my own bike serviced and maintained. This set me thinking about a bike dealership.

I had friends who lived on their farms on the fringes of Hassan. Ravi Khandige was one. He ran a mobile restaurant at the time. He had worked at the Taj and was an experienced hand in the hospitality sector. I sometimes went over to his place to share a drink and exchange ideas. One day I asked him whether he would like to be my business partner. I did not want to live in Hassan. This was largely because I thought the work I had done on the farm might go waste if I didn't live on the site. I was not the kind of farmer who could afford a manager and this would also serve to alienate me from the farm. I felt I needed to dedicate myself to the farm for at least nine to ten years, living it, breathing it, and working it. Only when the coconut plantation reached maturity would I be able to delegate its oversight to helpers. Until then it needed me.

Assuming that we would be able to get the motorcycle dealership, I told Ravi that as a business partner he would have to run the venture on a day-to-day basis. Ravi agreed to the plan and the deal was struck at five in the evening.

It was customary for established local business people to take up dealerships and franchises. Here I was, however, a complete novice, with no business experience or background. Even so, I never felt diffident or inadequate for want of it, I felt confident that as I had been riding the bike for the last four years, I knew how to cater to a customer because I was one myself. The customer's point of view was the most critical aspect I could bring to the dealership.

The matter was settled. That same evening instead of taking a bus back to Javagal as my motorcycle needed repairs, Ravi and I took a night bus to Chennai and went straight to the Enfield corporate office. The Enfield official asked us to find real estate to set up the business and handed a set of documents for compliance. He asked also to design the premises in such a way as to include a workshop, a garage, and other such components. They would come and inspect the premises before finalizing the dealership. I had it on my plate. Less than twenty-four hours later we were on our way to becoming businessmen. It all happened so rapidly that the enormity of the task ahead hit me only when I emerged from the manager's office. My friend too was surprised by the sudden favourable turn of events.

I knew that opportunities are lost if you don't seize them. I had the confidence that if the dealership came through I would be able to muster the resources. I knew too that if I hesitated on account of resources, I would lose my opportunity, and told myself that I'd find a way to fund the venture.

The deal was sealed and we received a letter of intent from Enfield India. For me it was more the beginning of a new journey. On the return trip, from Chennai to Hassan I dreamt plans non-stop. I would set up a showroom in Hassan and expand to twenty. Ravi and I decided to get a small place. From the money we made, we would move to larger premises. We found a very small building, 9 by 6 metres, facing the Bengaluru–Hassan–Mangalore highway. It had a large government field behind it. I reckoned that while the place was very small we could put all the bikes that came for repair in the open field without paying any rent. The front portion would function as the sales office. We settled on it. The asking rent was Rs 600. We put down an advance of Rs 10,000, an amount I had in my account.

In those days, motorcycles were in short supply in relation to demand. Customers would pay in advance, thereby providing us with working capital. Even then, we still needed some capital. We therefore went to a bank, gave a business plan, and asked for a loan. The bank, seeing the investment we had ourselves made, readily gave us the loan we sought.

That loan amount financed our purchase order for two Bullet motorcycles, each costing about Rs 10,000. We planned to launch the business with a display of these two motorcycles in the showroom. We also invested in specialized tools and bought some inventory for spare-parts trading. I was awash with a sense that from nothing we were creating something. From that something we were creating jobs and also serving a large rural customer base.

We got some interior decorators to do up the place. One day, while I was busy setting up the business, the head mechanic of the previous showroom approached us for a job. I took him on as head mechanic. He was our first employee. I hired a boy to look after the front office. The head mechanic's salary was Rs 500 and the office boy's, Rs 250.

I have always been fascinated with the creativity associated with naming something. These days, of course, naming is a major brand-building exercise, with companies hiring brand consultants. It has always struck me that the names of the great companies are the names of the men and women who founded them, whether it is Tata, Bajaj, or Ford. Your name is what your father gave you. You became famous or not because of what you did and not because of your name. Similarly, the brand of Tata or Bajaj or Ford became famous because of what they did. I took ten seconds to think of possible names. We were in the Malnad region, in the motorcycle business. We therefore combined the two and came up with Malnad Mobikes. We registered the name in Hassan, and it continues to exist there to this day. We decided on a date for the inauguration. We invited the superintendent of police and the local MLA to attend as special guests. We wrote to the head of marketing and sales at Enfield India saying that the showroom was to be launched and invited him. We put an announcement in the newspaper. These actions triggered an immediate cash flow. People rode-in on their bikes seeking repair, servicing, or spare parts. Others wanted to buy a motorcycle. We told our customers that they would have to wait for a while for the motorcycle and quite honestly told them that we had to send them—that is the company in Chennai, a demand draft. Only after its receipt would they send us the motorcycle consignment. As we were short of cash, they would have to pay upfront if they were in a rush, and even then it would take a few days. Customers paid us an advance and this became our working capital.

We have a tradition of 'grease monkeys', which even exists today. It goes like this. Fathers would come to the garage with an eight- or ten-year-old son in tow. The boy had shown no inclination to study, he had dropped out of school, or perhaps he was just a difficult boy with an impetuous or destructive tendency. The fathers asked to meet the head mechanic and beseeched him to take the boy on as apprentice and teach him the trade. The fathers hoped that by learning mechanical skills the boy might in the future be able to set up his own garage. We had to consider the issue of child labour, but there was also the question of the danger of the boys turning to begging on the streets or resorting to delinquency if they were not gainfully employed. They came from very poor families and such eventualities were commonplace. There is also the overwhelming tradition of 'grease monkeys' in India where 90 per cent of all mechanics joined the trade as 'runaway' apprentices. 'Don't give the boy any salary,' the father would say. 'Just give him his meals. He is a great mischief at home. Please teach him a trade. He can become a mechanic and set up his own garage in the future.'

This argument impressed me and we took on eight to ten such kids. These were extraordinary boys, as we discovered. They were naturals and loved the job. They went about with an almost permanent smear of grease on their faces and hands, and we affectionately called them 'grease monkeys'. In the West, a mechanic is a multi-tasking worker. He is conversant with all the tasks relating to a particular vehicle. He is a vertical integrator, to use modern parlance. In India however there is a head mechanic who is the boss. He sits or swaggers around the garage yelling instructions and supervising the job while the 'grease monkeys' go about loosening screws, jacking up, rubbing with lint, pouring out engine oil, and running engine tests. The head mechanics rise through the ranks. In short, the head mechanics groom the boys. He might, however, get a little rough in the process and it is the responsibility of the garage manager to ensure that he does not ill-treat the boys. The boys came in at eight in the morning and left at five in the evening. They were kept away from potential mischief for nine hours. They earned Rs 100 each from me as a stipend. Customers too gave them tips. In all they made anything between Rs 300–400 a month, good money in those times.

In three or four years, I was well known in Hassan and in the neighbouring district of Chikmagalur. People knew me as a farmer and also as an owner of the motorcycle dealership. There was some brand value and admiration associated with the latter. I soon added Luna mopeds and Honda scooters to the lines of two-wheelers we sold at the showroom. We also scaled up numbers. We opened branches in Chikmagalur, Kadur, Tiptur, and various taluq headquarters; in all eight showrooms in the region. Malnad Mobikes became a brand name in that area. In the initial years, when the motorcycle business was scaling up and increasing in popularity, I spent time between the farm and Hassan, with Ravi attending to the day-to-day operations. After a while he retired. The business had by then stabilized so I appointed a manager and lived on the farm, commuting daily on my motorcycle.

My daughter was growing-up. She needed to be admitted to a school. We therefore moved to Hassan and enrolled her in the Central School in town. My second daughter was born soon after we moved. When our first daughter Pallavi grew-up we enrolled her in Bishop Cotton School in Bengaluru, where she would continue to study as a boarder. The longer I stayed in Hassan, the more I began missing farm life. One day I admitted to my wife that I was missing farm life and said, 'I'm missing living on the farm. Pallavi is in boarding school. Krithika is still small and has two years before she starts school. Why don't we just move back to the farm?' My wife asked, 'When?' I said, 'Tomorrow morning'. There was a longing welling-up within me. I wanted to touch the farm, breathe its fresh air, milk the cows, be a dairyman, take long walks in and around the farm, see the sunsets. It was a primeval longing. My wife understood and agreed. 'Fine, let us go!' she said.

I called up Raju at the farm and instructed him to build an army toilet. Such toilets are common in battlefield areas. We dig a pit in loose soil. It's safe and clean. I asked Raju to have a room cleaned up and put up a thatched area outside for bathing. We would be arriving the following morning. He was shocked. He exclaimed in disbelief, 'Sir, there is nothing here.' But my mind was made-up. I told my wife, 'If you are ready to sleep under the trees again in the afternoons and take long walks, let us go.' Krithika was then only three years old. By the time she was born I had bought my first car, a 1950 model Dodge Kingsway sedan. A luxury carriage. It was powered by a P4 diesel engine and had a massive boot, Hollywood actors went about in this car during the 1950s and '60s. It could be useful to carry cattle feed, farm equipment, and other farm necessities. The previous owner had installed a P4 diesel engine because petrol had become expensive. I loved driving it. When I drove into small villages where people had never seen a car before, I was surrounded by hordes of children. They would exclaim and call it 'aeroplane caroo' (aeroplane car). It was indeed a huge car! I never realized that the nickname 'aeroplane' for the car would be so prophetic.

Although we had planned to leave the following morning, we couldn't bear to wait. We simply packed what we could accommodate in the boot of the car and left that very day, leaving everything behind as if we were fleeing the plague. When I eventually entered the farm I felt like a refugee having found a haven.

We moved to the farm for good. The farm was my best training ground. I was dealing with people, eating with them, learning the ways of nature, gaining insights into the larger things of life, throughout on land and in the open. When I was engaged in working on the farm or doing my business, I had a curious feeling that all this was the preparatory ground for something else altogether. I do not believe in superstition, but I was acutely aware that I was in the process of getting ready for much bigger enterprises. I did not know then what it would be, but I sensed it. When I left the army I had aimed to discover something. I had already known in a native way that to journey is better than to arrive. I did not entertain the idea of some grand denouement or a grand finale. If it led somewhere, that would be a good thing. But the journey—actually sensing the present, is the real thing.

The gentleman from whom we had rented premises for our motorcycle business was a well-known hotelier. His name, Kasturi, was quite famous in the district. He named the restaurant he ran after himself and called it Hotel Kasturi, and it was one of the best Udupi hotels in Hassan, famous for its dosa. Kasturi was also known for his social work and for his association with temples. He was the convener of the Ganapati temple and the annual Ganapati festival.

The Ganapati festival, a mega-event in Maharashtra, is also a major festival in Karnataka. It is an occasion for much religious and cultural activity and people look forward to it. For many communities, the festival has a religious connotation, but personally I loved the narrative evenings that used to form a part of the celebrations. The harikatha is an Indian bardic tradition in which the performer related stories from the Indian epics. As a child I wanted to be a harikatha performer. The tradition is still preserved in south India. The other cultural activities during the festival included classical music recitals. From early childhood, I nurtured a love for Hindustani and Carnatic classical music. My ardent love for musical forms was primarily due to my mother who had a keen appreciation of music and actively encouraged my sisters to learn and practise the arts. She invited the music teacher home. This was a common practise among south Indian Brahmin families. Boys learnt Sanskrit; girls learnt music. Hindustani classical music is the style of preference in north Karnataka; Carnatic is preferred in south Karnataka. The early study of music is a daily affair and is observed as rigorously as going to a temple or going to school. I woke to the strains of music floating in from my sisters' room. I never missed a musical concert. I somehow managed to make time to listen to many of the accomplished greats like Semmangudi Shrinivasa Iyer, M.S. Subbulakshmi, Balamuralikrishna, Maharajapuram Santanam, Mallikarjun Mansoor and Bhimsen Joshi. I continued religiously to attend their concerts for many years, and continue to do so even now when time permits. On the farm, I devoted my spare time to reading and listening to music.

Entry into the Hotel Business

Kasturi, or Hotel Kasturi as he was fondly nicknamed, was an extraordinary man. He wore his trademark white shirt and dhoti with a towel draped over his shoulder. He had made it big and was very well-off but he had had no formal education. I was interested in learning how he had made it big. At seventy, Kasturi was full of energy. He used to ride his moped to roam around the town. Once he came to meet me. It was a casual friendly visit. He was fond of me and appreciated my striving to achieve success. 'Gopi,' he would say in a friendly way. 'People spin the top (bugari in Kannada, lattu in Hindi) by winding a string around its base and then releasing it. You play it stringless.' This is also how he described me to others. I laughed it off. I, however had an education. My father had taken great pains to groom me. I had had the advantage of serving in the army. This man had neither social capital nor education. Yet that had not hindered him from becoming a successful businessman and a good citizen. In addition to his service to temples, he built a hostel for poor Brahmin children, and also a crematorium.

He used to raise funds for his projects both with his own seed money and through donations from the people. He had approached me for donations on several occasions. One day when he visited me at the showroom, I asked him to tell me his story. He did. At the age of seven or eight, he left his poverty-stricken family in the village and came to Hassan. That was fifty or sixty years ago. A relative of his, Raghavachar, had a very famous hotel in Hassan. Raghavachar was a Brahmin who had moved to Hassan many years ago and built a string of popular hotels. He ran a canteen for the Railways too. My father recalled having frequented Raghavachar Hotel some seventy-five years ago. Kasturi got a job at the hotel as a cleaner. In time, he became a waiter. He learnt the culinary trade by observing others and began helping in the kitchen as an assistant cook. Kasturi saw that Raghavachar was not a typical Brahmin: he smoked, drank and had a mistress. Raghavachar had also started out as a cleaner but had now acquired a larger-than-life persona. One day young Kasturi was passed some uncharitable remark on Raghavachar's mistress. The boss learnt of this and as Kasturi walked in to serve plates piled with idli and sambhar, Raghavachar came over to him from the till and slapped him hard. The plates of idli and sambhar went crashing all around. That was the last time Kasturi engaged in any kind of gossip. Sometime later, when Raghavachar died, Kasturi set up a small cafe in Hassan in a room that measured 2 metres by 2 metres. Kasturi was the cook, waiter, cleaner, and cashier. He poured batter, fried the dosa, served it to customers, cleared the table of the banana leaves on which he had served the dosas. He did this repeatedly through the day and for several years. He soon saved sufficient money to move to bigger premises. He met with a series of successes, moving to ever bigger premises in which to conduct business. Now a successful businessman, Kasturi built a commercial complex in Hassan and also ran the two most successful hotels in the district. He gave me space on the ground floor and basement of his commercial complex for my motorcycle dealership.

I saw that people like Kasturi succeeded because they had the courage, the determination, the energy, relentless persistence, and hard work without despair, to do more and do better every day. 'There is no short cut even for a genius' (Emerson). The path to success passes through fire. The treasure hunter is brazened like gold, tempered like steel, and beaten into shape by the hammer of adversity. Experience combined with energy, passion, and courage will get you there, but invariably it is the very journey that is the real reward!

One day Kasturi said he intended to build a restaurant on the neighbouring plot, which also belonged to him. Once that was done, he wanted to retire and engage in social service. He would also sell that off and his other existing restaurants and give away the complex to somebody to manage. Was I interested, he asked me. If Kasturi wanted to set up another restaurant in the plot adjoining the complex, he must have done his homework. It got me thinking. I did not need additional space at the time but at the same time I did not want the space to go to someone else either. I might require it in future, I thought.

It also occurred to me it would be a good idea to start a Udupi hotel of my own in the complex Kasturi was planning to build, as it adjoined my motorcycle business. Most of the property in Hassan was owned by Udupi hotel owners. I learnt subsequently that most Udupi hotel owners had joined as cleaners and risen through the ranks to become waiters and cooks, and some had gone on to set-up their own hotels. I liked the Udupi hotel concept. I thought it would be an adventurous experience to run one. I asked Kasturi to help me set up an Udupi hotel.

The name for the Udupi restaurant came to me on an impulse. I called my hotel Yagachi Tiffin. Commonly used in Kannada, tiffin refers to snacks. Yagachi is a tributary of Hemavathy that runs through my village, to which I had an emotional attachment. As I had already named my farm Hemavathy Farm, I decided to name the Udupi restaurant after the stream. Word got around that I was planning to set up an Udupi hotel. People said that Capt. Gopi had chosen a very beautiful location on the highway for the restaurant. While in the army, I had been mess secretary and wine secretary. I had taken an interest in the management and administration of canteens so the new venture excited me.

People looking for work began approaching me. A bhatta or cook from Udupi came to me for work. He had quit his job as head cook in another Udupi hotel. He said that if I hired him he would bring along other kitchen and hotel staff, including cleaners, and also manage them. He asked for a percentage of the sales in return. I thought it was a fantastic idea. It would solve the biggest problem of managing people. Kasturi had once told me that managing a hotel is like managing a circus company!

It was decided that the head cook would report a week before the launch, bring his team, start testing out recipes, compile a menu, and fine-tune processes. I felt free to devote myself to organizing other things such as interiors, kitchen equipment, utensils, plates, cutlery, and furniture. I had all the time in the world to design the modalities of the launch: identify and invite VIPs, get invitations printed, send them out, and devise the inaugural agenda. The local MLA and the municipal councillor were to be the special invitees. I invited all my friends and relatives, many coming from distant places. The countdown began. It was a week before the launch and the cook had not turned up. He did not turn up the next day either, or the following. He did however put in an appearance five days before the day of launch. He said he had not forgotten. He was held up because he had to attend to some work. He would go to Udupi and fetch the other cooks and workers and return two days before the inauguration. He promised much, but didn't keep any.

Two days to go and I had no cooks, no waiters, and no cleaners. I was at my wits' end. I was however dogged in my resolve that the launch would be deferred over my dead body. I set about cracking the plot. I recognized it as sabotage from competition: another Udupi restaurant nearby had planned this so that the setback would completely bury my plans to start a hotel. That made me even more determined. I decided I would find cooks and pay them ten times the asking salary if need be for the first few months. I would recruit them anyhow but would not abort or postpone the plan.

I hit upon an idea. I sent my brothers and cousins in my 'aeroplane' car to scour the district and find wedding cooks. These cooks specialized in cooking for weddings and also catered to other festivities: itinerant cooks who were turned on by the sights and sounds of a marriage hall. They loved their work and enjoyed being on the road. I planned to hire wedding cooks for a month. That would give me time to work other things out. After an entire day's search in Hassan district, the scouting group found one cook who agreed and came over the night before the launch. He brought a team of cooks, helpers, and cleaners. He dropped, as it were, from the sky as my saviour. That was how I inaugurated my Udupi hotel.

Running an Udupi hotel is like getting your daughter married every day. You get up at 5 a.m. and go and open the hotel. You make all the goodies with the care that you would accord to preparing dishes for your daughter's wedding because the customer does not care if it is three years or three days that you have been running the business! He wants the best each time he visits your restaurant!

It is also difficult to run the restaurant from a different point of view. Most people who wanted jobs as waiters and cleaners were runaway children. One day when I was sitting at the cash counter the kitchen supervisor came over and said the cleaners, three in all, had run away. The plates were piling up. I sought a reason. The supervisor said the boys had run away from home to escape cruelty or because they had flunked the exams, coming to the city or town to survive. Nobody knew them in the city. The Udupi hotel was an easy refuge because it gave them food and shelter. They picked up jobs in small hotels as cleaners and waiters. However, when a neighbour or acquaintance from the village visited the hotel and spotted the boy, his existence in the city was threatened. The neighbour would return and report the incident to his father. The father or some relative would come to the hotel wrapped in a shawl or towel that made them difficult to recognize. They would sit and wait quietly. When the particular boy came to the table, they caught their prey and hauled him back to their village. So whenever a boy spotted a nosy neighbour or a family member, he took flight.

That day I got down to washing the dishes myself because no one else wanted to do it. I still recall the runaway boys. They stood at the entrance of the hotel, a bundle in hand, looking anxious, a little pathetic, shivering in the cold. The bundles contained just a spare shirt and a pair of shorts. 'Is there any job?' they would ask. I was touched by the aspect of these kids who came looking for jobs. Many enterprising ones set up their own Udupi hotels years later; careers of some ended tragically.

I dabbled in other businesses as well. The farm was of course the focus of my activities. I only forayed into others when an opportunity came my way. V. P. Singh was the finance minister and the prime minister was Rajiv Gandhi. They initiated changes in the way the monetary market and stock exchanges worked. A friend who had lived in the US and returned to India wrote to me about a business prospect in stocks and shares. He said the Bangalore Stock Exchange had been set up. He was a member of the stock exchange and his company was looking for somebody to represent them in Hassan. He suggested that I operate the representative office at my existing premises. Those were the early days of stock market boom. My friend said,

'Why don't you establish a stock-brokerage firm in Hassan? You are well known there. You have office premises and require no additional investment. You would only need an officer to engage in day-to-day work.' The stock exchange in Bengaluru was new and stockbroking was fast becoming a business for educated people.

This particular friend, Satya Prakash, had an MBA from the US. He had set-up his own brokerage firm in Bengaluru and had taken the initiative to get me interested. I was drawn to the idea. It looked like a good learning curve. I therefore set up Hassan Investments and ran it for two years. People came and handed over their shares to be sold. I sold them for customers and I bought other ones for them. In order to understand the nuances of the business, I organized a seminar in Hassan and invited the president of the Mumbai Stock Exchange and the president of the Bangalore Stock Exchange to address it. The seminar was a success: participant registration was good and, newspapers reported on it. I did not however want to be a broker, so suddenly one day I decided to wind-up the stock-brokerage firm, having worn the stock-broker's hat for a short while!

Agricultural Consultancy

The silkworm business had become profitable, bringing in substantial financial gains. Its success had brought me into the limelight, making me into a celebrated farmer; it felt good to be recognized. I had also won the Rolex Award for Enterprise. People knew me already because of my other businesses. I now figured in the local newspaper and radio features mentioned my work. I had begun to write too, and my articles appeared in Kannada magazines and those published by the agriculture department. Journalists interviewed me.

I wanted to remain on the farm for a couple of years longer and ensure it was fully stable. My experience in farming and what I had seen in the US taught me both—how to and how not to farm. I also had to think of the future. As farming was something close to my heart, I decided I would do something in agriculture. Those were early days for micro-irrigation, water management, and horticulture management. I therefore teamed up with a friend of mine to explore these futuristic specialities. I had seen dealers in Hassan or Bengaluru selling hardware for managing water or for micro-irrigation, but these devices never produced a permanent solution. Some shopkeepers gave advice but there was no concept of end-to-end solutions for horticulture or agriculture. Water resource management and consultation for agriculture had not come to the fore. I had office premises, a computer, telephones, fax machines, i.e., the entire infrastructure required to set up a consultancy and undertake turnkey horticulture and agriculture projects. I thought end-to-end consultancy would be one stream of revenue; selling equipment would be another. I would therefore get into consultancy, design, execution, sales, and installation of micro-irrigation projects. Our solutions would integrate river water, groundwater, and rainwater, and deliver irrigation through effective systems. They would also help conserve water, soil, and electricity. It was a new field. Being a well-known farmer, I could count on other farmers coming to me for advice. At the time, there was a new company called Jain Irrigation, the first company to produce complete micro-irrigation systems.

Bhawar Lal Jain was an inspiring figure. He had started Jain Irrigation in a small building in Jalgaon and had moved on to build a Rs 100-crore business. He was a pioneer in agriculture related businesses. His most notable contributions were the manufacture of papain, an extract of the papaya fruit used in the pharmaceutical industry and as a meat tenderizer, and micro-irrigation systems. I had read about him and admired him. Just as I had done with the Enfield dealership, I went straight to Jalgaon. I met Bhawar Lal Jain and the company officials, and told them about my background. I asked them to give me the entire sales, distribution, and installation of equipment. I spent time with Mr Jain's children and tried to understand how he had built his empire from scratch. I said I would set up a team comprising agriculturists and horticulture graduates, technicians, engineers, and mechanics. It seemed a good idea to set up the business in Hassan as well as in Bengaluru. My farm, complete with dairy, sericulture farm, and coconut farm, would be fully functional in ten years. My second daughter would be growing-up and I would be able to move to Bengaluru in two years. I, therefore, needed to set-up the business in Bengaluru too, in order to extend service to Karnataka as a whole.

Accompanying me to Jalgaon was Harsha Gaonkar, an old friend of mine from Sainik School, Bijapur, and a retired air force officer. Harsha was already into farming in Bengaluru. I suggested that he partner me in the new venture. I offered him partnership too in my motorcycle business as well as in the irrigation business to increase his interest. He agreed and we set up the agriculture consultancy company. We hired 45–50 technical and non-technical people in Hassan and Bengaluru. They were mostly graduates from agriculture universities or civil engineers. Based on the human resource profile, we were in a position to take up landscape irrigation, horticultural advice, and end-to-end water management. We called the business Espak Agro.

I sold off the stockbroking business and the hotel business, and I sold the motorcycle dealership to my manager who had come to me as a small boy looking for apprenticeship. I had groomed him and he steadily grew. I withdrew from the other businesses because I needed to concentrate on my new one. In Hassan, for about two years, I loaded all the agricultural equipment that I set out to market in the car boot and hit the road. While on these business development forays, I combined the roles of MD, consultant, and manager of the company. I knew every aspect of the business and only booked orders from farmers. My manager would follow up and execute the orders. Every morning, I got into the car and travelled from farm to farm and from one coffee plantation to another. I did this every single day for two years, I found it to be the most difficult job in the world, the most challenging, and also the most rewarding. Each sale I made was an emotionally and financially rewarding event. Each time I missed an opportunity was a wake-up call causing me to hit the road once more with greater determination and aggression. I was often reminded of Arthur Miller's play, *Death of a Salesman*. It depicts the tragedy of modern-day America where a salesman wakes up each day to a job he does not like but must bring in sales if he has to survive competition. It ends in tragedy. I was also keenly aware of the parallel with Albert Camus's *Myth of the Sisyphus*. Camus tells the story of a man, Sisyphus, whose task is to roll a stone up to the top of a hill. He does not know why he has to do it, but does it every day of his life. That is god's punishment. When the stone reaches the top, it rolls down and Sisyphus has to begin all over again. It is futile, meaningless labour. The gods thought the best way to punish recalcitrant humans is to make them perform meaningless labour. Most jobs in large cities have become very much like the toil of Sisyphus. People do not love what they do, but do it nonetheless for the money it brings. The tragedy today, as was the case with Sisyphus, is that workers have no idea of the value they bring in. I realized how tough the job of a salesperson is, and also how important it is to get the salesperson involved with your vision and let him/her know what the true, not merely monetary, value of his labour is.

The knowledge that the product s/he sells to the farmer would help save money, increase yield, save energy, and benefit the farming community at large, brings a sense of purpose, and joy, to the work s/he does. This was what motivated me on the road. Going to every farm and telling the farmers how to save water had become a religion with me. I also shared many other insights I had gained as a farmer myself. I told them not to lose topsoil, not to destroy it by the use of chemical manure and chemical fertilizers. The farmers became great friends of mine; it proved a great life and learning experience for me.

4

Politics is supposed to be the second oldest profession. I have come to realize that it bears a very close resemblance to the first.

—Ronald Reagan

Dabbling in Politics

I began to get into the heart of agriculture-related businesses. Farming brought me close to people: farmers and farm workers, dairymen, donkey traders, silkworm growers, merchants, agricultural scientists and technicians, local and state-level bureaucrats, journalists, and the common man. In the best sense of the term, I was exposed to life in its rawest dimensions. And I witnessed, without blinkers, dire poverty, bureaucratic cynicism and indifference, corruption and apathy, and high levels of toil and struggle among the common people. It bothered me that this was rampant and that it often made the life of the common Indian difficult and miserable.

The system that functioned, if it did, was driven by the vagaries of political and bureaucratic decisions. It was arbitrary and self-seeking. We had slipped and fallen into a morass from which it was extremely difficult, if not impossible, to extricate ourselves. The morass was expansive, and it mattered little whether we faced the tentacles of this vast system in towns such as Hassan, or in villages, or in the larger urban conurbations. Most roads were indeed *no-roads*. Sanitation and hygiene were entirely absent from the diction and dictionary of villagers and small town dwellers. It was no better in the so-called district headquarters, commanding greater monetary and political resources.

It was a time when the government was only just beginning to wake up from its slumber, promising free power to villages. There was however insufficient electricity to distribute freely. While on one hand, there were the government, politicians, middlemen, bureaucracy, and the power brokers, on the other were the people: the consumers of government services, the payers of taxes, the large, middle and lower-middle income earners, the farmers, and landless labourers, all victims of the rot in the system. I set out to look at our own role here, conscious that we too were to blame. The manner in which many of us interacted and colluded with the system ensured that it continued to function in its indifferent, corrupt fashion. What were any of us doing to resolve the problems? What indeed was I doing to set matters right, I asked myself.

The system has its secondary-level charges: a euphemism for bribes. There is grease money, speed money, and as incidental charges you even get receipts for speed money from service providers: from lawyers and chartered accountants. You pay under the table if you want certificates issued by an authority. You pay a tip if you expect the electricity department, the telephone department, or the civic authorities to respond quickly to your problem or need and provide basic service, which is really what they are expected to do in the normal course. If you do not pay, your work does not get done. The equation of the bribe to the service provided is still a happy one; it can be considered to be a service charge. There is however a mathematical inequality entailed in the relation between bribe and work. Often bribes are paid but the work does not get done and there is no one to whom to appeal.

I was deeply troubled by all this. I realized that as I had myself, through sheer frustration, paid an occasional small bribe , consoling myself that it was merely a tip, I was both the perpetrator and the victim. Often, alone in my field, in a state of anxious agitation, I would think of the first sentence from Oliver Goldsmith's *Vicar of Wakefield*: 'I was ever of the opinion that the honest man who married and brought up a large family, did more service than he who continued single and talked of population.' I told myself, at such times, that doing one's job well was far better for society than mere cynicism and criticism.

I was in this deeply disturbed state of mind, when one day I got a call from someone in the Bharatiya Janata Party (BJP) asking me to join the party. The BJP was then making an attempt to establish itself as an alternative to Congress. The caller said, 'You are one of the most celebrated farmers in Hassan. Join the BJP and become the president of the party there.' The BJP barely existed in Karnataka, the state's political landscape being dominated by the old guard of the Congress, and Deve Gowda and Ramakrishna Hegde of the Janata Dal. The BJP was keen to make an inroad and field new faces. They thought I might be a suitable candidate to lead the party in Hassan.

I was on the horns of a dilemma: should I or should I not? I remembered the saying: 'There are only two tragedies in life: to have and to have not,' as Hemingway would have put it, and I was caught in this dichotomy. I wanted to play a part in public life but abhorred the idea of becoming a politician. On the other hand, it often struck me that while I was on the farm it was easy to spend two to three hours a day working for the party. I was however always consumed by the fear that rather than bring about change, it might be me, who became the subject of change and end up like any other politician. Many people from the party and well-meaning insiders from the local RSS unit called on me and said: 'What is the point of remaining outside and complaining, Captain? If you are so concerned you must take the plunge and clean up the rot!'

I spent many sleepless nights. Each time I looked at myself as a politician I hated the idea. The emotion changed its polarity if I looked at myself as a politician who could bring about positive change, I disliked the idea of my becoming a political agent of change. Prof. Thiru Narayan, teaching of marketing at IIM, Bengaluru, was one friend with whom I had long discussions on the issue. He said, 'You should give it a try if you feel so strongly about it.' I also thought it would amount to cowardice on my part not to take up the challenge. I must do my bit to improve the state of affairs.

My farm is in Gandsi Hobli, a legislative assembly constituency of Karnataka in Hassan district. I became the district president of the BJP and was appointed as a member of the national council and state executive council. I was determined that I would familiarize myself with the constituency even as I lived and worked on the farm. In that way I would not have to take my eyes off the farm, which remained my first love. I had also made it clear that I would accept party membership and the leadership responsibilities only if I was allowed to do things my way. I was uneasy about the reported links between the BJP and the RSS. I was apprehensive too about the party's communal overtones. This truly bothered me. I am not a believer. I do not, as a rule, go to temples. The party's association with the RSS might require me to take part in morning rituals or to profess a religious or RSS ideology. I wanted to have nothing to do with that. I have always cherished the idea of a pluralistic society that accommodates and nurtures a diversity of religions, belief systems, cultures, and traditions. The India of the dreams of Tagore, Gandhi, and Nehru was an India that was imbued with these characteristics. I was in favour of a multi-party system and it was necessary that an alternative be found to the decadent Congress. I nonetheless had my reservations and expressed them in clear and unambiguous terms right at the outset. The BJP assured me that the party was a separate and independent entity, and that there would be no interference in my functioning. I therefore joined the party at a time when it still had no clear form. It was led in Karnataka by a skeletal team comprising leaders like B.B. Shivappa, B.S. Yeddyurappa, and Ananth Kumar.

It was decided that Gandsi would be my constituency. I would visit all its 400 villages and study how they were faring. In this I was in my humble way emulating Gandhi. Gandhi had returned from South Africa and travelled the entire country by train before launching the freedom struggle. My father used to read to me episodes from the lives of great people. Gandhi's national expedition was one of them. I would do the same. I would go from village to village, house to house, meet people, and understand their problems at first hand. How then would I go about it? There was no such thing called BJP in my constituency so how would I actually, physically, go about visiting the villages? You couldn't simply enter any village and say that you are a BJP member and you have come to deliver them from their problems! No one would take you seriously if you did that. Probably that is why somebody said, 'A politician without a party is like a snail without a shell'. Then it suddenly struck me that I had to mobilize people to accompany me to visit the villages rather than going there on my own.

Who would accompany me? On any normal working day, people are busy at work, women staying home are busy cooking meals, and the children are away to school. The only people left in the village are the old people, the sick, the jobless, the idle rich and their hangers-on, and the lumpen. There is also the smooth-talking village tout who interfaces with the gullible villagers and the government. They are those who promise but who either have no intentions of fulfilling their promises or are unable to do so. The village politicians and their hangers-on are often also the local goons and the lumpen. It is they who eventually end up in the political process almost as a last choice. Of the nearly 550 members of the Parliament, the majority come from rural small towns and villages. It is this group which is politically active and engaged. Indifference keeps the educated out of the reckoning. There is an inevitability to the process: the best among them will rise to the top.

It is interesting to observe why an unemployed village youth becomes a party worker. As party workers, they get fed every day and have something to keep them occupied and dreaming future positions of power. There is a tendency among the urban educated classes to regard politicians from rural India, with some contempt. We must, however, remember that many of these leaders, MLAs and MPs, have risen through the ranks. The city-bred go to college, seek professional degrees and careers, and lead a cushy life. The village-bred politician, on the other hand, has no option other than to devote his life to politics. Many of them are passionate about local politics, some genuinely concerned about the state of the polity, but a large number become mere middlemen.

In recent times, there has been a huge shift of power from the Thakurs, Rajputs, Brahmins, and Gowdas to the traditionally backward and historically exploited classes in the villages. This class forms the real India. The educated, urban middle-classes have to figure out how to deal with this reality but without further dividing an already fragmented society.

On the positive side, these politicians have the keenest and most intuitive understanding of the lives of the people in real India. In my view, these politicians do more for democracy than those of us who are ensconced in our cozy urban cocoons. It is they who go out on the street to demonstrate against injustice and lopsided government policy.

Nelson Mandela was among the first to realize the new-age reality that the way forward to building a new order can only be achieved by not dividing society. This is beginning to dawn on new-generation Indian politicians to a considerable degree. In the initial stages, I went to villages wearing city clothes. They were ordinary clothes, not flashy nor particularly trendy. Hundreds of people move about in a city wearing such clothes and nobody bats an eyelid. To the people of the villages, however, I appeared to be a stranger. I, therefore, toned down my attire though I did not wear the characteristic politician's attire because that had acquired its own negative connotations. Neither did I want to wear designer kurta-pyjamas that politicians tend to wear today. I wore simple, unassuming cotton clothes: a bush-shirt and trousers. I saw the rural—urban divide as stemming from the utter isolation of the villages from modern urban life and the pervasive layers of caste and community distinctions. You can get an idea of the layers of community distinctions when you realize that there are two or more kinds of Gowdas, four or more kinds of Lingayats, ten or more kinds of Brahmins, and four or more kinds of shepherds, just to name a few of the hundreds of castes and sects that exist in India.

I wanted to understand these layers of caste and sub-caste distinctions. It is quite amazing that in India this complexity has worked for centuries, but there is a shake-up of the matrix today with modern thought and value systems taking root.

I wished to see how people lived, what their material basis of life was, how they coped with adversity, how they practised prudence in the management of the household. Many of them still observed traditional caste taboos, which came as quite a shock to me. One day on my farm, the party workers and leaders had gathered after a visit to some of the nearby villages. Everyone was very hungry. Raju, my man Friday, who belongs to the scheduled castes, had prepared a meal for us. I learnt from someone that some of the party members present—Acharis (carpenters) and Gowdas— would not eat because Raju had cooked the food. I sat with the group and asked Raju to serve me first. The army is a quintessentially secular institution in every aspect of its functioning. There is only the hierarchical distinction between officer and jawan but there is no caste, no community, and no religious bias. Indeed, there is only one caste, one community, and one religion: of being an Indian. Anybody who has served in the army knows that when an injured soldier needs a blood transfusion to survive, he will accept blood of any colour or creed. A soldier has the same attitude to food: meals are consumed from the same dishes and everyone eats at the same table. On that day at my farm, I decided to give lead and began eating what Raju had served. The others took the cue. They were so hungry that they just needed the reassurance that caste taboos could be broken without a prick of conscience, and they too joined in.

I had spent seventeen of my formative years at school, the NDA, the IMA, and the army. At all these institutions I had never witnessed a single instance of discriminatory behaviour and had lost track of the caste and religious divide that runs so deep in our country. Although I found it a little amusing at one level, that incident was an eye-opener of sorts. Even Manje Gowda initially hesitated to eat at my house, but today is quite comfortable doing so and readily accepts what Raju cooks. On that day, I believe, the caste taboo had been broken in my farm at a stroke.

I cobbled together a small band of local unemployed young men who were ready to accompany me on my visits. I decided that I must feed them, and this was a tacit understanding between us. I took my car and we drove to one village each day. I met everyone: the temple priest, the village headman, the panchayat member. The Congress and the Janata Dal had long been a presence in the villages, the BJP was very new and I had to break the ice. It was quite an uphill task. The villagers shared their problems and their aspirations with me. Their backwardness was stark. They lacked simple amenities but they lived their lives intensely and worked hard. I was touched; the entire experience had a profound impact on me. I realized that the host of odd-jobsmen in the villages undertaking basic chores like thatching a weather-beaten roof to collecting, patting, and selling cow-dung cakes, actually keep the country running. From farm labourers, carpenters, and blacksmiths to the goatherds, the plantation and orchard workers, the bee-keepers and honey-gatherers, millers, and the dairymen, a multitude of people toil day and night and help the state's economy function like a well-oiled machine. Their work is however neither recognized nor given due socio-economic importance by the state.

The task of creating jobs for people in the villages is enormous. Indian farming practices are not conducive to the creation of wealth per capita on a large scale as the case in America and Europe. In those countries only three or four per cent of the population at most is engaged in agriculture. Their farms are vast and run into thousands of acres. Their levels of automation are very high and very little human agency is employed in farming. During my visit to the US in 1984, farmers told me that agriculture on landholdings of less than 3–4000 acres was considered unviable. Farmers with large tracts of farmland also found it difficult to make ends meet and were heavily subsidized by the government.

India has an agrarian economy. However, given its poor infrastructure and the lack of technology, much of the farming effort goes to waste. Eighty per cent of Indian agriculture is rain-fed. Rains are erratic and unpredictable. There are also problems of plenty; excess produce lowers prices and a substantial part of the produce is lost due to poor storage which makes it imperative for the farmer to sell off the produce immediately after the harvest. Transporting produce to the market is a strenuous exercise too.

Sugar cane is a water-intensive crop and takes one-and-a-half years to mature. On my own farm, there was once an occasion when the cost of harvesting sugar cane proved to be more than the price I could get from selling it. In such circumstances, farmers simply burn the sugar-cane!

There are occasions when bumper harvests deprive farmers of a fair price. There is no equitable supply chain that operates between the farm and the market. Once in Hassan the main roads had become unusable because farmers had dumped tons of chillies there. There was a glut in production and the price they were getting did not support the crop. The rates fell and reached rock bottom. Cold-storage units are limited in number and are besides unaffordable by the small farmer. During that time, the black tarmac became a green tarmac with chillies squashed by passing vehicles. The chilly fumes were so pungent that nobody could approach the road for an entire day. Under these circumstances, the middleman buffers against the fall in price and makes money. We cannot blame him for this either because has to buffer against the fall in price. In such situations no one will buy something at a higher price when the produce is available at a lower price.

Returning to the original question, 'How do we create meaningful employment in agriculture? How can agriculture become viable as an economic activity? And how can profits accrue to enable the farmers to live a better life?' There is no easy answer to this.

The conditions I witnessed in the villages were appalling. The villages had degenerated. Farmers worked their half-acre, one-acre, and two-acre plots during season when water was available. The rest of the year they sat idle. Children dropped out of school because a degree or certificate did not guarantee a job and also in order to help the family at work, or by doing odd jobs. I wondered how I would tackle these problems even if I got elected. How would I eradicate unemployment and create profitable agriculture? How would I ensure minimum sanitary amenities in the villages? How would I provide clean drinking water and electricity? I was overwhelmed by the scale of poverty and deprivation and often moved from village to village in a daze.

Village life is idyllic in its rustic charm and the simplicity of farmers. Their lives are in tune with the rhythms of the seasons and there is apparent harmony. However, beneath what meets the eye is harsh reality and abject poverty. The material quality of life is poor. Farmers resent their inability to send their children to a good school and lament the absence of basic civic amenities. They realize that the traditional Hindu laws of inheritance result in the fragmentation of land from one generation to the next, making it difficult to sustain decent and united family life . They have seen the relative comfort of the city dweller on occasional visits to relatives or through films and television. However, a collective effort to infuse fresh energy into the village economy remains absent.

One thing that never ceased to amaze me was the strength and spirit of the villagers. Barring the odd farmer who finds himself in a debt trap and commits suicide, the people are strong. I often found strength in their spirit. The typical village dweller does not lose hope of a better life. Whatever their degree of poverty, they find the means to celebrate festivals. They share in each other's work in the peak season of harvest and sowing. On the other hand, it also amazes me and makes me wonder why farmers do not bond together to work for better sanitation.

This inexplicable contentment is also why India has not seen the violent upheavals other countries have witnessed. There is however no room for complacency, and if the villagers are pushed to the wall, the balance can tip. It is particularly important for the other, prosperous India, which is enjoying the fruits of development, to take note and put an end to exploitation. There is a strong dichotomy between the two Indias, and such a discrepancy cannot nurture a stable society.

I asked people in the villages what their fears and problems in life were. I wondered what went on in their minds as I spoke and was sometimes a little self-conscious about the role I was playing. I was reminded of a particular cartoon by R.K. Laxman. It is set at election-time and depicts a fictional village that has every amenity. The politician looks a little anxious and says, 'If these villages have everything, I can't promise them anything to win an election!' I felt comforted that I was not a candidate seeking votes during the final days of poll campaigning. Elections were at least four years away.

My village visits continued over the next three or four years. On one occasion, BJP stalwart Atal Bihari Vajpayee visited Hassan. As president of the party in Hassan, it was my responsibility to organize a rally and persuade a large crowd to attend it. I was expected to make other arrangements too. I realized that political events are not easy to organize, and becomes particularly challenging when people of Mr Vajpayee's stature are visiting. The state party president gave me a pep talk. He expected me to organize the event and to bring in the crowds but there was a severe shortage of funds. One needed banners, pamphlets, signages and hoardings to be put up everywhere to ensure visibility, and tractors and trucks to bring in people from the villages to attend the rally, otherwise the national leader would have to address an empty maidan. That is probably why politicians have glamorous film actors and actresses accompanying them!

It was my test as a political leader in the making to attract large crowds to attend Mr Vajpayee's meeting and I had to devise ways of mobilizing funds to do so. I met many newly recruited local BJP leaders and wealthy businessmen. They did not want to give donations to the party and I soon realized that if I embarked upon a venture to bring in lakhs of people from the villages in tractors and trucks I would soon become bankrupt. I therefore abandoned the idea and decided to publicize the function as best I could with my small band of party faithfuls and hoped for the best.

I hired extremely talented local artists for the job. They went from village to village, painting signages and creating posters. They were paid in kind and for food. They also hoped to benefit if I were to come to power. Many of the local traders and contractors who allied with me were also investing in that hope. Significant funds are given to village panchayats to finance development contracts and for the repair and upkeep of infrastructure. These contracts were always given to party workers who supported the local MLA. The nexus is a strong one with many links to the chain: from the contractor to the MLA. The party that comes to power gives the contracts to its party cadres and very little translates to development.

Many such small traders and contractors supported me with this in mind! I had no intention of going by the rules of this dubious tradition. If these men were under the impression that I would reward them with contracts or plum doles, how was I to refuse them and remind them that ability and track record alone would determine the beneficiary? I began to wonder how I would keep my brand of politics clean and different from the rest. I was however too pressed for time at that juncture and rushed along.

Mr Vajpayee arrived as scheduled, and his charisma attracted a huge crowd and saved the day for me. One positive spin-off of the political campaign was that my Kannada improved immensely. I had been religiously attending all the village meetings and soon I could make a fiery speech in my mother tongue. I lambasted the government and the other political parties. Addressing the crowds gave me an adrenalin rush. I waved my fists in the air, gesticulated, and proclaimed drastic change for the future. When I returned from these meetings I often wondered whether I was simply falling into the classical mould of Indian politicians.

Mr Vajpayee's visit to Hassan concluded with a dinner at my house. Leaders of the state BJP accompanied Mr Vajpayee. Among them were Ramachandra Gowda, Ananth Kumar, Yeddyurappa, and V.S. Acharya. That dinner was marked by one memorable incident. Those were the days of only two government-run Doordarshan channels on Indian television. There was dinner-time banter as well as serious discussion at the table. During one such exchange of words among the guests, I posed a question to the guest of honour. 'Mr Vajpayee,' I said, 'as you now criticize the government for misusing and usurping the media, why don't you plan to change that forever? Why can't you announce that you will allow a thousand TV and radio stations to come into being if you became the PM?' Mr Vajpayee was visibly shaken . Recovering his poise , he said, 'Young man, can you imagine what would happen if terrorists took over a TV station?' I was ready with a quick repartee and retorted, 'It's easier to take over one TV station than a thousand'.

We got into a debate. He lost his temper and in the heat of the debate the tenor of my voice too had risen. At that moment, somebody gently tugged at my kurta and intervened, suggesting that I change the subject. After dinner I went up to Mr Vajpayee and said, 'I am sorry, sir. I did not mean to offend you. I thought I must confront you with this.' He said, 'Young man, I enjoy fights and repartees!', and broke into a guffaw. I got an insight into a seasoned politician's mind through this incident and realized they are a mix of the biased and the good, as in any other profession.

The political campaign and the meeting with Mr Vajpayee steeled me and lent me the confidence that I lacked. It gave me extraordinary insight into politics at various levels: the panchayat, the taluq, and the district. At the national level, I got to meet leaders from other parties too. The BJP was a young national party and I happened to be a member of the national and state councils, so I enjoyed a fair deal of national exposure. I met leaders like Pramod Mahajan, Venkaiah Naidu, and L.K. Advani.

Indian political parties, whatever their hues and ideologies, suffer from one major shortcoming: the absence of inner party democracy. This does stand out rather like a sore thumb in the Indian democracy, the largest in the world. India's government is chosen by a process of secret ballot but such a process does not exist within parties. Political parties have legally drafted their constitutions and internal democracy is an important clause. This provision requires leaders to be elected at all levels, and the elected representatives at the village and district levels together elect their state and national leaders. As a rule, however, this never tanspires and parties are afraid to conduct elections. The reason for this is the belief that elections within a party would lead to rifts and jeopardize the party's very integrity. When a political party wins a majority vote in an election, party legislators do not choose a leader by open or secret ballot. All parties follow the rather dubious practice of asking individual legislators whom they favour through a private exercise, usually conducted by the so-called party observers, who are in turn instructed by the high command of the party in New Delhi. As there is no inner party democracy, a leader who feels slighted by the party has only to send in, his or her resignation papers for the central leadership to sit up, take note, and intervene through an offer of sops or bargaining positions within the party. It is ironical that the champions of democracy at the national level, act as dictators within their own parties.

Elections to the state assembly were announced. The party asked me to contest from my constituency of Gandsi. Constituencies are determined on the basis of population and according to taluq demography. Gandsi was a large constituency with 410 villages. Only two political parties were dominant there: the Congress and the Janata Dal. Congress MLA Shivaram was serving his second term and the party held sway over the region. The BJP was still scouting for grass-roots leaders. The Janata Dal was headed by Ramakrishna Hegde and Deve Gowda. Both leaders were powerful and popular. Deve Gowda had great clout in my area, which had a significant Gowda population. His sons were with him in politics. They had strong grass-roots cadres and leaders. The fight was clearly between the two major parties, with the BJP making an attempt to join the race. People advised me to contest from Malleshwaram or Basavanagudi in Bengaluru, or from Hassan city. These had large Brahmin populations. This idea did not appeal to me as I was not seeking caste votes. I was ex-army, well-educated, hard-working, and well-known as a farmer. People in my party got together and coined a slogan 'Model Farmer, Model Soldier'. I glanced at the slogan and was delighted! It looked catchy enough to sell my brand name! I would be the candidate of choice for farmers and people in the villages. I, therefore, remained in Gandsi reckoning that I had a good chance of winning as I had a clean track record in the region, as a hard working farmer. I began preparations for my election campaign in right earnest.

I received healthy press coverage in all Hassan's local newspapers of Hassan but was mortified that nobody in the villages knew me. The BJP as a party did not exist for them. It was a big challenge for me to create an image for the party. I delved deep into my psychic resources and spent sleepless nights. I felt certain that people would look up to me if they learnt about the serious work I had been engaged with, as a farmer. I was elated at the thought of the good work I could do for the people if elected.

Candidates spent Rs 15 to 20 lakhs on their election campaigns. I decided to keep mine low-budget and compensate with my energy, passion for work, and my immense lung power. I met people personally and visited every nook and cranny of my constituency. I began a second loop of village visits three months before the elections. I bought another second hand car and together with a few supporters, I set out for every village. Local supporters had put up posters with the slogan, 'From Model Farmer to Model Leader' next to my photograph. I attempted to create a highly visible and catchy campaign through specially designed peak caps, lapel-pins, and paper badges featuring my photograph.

Doordarshan, the only TV channel in the country, had begun to air programmes. There was one TV tower in Hassan with a footprint of 15 to 20 km, which meant that the rest of the district, about 90 per cent, lay in an information-blackout zone. I therefore decided to make a short film about my life and work. We planned to hire a few television sets and video cassette players to screen the film. That would ensure maximum coverage and publicity in the villages.

We sent word around that there would be a movie screening at 10 p.m. The equipment was placed in the village square and the entire village turned up to watch my film prefaced by my speech (which actually rode piggy-back on the promise of a film screening). I found it impossible to visit all the villages in the twenty days allotted to campaigning so my party workers screened the film minus my presence and speech in many villages.

There was enthusiasm and euphoria in the villages during the campaign. My wife and I visited about 200 villages. In each I was welcomed traditionally with incense, vermilion, and garlands. I would make my speech at the village square. Following this they gave us panaka (sherbet) made of bel fruit, bitter lime, and jaggery. If I finished around lunch-time they offered us a meal. Sometimes we were greeted by poornakumbha, a group of fifteen to twenty girls offering us the traditional welcome. Each of the girls carried on her head a kalasa topped with a whole coconut and four betel leaves arranged like petals. There would be folk music and the girls swayed gracefully to the gentle rhythm. People touched my feet, sang for me, made me feel like a hero.

It is customary for a party to organize at least one or two large election rallies. The party sends star campaigners to attend such rallies to boost the morale of the local party candidates and to help improve their prospects of victory. Former Bollywood star-turned BJP leader Shatrughan Sinha was assigned to Hassan to campaign with me. A Kannada film star was also asked to attend the rally, which was supposed to be held at 11 a.m. at the weekly market or shandy where people gathered. We were assured of a large captive audience.

T.N. Seshan, the then chief election commissioner (CEC) had put in place a very strict election code. Shatrughan Sinha was to stay in Hassan district for two or three days. Most people in the party seemed to be aware that Shatrughan Sinha is not an early bird—I was not. The actor was spending the night at ITDC Ashok Hotel at Hassan, from which Javagal, the venue of the rally, was an hour's drive. My people went to fetch him from Hassan and waited from 9 a.m. until it was half past ten. I was nervous: the crowds were likely to become restive, and we had already announced that Shatrughan Sinha and the Kannada actor would be attending the function.

My party workers told me the crowd was getting edgy. Shatrughan Sinha was nowhere in sight. Like many of us, he liked a drink and a drink too many!

The actor had crashed out the night before. When reports last came in, he had not yet been salvaged for the morning chores. This made me quite wild. I asked my brothers and fellow party workers to keep banging on the actor's door, till he opened it. Shatrughan Sinha eventually emerged from his hotel room at 11.30 looking as fresh and as well groomed as ever. Actors, regardless of where they are, are very particular about their appearance and couture. He emerged and told the reception party, 'Look here, it's already too late! I don't think I can do the first two meetings.' He was desirous of skipping my meetings, his manner was brusque and dismissive: 'I apologize, but I cannot come. I'm unwell. I'm only human. How can I be expected to attend so many meetings every day?' he retorted.

I asked my brothers and party workers to be aggressive. 'Physically stop him. Tell him you will not let him go. I will not allow him to ruin my campaign; not permit him go back on his word. If he has begun late he must finish late.' The star reluctantly agreed. Back in Javagal we had managed to keep the crowds regaled with songs and jokes. Shatrughan Sinha arrived by mid-day. I made a very powerful speech in Kannada. As many Kannada words are derived from Sanskrit, Shatrughan Sinha understood what I was saying. He complimented me by saying: 'Had I only known that you are such a good orator, I would not have come.'

Sinha himself was of course a very powerful orator. Tall and solidly built and gifted with an arresting personality, he exuded an impressive aura and spoke to the audience in his trademark rich baritone. His speech was passionate, in very fluent, chaste Hindi. The crowds were delighted.

He smiled at me and said, 'Your people physically arrested me and brought me here. Anyhow, I admire your guts and your determination. Hats off to you!' The Kannada actor was there too, and between them the function went off well and the rally concluded on a happy note. Shatrughan and I became good friends and remain so.

On another occasion I campaigned with Kannada actor Rajesh. I was supposed to start my speech at 11 a.m. We were assembled at the village square in Gandsi. In contrast to Javagal, where no other election rally clashed with ours and therefore the time factor was not critical, in Gandsi the speech had to begin at an exact time. The EC was strict about timing, not wishing politicians to arrive late and block public places from general use. There was no grace period and no adjustment of slots. This code of conduct kept politicians on their toes. More importantly, it helped provide security to all party leaders.

On the day I was to address the rally with Kannada actor Rajesh at a busy market-place, the next slot had been allotted to Janata Dal supremo Deve Gowda. My speech was to be at 11 a.m., Deve Gowda had been allotted the noon slot. We had distributed pamphlets announcing that actor Rajesh and Capt. Gopinath would speak. People had turned up in substantial numbers for the village fair and had drifted close to the elevated platform. It was a circular dais partitioned by a delicate, translucent curtain at the centre. The leaders of one political party could take their position on the other side and as the party on one side finished its speeches, the other's began.

Our function got under way. A few leaders spoke before me. I had only just taken the stage and spoken a few introductory words when there was a deafening sound of crackers, the noise drowning out my speech. There was a stunned pause. People turned to see where the sounds were coming from and witnessed a spectacle. A sea of people, numbering thousands was marching like an army towards the venue, many perched atop hundreds of tractors and bullock-carts. The huge march was accompanied by the palpably loud rhythmic thudding of drums, the rhythm shattered by the bomb-like bursting of crackers. Some of these were staccato and could be heard for a long while. In the din you could not hear your neighbour shouting. The procession also presented spectacular visuals. A burning, giant bullock-cart wheel was held aloft, spinning on its axis, resembling the Vishnu Chakra. Right in front of the Vishnu Chakra stood Deve Gowda, suggesting it was he who wielded the invincible weapon of the gods. Deve Gowda stood tall in a cart, his hands folded in a humble namaste. His son, Revanna, who was also a contestant from one of the constituencies, was by his side.

Hassan was Deve Gowda's constituency and he had a huge following. He was the PWD minister and a prominent leader of the Gowda community and a powerful politician. The audience who had been cheering and hailing me, without exception rushed off to join Deve Gowda's procession within seconds. These even included my BJP workers. Gowda's charisma had acted as an electrifying switch. He is a master tactician and politician, and every vacant spot at the venue was now filled with people eager to listen to him. People danced, gyrated, tottered. Many of them were drunk on liquor and the rest on his charisma.

Rajesh, the Kannada actor, went white with anxiety and fear. He whispered in my ear, 'Can we call off the meeting? There might be violence.' I, however, had no intention of calling it off. I was facing my first real test in public life. Fleeing at that juncture would spell the end of the road and a goodbye to politics. As for the actor, I quickly realized that he was a hero only on the silver screen and I could not expect any support from him. I also realized that by standing my ground, I would be taking on someone politically very powerful. I therefore stood my ground and looked at my watch, which indicated that it was 11.35 a.m. Deve Gowda's meeting was scheduled to begin at 12 noon. He had reached early and was depriving another candidate of his rightful time and space. This was in violation of the rules. I knew that Seshan, the CEC, considered these transgressions very seriously, and this lent me added confidence.

I began and continued to speak to the empty ground before me, mounting a sharp, strong, and articulate attack directed against Deve Gowda. 'Come back!' I hollered to my supporters. 'This is unethical. This is high-handedness. This kind of tamasha will not get us anywhere. This is precisely why Gowda should be removed from power.' In the meantime, without my realizing it, Deve Gowda was standing right behind me, just behind the thin curtain. The circle inspector came; other police officials came. They urged me. 'Sir, why don't you stop for just twenty minutes. He has come a little early. Yes, we understand, but please wait for twenty minutes. He will be done. This crowd will come back to you.' Far less polite were the Janata Dal goons who were gesticulating quite threateningly at me and at my supporters. Some of the party workers of Deve Gowda, who knew me, came over and requested me politely to stop my speech.

As the speakers faced both directions, my remarks had been heard by everyone including Deve Gowda. He would have been unable to match the sheer stridency and the high decibel level of my voice unless I stopped. It was a narrow podium. At the time I did not realize I was on the mike and my explosive response went something like:

Over my dead body will I leave this stage. I will file a complaint with T. N. Seshan to have Deve Gowda disqualified from the election. It's a violation of the election code of conduct. I have my permission letter here. I am allowed to speak here from 11.00 a.m to 12.00 noon. Deve Gowda can speak only at 12.00 noon. I am not going to leave the stage. You may ask him to wait for twenty minutes or leave.

I also let fly a string of expletives in Kannada, my voice booming. I then heard Deve Gowda making enquiries in Kannada, '*Yaaru avaru?*' (Who is it?) He was told that I was a BJP candidate. He knew I was inconsequential, his real battle being with the Congress, but there was no way he could continue with me shouting over the mike. While this was going on the crowds took notice of my firm voice, my fearless use of expletives, and my gumption and edged towards me. Among them were Congress sympathizers in addition to BJP workers. They began booing and shouting at Deve Gowda. I remember one man coming over to me and screaming in Kannada, 'You are a tiger, Sir! You must continue!' Another said, 'You are a man, Sir! We are with you. We want to hear you.'

I felt greatly encouraged and continued my tirade. I then overheard Deve Gowda tell his associates, 'Don't trouble him. I'll come some other time.' He was unable to deliver his speech but his party workers and associates did not leave with a whimper. They made a raucous noise and burst a volley of crackers. Deve Gowda mounted his Vishnu Chakra-adorned truck and departed with dignity. From that day's experience I learnt that nobody is inconsequential in politics. If I had thought of myself as a political non-entity I would not have been able to assert my legal rights against someone as powerful as Deve Gowda!

The polling took place and the counting began. It was a thrilling experience. I was in the counting hall along with politicians from other parties including Deve Gowda's son Revanna. I was certain of victory as were my supporters. We expected a landslide victory but I had overlooked one important cultural aspect of village life which perhaps applies also to cities. When I went campaigning, people escorted me to the village temple. The head priest would tell me he had prayed for me. He had placed flowers on the lingam and the flower had fallen on the auspicious right hand side, meaning victory for me. I did not believe in temple rituals, but it crossed my mind that every politician went to the temple and made an offering to the deity. My opponent had visited the same temple, explaining why every candidate brimmed with confidence about victory. Diehard sceptic that I was, even I was taken in!

I was reminded of the story, 'An Astrologer's Day', by the well-known writer R.K. Narayan. A man murders someone, flees his village, and moves to the city. He has no skills and cannot find a job so he decides to become an astrologer. He becomes quite a popular fortune-teller. He knew no more of what was going to happen to others than he knew what was going to happen to himself next minute. He was as much a stranger to the stars as were his innocent customers. One day he has a customer. The pseudo astrologer recognizes the customer as somebody from his shady past: the man he had thought he had killed in a drunken brawl was alive. The fugitive is able to recall in close detail the events of the past. He speaks of the past; the future remains unsaid.

Years later, when Deccan was going through a rough patch, I was advised to seek help from an astrologer. It still puzzles me how even the highly educated and successful politicians approach these god-men and god-women. Politics is like a game and the anxious electoral candidate clutches at anything, even a flotsam of straw, to ascertain his win. I was carried away too and did likewise, even believing that there could be some hidden power in the utterances of fortune-tellers. I was also compelled by the absolute faith of my supporters to believe in the powers of the divine spirit. By scoffing at it, I would have hurt their morale.

The result of the polls was independent of fortunes foretold. The counting began with me still believing with certitude I would win. If I lost, I reckoned, it would be by a small margin. Such was my optimism. In the event, however, after the count was closed, the vote tally was dismal. Of the 1,40,000 votes polled, only 7000 had been cast in my favour. As I had initially, correctly suspected, the votes were split closely between the Congress and the Janata Dal. The latter came to power and Deve Gowda became the chief minister.

I returned to my farm. Those three months spent campaigning were the longest I had stayed away from it. I would begin campaigning at eight in the morning and spend the whole day on the road. I often returned as late as two or three in the morning. I had lost in the election but I had won in the battle because I had discovered this source of great strength and stamina within me. My election debacle did not sadden me. Yes, there was disappointment, but there was also a curious sense of exultation. I had discovered a strange power within me. I would assume charge of a situation and do all that was necessary for its accomplishment. I had no money but I was able to raise sufficient resources from friends and well-wishers to fight the elections!

My focus reverted to the farm. The crops that I had planted were ready to be harvested. The cycle had commenced and the trees yielded fruit, season after season. The farm had been freshened by the rains and glistened in the sun. My heart was filled with music. The wind rustled among the coconut fronds, bees buzzed, birds hummed, and I was aware of an intense sense of joy. The trees I had planted and watered with my own hands were now bursting with fruit. Wild berries and nuts that had flowered in the thickets were a bonus. Sometimes I felt like a tree among trees, bird among birds, and bee among bees: an inner soul of all I perceived: a true romantic.

5

*You see things; and you say, 'Why?', but I dream things that never were;
and I say, 'Why not?'*

—George Bernard Shaw

The Foundations of a New Venture

The strange stirrings within me were pregnant with the prospect of a new beginning.

The farm had been established. Raju, the farm boy, had grown into an adult. I built a small hut for him, got him a motorcycle and a television set. He got married. The couple lived on the farm and they had a son. His family became as much a part of the farm as the trees we had planted. Raju was uneducated but he had an innate sense of management and managed the farm, including its finances. Every week he produced before me farm accounts with the right numbers. He had taught himself numbers but enlisted the assistance of someone who could read and write. As happens in the case of people deprived of one sense—their other senses become far more acute than normal, Raju's lack of literacy made him keen and intuitive about numbers. From one end to the other, the farm was covered with coconuts, areca nuts, bananas, some fruit-bearing trees, mulberry, and was now fully established and yielding. Pallavi was in boarding school in Bengaluru. Krithika was waiting to go to school. I now considered the idea of moving to Bengaluru and dividing my time between Bengaluru and the farm which now needed less attention. The agriculture-consultancy business I had set up there three years ago was beginning to show promise and had main branches in Bengaluru and Hassan, and franchisees in other parts of Karnataka. I had one hundred people working in the two branches together. The HR included horticulturists, civil engineers, mechanics, and salesmen. They handled projects principally relating to agriculture, horticulture, landscaping, water management, and rain-water harvesting.

I moved to Bengaluru. Once there, I discussed the distribution of responsibility with my business partner so that we could complement each other. I soon got busy dividing time between Bengaluru and Hassan. By 1993, my move to Bengaluru was complete. I found a small apartment close to Bishop Cotton Girls School where Pallavi studied. Krithika joined her sister in the same school. The apartment block was right next to Cubbon Park where I took walks in the morning and evening. I was also close to the Army Club and began playing squash again. The apartment was on Grant Road, now renamed Vittal Mallya Road. It was, and still remains, a very beautiful part of Bengaluru. It captured my heart because the area was full of rain trees. Some of them were perhaps the most magnificent trees in the world, some centuries old. There was a variety of flora including rain trees, gulmohars, neem, jacaranda, *Cassia javanica*, and *Tabebuia spectabilis*. In those years, not so long ago, if you took a helicopter ride over Bengaluru, you could still see swathes of lush green tree cover. The trees on Vittal Mallya Road created a canopy so wide you were wholly enveloped by the arching green glade.

I used to walk the short stretch of Vittal Mallya Road, and amble along Lavelle Road, an equally shaded street that intersected the former. The avenues were dotted with old-style bungalows. These were parts of the old Bengaluru cantonment where the military officers and the cadres were provided quarters, both during British rule and after independence. The army centres included MEG (Madras Engineering Group), the Pioneer Corps, the ASC Centre, the Services Selection Board, and several army officers' messes and the RSI club. These large campuses constituted the city's lungs.

Even in those days, however, during my frequent helicopter sorties over the city, I saw in the midst of large swathes of greenery early signs of denudation. I also saw the famed lakes of Bengaluru, had once been agriculture tanks. These great waterbodies could have kept the city cool and been used for rain-water harvesting and constitute as world-class recreation zones. The lakes were however choking with sewage and non-biodegradable waste. Tree cover was being eroded. In any part of the world, the Ulsoor, Hebbal, and Yediyur Lakes in Bengaluru, would have formed the magnificent backdrop for the best lake-front properties. They could have featured water parks that would have been the delight of urban architects and designers. Urban landscape is a delectable speciality in many schools of western architecture. Many students initiate graduate projects on the best ways of incorporating the lineament and ecology of inner-city waterbodies and old heritage buildings within urban housing or commercial developments. The lakes in Bengaluru were however clogged and dank from rotting weeds and sewage. The beauty of Bengaluru was already being destroyed at a frightening pace. Today, 95 per cent of the tree cover and grassland in downtown Bengaluru has vanished. All that remains is greenery preserved in the army-command areas and some government-owned properties. The old bungalows have vanished too. City expansion should be so planned that it preserves historical and cultural legacy.

I also loved the other, older Bengaluru. I loved Basavanagudi, Shankarapuram, and Malleshwaram. I enjoyed visiting the markets there and Russell Market in Shivajinagar. There is a labyrinth of history among these landmarks of the city. Their legacy and the old-world charm is unique. The Gavipuram temple for instance, is nearly 2000 years old: it's a temple within a cave. In comparison, a glitzy shopping mall is just the same be it in Paris, Singapore, or New York. If you are in any mall and looking at any Louis Vuitton or Armani outlet, they look the same, they all feel the same, and they sell the same types of goods. Nobody can therefore identify where you bought your goods from. The danger facing most growing cities across the world is the loss of character and culture. The challenge to urban planners is how to build clean modern cities to accommodate the new immigrants and how to house them without losing the heritage and tradition, and snapping the cultural moorings. I heard V. S. Naipaul say that India should not use Dubai or Singapore as models of emulation because a city is not just a conglomeration of glass-fronted buildings, shopping malls, and dry statistics of per capita income and GDP. A city becomes a great city when it is the repository of learning, art, theatre, and literature.

At festival time, the market in Basavanagudi is decorated and sports its best colours. The aesthetics of colour, scent, and sound have evolved over generations. Covent Garden in London has been rebuilt to accommodate pubs and other watering holes; the Covent Garden of legend where traders and horsemen came to buy and sell horses has vanished. We have to learn from, and caution ourselves, against this form of inordinate urgency to destroy the old. There is another story that straddles the old and new. Some fifty-five years ago an Iyengar gentleman came to Bengaluru and set up a bakery in Vishveshvarapuram in Basavanagudi which became very famous. The owner named it V.B. Bakery. It specialized in savouries that are redolent with flavours of old Mysore. The repertoire included vegetable-stuffed buns and puffs, spiced buns, buns with coconut icing, sweetened milk bread, sponge-textured ordinary bread, and other snacks, hot and cold. The aroma of baking bread wafted over hundreds of metres from where the bakery stood in the famous Sajjan Rao Circle, the old quarters of Basavanagudi. It was a landmark for the hungry; for those unable to resist temptation. The

bakery was and remains a landmark, even metaphorically. The Iyengar who
came and set up the bakery was my brother-in-law's father.

The Iyengars, some of them relations from my father's side, migrated to
Bengaluru from nondescript rural nodes of Hassan district and set up what
has become a brand name: the Iyengar Bakery. The migrations have taken
place over a period spanning more than a hundred years. The migration
continues. Just like Udupi hotels (read 'restaurants'), the Iyengar Bakery is
supposed to offer certain standards in terms of product quality and service.
The Iyengar Bakery is operated by Brahmin bakers, and they are expected to
observe cleanliness and hygiene of a high order and use the finest ingredients.
They are also expected to be fastidious about taste and about the segregation
of food types, to ensure that the more quickly perishable grade of food
items are not brought into contact with those that have a longer shelf life.
Above all, the Iyengar Bakery provides a nutritious snack at a reasonable
price. They form a ubiquitous feature of the Bengaluru landscape, and there
must be over a thousand bakeries in the city. It is still a mystery how the
puritanical, orthodox Iyengar Brahmins, who had no vocation for business
took to baking as a profession, a legacy of colonial India.

A visit to Bengaluru is incomplete without a visit to the Lalbaug, the
gardens laid out by Tipu Sultan in 1776, MTR, the legendary Udupi Hotel,
and the Iyengar Bakeries. The bakeries are to be found all over Karnataka,
Andhra Pradesh, and Tamil Nadu. Lalbaug has delights for scholars and lay
people. MTR was in those days the mother of all Udupi hotels.

My friend Prof. P.N. Thirunarayana of the Indian Institute of Management,
Bengaluru, who later became a director in our company, and I were at one
time frequent visitors to Lalbaug and MTR. I asked the professor to join
me for a morning walk in the Lalbaug whenever I needed to pick his brains
and discuss some pressing matters. We met at six at Lalbaug, walked and
talked for an hour and half, and then sauntered across the street to MTR
for a wholesome breakfast of idli and dosa. These little things gave me joy.
Happiness is a mirage if you look at it as a destination to arrive at. If you
take joy in the everyday things of life, you will never need to embark on a
journey towards an elusive destination. If work is your joy, you never need
to toil at all in life!

My father told me about how one day Gandhi, while still a lawyer,
decided to walk to work. He hoped the walk would give him time to think
and to sort out problems, as well as some physical exercise. On most days,
therefore, I too began walking to and from work.

I learnt to live each moment intensely. These were moments with family,
moments with friends, moments spent strolling, and moments exchanging
banter at the vegetable market. Happiness is no pinnacle to be attained. It

doesn't exist as a destination and is meaningful only as a journey. What you want to be is a vision. It's an ideal. If you have reached it, you may have reached a goal but a vision is something that drives you because it is almost impossible to achieve. It is something virtual. This was the case with me. I was vaguely conscious of seeking something more. Unknown to me, I was reaching out to a new beginning.

My move to Bengaluru had two important consequences for my future career. I resumed socializing with old friends from the army at the RSI (the army club). The other thing was bumping into old buddy, Capt. K.J. Samuel—Capt. Sam—for all of us. This was a watershed moment for me. Capt. Sam was with me at the NDA and at the IMA. We were also bunker buddies and room-mates at the School of Artillery in Devlali. Sam is a wonderful guy with a heart of gold. He is unassuming and very lovable. We reunited amidst much rejoicing. We had a lot of catching up to do. Things had happened to our lives and we needed to share notes. Sam loved his rum and was a touch wild in his younger days. He could drink a bottle of rum and remain unaffected and sober. Now he was no longer the old tippler! He had given up drinking and become as sober as the Pope! I did not like either of the extremes because I enjoyed a drink with old buddies. I tried to preach to him that moderation is good as the ecclesiastics said but Sam was a disappointment. Just as the sun was setting and the need arose for some old style camaraderie, Sam would say he had a family to take care of and had to leave. Even then he retained an infectious zest for life, and remained my buddy of yore! We met frequently at the club to play squash and tennis. We talked about what each of us planned to do in the future. I told Sam about my return from the army, my decision to become a farmer, the move to Javagal, the coconuts and the mulberry, the sericulture and the success of the farming enterprise. I narrated my story as a businessman and my entrepreneurial essays: the motorcycle dealership, the restaurant, and the agriculture and water management consultancy. I told Sam the circumstances that had taken me to Javagal, to Hassan, and now brought me to Bengaluru. I updated him on my family. My first daughter Pallavi was a day scholar in the fourth standard and Krithika was in LKG. She was four years old. Bhargavi took care of the family. Sam told me his story. He had married earlier than I did. He had a daughter and two sons. The children were grown-up. Sam had resigned from the army and was working as a freelance helicopter pilot. He was looking for something gainful and steady.

As a freelance pilot, companies hired him when there was need. His assignments took him all over, from the north-east flying for the Oil and Natural Gas Commission, to the west flying for some private business.

He did not know where the next assignment would be. He did not know if there would be a next assignment. Things were fluid; were unsettling. Work he had to, for a living. He wanted to be in Bengaluru after twenty years of service in the army. He was energetic and fit. He had a great sense of humour. He was young in civil parlance. In army slang, for me, it was always 'Hi Sam, Old Man!'

Post-NDA one becomes a commissioned officer at the age of nineteen or twenty. After twenty years of service, an army officer is relatively young. Jawans who did not get promotions used to retire at thirty-five and are younger than officers at retirement. It is a great tragedy that after giving the best years of their lives to the country, they are left to fend for themselves. A retired jawan received a measly Rs 300 or Rs 400 as monthly pension. The only jobs they get after retirement are that of security guard's. They are however excellent human resource given their meticulous training. They are hard-working and highly disciplined. It is a huge challenge for the country to ensure that this wonderful resource does not go waste.

Sam, was in his early 40s when he left the army because he wanted to settle in Bengaluru and find himself a steady job. He had lost interest in army life and did not wish to continue.

Visit to China

It was around this time that I had the opportunity to visit China. The government sent me to China on an exchange visit. The purpose was to study silk-rearing practices there. I was a kind of silk farmer celebrity and that must have weighed on the government's decision to select me. I have always liked visiting other farmers, be they my neighbours in Javagal or farmers in the US or in China. It was a month-long visit and included both Thailand and China in its itinerary. As I look back, I can see the truth of Somerset Maugham's words when he wrote, 'Often life is influenced by and steered by chance events.' Life is driven by chance events. The direction it takes is often determined by simple decisions like taking one road or one turn at a corner rather than another. Sometimes a casual decision to watch a play and not go to the shopping mall might make a big difference. Chance events have the power to dictate our lives. If you call these events, fate or destiny, so be it. Maugham tells the story of a man whose life took a dramatic turn because of a chance meeting with someone who he would not have met had he taken a different road. That is an extraordinary story, tellingly narrated. The moral of the tale applies to me too. It is significant that I met Sam on that particular day, fateful by hindsight, and not on any other, before or after. It was equally an event of chance that I was sent to

China. Together these two events took me on a course that would not have otherwise been taken.

Almost every other day, in the first six months to a year after we met, I asked Sam if he had got a job. I was curious about the life of freelance pilots and was concerned about him. A freelancer tends to be a drifter and it is difficult for him or her to settle down to a reasonably predictable routine and lifestyle. It becomes a greater concern when there is a family to support. I once asked Sam point blank, 'Sam Old Man! How come you are not getting a job?' He had been to several interviews for the position of a helicopter pilot. He was not selected. I could sense that he was bothered by a vague sense of unease. Sam was positive and not depressed but I discerned a dark line of worry beneath his poker face. He had a family to support. He was young and that made a lot of difference. Most of us will fall apart if we don't have work to do, which is an anchor, necessary for happiness. Human beings need to work, but individuals need to reason and discover for themselves the unique secret of the kind of work that suits them, is productive, and makes them happy in the long-term. More people these days are unhappy at work than ever before. Most of our waking hours are spent at work. The majority looks at only one consequence of that work as the most worthwhile: money. Money is one or more steps removed from happiness. Only for the miser, who counts his money before going to bed or looks at the interest accruing to his savings bank account, can money be an end in itself. For the rest, it is what money can bring and buy that matters. There is a direct relationship between the consumerism of the world today and the work that people do. People seem to be happy and enjoying life when on a buying or shopping spree at the mall, but for many if work does not offer challenges, it is not worthwhile.

As time passed, with Sam and I continuing our morning game sessions without a break, the line of worry on Sam's brow began to deepen. Restlessness had begun to border on dejection. Sam's face began to wear a shadow. He was predictably taken to the edge, and it is at the edge of one's existence that one is most creative. Danger stimulates the adrenal glands. Sam's acute concern about the future made the creative juices flow. He had begun to think and look beyond the narrow confines of a job which had boxed him in. One day I got a flavour of his idea. 'Gopi,' began Sam. 'Why can't we do something with the helicopter?' There was a pause and a deep breath. Rather, there was one conflated pause and two audibly deep breaths. 'What do you mean, Sam?' I quipped. It was that inchoate moment, before a new line of thinking opened up. Sam did not apprehend the idea he had just authored. 'I don't know,' he said. 'Let's just do something with the helicopter. I mean let us do things on our own.'

He knew I was in business. He said, 'We could set up a business for crop spraying using helicopters.' As a businessman, the idea appealed to me. As a farmer, it was abhorrent. I had just won the Rolex Award for Ecological Farming. I retorted, 'Oh! No, Sam. I don't want to spray pesticides.' I said, 'Look, Sam, this is dirty work. The world is going green.' I knew the commercial aspect of pesticides as I had now been engaged in farming for fifteen years. I was aware of what kind of pesticide applications there were and that perhaps only tea and rubber plantations could afford aerial spraying. In coffee plantations however their tree canopy makes aerial spraying an impracticable idea. Tea plantations could also afford it, but tea prices had collapsed. Rubber plantations could afford it, but the terrain was dangerous for flying. Overall the prospect of pesticide spraying seemed to me dirty and erratic flying. It would also not make for a steady source of income. I refused, but the idea remained with me.

One day when I met Sam, he said, 'Gopi, I got a job!' I was thrilled for him. 'Where?' was my next question.

For most people, the job of a helicopter or airline pilot evokes images of glamour and abandon. I was happy for my friend. I assumed he had a job as a pilot, at last, but was taken aback by what Sam told me. He had been offered a job not as a pilot but as administrative-cum-security officer in a courier company! Sam said his salary was Rs 10,000 a month. He had reported to work the previous day.

The news was shattering. My friend is an outstanding personality. He was a colonel in the army, had led men, had fought wars, had won the Sena Medal which recognizes a soldier for exceptional bravery. He had won the medal for his dare-devil display of courage in Kashmir against the Pakistan Army flying helicopter rescue missions. Such a noble and brave heart was ending up as an administrative-cum-security officer! This was bad for morale. I felt sad and disturbed.

Lessons from China

Meanwhile, the visit to Thailand and China was organized. This was in 1995–96. We spent the first two weeks in Thailand and were in China for about twenty days. In that country we travelled to the province of Guangzhou and were taken to the deep interiors. We saw and experienced Chinese agriculture at first-hand. I noted a similarity between Chinese and Indian villages, in terms of the poverty, ignorance, and lack of hygiene. The principle occupation in the villages was farming. People were largely naïve and uneducated. The trauma of communism was slowly making way for the trauma of capitalism. There were a few scattered shops. Farmers owned property. The government had redistributed land that had once been collective property. Peasants owned anything between half an acre to two acres. It was a time when there was a huge social churning going on and, stunned by its own economic success, China was unable to integrate vast populations of the rural uneducated poor into the mainstream of largely urban islands of prosperity.

Silk farmers produced cocoons and sold them to government-owned mills, the size and scale of which truly surprised and amazed me. China is the country credited with the origin of silk. There is a legend about how it came to India. Some 2000 years ago a Buddhist monk was supposed to have smuggled a few moths out of China and brought them to India. They laid eggs and the story of Indian silk began.

The Chinese created a habitat for the silkworm indoors. They evolved a method of breeding cocoons and drawing out yarn on a spinning wheel. This is their contribution to the silk industry. They bred the worm in such a way that one single variety produced more silk than the others. They evolved worms that—fed on mulberry—to an exclusive fine breed that yielded the finest gossamer thread and had the finest lustre. The West has always shown a preference for the fine varieties of silk produced in China and Japan.

India has been producing silk for over 2000 years. The industry produces many varieties of worms. Mysore silk is among the most famous and is produced by a variety of worms native to Karnataka, the regions of Kunigal, Chamarajanagar, Kolar, Mysore, Bengaluru, and Ramanagaram abounding in this variety of worm. The yarn produced is used to weave Benares and the Kanjeevaram silk saris. It is silk that is wonderfully suited to Indian fabrics, lending them the peculiar stiffness that gives the saris the right fall and crispness. Weavers throw in woofs of gold thread to make the saris look grand. The classic Kanchi, Benares, and Dharmavaram saris are rich in texture and weight.

There is another variety of silk in India which is harvested by native forest dwellers. The tribal people pick the cocoon from the forest trees, made by worms that feed on a variety of forest leaves from oak and castor oil plants. The silk produced by these cocoons has its own distinctive texture and colour, and is amenable to traditional methods of weaving and printing. They produce varieties of silk such as moga, eri, and tussore. The original Indian silk may have been derived from native varieties. Indian farmers later bred them. India also has a greater variety of silk traditions than China. In China, silk is accorded the status of family heirloom on the lines that gold ornaments in India are passed on from generation to generation. Chinese emperors wore grandly crafted silk robes and silk slippers. India however produced silk both for the rich and the commoner and has perhaps more varieties of weaving and printing techniques.

I became aware of some of these techniques and traditions as a farmer. I was interested in understanding Chinese techniques and looked for them when I visited that country. However, in the immediate aftermath of communism, China had not accorded the kind of importance silk originally held. In the process Japan assumed a leadership position in silk, India was the second largest producer at the time with China in the third place, and Thailand following it. However, after China decided to open up its economic sphere, in a style typical of the Chinese, the government set-up massive silk yarn and textile mills. Overnight, China became a giant in silk production and began unprecedented dumping in India. The Indian silk farmer reeled under this onslaught. This was the backdrop of my visit to China. I visited mills and workshops. The size and scale of their industry was overwhelming, and they had acquired the most sophisticated machinery. The West loved the soft, lustrous silk produced in China of a kind which in the past was made in Italy, France, and Switzerland. These countries had the machinery needed to lend a lustrous finish to the silk. Silkworm disease and shortage of labour led to a collapse of silk farming in Europe, and was part of the large shift that took place there from manufacturing to services. The European silk industry eventually collapsed, surviving in only a few insignificant pockets as a cottage industry. Japan, India, China, and Thailand took over. The Chinese silk farmer was given a massive support to boost silk production as the Chinese government decided to produce for the West and imported sophisticated machinery for this purpose. Virtually overnight China became the world's leading production centre. Being a communist economy with total state control, they changed policy to an investment-oriented regime and bulldozed their way. Japan slid from its position as number one, with China soon regaining its top slot with India a distant second. China's unimaginably explosive economic growth, dating to as far back as in 1995, simply astonished me during my visit.

Silk farmers in Karnataka and Andhra Pradesh had been hard hit and were going bankrupt. They protested 'government apathy' and wanted the government to salvage their industry. They said that the Chinese government had been able to control the import of silk into their country while ours had not been able to follow suit.

A new regime was beginning to operate in international trade. General agreement on tariffs and trade became more inclusive and more globalized. Trade barriers broke down, textile manufacturers were told they could import yarn if they were in a position to match the value of import with export. When things go wrong, we find it easiest to go for the government's jugular, though it is true that governments often make rules to suit particular industries.

I am not an economist but I understood the complexity of world trade as a farmer and an entrepreneur. The issue of raw silk yarn imports from China, on one hand while protecting Indian silk farmers was always complex. I pondered about this while touring the large Chinese cities. I wondered at the scale of progress and the social changes they had brought about, but such reflections were tinged with a sense of sorrow. The cities were experiencing unprecedented escalation in business activities. Along a 150 km stretch of road from Guangdong to a rural town, the name of which I forget, there was not a square centimetre of vacant land. The highway was dotted on either side by marble and granite-cutting mills that were feeding the insatiable appetite of the construction industry and providing for the new high-rises and the development activity in Beijing, Shanghai, and Guangdong.

The government campaign to attract foreign investments was wholehearted. The hotel in which I was accommodated boldly solicited investment proposals. The government advertisement publicized a free trade zone in Guangdong, just outside my hotel. It said investments in the free trade zone were eligible for tax benefits, income tax breaks, and concessional tariffs, with single window clearance. The government sought to impress upon foreign guests at the hotel where China had kept its doors ajar, with economic free trade zones open to foreign investment.

Anticipating a flow of foreign investors, China had built massive five-star hotels to accommodate them. I had seen hotels of such a scale only in Las Vegas. Compare the 300 to 400 hotel rooms offered in India's best five-star hotels to the five-thousand-room hotels of Las Vegas. The social infrastructure had also changed beyond recognition with more hospitals, schools, parks, and nightclubs.

The Chinese realized that for infrastructure nightlife was crucial if investors were to be wooed to visit the country. I do not mean legalized or licensed prostitution as in Amsterdam or Las Vegas but good restaurants, pubs, theme parks, music, and places to unwind after a hard day's work. Nightlife implied that these amenities and attractions would remain open throughout the night. Expatriates appreciate such facilities because, separated from family and friends, they usually work late into the evenings. Notwithstanding the wholesale development that was taking place across China, including economic, physical and social infrastructure, there was one thing that saddened me. In the midst of all this I could see the future—massive devastation of the countryside. I could visualize large tracts of farmland and wilderness built over by massive construction projects, relentless mining, and the bulldozing of everything that stood in the way of 'development'.

China was taking a giant step forward and was the envy of many other emerging economies. It seemed to have overtaken India in many areas. Deep within me, however, I did not want India to follow China's path to development. This path of irreverent modernization made me fearful for India's future. These feelings were in line with the lessons I had learnt on the farm. Besides, China's experiment would have important consequences both for India and rest of the world. Destroying the topsoil to create buildings would ultimately mean destroying the world. In China I could sense disaster waiting to unfold. The picture was the same everywhere: in the countryside, in district towns, in sleepy hamlets, and in busy cities. On the positive side, the frenetic, relentless pace of industrialization had taken China twenty years ahead of us. It actuated a train of thought in my mind: what did China do to become what it is today?

Foundation of Deccan Aviation

The question did not leave me for a long time. It burrowed away like a worm in my head. I think I had a flash of insight one day. It could have been in Shanghai or Guangdong or Singapore. I was reading a newspaper story about a Vietnamese girl. During the Vietnam War (1969–75), almost the entire country was razed to ground. Buildings, factories, villages, and homes were burnt down. Rice fields, woods and forests were carpet-bombed. Millions had become homeless refugees. There was a refugee crisis on a massive and tragic scale. Thousands fled the shoreline in makeshift boats. The US and France evacuated thousands. Many of us can recall the picture of a nine-year-old Vietnamese girl fleeing the site of Napalm bombing, her back still in flames. The bombing was carried out by the US air force. That day in the newspaper was the story of a similar girl orphaned by the war. A French couple had adopted her and taken her to France. She grew up with her French-foster parents and became a helicopter pilot. After Vietnam became independent and the North and South united, western countries, particularly America and France, were consumed by the guilt of what they had done to that country and hoped to assuage this through positive engagement in development. It occurred to the benefactors that they could combine altruism with self-interest. A campaign was launched for the rebuilding of Vietnam. Rebuilding efforts were a great opportunity for American and French businesses. The Americans, French, British, and Japanese returned to Vietnam in the early 1990s. They came with huge investment packages. They also issued an accompanying caveat: construction contracts must be awarded to American or French companies. If a donor gave a billion dollars as aid for setting up a hospital or a factory, the equipment required for it would have to be purchased from businesses in the donor country. Jobs are created back home and profits accrue to the investors. All this happens even as Vietnam gets what it badly needs. It is a win-win situation. This is an accepted practice on the global diplomatic stage. India should take the cue and learn from this example.

With investments flowing into Vietnam, a need arose for interpreters to help western investors connect with Vietnamese culture. The girl in the newspaper story who became a helicopter pilot returned to Vietnam with investors to participate in the rebuilding effort. She brought a helicopter because the surface transport infrastructure was in shambles. It was impossible initially for people to move from one place to another because of the scale of devastation. There were no roads, no highways, no bridges, no railways, and no airports. The entire country was littered with unexploded mines, a terrifying legacy of the war, compounding the problem of travel. The safest and speediest way to travel was by helicopter. The girl did just that. She flew investors and aid workers to different parts of Vietnam in a helicopter and became a national icon.

Reading the story of her life suddenly prompted an idea in my mind. It occurred to me that our infrastructure was as bad! Helicopters were a great innovation for transport in Vietnam. Helicopters in their majestic flight may look glamorous from the ground below, but the sky is the highway along which helicopters fly. I saw that a country as large and as diverse as ours has enormous untapped potential for helicopters. A list of business uses unfolded before me. VIP visits were one. Then I could use helicopters for surveys of power lines, gas pipelines, for mining and land-use mapping. A geophysical ground survey of a mining area running to 500 sq km would take a year, while a helicopter-based survey would take a day. The helicopter flies low to undertake geophysical and electromagnetic survey. The scientist is able, at this low altitude, to carry out measurements for the location and type of ore, its extent, the veins along which it can be found, and form a rough estimate of its worth. This, however, calls for highly specialized flying.

I could see many other applications too: in tourism, for surveys in the petroleum and mining industries, in urban and rural land use mapping, for aerial photography and videography, for 3D mapping, for film shoots, and medical evacuation. I decided that on my return to India I would go straight to Sam and discuss the matter with him. I would share with him what I thought about the many applications of helicopters. As ever, my dreaming and my decision making were simultaneous.

It was reform time in India. P.V. Narasimha Rao had come to power following the assassination of Rajiv Gandhi. Rajiv Gandhi had set the reform process in motion. He had been a young and dynamic leader who recognized the role of technology in shaping India's future. Fortunately for India, the momentum of reform did not die with the leader.

The BJP was right wing to its core. It was right wing on religion, right wing on reforms and capitalism. Congress began left of centre but moved rightwards towards the centre. P.V. Narasimha Rao as prime minister, Dr Manmohan Singh as finance minister, and Dr P. Chidambaram as commerce minister successfully ushered in economic reforms. The Congress was however losing its hold as a monolithic ruling bloc. It had ruled almost uninterruptedly for forty years and remained staunchly left of centre all along. Now that it had begun moving right of centre, and had also begun losing its stranglehold over the electorate, it was obliged to acknowledge the emergence of powerful regional parties in the states.

I sensed that at the time an impetus was hiding in the womb of history. In very lucid moments I could see the future trajectory of events. The only question was where to begin. I could see in my mind's eye the irreversible shift of history. There were strange, almost vulgar, high points to the tumult that was afoot in Asia. China had brazenly embraced capitalism without abandoning communism. Events that had taken place at Beijing's central square in 1989 had cast a shadow over China. It seemed eager for economic reforms; almost with inordinate haste. The end of the 80s was the vulgar high point of China. It almost seemed as if the economic edifice of China was being erected on the tombstone of failed democracy.

The other major event was the collapse of the USSR. India had relied heavily on Russian support after independence.

How does one look at the India versus China equation? India has always looked at China as a kind of rival. There are both similarities and dissimilarities. There has been a question of regional hegemony between the two. After both Russia and China discarded old beliefs, abandoned the communist path and adopted the capitalist mode of organization and production, with China making enormous economic strides, India had to seriously rethink its approach based on socialist pretensions and find itself a new lodestar. Leftist ideology in India had weakened. Left-leaning politicians realized they could not return to power unless they created new jobs by supporting the private, corporate sector. Non-Congress led governments in many states (Tamil Nadu, Andhra Pradesh, Karnataka, and Maharashtra, among many) saw that they just had to attract investment help in order to create jobs. It became a matter of regional pride to outdo other states in terms of inward investment. Chief ministers made a beeline to large corporations such as Toyota, Hyundai, and Volvo, seeking investment and inviting them to set-up manufacturing units, offering inducements in the form of huge tax breaks and investment incentives. I felt the reforms under way were irreversible. All pointed to a future that had a favourable environment for growth.

There were two other factors that gave the idea wings. One was that there were no helicopters in the country's commercial space. The few that existed were owned by large industrial houses in the private sector. These houses kept them for private and personal use or used them as a tool to gain political patronage, not for public benefit. There was not a single helicopter company apart from Pawan Hans in the public charter space. I would therefore have no competition whatsoever. The second was that there were thousands of pilots and engineers who had retired from the army, air force, and navy who were still young, capable but had no jobs. It then suddenly struck me like lightening, 'My god, this is a combustible mix of factors! One can't go wrong!' It then immediately dawned on me why Sam was not getting a job. The trail of my thought went this way. As a first-generation entrepreneur if I were to enter any entrenched business space, I had no prospect of success unless the idea had countrywide resonance and caught the imagination of the people. It is always simple in hindsight but it then occurred to me that I had no competition!

Entrepreneurship has a lot to do with marketing. You have to get noticed to get started. You must stand out in the clutter of new products and services. You need to be in a space which is new, different, has no competition.

According to Peter Drucker

> An entrepreneur is often defined as one who starts his own new and small business .... But not every new small business is entrepreneurial or represents entrepreneurship. The husband and wife who open another delicatessen or another Mexican restaurant in the American suburb surely take a risk. But are they entrepreneurs? All they do is what has been done many times before ... but they create neither a new satisfaction nor a new consumer demand. But a true entrepreneur is one who creates wealth where it did not exist earlier by creating a new market and a new customer. They create something new, something different; they change and transmute values; and, on a size and scale that will impact society.

I picked that last sentence out of the quote: must impact society for the better. Summing up Drucker, a true and great entrepreneurial venture must impact society for the better; must focus an unexplored area; must benefit as many people and as vast a geography as possible.

I had heard of but not read this particular book, *Innovation and Enterprise* by Drucker at the time. I had read about Sam Walton and read his story where he scaled up one pop-and-mom grocery store on the basis of the simple idea of *low prices every day* and turned it into the largest corporation on the planet, Wal Mart. I had seen Gandhi's algorithm for scaling up a simple idea and galvanizing the entire country. I, therefore felt, I was on the right track and had the conviction. One factor weighed heavily against me. As a first-generation entrepreneur, I had little money. The factors that weighed in my favour were ideas, energy, and enthusiasm. The idea was a powerful one. Nobody who owned helicopters saw the enormous consumer space lying vacant for me to tap. There was no existing clutter of products like toothpaste or powdered milk. This was my epiphany. I was confident helicopters were the infrastructure of tomorrow, and there was no one for me to compete with. Existing helicopter owners were not customer-focused because they were not customer-dependant. Rahul Bajaj needed to sell scooters to fly his own helicopters. Anand Mahindra had to sell jeeps and tractors to get airborne on his own flying machine. Vijay Mallya had to sell beer to take off. Their helicopters were not dependant on paying customers. It seemed incomprehensible to me that the country was chugging along the reform track and did not have a single helicopter company.

The combination of factors for a dedicated helicopter business was just right. India had a well-trained and handy pool of pilots and engineers, the market was untapped, there was no competition, a congenial political and policy environment seemed to be unfolding with reforms in process. A fleeting shadow of a doubt occasionally flitted across my mind. I asked then: 'Is the risk worth taking?' The answer was always driven by the inextinguishable optimism that the reforms were here to stay. Parties on the leftist horizon did raise an outcry against reform and liberalization. They perceived the threat of a neo-imperialist invasion and saw an 'invisible foreign hand'. These were not frequent, so I made up my mind. I did not know how much a helicopter cost. Fortunately, I never asked!

On my return flight from China, I was a man possessed. Plans unfolded in my head. I would get buddy Sam to join me. I would also get Col. Jayanth Poovaiah to join me; Jayanth was another friend from the army, a helicopter pilot still serving in the army. I knew other helicopter pilots and would handpick them. Not once did it occur to me to ask: who would I approach for the finances? Had I thought along those lines, there would perhaps have been no helicopter company!

When I returned, I went to Sam. 'Let's play squash tomorrow!' I said. On the court I said, 'How is the job, Sam?' He said, 'I hate it, but I do it. I have to. I hated freelance flying too.' He said his boss was a 28 year-old guy; an MBA. Sam had to report to that 'kid'. The time was ripe to throw the bait. I said, 'Sam, I've been thinking about what you said. I now know exactly what we can do. Let us set up a proper helicopter company. We will begin by carrying VIPs and the rich and the famous. We will be the first movers. The sky is the limit!'

I went on to explain to Sam how the economy was opening up for us to seize the opportunity. I said, very solemnly. 'Sam, resign from your job and join me in setting up this company. I know nothing about helicopters, you know nothing about business. You look after operations, I will look after business. I will get the investors and create the brand. I will drive the company. Give it a thought, Sam old boy!'

I planted the idea but did not want an oversell. I loved Sam as a friend and wanted him to join me but I would set up the company anyway. A chartered accountant friend of mine from my early days of business in Hassan, Balakrishna Achar had once alerted me. He said most businesses fail in the initial stages because of ego problems between partners and incompatibility. He also cautioned that this could occur between the best of friends. Achar said that under the Indian Partnership Act, incorporated in 1932, 'it is easier to divorce your wife; it is harder to get deliverance from a partner in business.' One of the partners has to be willing to take a back seat. I firmly believed only one person can lead a business and I knew Sam would let me lead. He has a wonderful temperament. I would structure the company in such a manner that a parting of ways between partners would not kill the business. I also bore in mind the words of Henry Mintzberg, a friend and one of the greatest management thinkers of our times. Mintzberg said, 'All great businesses involve only two things. One is having a great idea. Two is having great people around you.'

I would add a third factor to Mintzberg's list. Your ability to retain good people is what will count most. An entrepreneur is like the Pied Piper. He needs the people who come behind him. All through history everything that has been achieved has been achieved because a leader sold an idea, sold a dream, and people followed him.

I wanted Sam too to be possessed by the idea. I did not want to say, 'Join me, Sam, and this is what I will pay you?' That would make it a non-starter from the outset. Instead, I said, 'This can't fail. It can fail only because of our stupidity. The only thing between us and success is our willingness to commit ourselves to this dream.' I quoted some figures to Sam. 'Brazil has 400 helicopters. India has 25. That should ring a bell. The message is writ large and clear. The market is staring in our face.' I described to Sam what I had seen in China and Vietnam and left it there.

We met regularly over the next two to three months. Sam never uttered a word about the helicopter business. I did not press him. If the idea had not set his heart aflame he should not be there in the first place. A lot of people come to me and say, 'I have set up a business. My boss does not know. My company does not know. When the business succeeds, I will resign.' My reply is, 'That business will never succeed. Your business will succeed only when you can't pay your rent, you can't pay salaries, you can't buy your wife a sari, and you can't pay your children's school fees. Then you will learn to innovate. You will be forced to improve. Nothing breeds invention like necessity. Necessity will ensure you do not become complacent. You will be unable to sleep because your business may go bankrupt. This is how your business will succeed. Any other way of setting up a venture is a recipe for disaster.'

It was 1995. One day in April that year, a few months after Sam and I had this conversation, Sam dropped into my office. I still ran my agriculture business from a small office off Infantry Road. I saw Sam walk in. My army friends occasionally dropped in for a cup of coffee. I preferred to catch up with friends in the evening. During office hours I would get impatient. Sam, I saw, did not seem inclined to leave. I did not ask him to do so but got up myself to say goodbye. Sam said, 'Hold it, Gopi. I have come away.' I did not understand what he meant. He said, 'Gopi, you asked me to resign. I have left for good this time.'

Sam has this habit of saying the most serious things with a poker face. He has large, gentle eyes. You can never tell whether he's joking or means business. It took a while but I suddenly I realized the import of his move. He had resigned from his job to follow my dream. He had placed his future and security in my hands. At once I saw what a huge responsibility we had on our shoulders. A kind of shiver ran down my spine. I recovered my poise and said, with solemnity, and a touch of laughable pomposity, 'The helicopter company is hereby formed.'

I moved across to Sam and hugged him. I said, 'Sam, that's great! Sit down. Don't leave!'

That small office in Infantry Road was where Deccan Aviation was born. It took a nudge from Sam for the idea—I had been incubating to come into the world. I said, 'Sam, I am in a state of happy shock; stupefaction. This is the beginning of a great journey. Let's start right away. I want to know all about helicopters. What kinds there are, their make, the list prices. Make operational plans. Let's get going.'

I began preparing a blue-print for Deccan but still did not ask 'How much will the project cost?' I knew I would have to come to that eventually! I took a piece of paper and jotted down a few things that needed doing immediately. I also needed to test my ideas on others to figure out who I could take on-board. I would have to form a company. I must figure out how to raise the money. Money, I was certain, would be the least of my problems. Getting a licence from the government, getting the clearances, getting the people together—yes, those would be the real tasks.

I decided not to put the cart before the horse. I told Sam, 'Let us get the licence'. Those were still the days of Licence Raj. The aviation sector was perhaps the most tightly controlled. I suggested we used my current office space and secretariat as our registered working place. I had a computer, a fax machine, and basic office infrastructure. I asked Sam to set about devising a plan and setting up operations.

Sam too felt overwhelmed by the decision. It was a tough one. I had taken the decision twenty years ago without any money, he had taken it now. He, however, had three children and a pension of Rs 7000. That was not enough money to look after a family in Bengaluru. I was conscious of these considerations and therefore decided I would put whatever income I had into the new venture and Sam would similarly put in all his savings.

Sam was entrusted with obtaining the licence and creating the operational base of the company. He would have to get the parameters right, find out what conditions needed to be fulfilled, and look for ways to see that those conditions were met. There would be bribes to pay. I knew, however, of ways of doing things without paying bribes. I believed then, and continue to believe, that even in the corridors of power not everybody is venal or corrupt. There are people who have ideals, who have dreams for the country's future and are patriotic. If one person is not willing to help, there is always another who is. Eventually you will meet someone with integrity and vision. That will not however happen unless you relentlessly pursue your objective with focus and vigour. Sam and I decided to start doing our homework. Then we parted. We met again a few months later.

Sam visited Delhi and went to the DGCA, the regulatory body that issues licences. He learnt what needed to be done and made a list of conditions for the licence. We settled for a two-pronged approach. Sam would proceed from the bottom and move upwards. He would approach the grass roots of ministries, prepare the documents. He would tie up loose ends as he went up. I would go top-down. I would approach the ministerial entourage and the bureaucrats. We took a vow that we would not give up until we obtained the licence. There was no deadline: the objective was to keep going till we reached the goal.

This is a good way to approach a project. When you decide that you won't give up till it happens, then it happens. It is relentless pressure that creates the crack. If a bureaucrat is like a rock that won't let the river flow, muster a will that is as powerful as the rapids that swirl, whirl and drill a hole through, bursting forth and rushing on unchecked. The river has only one purpose: to join the ocean. Your will has to be the metaphoric river rapids. You have only one purpose: to reach the goal. To achieve—that you just have to do it.

When you start something you cannot give yourself a time-frame for success. You can't say: if it doesn't work out in six months I will give up. Your only task is to keep doing whatever it takes to achieve the goal. That is what Sam did. He never asked a question. He went to Delhi several times a month. Delhi is a den of power-brokers who know how objectives move and how to navigate in the flurry of hundreds of power brokers. Coming from another city, it is difficult to find one's way out in the maze of bureaucracy.

There was a new kind of financial institution with which India was not familiar. I had heard a lot about venture capital, as it was called, which had been the force behind the rise and success of American industry. It had created and sustained the Silicon Valley. I began my search for money with venture capital.

There was a company called TDICI, an offshoot of ICICI headed by Vijay Angadi. I called him and said I had a great idea and would like to meet him. He gave me an appointment. I told him the story. Opinions are made within the first five minutes of meeting so the story must be attention-grabbing. I said plainly, 'Vijay I want to set up a helicopter company'. I focused on the proportion of helicopters to the size of the country. India had about thirty helicopters. Though about forty were registered, ten of them were relics. Malaysia had twice the number, Brazil about 500. I deliberately did not compare India to Germany, the UK, France, or Japan. I compared India to the emerging economies which had recently stolen a march over us. I said, 'You are a venture capitalist. You can see these figures for yourself. India has to get there.'

The idea seemed to have grabbed him. 'Captain, this is a fantastic idea,' Vijay Angadi exclaimed excitedly. His colleague was an IAF officer's son and said, 'You know, Captain, I have an air force background. I understand helicopters. I think India needs this kind of project. We are excited about this. We will talk to our head office about your proposal. Meet us in a fortnight's time.'

I left, a happy man. It was the first attempt and by the manner in which they spoke to me, it appeared I had hit the bull's eye.

I was a little too quick to rejoice. After fifteen days, I called up Vijay. I asked him if I could come and meet him. Vijay received me warmly and we got chatting. He offered me coffee. We talked of this and that. Vijay did not broach the subject I had come to discuss. I was even expecting some kind of offer letter and imagined we would be advised about the application process and documentation for funding. It showed that I had been naïve. Vijay took his time and said, not without some embarrassment, 'I am extremely sorry, Captain. I spoke to my head office about your proposal. They are excited about your story but they have given me a mandate only to invest in IT and software, and perhaps to an extent biotechnology.' I was deeply disappointed.

Those were the early days of venture capital in India, which had just started investing very small amounts tentatively in IT. The government had laid down several rules and regulations to govern it, and TDICI was the first venture capital company operating with a very small fund base. I could understand the caution with which my project had been received, but the response fell on me like a bucket of cold water. I sat for some time digesting the news. Before leaving I said, 'Vijay, that's fine. I can understand your compulsions. But can you do me a favour?' He looked surprised. I said that since his job was to meet entrepreneurs and evaluate their proposals, he must have also met their financial advisors. I had pilots and engineers on board. I now needed a very solid financial adviser; someone who was sharp and had a long-term vision; one who could figure out ways of raising finance and also stay with me long-term. Most importantly, I could not afford to pay huge sums upfront. The compensation would come in good time.

The ability to gauge my own inadequacy in locating a good financial advisor was the key to the success of my future ventures. I therefore asked, 'Vijay, among the many finance people you have been meeting, is there anyone who has impressed you with the attributes I am looking for?' Vijay asked for two days to think over.

He was prompt with his phone call. He said, 'Capt. Gopi, I have found someone for you. His name is Mohan Kumar. He has an exceptionally sharp mind and has an incredible way of thinking out of the box. For that alone I think he will fit your requirement. Besides, he has a way with supporting new ventures.'

I thanked him. Looking back, I am glad TDICI did not pick up equity in my company. Had they done so I would have been left with next to nothing of my own equity. I had hardly put in any money into the venture at the time.

Without losing a second, I got in touch with Mohan Kumar and asked if he could partner me in this venture and join me on this exciting journey. 'We do not have much by way of funds, but Sam and I are ready to mortgage whatever little we own.' Even if we had liquidated all our assets at that point in time we would have been unable to buy even a pair of helicopter blades which in those days cost $60,000! I said I did not want to build a company for Bengaluru but a great aviation company for the country with enduring values, and in consequence create jobs, customer value, and wealth for all partners. Mohan Kumar said, 'I understand you, Captain. You can count me in.'

Mohan Kumar is easily the single most important factor in the success of my endeavours. This is not to detract from the role played by others. They were pillars of the company, and organic to its growth, but Mohan joined the company at an embryonic stage. He laid the foundation for sound financial structuring and processes, and with his innovative way of looking at things, raised future capital for the company. I did not receive a bill from him for the first four years!

We need to accept that there is dichotomy in the world. There are great, dynamic bureaucrats; there are wooden ones. There are great business visionaries with foresight and integrity who contribute to nation building; there are also people who run their businesses in unethical ways. There are committed environmentalists; there are politicians of the environment. The economy is astir with contributions, big and small, from the private sector. The Supreme Court has said that in a democratic state the government must recognize the private sector as the nation's pool of workhorses. For the private sector to survive and thrive, it must be profitable. According to Peter Drucker, 'Profit is a sacred word'. The only reason for businesses to exist is profit. A country sustains itself and grows on the strength of profits. The political, bureaucratic and social machinery of a country is maintained by profits. India's public sector investment is approximately Rs 2,00,000 crore; the return on that investment is less than two per cent. A robust private sector then becomes the backbone of the economy. For the private sector to be healthy the government has to create the right socio-economic framework and environment, and implement the right policies. The government is better off regulating the economy than constructing things and offering services. It is best to leave the manufacture of consumer items like bread or production of commodities like power or steel to the private sector. The government must regulate the environment and prevent monopoly operations. It must ensure that the environment is conducive to the growth of the private sector. A conducive business climate and environment are as important as the appropriate forest cover to regulate the earth's climate. In such a forest nobody plants anything but growth is abundant yet balanced because of the right ecology. The government has to ensure equitable economic growth, to see that reforms, infrastructure, and opportunities percolate to small towns and villages in the country's interiors. It should also ensure that the environment is conducive to the growth of the private sector but be ever alert to the formation of cartels.

The reforms have operated in such a way that instead of being alert to the formation of monopolies, government policies have either favoured particular large business houses or allowed cartelization of some sectors of the economy. Reforms should have entailed the percolation of new and beneficial provisions down to the smallest towns, so that millions of entrepreneurs, across the length and breadth of the country, are enabled to operate in an entirely equitable environment.

Mohan had his own company. He combined three institutional endorsements: he was a chartered accountant, a company secretary, and a lawyer. He helped entrepreneurs set up new businesses. The task accomplished, he moved on.

We got to work immediately. The first thing was to set up a company, and name the board of directors. We had to name the company. I asked Sam for suggestions. He suggested 'Gopi Air'. I said why not 'Sam Air'. Sam rejecting this, suggested Gorur Air, Silk Air (because of my connection to silk farming), Garden Air, and Deccan Aviation. Deccan Aviation sounded right and I decided to keep it. I wanted a generic name and it took me just five seconds to decide. I said, 'Let us settle on Deccan Aviation.'

Mohan Kumar had the company registered. The word 'Deccan' represented the Deccan Plateau which covers almost all of south India. It evoked geographical connections, space, cultural and historical lineage.

Within a week Mohan Kumar had incorporated the company. I was managing director and Sam, executive director. I was very clear—there had to be firm and clear leadership. A good leader generates other leaders and sets in place democratic processes in the company. Great leaders, have an innate ability to create consensus. They led from the front and from behind: they went to the grass roots and carried everyone along. Notable examples are Abraham Lincoln, Mahatma Gandhi, Nelson Mandela. There is another characteristic to leadership. It depends on your willingness to bring in people smarter than yourself. It is a general malaise that people in senior positions are reluctant to recruit people they believe to be smarter than they are. To do so would tend to make them feel insecure because they seek to become indispensable to the company. The result is that they end up being surrounded by nincompoops. In reality the logic works the other way. If a smart manager surrounds himself or herself with poor talent, what they deliver will be of poor value and they will eventually be judged only on what is delivered. We were creating a company of enduring value. It should not have to depend on me or Sam as individuals. David Ogilvy did not come from an advertising background but became an advertising icon. He writes in his book *Ogilvy on Advertising* that when someone was appointed head of an office in the Ogilvy & Mather chain, he sent him a Russian Matryoshka doll from Gorky as a gift. The big doll had a smaller doll inside, and then a smaller one within that, and so on. The last doll contained a note which said,

'If each of us hires people who are smaller than we are, we shall become a company of dwarfs. But if each of us hires people who are bigger than we are, we shall become a company of giants.' What Ogilvy says in the context of the advertising business is universally applicable to other businesses too. As a foreword to his remarks on dwarfs and giants and almost as a flip side to his earlier observation, Ogilvy said, 'It is a tragedy of the advertising business that its best practitioners are always promoted into management. I was infinitely more useful to my clients when I wrote copy than when I was chairman of the Board.' People do it unknowingly or consciously, but most of us do tend to create indispensability in our departments and our companies. Great leadership requires great humility and the vision to look beyond one's own role and create value and sustainability without arrogance. This is what I set out to do. At every stage I sought to choose the very best.

I had to build my core team. I said, let us get a chairman. I remembered General (rtd) Narahari. He had had a deep influence on me during my army days as my commanding officer. There were two reasons why I wanted to ask him to be our chairman. One, I looked up to him, and secondly because he had high moral and ethical standards: he would be my conscience-keeper and the company's ethical watchdog. Each time I made a decision, I would have to evaluate whether that action would bring dishonour to the chairman of the company. If it did, then I wouldn't do it. It is tempting to take short-cuts in business. Having Gen. Narahari by my side would deflect such temptations. I called the general and went over to meet him at his house. I asked if he would be the chairman of my company. He readily agreed. He set one condition. He was not joining for money. He would not accept an honorarium of more than Rs 3000 a month. I was touched by his approach. Gen. Narahari was appointed chairman and suggested two other names for the board. One was Air Vice Marshal Satya Pal, an accomplished air force veteran who had inducted the Jaguar fighter aircraft into the IAF. He was highly principled and had risen to high rank in the IAF.

Gen. Narahari also suggested A.D. Sinha to provide a civilian perspective. Sinha was on the advisory board of several large companies and had rich experience in business and management, having served in a few multinational companies.

Getting Gen. Narahari on board was as I said, essentially to voluntarily have someone, who will have no hesitation to rein me in from straying. It reminded me of a story by Leo Tolstoy—'Father Sergius', who punishes himself brutally to save himself from temptation. Leo Tolstoy's long story is about a young and brilliant officer of the guards tipped for royal adjutancy, to the Czar of Russia who becomes a monk. He is poised for a great career.

The young officer is engaged to a woman with whom he is madly in love. He dotes on her and sees in her the epitome of virtue. He marries the woman of his dreams. On the wedding night, the bride confesses to the young officer that she has been the Czar's mistress and asks for his forgiveness.

The young captain is stunned as if struck by a bolt of lightning. He recalls the Czar's knowing smiles at the wedding. That night, he quietly leaves home without telling a soul, travels far and wide, and comes into contact with mystics and wanderers. He becomes an ascetic and joins a monastic order, wishing to renounce the world and abolish desire. He reads the scriptures, studies the lives of saints, does rigorous penance, gets absorbed in various meditation practices, subjects himself to extreme hardship and suffers corporeal pain, to rise above the physical trappings of pleasure and pain.

Word spreads about the saintliness of a monk who practices extreme austerity and who can cure incurable ills. People begin to regard him as saviour and messiah, and come to seek his blessings. The monk is aware that he himself has been unable to transcend physical longings and the desires of the body. He knows that he is as weak as those who come to him for help.

Tolstoy goes on to describe a hunting party. There is a woman among them of exquisite beauty, and the irresistible charms of a seductress. During light-hearted banter among the hunting party members, there is talk of the redoubtable austerity of Father Sergius. The woman claims that no one can resist the charms of a woman and undertakes to seduce the monk before dawn. Her friends drop her off at the monk's cave and leave.

The woman calls out to Father Sergius to let her in, beseeching him to save her from certain death in the cold and rain. Sergius knows that letting her in would be his undoing but he cannot ignore her entreaties. He asks her to come in and is soon bewitched by her physical beauty. When she asks him to help her undress because her fingers are frozen numb in the cold and rain, he realizes that nothing can save him now. He however suddenly spots a razor blade lying nearby, picks it up and without hesitation he brings it down on his little finger and sunders it. In this way he saves himself from certain perdition.

It may be a good idea for many of us to keep out of temptation's way by surrounding ourselves with people of high moral fibre.

Because of security concerns in the aviation sector, directors appointed on an aviation company board have to be approved by the home ministry. All the directors needed to be minutely vetted by the RAW, the IB, CBI, the state police, and several other agencies. It usually took six to seven months to receive the clearance. I therefore hand-picked a very small board with impeccable credentials so that I would not have any hitch with security clearance. I could add more names later. We formed a board and Deccan Aviation was incorporated in May 1995.

The helicopter company took birth in a small office in a gulley off Infantry Road. As a farmer, I used to check on the incremental growth of my saplings with the expectancy of the birth of a child. I ran out of my hut early one morning, my wife in tow, to see the first coconut seed burst through the sod and put out a shoot. We did the same for the first inflorescence of my 5,000 banana plants. I experienced similar sentiments when Sam and I incorporated Deccan Aviation Pvt. Ltd.

Sam came to office every day. I issued a press release that Deccan Aviation would establish India's first one-stop helicopter charter company. In the release, I said: 'We want to make getting a helicopter easier than finding a taxi.' In 1995 there were not many taxis in Bengaluru. The old yellow and black taxis had to be booked in advance. There was nothing remotely like the phone-to-order cab service Singapore had. I wanted to break the veil of myth attending the hiring of a helicopter. In general, people thought it unaffordable. Middle-income families couldn't even think of it. People with money were apprehensive of flaunting it; it might suggest that they had black money. Some politicians used helicopters, but most shied away, fearful of tainting their populist image. I wanted to break the mythical barrier that only rich tycoons could use helicopters and bring them into the sphere of public use.

Even as a new corporate culture was beginning to take a foothold in India, the first news story appeared in *Deccan Herald* and the *Economic Times*. Deccan Aviation was in the news every day. Somehow, I managed to keep putting out stories about Deccan Aviation and its prospects while it was still in its formative stage so that people increasingly learnt about the company. The newspaper articles helped put us on the radar of new companies. We boldly made our plans public. There was no competition to be wary of. News columns are better vehicles than advertisements for projecting a company's profile as they have greater credibility, and build up word-of-mouth publicity at no cost.

The newspaper story had its impact. I received a call from a gentleman called Mike Robins. He said he was the managing director of Bell Helicopters, Asia. He had read that we were starting a helicopter company and would like to meet me. I was thrilled. We were attracting attention. Bell Asia was headquartered in Singapore. Mike Robbins flew down and we met at the Taj West End. The hotel is a personal favourite of mine with its lush setting right in the heart of the city. Many of my subsequent business decisions were made with the West End as the backdrop.

Mike was a very resourceful salesman. He made me sit through a presentation created by a group of students at MIT (Massachusetts Institute of Technology) and commissioned by Bell Helicopters. A study of the market for helicopters in India, it was one of the most powerful presentations I have come across. Rather than an unwieldy 300-page report, it comprised only 10 slides with bullet points. The presentation discussed the market potential in India and what Bell must do to capture that.

I looked on with the wide-eyed astonishment of a village boy, sometimes conscious of not having an IIT or IIM background. That did not however stop me from asking questions. Bertrand Russell once said, 'In all healthy affairs it's a healthy thing now and then to hang a question mark on the things you have long taken for granted.' Such an attitude was good for individuals and also for companies. The study recommended that Bell set up office in India to develop and capture the Indian market. Bell obviously had not been able to crack the Indian business massif. Helicopters in India were owned only by a very few individuals and corporate entities. Bell desperately wanted to break into commercial charter space. No one operated there.

Mike realized I was a first-generation entrepreneur and that I was setting up the first helicopter service with a public charter licence. He also realized that I would go bankrupt if I did not find customers as I was not intending to buy a helicopter for my personal use. Mike knew too that I did not plan to buy a new helicopter but only lease an old one. However, unlike a typical salesman who made money selling a new product, Mike did not lose interest. He saw beyond the present into the future; saw beyond his nose and took a keen interest in my project.

Integrity and enthusiasm were Mike's characteristic traits. He did not write me off yet but kept returning every two months and advising me. Having me as a Bell Helicopter customer for used helicopters would automatically establish the Bell brand in India. One day, he reckoned, I would buy brand new helicopters. The business would grow. It required patience, ingenuity, and integrity. One sale of a helicopter, used or new, would trigger a supply chain event. Mike understood that. The market for new helicopters depended on the market for resold ones. Mike proved a godsend. He translated for me the byzantine scale of the aviation market for used helicopters. With his help we began corresponding with a number of companies that were in the helicopter lease business.

Obtaining the government licence was my first priority. Next was funding. Infrastructure-creation and hiring people followed. I was not in a tearing hurry to buy or lease the helicopter. I wanted to hire people at the optimal time: not too soon, not too late. The focus was on getting clearances and licences from the civil aviation ministry, the DGCA, and the home ministry.

People asked me for my business plan. The DGCA wanted one. The civil aviation ministry too asked to see it. I did not want a consultant's advice. There is a point beyond which analysis can go, no further. At that juncture, as the entrepreneur you have to believe in your guts; in your intuition. As Ralph Waldo Emerson said, 'The inquiry leads us to that source, at once the essence of genius, of virtue, and of life, which we call spontaneity or instinct.' We did of course need a market research and business plan to place before various ministries and banks. I knew it had more weight than value. When you submit to a department bureaucrat a 300-page tome with a covering letter, the bureaucrat will only read the covering letter. I had to choose a consulting company to write out a report, and one with a weighty-sounding name like McKinsey, KPMG, PriceWaterHouse Coopers, or Ernst & Young. Instead I chose an Indian company, Tata Consultancy Services (TCS). First, I knew they would be cheaper. I also thought TCS, being an Indian company, could possibly provide me with some valuable insights. Of course the name of the Tatas carried weight, but even their research was likely to be in the nature of a hunch because they too would be asking whether people would use a helicopter if one became available. We already knew that for an emerging economy such as India, market research relating to a non-existing sector would not be very relevant. The TCS report took six months to compile and was over 200 pages long. They conducted extensive research and explored local and NRI demands for helicopter services.

Sam and I began rounds of the Civil Aviation Ministry and the DGCA. Most people fail because they give up at a time when they are unaware how close to success they are. Sam and I had decided not to stop till we got the licence. Sam fixed his sights on DGCA, I took aim at the civil aviation ministry. We, however, went around in circles pursuing clearances and approvals relentlessly.

There were other events that spurred the process on. I ran into another course-mate and friend, Capt. Vishnu Rawal, nicknamed 'Flying Saucer' because the only thing he loved doing in life was fly. We were from the thirty-eighth course at the NDA and also together at the IMA. He had become a kind of legend in the army, volunteering to fly at any time, anywhere. If a colleague was reluctant to undertake a sortie for personal reasons, he would volunteer to fly in his place. The most number of hours of those flying for the army log, after 15–20 years of service, are 1500 or 2000 hours. Vishnu logged over 6000 hours of flying. He had quit the army and joined the UP government as a helicopter pilot.

Vishnu called me up one day. He said he was in Bengaluru to fly a UP government helicopter that had been brought to HAL for routine maintenance. He was to take off the following day and said he could give me a joy-ride in his helicopter if I went over to HAL. For some strange reason, rather than accepting his offer of a joy-ride, I asked him which route he would take, flying back to Lucknow. He said he would be doing a zigzag detour. He would be flying first to Mangalore, and then would fly on to Goa, Pune, Nagpur, and on to Lucknow. I realized at once that he should be flying over my farm or thereabouts. I asked if I could exchange his offer of joy-ride with a ride to my farm instead, as it would be on his way.

Vishnu asked where my farm was. I said it was close to Hassan, off the road to the famous temple town of Halebid and a few kilometres from a village called Javagal. Vishnu had an army map with him and he had already located Javagal. He wanted to know where exactly—near Javagal, the farm was and I told him it was north of Javagal and just short of the next village of Bidare. He said he had it on his map and he would be pleased to take me to my farm. I asked if it would be okay for me to bring Bhargavi along, as well as Jayanth and his wife Ponnu. He said it would be a pleasure, but we must be at the HAL airport before 9 a.m.

It sometimes seems as if my mind is a seed-mill of ideas. When the time is ripe and the soil fecund, an idea quietly germinates. One such seed seemed to have coaxed its way to life at the time I was talking to Vishnu over the phone. It was still incipient, but I imagined people taking a helicopter ride to the wondrous spots of Karnataka; to the temples, to the ancient monuments of Hampi; the statue of Bahubali in Shravanabelagola; the Jog Falls; to just anywhere their fancy took them. In those days, only the very rich could afford to ride in a helicopter. If a business magnate wanted to ride his own helicopter his company executives used to initiate preparations much in advance. Vishnu was able to locate the farm in less than a minute, so it should be possible using good maps to take people to where they wished to go at short notice. I remember the vague stirrings of a thought. Could we make it possible for just about anyone to fly—and at short notice?

In preparation for the landing on the farm, Vishnu asked for a field to be cleared and a fire lit up to help him locate the smoke and find the landing spot as also the direction of the wind. I called Raju in Javagal and asked him to make the necessary preparations for our arrival the following morning.

We were to take off at 9.30 a.m. Vishnu would get his Chetak helicopter ready for the journey. The Chetak helicopter was the same as the French-made Ecuriel. The Ecuriel had a 180-degree view and was unsurpassed in its ability to negotiate difficult mountain-flying conditions. It was, and remains, the backbone of the Indian army's helicopter operations. HAL made the helicopters under a French licence. Vishnu asked me to sit with him in the cockpit to help with micro-navigation when we approached Javagal. I sat with a map spread out on my lap.

The engines whirred, rotors turned, and the helicopter was airborne. I felt a surge in my heart. I wished I were a bird; wished I could fly at will. This is what helicopters and airplanes do to human emotion.

The army had made a good map reader of me and I expected to be able to correlate ground objects with markings on the map. However, when you fly 200 km an hour you are in another dimension. By the time I could note my bearings, we had crossed Bengaluru. It would have taken an hour or so to get from HAL in the south-east to the city exit on Tumkur Road in the north-west. Before I knew it we had crossed Nelamangala. Landmarks flitted past on the ground below: streets, buildings, farms, and orchards, lakes and hills. Objects looked a little warped as we flew over. As we headed out I experienced a sense that it was a divine hand that had scripted this incredible helicopter ride so that I would actually go forth and set up a company for aerial sightseeing and helicopter tourism.

We skirted Shivagange and as we approached Shravanabelagola, the world's largest monolithic statue of Gomata on the hill, rose before us on the western horizon. I asked Vishnu if he would like to take an aerial view of the 1000-year-old statue. He veered the helicopter south-westward and we circumambulated the statue from about 600 metres. The view was magnificent. There was an added serenity to the placid defiance of Bahubali. Totally exposed to nature, the Gomata was wholly defenceless and completely vulnerable but he appeared invincible.

We then flew over the towns of Channarayapatna, and Arsikere. Before I knew it we passed Javagal. As we flew over my farm, it looked verdant and far more luxuriant than it did on ground. It was beautiful. One transient moment I saw before me a parade of past events: the first expedition there, life in a tent, the stream and the flood, life with donkeys, the first rains, the mulberry, the silk-rearing house, Manje Gowda and his family, Bhargavi and my marriage. It was an oasis now. Raju had lit a fire in a nearby patch of ragi from which rose a wisp of smoke. Raju and a host of neighbours and many others who had got wind of the event—momentous for a village milieu—crowded around the ragi patch when they heard the sound of the helicopter. There were perhaps a thousand people—farm workers, women and children, and the more preoccupied-looking elders swarmed closer to get a view of the flying wonder. A gust had been whipped up while landing and the loose ends of their clothing flagged and fluttered. Everybody looked on, dazed and wonderstruck. For those who had never seen a helicopter, and there were hundreds of them, it was like a page from mythology: the mythical bird had landed in their midst. The journey had taken less than fifty minutes.

We alighted. Raju brought us tender coconut water to drink. I knew after the aerial journey in the helicopter that there was no going back: I would definitely set up a helicopter company in commercial space. I asked Vishnu if he would like to join me. Without hesitation he said he would be thrilled to team up with us.

We took a short break, walked around the farm, and ate a simple meal. Vishnu took leave and was off.

The journey back to Bengaluru in my old Tata Mobile pick-up truck seemed far longer than the six hours it actually took. The ease with which we had travelled to Javagal in the helicopter made it seem like sixty hours. During the drive, my mind was full of images, dreams, and plans for the new venture.

Col. Jayanth Poovaiah, Sam, and Vishnu were my course-mates at the NDA and the IMA. Jayanth is an outstanding pilot. He had fought the Bangladesh War in 1971, fought the LTTE in Sri Lanka, and flown helicopters. He had also flown extensively in Kashmir. I realized that as Jayanth and Vishnu had both flown in arduous wartime conditions, flying passengers in normal times should be quite easy for them. In addition to their flying skill, both were good administrators and logistics experts. It is true that former armed forces officers initially find themselves unsuited to civilian life. However, with training and some adjustment, they make good leaders and managers.

Jayanth and I got talking on our drive back. Jayanth said he was studying for a BA degree to help him fit into civilian life after retirement.

Officers in the army have a degree in military science. For them, post-army, a BA degree is quite redundant. When I heard that Jayanth was planning to get a BA degree, I suggested that he get a flying licence instead. I revealed to him my plan. I said, 'Jayanth, I am setting up a helicopter company. Get a flying licence and perhaps you can join us.' Jayanth had a habit of looking incredulous. He did not say a word, not knowing what to make of my words. As I drove on towards Bengaluru, I got the feeling that the idea was taking hold of Jayanth. He had fallen into a reverie and seemed to be clutching at a new dream. It may have appeared far-fetched but a dream is irresistible especially when it sharply contrasts with the humdrum life of an administrator or clerk. Oh! how wonderful it would be to start flying again! At the end of the journey, Jayanth woke up from his dream and asked me what was the first thing I wanted him to do.

I asked him to get a posting to Bengaluru. He was then to wait until we got the helicopters. He had done twenty years of service in the army and was entitled to premature retirement with pension and was also in his early forties. Because he was close to pensionable age, he could choose the location of his posting. I also advised him against quitting the army before we received our helicopters.

Soon Jayanth called to say he had got a posting to Bengaluru. 'Welcome aboard!' I said.

Sam, Jayanth, and I formed a threesome. We went to the langar or the jawan's mess for a good army meal. It had been fifteen years since I had last visited a langar. We ate and chatted till the wee hours of the morning.

Jayanth's brother-in-law, Dr Ashok Pandey, was a very senior IAS officer. He was a secretary in the Lok Sabha and his wife, Jayanth's sister Reena Pandey, was a senior officer in the Indian Foreign Service with the ministry of external affairs. She went on to serve three prime ministers. She is now an ambassador. The most ardent words of gratitude would not sufficiently express how beholden I am to them for their help. In all probability, but for their unstinting help and encouragement, the venture would have got aborted in the labyrinths of bureaucracy. In my less agnostic moments I think they had been sent by God to help me and my team. Perhaps it is true that people determined to achieve their objective receive god's help at critical junctures. Ashok and Reena Pandey repeatedly made efforts to ensure that our files got pushed forward. I had experience with the tardy way in which files moved at the electricity board and the government offices at the district and taluq levels. I had prided myself that as I could surmount those hurdles I should be able to do likewise in Delhi. Delhi is, however, an entirely new species of bureaucracy. Despite our efforts over a two-year period, our application for a licence and the NOC had not moved an inch. The exercise involved frequent travels to Delhi. It was extremely frustrating and a complete drain on our meagre resources.

Jayanth arranged for us to meet Reena Pandey at the external affairs ministry. We met her and gave her an idea of how the files had moved to one place in the hierarchy and got stuck. Reena called up contacts and friends in the bureaucratic echelons. The bureaucracy is well networked and the web of contacts came in handy. Reena and Ashok did all they could to speed up the movement of the files through the tangle of red tape. We did not want to bribe as a matter of principle, and had we even been inclined to occasionally, we did not have the resources.

Sam and I worked in tandem. Sam prepared the groundwork to create training and engineering manuals as per the requirements of the civil aviation ministry. These had to be meticulously prepared and needed to be accurate to the last technical detail to satisfy DGCA rules and guidelines. I busied myself with the licence process. It is difficult to describe how frustrating it was getting the licence cleared. Each visit to Delhi, over two prolonged years, was as agonizing as another, and each ended with no result. I have selected two incidents to shed light on the gargantuan size of the bureaucracy and the intricate web it weaves around the unsuspecting supplicant. Most return overawed by the size and unable to extricate themselves from the tangled mess of this web.

The joint secretary is the officer who deals with the initial stages of an application. It is at this level that an application is translated into a file. Thereafter it is the file that is at the core of everyone's attention. The secretaries of the government are forever attending meetings. I filed my application and waited all day for a meeting with the joint secretary. When I eventually I got to see him, he asked me why I was there. I said I had filed an application for a no objection certificate to operate a helicopter service. He said, 'We will look into it.' That was it.

I was relentless in this pursuit. Months rolled by but there was no sign of the NOC. The file had got stuck at the joint secretary's table for six months. The answer was the same each time, 'We will look into it.' By the time I had made fifteen visits to the joint secretary's office, three incumbents had come and gone. On my sixteenth visit I met the official. Wearing the standard expression of impatience, suggesting that he had more important tasks to attend to, he asked me curtly what I wanted. I said without losing my cool that I had applied for a NOC to start a helicopter charter service and that the file needed his attention. I also said we did not have the funds to make endless trips to Delhi. He seemed to be getting even more impatient after listening to my litany. The officer managed to smoothen the crinkle on his brow and, putting on a deadpan expression, he said, 'We will look into it'. I was not easy to shrug off this time. I drew his attention to the fact that three joint secretaries had come and gone but the file remained steadfastly on the table. He looked perceptibly annoyed. He glowered at me as though I had transgressed the line. Then with a flourish of the hand he brought the wrist watch in front of him, indicated to me that he had given me sufficient time and, with a noisy shuffle of his official chair, stood up and motioned to me to leave.

Subsequent meetings with the officer were enactments of a pre-recorded video of the officer and me. Each meeting ended with a brusque dismissal. I did not give up. I dogged him even if it meant making more trips to the capital and a further drain on resources. I think he was fed up with me and eventually said he had sent the file to the secretary. One small step for bureaucracy and a giant leap for me! That was how I felt.

Bureaucracy had tested templates for dealing with applicants. Mine comprised the following series of actions: make him wait, give him short shrift, browbeat, dissuade, and procrastinate. There is a shorter secondary loop between the secretary and the joint secretary. The secretary does this to seek clarifications on the application. This took some more time. I continued in my routine and was not easy to shake off. Finally, the secretary told me he had sent the file to the minister. On my third visit to the secretary, he said not without some annoyance, that the minister had neither signed the file nor rejected it. 'So please don't come to me. Go to the minister.'

When I asked the secretary to remind the minister about the file, a very knowing smile appeared on his face. He was a little sheepish at the message he intended to give me. He said, 'Once a file is sent to the minister, if he neither approves nor rejects it, I do not go and remind him, especially when it concerns private sector licensing. If I did, the minister would impute motives to me. The minister does not need reminding and knows your file requires to be signed. He has kept it aside. It obviously means that he's expecting you to meet him.' I understood that when a minister sets a file aside but does not approve nor reject it, there might be certain expectations.

The corridors of power in Delhi are colonized by wheeler-dealers, touts, and fixers. They charge a professional service fee plus speed money. I abhorred this practice. People are not willing to go direct to a minister, assuming that he will not do their job. They are convinced that the only way to get their work done is get hold of a middleman. From my younger days, I have not resorted to this practice. I did not want to do it now. The minister of civil aviation was Ghulam Nabi Azad, so I decided to go straight to him.

I sought and was given an appointment. At the meeting, I told the minister that I was an ex-army officer seeking to set up a helicopter company. The application for the licence had been on his table for quite some time. I was running out of time and resources. I had used up all my savings, shuttling to and from Delhi for two years and had reached the tattered end of my tether. I wanted him to grant me the licence.

Many of us don't get what we deserve because we do not ask for it. I have found that most official work actually gets done without people asking you for money. If you are on the right path you don't need to fawn. You can be direct and honest and ask what is rightfully yours. You will be amazed how the political–administrative machinery often yields to honesty and integrity.

I told the minister what I had been through, and said I could not believe that it took so much time for an ex-army officer to get what he had a legitimate right to seek. The minister asked his secretary if there was a file on the application made by Capt. Gopi. The secretary brought the file to the minister's table. Politicians as a class in India are corrupt; so are businessmen as a class. Individuals can however, and often do, hold back the urge. The minister said, 'I am approving your application and will sign it today.' I did not believe him but the minister was true to his word. He gave me the government's approval-in-principle to establish an airline. He referred us to the DGCA for further processing. Two years of unrelenting effort had paid off; two long, years of torment just to get those two sentences on the NOC: 'The government hereby has no objection to your starting a helicopter company.'

I had two friends in Delhi. One was Capt. D.V. Singh, who later joined the venture. We stayed with him during our visits to the capital. Capt. Abraham Ben was the other friend and was associated with Nirula's in New Delhi. Ben got us lunch and helped us with printing and faxing letters and our correspondence. We did not of course have the money to pay business centres.

The egg had been hatched and had broken free of its shell. We needed to give it wings and get the helicopter. Sam pored over aviation magazines and newspapers and jotted down the addresses of prospective suppliers. He wrote letters asking whether they could lease us a helicopter. Brokerage firms asked us to deposit $10,000, which they said would be adjusted against the brokerage fee once the leasing deal actually came through. We did not have that kind of money so we abandoned brokerages. RBI foreign exchange rules were stringent. Leasing companies asked for a bank guarantee. Banks said that if they could provide a bank guarantee, they could as well give us the money. Indian banks, a majority of them nationalized ones, did not have exposure to structuring loans and instruments for the aviation industry, having no knowledge of aviation financing. Helicopter leasing is a sophisticated business and they did not have the financial instruments to address its requirements. They were unaware of how an aircraft could be repossessed if a lessee defaulted or went bankrupt. An aircraft cannot remain idle in the hangar and requires daily maintenance even on ground or else it will become worthless. All these factors made banks wary of aviation projects.

We went from bank to bank. On these visits we, Sam and I, Gen. Narahari, and our CFO Mohan Kumar, dressed formally. This was something I had not done since I left the army. The managers said they would get back to us. It was very much like my experience with banks as a farmer when I went seeking a project loan. The only difference this time was that the banks got back to us after a month or so to say that the proposal did not appear to them to be viable and therefore they were unable to fund the project.

Helicopter leasing companies too, were also not interested in India, viewing it as a remote and risky country. They were wary of not being able to recover costs if their helicopter encountered problems here because Indian courts took a sympathetic view of tenants and lessees. It was only much later that I realized why leasing companies were so hesitant: Indian laws were unfavourable to the lessor and the laws governing helicopter lease made it difficult for companies to recover their helicopter or payment dues.

Karnataka State Industrial Investment Development Corporation (KSIIDC) is an investment arm of the state government with an investor-friendly mandate. We hoped to get money as loan or as equity from them to buy two helicopters and asked for Rs 10 crore. After considering our application and the general investment scenario, KSIIDC told us they could give us Rs 43 lakh as loan to fund our spare parts and hangar requirements.

Even more shocking was the fact that KSIIDC asked us to get our business plan approved by Pawan Hans, the only helicopter company in India. Pawan Hans was a public sector undertaking controlled by the ministry of civil aviation. They undertook government contracts and oil contracts but they were not into general charters. I vehemently refused to reveal my business plans to Pawan Hans, my only competitor. Finally, KSIIDC waived this condition and issued a letter of offer to us.

Now that we had the licence, we began to work on various fronts. Sam continued to explore companies that would lease us a helicopter. I looked for a place to build an operations base and hangar for the helicopter. Bengaluru has three airfields. The Yelahanka air force base, HAL defence airport, and the Jakkur state government airport. The only user of the Jakkur airfield was the flying school which had been in existence for over fifty years. I discovered that the Jakkur airfield fell under the jurisdiction of the office of the chief minister.

When we got the NOC, the Indian political and economic scenario were both undergoing a change. The government at the centre was led by Narasimha Rao during the last days of his government. Narasimha Rao had teamed up with Manmohan Singh as finance minister and P. Chidambaram as commerce minister. Their team had initiated, and taken forward, a fundamental economic reforms process. Sonia Gandhi had become a recluse, the stoic woman in self-imposed mourning after the tragic death of her husband, Rajiv Gandhi, some years earlier. Narasimha Rao had become quite well-accepted as the new leader of India and was respected across the political and social spectrum. He had brought new hope to a moribund economy. International observers had hailed him as the leader who was pushing India, for a long time written off as a struggling economy, on the road to economic transformation and long-term success. There was a general euphoria about India.

We had the licences and the people but no helicopter. At just about that time, one day out of the blue, Mike Robbins called. He had continued to look around for a used helicopter for us. This time he had news. 'There is a company in Japan,' he informed us. 'It is a leasing company and has fifty helicopters across the world. I've spoken to them about you. They want to set up a meeting with you.'

I contacted the leasing company, ITC Leasing International. A senior representative of the company arrived in Bengaluru. We met for dinner at the Taj West End and spent three or four hours talking. We talked about India, about the upward path of the economy, about the reforms, about how this was not a flash-in-the-pan project. I said that if India succeeds, we would need not one or two or a dozen helicopters but thousands. I spoke of my dream with conviction and feeling.

The visitor said nothing. The Japanese say little and I have often been tempted to think they are dumb. But individually they are like members of an ant colony. Alone, an ant does not survive but a million ants together constitute an architectural masterpiece: the anthill. So it is with the Japanese. A few of them only buzz: a few more and they make a Sony.

The gentleman asked no questions; answered none. He listened. Dinner over, he wished me goodbye and returned to Japan.

The email had begun to find favour among early users but we were not yet email-savvy. It was still a curiosity. Instead, we had plain old fax machines. The following day I received a fax message when I was at my agricultural solutions office. The office was busy with farmers, agricultural and horticulture workers, mechanics, among others. Above the din rose the voice of my secretary. He said there was a fax from ITC Leasing. Wearing my heart on my sleeve and clutching at it with both hands I ran my eyes over the A4 message sheet. It was a one liner. 'We are very pleased to inform you that our board has decided to offer you one helicopter: Bell Long Ranger L3.'

I was overcome with emotion. Sam and I hugged each other. At last, we had a licence, a helicopter, pilots, and engineers. All we needed was the money, and now nothing could stop money from coming our way!

However, the joy the fax message brought us was short-lived.

Parliamentary elections were held in 1997 and belied the predictions of the poll pundits and astrologers. The Rao government was denied a second term of office. It was a hung parliament and the country was plunged from the relative high of economic reforms to the low of an uncertain future. The single largest party was the BJP but it was short of a simple majority. Atal Bihari Vajpayee cobbled up a coalition of various parties and staked a claim and the president invited him to form the government. His government was, however, unable to muster majority support and fell in exactly 13 days. Vajpayee was asked to become caretaker prime minister. That election marked a churning in the Indian polity, in the form of an emergence of regional parties and major electoral gains by the Left.

Overnight a country on the rebound, a country embarked on a successful market, financial, and licensing reforms had suddenly been brought to a halt. Every major global newspaper wrote obituaries on the Indian economic reforms. The constitution provides for presidential rule in the states if there is a hung assembly; but it does not provide for president's rule at the centre. People outside the country interpreted the chaos as the end of India's march towards stable democracy and the end of reforms.

The hung Parliament had melancholic consequences for our business. The euphoria of the first fax from ITC Leasing, Japan, offering us a helicopter had buoyed our enthusiasm and kept our morale high but we received a second fax from the company. It was another one-liner: 'We are nervous about India. We are withdrawing our offer to fund the helicopter.' I was reminded of a few lines from a Robert Burns poem 'To a Mouse':

> But Mouse, you are not alone,
> In proving foresight may be vain:
> The best laid schemes of mice and men
> Go often askew,
> And leaves us nothing but grief and pain,
> For promised joy.

Sam was completely shattered and the entire team shrouded in a pall of gloom. I managed to stay calm and did not lose faith or courage. Something in me prevented me from breaking. My optimism continued to burn. I said this was just one more obstacle. We had to overcome and we would. I told Sam, 'Look, if one door closes, another one opens. Don't worry, we mustn't lose hope.'

We, therefore, began afresh. We knocked at new doors, wrote new letters. Sorrow and self-pity consume enormous quantities of energy. If you only can desist from feeling victimized by fate and look for a new solution instead, not only would you conserve old energies but at the same time also feel the surge of the new. New hope is kindled in the process.

All battles are essentially fought in the mind, and it is what happens there that makes or breaks us. Action is another fantastic antidote to despair. I did not waste time in wasteful regret and sought an alternative opening; a new way out.

One day, in the midst of the gloom, I received a letter from a gentleman called Vidya Babu who worked for a helicopter company in Macau. He wanted to know if there were opportunities for a helicopter engineer. I was indeed looking for an engineer. Vidya Babu was a typical Indian émigré from Tamil Nadu and possessed a sharp, critical mind capable of problem-solving. He was among those who worked within budgetary constraints and yet delivered great work. A company like ours was in no position to spend money on frills. I signed him up. That completed the entire resource pool.

Vidya Babu suggested that we operate from a tent or shack to begin with and later add a hangar and other facilities. I, however, took a different view. People using our helicopters would be corporate or wealthy people. A shoddy makeshift office or hangar would not inspire their confidence. I wanted the helicopter company to be a 'ten-star' one. We would save money and cut costs elsewhere but the engineering and maintenance facilities, customer reception area, the VIP lounge would need to match international standards. The frontage should inspire confidence or customers would feel they were using an inferior-quality helicopter service.

Where would we build the facility? There was HAL airport but Sam said it was better to be outside the city or the visibility would be poor. There was Yelahanka belonging to the air force and Jakkur airfield on the outskirts of Bengaluru. Built around the village of Jakkur, it had one of the earliest and most highly reputed flying schools in India. The chief minister was the decision-maker with regard to the airfield. The best thing was to go and meet the CM, J.H. Patel of the Janata Party.

On my way to see him, I thought about Singapore. About how, although a small island, Singapore hosted the offices of major engine and aircraft manufacturers including Pratt & Whitney and Rolls Royce, Boeing and Airbus. Singapore had become the regional headquarters for most multinational companies and especially for aviation majors. Why did these companies choose the tiny island of Singapore and not India?

Singapore was not in the logistical proximity of Nepal, Pakistan, Bangladesh, Sri Lanka, and Myanmar. Logistics do play an important role in aviation. Aircraft require a continuing overhaul and replacement of parts. The safety standards are extremely stringent and companies are extremely particular about meeting these standards. A helicopter engine rated for 3000 hours of flying had to be replaced exactly at the 3000th hour. Some parts have a calendar life and some are replaced on the basis of usage, in

terms of number of hours. Ninety-five per cent of all helicopter parts had to
be completely replaced and not allowed to run even for a minute extra. It
was possible however, to have a new aircraft or a slightly older aircraft with
all parts brand new.

Aviation companies would not however use services if offered in India
because of delays and the cost overheads stemming from the bureaucratic
process. Landings were delayed at airports, there were other restrictions
and checks at the airport, high tariffs added to the cost of operations. India
would not be able to match Singapore in the promptness of service. It would
be impossible to bring in an engine from Nepal or Pakistan into India, repair
it, and send it back the same day.

I thought it was absurd for India to lose this business. India had the
talent. Of thirty-one engineers at Singapore Technology Aerospace, nineteen
were Indians. Air India and the Indian government initially helped set up
Singapore Airlines. Half the airline's engineers and pilots were Indian. Indian
airlines and the Indian aviation sector had declined but Singapore Airlines
had grown to become an aviation icon. The absence of similar facilities
in India also meant that Indian aviation companies had to spend a lot of
money on maintenance. Just to replace a bearing, an engine would have to
be sent to Singapore. For a part costing $500 you would end up spending
$50,000. The cost of shipping to Singapore, repair, and part replacement,
and return shipping was twenty times the cost in India. Aviation companies
would besides have to bear the cost of freight charges, insurance, and loss
of operational time, custom formalities, and high labour costs.

These were the thoughts flitting around in my head as I went to meet the
chief minister by prior appointment. I spoke with conviction and tried to
convince him that Bengaluru had the talent and the infrastructure, and the
potential to become the aviation capital of the world.

I explained to him that to set up a helicopter company I could go to
Chennai or to Hyderabad, 'But I am from Karnataka and it is my dream to
set up an aviation industry in Bengaluru. Can you help me?' I asked.

The chief minister asked me to state clearly what I wanted. I told him
that what I wanted was to set up a helicopter charter service; build a world-
class facility; set up an engineering facility; but more than anything else, at
the outset, to build a hangar. For that, I said, I wanted an acre of land at
Jakkur airfield. I reminded the chief minister that the airfield fell under his
jurisdiction.

The CM replied, 'Captain, I will give you land and I will also be your
first customer.' The joy and relief I felt was unbounded. CM Patel called his
principle secretary, N. Vishwanathan and instructed him to assist me.

The IAS had become very powerful over the years and for a number of reasons, so much so that they controlled the economy. In the early years, the Indian political climate was semi-socialist; the regime was bureaucratic. Administrators interpreted and implemented policies. Being socialist, translated into control over licensing. Besides granting the licence, the joint secretary of industry also decided how many scooters Bajaj could manufacture. If the bureaucrat, in his wisdom, decided that steel was better utilized in making goods for use in the rural economy rather than in cars or scooters, there would be a reduction in the steel allocated for scooter manufacture. If Bajaj manufactured more scooters than the licence permitted, the company would be penalized.

Power endowed prerogative and bureaucrats learnt to dispense favours. Most were honest and well-meaning but went by the rule book and controls choked the economy. The state got into producing everything from bread to steel. It also controlled private businesses that manufactured bread and steel. The bureaucrat was aware that excessive control was bad for the economy but the exercise of power was an ego-booster. Control was therefore the source of bureaucratic discretion and nothing moved in corridors of power without the sanction of the IAS lobby. The IAS officer's tenure was fixed, and his or her performance was rarely questioned.

Many officers were, however, well-meaning and bent the rules to support a good cause. Mr Vishwanathan was outstanding in this sense. He was part of my good fortune. The documents had been prepared by that evening and I received a letter signed by the chief minister the following evening. It said our company had been sanctioned one acre of land at Jakkur airfield.

It was good not to take moral high ground and be judgmental. If you had the determination to desist from corruption, there were good people who would help you out. None of the IAS officers, barring one, in my last twenty years, asked me for a bribe.

The actual handover of the land took some time. The principal of the flying school in Jakkur had raised an objection to the CM's decision to give us part of the land. He had complained that helicopters would hamper the operations of the flying school.

I met Mr Vishwanathan about this and we spoke at length. I expressed shock and pointed out that the flying school was defunct. It had a total of six aircraft which had been grounded due to internal politics. The principal was not permitted to fly for medical reasons. Besides, airports handled hundreds of flights a day: Chicago Airport operated 3000 flights, Singapore Airport 650. Rather than asking helicopters to stop flying we should be addressing the question of how helicopter and flying operations could be made seamless. It was only a matter of sequencing, landings and departures. I said I could not imagine how someone from a defunct flying school could write such a letter. Whoever had written it was totally unaware of how things worked in the real world, and demonstrated a destructive tendency.

Mr Vishwanathan responded with a smile.

There were administrators who are quick to help projects, others who were quick to scuttle projects. Vishwanathan belonged to the former category and did not misguide the CM. He said he would form a committee to look into the matter and make a recommendation. I suggested a few names. Well-known aviator Air Marshal Lamba was one. There were a couple of other names from Indian Airlines and Air India. The committee examined the issue and made its recommendation. It said there should be no problem once the right processes and systems were in place. Mr Vishwanathan then formally handed over the land to us.

Jakkur airfield is a beautiful expanse of 250 acres. A chunk of land about sixty metres by sixty metres was carved out of the larger tract, and that became ours. The first thing we did was to pitch a tent and hired a security guard. I love tents. My school was run in a tent, much of my army life was spent in tents, and on the farm, a tent was my first abode.

In those early days when the WTO had just been set up, countries seeking vast, open markets suddenly became protective about their own. India was seeking the opening up of some areas while trying to protect some others. It was a very complex web. As with climate change, if you destroyed the rainforests of Amazon Basin, or of Myanmar or Indonesia, India's climate too would be affected. The analogy could well apply to the political, financial, and social climate of the world. An upheaval in one country affected life elsewhere. What I experienced illustrated this closely-knit web.

At about the same time, during 1997–98, the world's financial market seriously disrupted by the Asian currency crisis. It was like a Tsunami. The value of Asian currencies collapsed against the US dollar overnight. Most countries in the Asian east were affected, especially the so-called Asian tigers. Only Singapore seemed relatively unscathed by the battering. Major companies went bankrupt as a consequence. For companies that had imported heavy equipment from overseas and were servicing the loan in dollar terms, the servicing tranches suddenly rose several times, other terms and conditions remaining unchanged. It was only the dollar conversion rate that was affected. Overnight, businesses became unviable, juggling with their existing overheads and higher loan-servicing rates.

One consequence of this for Deccan was that among the companies becoming bankrupt were those that had leased helicopters. These helicopters were now grounded. This crisis gave me an idea. Suppose the Japanese leasing company had helicopters in Malaysia, Thailand, and Korea. Assuming that some of these had been grounded, there could be nothing more useless for a helicopter leasing company than to maintain grounded helicopters. I called my friend Mike Robbins for information about grounded helicopters.

Mike was in India, on his way to Bengaluru and wanted to meet me. We met for a drink at the Taj West End. I updated Mike on the current status of the company. I said we had the land, the licence, and the team in place. A helicopter was all I needed to take off. The political scenario had just about stabilized with Deve Gowda becoming the PM. I asked Mike whether he could speak to the Japanese and tell them, that the political scenario had improved. True, Deve Gowda headed a somewhat messy coalition of MPs, and had had the support of a mere 16 against the 272 necessary for a simple majority

━

Deve Gowda as PM had to perform a tough balancing act. Nobody believed he would last for any length of time in office. It was only a question of time.

Mike Robins got in touch with the Japanese helicopter leasing company from whom I once again received a one line fax. It said: 'We have decided to give a helicopter to you,' adding that Mr Douglas Cavanaugh, the president of ITC Leasing, would get in touch with me to finalize the formalities of the contract. We were elated. It seemed as though things were at last falling into place.

Douglas Cavanaugh called me the next day, and I could make out that he was British. Douglas said he would be coming to meet me. He arrived and checked in at Taj West End. Having told him about my dreams; we spoke about our background and lives.

Doug had a very unusual background. He had been a British air force pilot. He flew fixed wing aircraft and served in the RAF for twenty years. He was also a helicopter pilot and had undertaken various assignments after he sought release from the RAF, including some for the CIA in Canada and the USA. Those assignments often entailed adventurous flying. This was under the auspices of a company called Evergreen headed by a certain Dell Smith, who I met subsequently when he visited India. Evergreen specialized in offshore flying for oil. The company had another USP: lending its helicopter for clandestine missions for the CIA, targeting illegal trafficking of drugs. The company's helicopters also carried out missions in Iraq and Iran. Evergreen was in other sectors of aviation too, for instance adapting its Boeing 747s to carry space shuttles. Indeed, the company was pretty much involved in every aspect of aviation.

Doug had a reputation of being capable of a variety of covert and overt flying operations. He used that to his entrepreneurial advantage and was a walking encyclopedia of aviation.

He recounted his story. He had flown as a mercenary in various parts of the world: in Oman, the Middle East, and Papua New Guinea. He had ferried aircraft, flown offshore for oil prospectors, and had flown African rulers. He was eclectic in the best sense of the term. Doug later worked as sales manager for Eurocopter Helicopters. He had flown in Hong Kong and married a Chinese girl. Like other white men, having married a Chinese girl, he stayed back and rarely visited the West. There is a large expatriate community in Hong Kong, Singapore, and Thailand of westerners who married local women and settled. Chinese women, I learnt from talking to the expatriates, made good housewives and took care of husband and children. Western women, they confided, tended to be domineering and independent-spirited. For Chinese women, family was their first priority. That explained why Doug had stayed back in Singapore.

On the first day, before Doug and I spoke about our individual lives and families, Doug said, 'Captain Gopi, I have had hundreds of letters from Indian entrepreneurs. You are the first who has everything to take off. Many people have wanted a helicopter. Some had money but no plan, nor people, nor vision, nor a road map. You are the first I have met who has a team, fire in the belly, and a clear idea of what you want to do. You have pilots, engineers, land, and licence. I am confident we will together make this work.'

His words were like a balm and brought solace. I saw what Doug meant. I had everything except a helicopter. If it were the other way round I would have been putting the cart before the horse; I would not have been sufficiently credible. I realized that the Japanese had also looked for my commitment and a roadmap. I saw people who got into this field quit in two or three years because they got the money or helicopter before setting up their company and team.

Doug and I met again at ten the following morning. Doug had no assistance; he was a one-man army with a laptop. Everything that he needed to know about leasing and aviation was on his laptop. He had no lawyer, no secretary, and no chartered accountant. This leanness seemed to add to his efficiency: his depth of knowledge amazed me. It took us three hours to hammer out the lease rental and the financial terms.

My homework had suggested that helicopter lease rentals across the world were 1 per cent of the cost of the machine. I began at 0.6 per cent. I told Doug, 'It is in your interest that I succeed. It is not one helicopter. It is the first.' I told him about the debt trap created by local money-lenders in India in which I had myself been once or twice enmeshed.

I related stories of how money-lenders kill the businesses they fund. Doug was amused. I made it quite clear that I wanted the project to be sustainable, and I would leave that part to him to attend to, in such a way that I would not need the assistance of a lawyer or accountant or both. Once we shook hands, I called Mohan Kumar over to West End. He had some issue with taxes and that was smoothened out. In the end we had a fifty-page document: the contract.

I usually read all agreements and contracts. Regardless of how good a lawyer you have, it is better you read it yourself, word by word. What you don't understand you ask to be explained to you. A trained eye looks at it in a trained way. You have a fresh eye and that helps. You can even overrule the lawyer or consultant. If you leave everything to others, things will never get closed. Whenever I took charge I never had a single instance of litigation. Deals worth millions of dollars never gave rise to any legal wrangles, while cases of joint ventures and partnerships went through huge legal scrutiny and litigation when the relationship was based merely on legal documentation, as if that was the natural outcome. Relationships forged by us on the basis of mutual trust, goodwill, and common sense, invariably worked.

The following day Mohan and I sat together and ironed out the burrs and edges relating to double taxation. Doug got on the phone and talked to his people. I was keen to close and seal the contract, fearing that any further delay in execution would prevent the company from taking off. There were many things at stake. I could lose team members, the political climate could worsen, and infrastructure issues could crop-up, and on the like.

Within each of us there is an inner compass. It points to the final fact beyond which analysis cannot take you. You need to draw on that inner resource and follow it. 'Fine, let me take the plunge,' you must be willing to say. That will win the day for you, because even with the most foolproof document, you may lose the deal. Shakespeare said, 'Indecision is in itself grief.' One remembers in this context, what Brutus says in Shakespeare's play *Julius Caesar*:

> There is a tide in the affairs of men.
> Which, taken at the flood, leads on to fortune;
> Omitted, all the voyage of their life
> Is bound in shallows and in miseries.

> On such a full sea are we now afloat,
> And we must take the current when it serves,
> Or lose our ventures.

I sensed this tide in the life of Deccan, in Sam's life and mine. Catch the tide I must. I took a call and said, 'Doug let's shake hands.' We signed the documents.

6

If you wish to advance into the infinite, explore the finite in all directions.
—Johann Wolfgang Goethe

Acquiring a Helicopter

ITC Leasing had leased helicopters around the world. Doug said he would give me either the one stationed in Singapore or Kathmandu. We now had everything to launch the company: the lease contract for a helicopter, land allotment within an airport to operate the helicopter, a complete team of pilots, engineers, and technicians to fly the helicopter, and most important of all, the treasured licence from the government. What we still didn't have was the money to launch the business! It had taken us two-and-a-half years to get here and all the money we had, about Rs 20,00,000–Rs 10,00,000 each from Sam and me—had already been spent. We were now closely poised for take-off but it suddenly dawned on me that if we didn't get the funding in the next two months, the team and the dream would dissipate like the fortuitous monsoon cloud because the licences would lapse, and it would be a Himalayan task to start all over again!

While Sam got busy getting the technical details ready for the commercial licence, Mohan and I teamed up in the hunt for the so far elusive golden stag. Both of us were fully aware that the sand in the hour glass was rapidly depleting!

One day an angel appeared on the horizon! Mohan suggested that as it was now almost certain that no bank would invest in this project, I should consider meeting an old friend of his. Mohan had spoken to his friend about my helicopter project; the friend was keen to meet me and ready to invest. Mohan's friend's name was S.N. Ladhani, a Sindhi businessman who owned the largest Coca Cola bottling unit in India. Sindhi businessmen are shrewd investors. Some of the astutest businessmen in the country are Sindhis, Gujaratis, and Marwaris. While the Sindhis and Gujaratis, besides setting up their businesses in the major cities across India, also ventured overseas to set up business colonies, the Marwaris remained largely rooted to Indian soil, penetrating the farthest corners of the country. They command a presence in the remotest taluq headquarters and even at the southernmost tip of India.

They once owned 90 per cent of the business operations in the country. The Sindhis, like the rest, had a yen for money and were like homing pigeons. I admired them and felt it would be good to have a Sindhi investor in my business to keep a check on my evangelical zeal. I also knew that they could guide me instinctively, without the trappings of detailed market research, balance sheets, analysis and counter-analysis. I also clearly needed someone who could advance money when I asked for it. I remembered the advice of Balakrishna Achar, my accountant in Hassan, about how to choose a business partner. I asked Mohan only two questions. 'Is the prospective investor a good man?' 'Is he someone who can identify himself with my dreams?' Mohan answered in the affirmative to both questions, and also added that Ladhani would be a good business partner.

Mohan had known Ladhani for fifteen years. He described him as a tough but a good man with empathy for others. Like all Sindhi fathers, he treated the money given to his sons as a loan and expected interest on the return. Timely interest payment was a barometer and a monitoring tool. If his son failed to pay interest on time, it meant that he was not doing well in life; needed to be counselled and perhaps warned. Sindhis believed in nurturing values such as fiscal discipline and respect for money in their offspring.

I found Ladhani to be a fascinating man in his own way. He had a harrowing tale to tell about his past. He had suffered the grief and trauma of Partition. He and his parents fled the persecution in Pakistan, and after moving from place to place in India, had for a while settled down in Ayodhya. He was only eight years old at the time. Under the most trying circumstances, Ladhani, like many others who shared his difficult destiny, took up small business contracts in remote parts of UP and Bihar. He was only fourteen when he began his businesses. He gradually rose through hard work and perseverance in the face of odds to become a giant in his line of business in India. He had launched small, soft-drink bottling plants in Bengaluru and gradually become the largest bottler of Thums Up. When Coca Cola bought over Thums Up, they offered him a large compensation in return for his bottling company in Bengaluru. They also gave him the job of setting up a bottling plant in Faizabad in UP.

Ladhani's story is akin to those of many like him who fled Pakistan during Partition and who, persevering and, picking up what came their way without complaint, went on to rise to positions of wealth and prestige in society. One does not need to read 'How-to' books, routinely churned out by the American publishing industry, to learn how to make a success of one's life. It is sufficient to sit with people like Ladhani and listen to their life stories. Their tales are hair-raising, dramatic, and compelling. They are tales of courage, resilience, sheer dogged persistence and optimism in the midst of darkness. Hidden under layers and folds—in these tales of boldness, in the face of adversity are all the management and human resource development tips that no 'How-to' book will ever tell.

Ladhani maintained strict discipline in the handling of money. He once told me, 'Main bukhar bhi free mein nahin deta hoon.' ('I don't give away even a fever for free'). The Americans say it differently: 'There is no such thing as a free lunch.' I liked that attitude, but I was also aware that the Sindhi rate of interest could kill a business. Mohan advised me not to give away equity too easily, because that might dilute my equity and erode my prerogative to steer the company. We decided that I would give Ladhani a small equity and negotiate a large debt at a reasonable rate of interest. I planned to offer him a larger equity stake as the company grew.

I met Ladhani and took an instinctive liking for him. Soon, the relationship strengthened, took on a different hue, and we were almost like two brothers. I patiently told him what had by then become standard pitch. I told him the story of the helicopter company and its business potential for India. I reeled out statistics. He understood numbers. Coca Cola was an American company and he dealt with numbers all the time. He saw the analogy between Coca Cola consumption in America and its consumption in India and understood the tremendous significance a small increase in per capita consumption in India had for the business. The per capita consumption in 1995 was 120–30 bottles in the US and about two or three in India. By increasing that figure to five or six per capita would result in an enormous increase in the total production and consumption volumes, because India's population was four times that of the US, resulting in huge sales figures. Ladhani got my point instinctively. India had only a few helicopters. There was immense potential for the deployment of helicopters in mining, construction, oil exploration, and tourism. He saw there was a great future ahead and agreed rightaway.

We got down to negotiating the deal. He agreed to take 10 per cent equity at a capital infusion of Rs 21,00,000 . Ladhani made an interesting statement. He said, 'The faster you run, the more money I'll put into your venture.' We agreed broadly that when I needed money he would fund me on the principle that the amount would be paid back with interest. It was an important moment for the company, which I believe was born in flesh and blood, that very day! I now realized why there exists a term in American business parlance, called 'angel investor': Ladhani had come to me in the form of an angel and I was even better pleased to discover at a later date that Ladhani's rate of interest, although much higher than the bank's rate, was much lower than the standard Sindhi rate of interest!

Vishnu Rawal was at the time in Macau, flying for a Chinese company. Macau was still a Portuguese protectorate. Portugal had bought the island on a 150-year lease from China and the period was drawing to a close. Macau followed a laissez-faire form of economy under the Portuguese, as Hong Kong had done under the British. Macau, however, more laid back and fun-loving than Hong Kong, was an hour's boat ride to the west, and focused on the fun and leisure industry with hospitality and casinos as its principle driving forces. The country's laid back economy was a well-planned strategy of the Portuguese. The island did not become a global source of capital like Hong Kong but built a string of gambling houses and casinos surrounded by nightclubs and restaurants. Stanley Ho, the eighty-year-old Chinese strongman of Macau, controlled eighty per cent of its casinos. He owned four helicopters which shuttled between Macau and Hong Kong, ferrying high-profile tourist-gamblers. Vishnu called me one day and offered to chip in by taking some equity. His CEO too wanted to invest a larger amount and take equity.

Kennichi Miyagawa, his CEO, a Japanese by birth and now a US citizen, had previously been a helicopter pilot with the US Air Force. I thought it was good to have a Japanese in the company. It would be useful in dealing with the Japanese leasing company for helicopters, the only one in the world to offer me a helicopter on lease after a two-and-a-half-year search. It would also lend a lot of credibility to a start-up company like ours.

Miyagawa called me up and said, 'I don't need to see you. Vishnu has spoken for you and has inspired confidence in your venture. I do business on trust. I can give you $100,000.' I discussed this with Mohan Kumar. We concurred that the $100,000, KSIIDC's small contribution, Vishnu's money, and Ladhani's tap should now enable us to kick off! When finally the funding was in place, I realized the truth in the saying, 'When you have an iron will and an indomitable spirit, the gods themselves join in the combat and the universe conspires to help you succeed!'

It suddenly dawned on me what a huge responsibility I had on my shoulders. People had invested money and trusted me to deliver. I realized that we had to work day and night keep our heads over our shoulders, stretch every rupee, and scrub the floor if necessary. We would not waste a single paisa of our investors' money. Just as during my early days of farming, the money we had raised was just sufficient to take the project off the ground. We would have to ensure that not a rupee was unproductively spent and that revenues were generated quickly and ploughed back into the business to reinforce the workflow of the venture. I had to protect the investors' faith in the venture and in the process fulfil my own dream. This was sufficient to inspire me.

I remembered the words of the legendary founder of IKEA, Ingvar Kamprad, the global home furnitures chain. One of the world's richest, he had said, 'Whenever I write a company cheque, I only ask one question. "Can my customers afford it?" If my customers cannot afford it, I don't write that cheque.' This should be the guiding principle for all entrepreneurs dealing with public money. They must want to deliver value to the customer and bring value to investors. This is a huge responsibility. I was the trustee and all these people were friends. They had put their money on the basis of blind, implicit faith in me and the dream I had structured for them.

We were in the month of August. I chose 5 September 1997 as the launch date. It was like zeroing in on a daughter's wedding. Unless a date is fixed it won't happen. Once a date is set, you will die to ensure that your daughter gets married. There had been many clearances required and many bureaucratic hurdles to cross. The biggest hurdle had been getting the land, the licence, the people, and the money. We had all that. Still, scores of minor clearances and licences had to be secured. By not fixing the launch date, matters would drag on. The company would bleed to death.

Several steps needed to be taken before the Japanese company released the helicopter for our use. The helicopter would have to be written off their books; clearances from their DGCA sought and secured; it had to be de-registered and placed in the inventory of another offshore company. These measures would help the company avoid double taxation on earnings. All this cost the company a lot of money. The leasing company was therefore very particular that their machines began earning the moment they left their corporate jurisdiction.

Once the helicopter was transferred to our name, whether or not I took delivery, I would have to start paying interest and lease rental. Procrastination would have been suicidal. What I did, may have appeared too ambitious and foolhardy. This was the beginning of a pattern of behaviour I would begin to manifest each time I launched a new venture. I would fix a date and force myself and everyone else into a schedule we would have to meet. There was no going back. Beyond that date, I would say, I am a pauper. This I felt in my bones, my heart, my blood, and my cells. The one and only way to make anything work was to fix a date; make a commitment. I had decided on 5 September and I would make it happen.

The choice of date was not entirely random. There were reasons.

During lean periods, before things began to happen, especially when things did not seem as if they would work out soon, I had received a call from management professor Thirunarayana of IIM, Bengaluru. He is the son of a major literary figure of Karnataka, Pu Thi Narasimhachar (fondly remembered by the people of Karnataka as Pu Thi Na). He had called to tell me about a management programme initiated by Henry Mintzberg. He said Henry Mintzberg was one of the greatest among management thinkers, and ranked him among twenty thinkers who had changed the course of management thinking.

The professor said Mintzberg had initiated a management programme. Participants would receive a master's degree in management at the end of the course. I did not need a master's but the programme was itself unique. It was designed to happen over eighteen months and at five different locations across the world. These locations were well-known management schools. It was a very eclectic programme designed to initiate new ways of looking at management practices. It had experienced people from the industry and academia discussing and debating alternative approaches and perspectives. There would be structured classroom curricula with the difference that there would be intensive cross-industry interaction. Real-life situations would be built into the curriculum based on Mintzberg's philosophy. Mintzberg had published a celebrated article in the *Harvard Business Review*, 'The Manager's Job: Folklore and Fact', (*HBR* July–August 1975), which had a very high citation index and was one of the most frequently reprinted articles in *HBR* and had brought him a considerable reputation. Prof. Thiru asked me to read the article before making up my mind about the study programme.

When Henry Mintzberg had just graduated from management school, he wanted to complete his internship in a novel way. He identified some leading CEOs and asked if he could follow them, without disturbing them or asking questions. He would only observe the way in which they handled situations. He shadowed five or six very well known CEOs and made notes on their lives. After pursuing his subjects, Mintzberg drew the following conclusion: The difference between what they teach you at management school and what happens in reality at the workplace when you begin to manage is startlingly different.

Mintzberg's key observation was that the CEO goes with a structured mind to the workplace. He has a predetermined plan worked out and ready to be applied to the problem at hand. At the workplace, however, the unforeseen occurs and the CEO is caught completely off guard!

Since Mintzberg wrote his path-breaking first essay over thirty years ago, he has written extensively on management and strategy and gained reknown across the world. Tom Peters, of *In Search of Excellence* fame, considers Mintzberg to be the most influential iconoclastic management thinker of today. Mintzberg's management programme is for senior-level managers occupying positions of vice-president and general manager.

They bring experience from their workplace and share it with peers to evolve management perspectives. Instructors from five well-known schools and professors with industry experience conduct the programme. Henry Mintzberg wanted at least two enrolments in the class who were first-generation entrepreneurs.

When we met, Mintzberg said, 'You are an entrepreneur who has come from a village, has been on a farm, dabbled in various businesses, and fought an election. You'll bring a different perspective to the whole thing. Why don't you consider enrolling?' He said the programme would involve moving from one B-school to another, five in all. The schools were Lancaster Management School, UK; McGill University, Montreal, Canada; IIM, Bengaluru; Hitotsubashi University, Tokyo; and INSEAD in Fontainbleau, France. He said the course was designed so that managers of corporate companies would be able to continue their work and yet pursue a master's management programme and also choose projects applicable to their companies.

I was fascinated. As I was getting into the business of helicopters, making me somewhat corporate, I thought it might be a good idea to get under the skin of managers. I did not want a degree but I needed to put the chaos in my mind into some form of order. I needed to understand the world of management. There were questions to which I needed answers. For example: how do managers think and behave in various situations? I looked at the list of participants. Five were from Motorola, five from Lufthansa, five from the Royal Bank of Scotland, five from the Red Cross, and five from Panasonic. The remaining three or four were entrepreneurs. The participants were senior-level people with excellent academic backgrounds. They were rising stars in the companies that had sponsored them. I signed up for the programme, and it also interested my brother-in-law, head of the legendary V.B. Bakery in Bengaluru, who also enrolled. There was another entrant from India, an entrepreneur like me. I found the nature of the programme and the prospect of associating with Mintzberg exciting. The licensing process and finding the funding for the helicopter venture was taking very long so I thought it might be a good idea for me to educate myself in the meantime. I accepted Mintzberg's programme offer for the sheer 'adventure of ideas' it offered.

The first leg of the programme, held in May, was in Lancaster. Lancaster was chosen for its rich tradition in the humanities. Management education in the UK, unlike in India and the US, does not focus entirely on the engineering and technology streams. Both Oxford University and Oxford town have a long tradition of exploring human society and human endeavours. Cambridge has a rich tradition in the pure sciences and philosophy. Any form of education in the UK has the tempering influence of the arts and humanities. This is guided by the fact that human beings are agents and creators. What concerns them provides an understanding of the conditions that make human creativity possible. These institutions serve as intellectual breeding grounds. Indeed, most management graduates had a largely arts and humanities background. This was an agreeable thing for me as my own philosophy concurs with the spirit of academia in the UK, that management is about dealing with people.

Each leg of the programme lasted two to three weeks. The Lancaster module was called *Reflective*, its focus a reflection on the larger issues of management, people, history, and the evolution of business. The McGill module was entitled *Analytical* and explored finance and accounting. The third leg, at IIM Bengaluru, was devoted to *Understanding China and India: Economy and Culture*. The fourth limb of the course was hosted at Hitotsubashi University in Japan. This module sought to dip into the large repositories of knowledge residing in the large Japanese corporations. The last component was at INSEAD in France, considered the Mecca of Management in Europe, and dealt with *Change*.

The Lancaster module featured inspiring lectures by business historians, philosophers, and great management thinkers. There was an eclectic reflection on various aspects of management using philosophical heuristics. The speakers referred to A.N. Whitehead and Bertrand Russell, quite an unusual idiom of discourse. They moved from one end to the other of the spectrum of the British management tradition.

At McGill, I met the acclaimed author and academic Kunal Basu. I also met Jonathan Gosling, who has done a lot of different things from business to teaching. In the late 1960s, the young Jonathan became a hippie sanyasi and roamed the Himalayas in search of an elusive nirvana. By a strange design of destiny, he met the same woman, Susanna, a German, in three different places, over a period of a year; meetings that seemed to defy the laws of ordinary probability. Jonathan read these meetings as the trajectories of fate, proposed to her, and the two married. Jonathan's lectures on management often contained mystical elements which left many in the audience bewildered, especially those who had no idea of Indian culture and philosophy.

I met many other people, each with significant accomplishments in his/her sphere of activity. However, the person who had the greatest impact on my thinking was Henry Mintzberg himself. His lectures, two or three in each module, reflected a rare genius. He was a man of deep insight into business, and employed vivid imagery to render concepts palpable.

I took Mintzberg to my farm. He loved cycling and trekking, and we often escaped to my coffee plantations, cycling or roaming the hills. To me this was an extension of the programme. I was able to observe from close quarters how his keen enquiring mind worked. During ambles among the hills, Henry often came up with utterances that were nuggets of insight. He was a livewire of observation and always carried a notepad and a pen with which he jotted down whatever he found interesting or unusual.

Henry came across as both a keen student of the world around him and a very sensitive human being. On the farm, we slept in the same room on different charpais, separated by about five or six feet. On one occasion I had fallen asleep and was awoken by a faint rustle around three in the morning. A pale moon had cast its light into the room and I saw a ghost-like figure, silhouetted against the wall of the charpai where Henry had been sleeping. I peered into the darkness and was surprised to find that the figure was crouching with a blanket over it, not in a supine position. A sliver of light came through a slit in the blanket. It was all a bit eerie. I was curious and called out, 'Henry, is that you?' Then Henry removed the blanket from over his head and a torch-light shone from inside the blanket: he had been jotting down notes and had covered himself so as not to let the torchlight disturb me. I was touched by his concern and amazed at the way he was capturing his thoughts which must have woken him up in the middle of the night!

The programme required observing at first hand the conduct of business. We visited legendary companies like Lufthansa, British Telecom, British Aerospace, and Fujitsu. We were formed into several learning and discussion groups. We saw the differences between how a Japanese company operated and how a Dutch company operated. We got to interact with CEOs of many large companies who spoke on a variety of subjects.

At Hitotsubashi University in Tokyo we were fortunate to spend time with Professor Nonaka, considered the sage of knowledge management. Ikujiro Nonaka had co-authored the well-respected book, *The Knowledge-Creating Company* with Hirotaka Takeuchi. We visited the famous Japanese garden at Shinshin-an in Kyoto where Konosuke Matsushita, the legendary founder of Panasonic, had built a guest-house. Overcoming difficult beginnings, Matsushita is credited with contributing very significantly to the Japanese economic miracle after the Second World War. The hardships he faced early in his life made him conscious of the value of hardships in life. 'Hardships,' he said repeatedly, 'can be very useful, for building character, forging motivation, and forcing honest self-assessment.' From his realization of this Matsushita incorporated hardship as a part of the learning process in his Matsushita Institute of Government and Management, a school he founded near Tokyo. In that school, 'students would not sit in luxurious dormitories and be spoon-fed assignments and ideas. They would live in modest surroundings, work hard, and be asked to devise much of their own curriculum.' It is indeed true that 'nature, when it adds difficulty, also adds brains'. Matsushita often took to a garden retreat to reflect on business solutions and innovations for which Panasonic became recognized globally. We spent a day there with the senior management of Matsushita. Every component of the garden—every pebble and boulder, stream and bridge, blade of grass, and plant that grew in it—had been placed or trained and composed so as to provide pure tranquility. The garden is now a heritage site and is held in great reverence by the Japanese and has attained the status of a temple shrine.

At the end of the Japanese leg of the programme, I made some time to trace Masanobu Fukuoka, the global god-figure of organic farming. I was told that he lived 1000 miles away on a remote island known for its thermal springs. I took a bullet train, Japan's icon of modernity, to get there. Fukuoka's farm was set deep in a small forest on top of a small hill. Entrepreneurs had built small cottages with rooms and small hotels all catering to the various hot springs in the village. Many of the springs were set indoors and some were set outdoors with a view of the mountains and the sky. Guests at the hotels were given a robe and a pair of house slippers, and there was a regular procession of people in robes walking up and down, to and from the springs. It was a strange feeling. I must have been the only Indian in a sea of Japanese robes moving along the street. I was almost reminded of the temple streets of south India where thousands of men and women move about during temple festivals attired in the south Indian equivalent of the Japanese robe, the panche and sari. Separate areas were earmarked for men and women. In the men's section of the spring, guests had taken off all their clothing and got into the pool. This is the normal practice. I did as the Romans do and enjoyed a healthy dip in the steaming sulphur spring.

The following day I hired a taxi to take me to where Fukuoka had his farms. The cab driver stopped the car at the edge of the forest and said I would have to walk a couple of kilometres to reach the sanctuary. I made my way through the woods and finally found the house where Fukuoka lived. It was a traditional Japanese house on stilts with a wood-and-bamboo roof and wooden flooring. It had a flight of steps, made of wooden slats that led up to a large room on top. I walked up the steps. In the room, seated on the floor, smoke rising from a wood stove, was the man himself. He looked old and frail, his hair tied in a bunny knot above his pate and a long flowing, straggly beard. The room was a little cold and the wood stove had been lit to provide heating. There was a samovar in which water was boiling and a table with tea crockery on it. A few students were present too, listening to the old man and attending to him. I was welcomed in and offered a seat on the floor at the master's feet. The atmosphere had a touch of the mystic. I was served tea and later a meal cooked in the kitchen. I spent a few hours with Fukuoka, a student acting as interpreter, and we were able to exchange a few words. Fukuoka, whose *One Straw Revolution* is treated as a bible of organic farming, was probably in his mid-eighties at the time. He instructed his students to take me around the farm. I fully savoured the silences of the farm. On my way back, when the rumble of earthmovers and caterpillars in the distance fell on my ears, I realized that the world had ignored Fukuoka's warnings and had busied itself with incessant development, paying no heed to nature and its vulnerabilities. I realized that the world was moving in pincer-like on Fukuoka's fragile haven and felt a twinge of nostalgia for the purity of the nature and life I had just left behind on Fukuoka's farm.

At INSEAD in Fontainbleu I was fortunate to meet and spend time with Yves Doz, professor of global technology and innovation. We became friends and met later on my subsequent visits to France and during his visits to India.

We were expected to write a thesis at the end of each module of the programme. We had three months to write on a topic of our choice that captured the principle themes of the previous module. This was required to be completed before the next module. Each of us had a tutor assigned and were in touch with her/him over the phone and via email. Subsequently, the tutor visited the city where the participant stayed.

I produced four theses, and each was in itself a learning experience. After clearing that, participants had to write a fifth. This thesis would entitle them to a degree from any of the five universities. I was not so much interested in a degree as in acquiring knowledge and insight into management, though perhaps I was a little over-anxious about failing. I had, however, been sucked into the whirl of my helicopter company, and indeed when Henry Mintzberg and his team visited Bengaluru, Deccan Aviation was just a month old. They made Deccan a case study and they provided me with very valuable feedback.

I had settled on 5 September as the date of the launch because on that night I had to take flight to Montreal for the McGill leg of the course. I would be away for almost a month and I wanted to launch the company before leaving. Others in the team felt we should fix a date after the helicopter was actually inducted into the company but I was firm. I said, 'The helicopter will arrive in India and 5 September is the launch date'.

The helicopter was to fly into Bengaluru on its own power. It occurred to me that a flight-worthy helicopter should have no technical problems because it had to be certified by the DGCA of the exporting country for export-worthiness and air-worthiness. An aircraft is subjected to stringent safety checks and documentation at all stages and modes in which it has existed right from the day of manufacture. The DGCA of every country is punctilious about documentation and insists that the operator strictly follows the rules and guidelines set out in the manufacturer's manual. I realized that the Indian DGCA would be as stringent about documentation as the others. Without in any way intervening in the documentation and certification processes which are very important from a safety point of view, I asked myself whether we could request the Indian bureaucracy to compress the time from twenty days to two. The DGCA, like other departments in India, tended to take longer than similar agencies elsewhere in the world. I checked with my engineer Vidya Babu who had worked both under the Indian DGCA and various foreign ones. He knew all the nitty-gritty and was intuitive about such issues. Babu said the issue was not safety but documentation. I then decided that I would not allow more than two to three days between the arrival of the bird and the launch of the inaugural flight. The Indian bureaucracy is not used to such short notice. Bureaucrats take their time either because they expect something or because they are 'bureaucratic' in the worst sense of the term. I have however also come across, in various departments, including the DGCA, many committed bureaucrats who are ready to help and expedite when the cause is just and honourable but who feel strapped because of systemic constraints. Being the incurable optimist that I am, I shocked not only the DGCA but also all my colleagues by providing for only a two-to-three day hiatus between the arrival of the helicopter and the launch of the first flight.

There are people in government service who are honest and and have impeccable credentials but they can be frustrating because they are obsessed with rules and regulations. I had decided to use every resource at my command and invoke every influence I could, to ensure that the helicopter took off on the date fixed for the launch. The helicopter was expected on the morning of 1 September. The die was cast and no one could change it, not even me. People were incredulous. Some thought I was crazy. It would have been safer to get the aircraft first, obtain the licences and clearances, and only then schedule the date of the launch. I realized that if we played too safe we could go bankrupt before the business even took off.

I hit upon an idea. I would approach the minister of civil aviation, C. M. Ibrahim, in prime minister Deve Gowda's ministry. Ibrahim hailed from Karnataka with a not overly encouraging reputation. He was rumoured to have stopped Tata–Singapore Airlines from taking off, he and his colleagues opposing the venture and grounding it. I was visibly nervous. How would I tackle roadblocks that he might place in my path?

I went straight to him and told him abut my company. I said, 'I want you to come and flag off the inaugural flight'. Ibrahim readily accepted. The meeting ended in two minutes and I was speechless.

I had figured that if he agreed to bless the occasion, all clearances would fall into place. People in power who can dispense favours are able to see through you instantly when you ask for something that is not legitimate and beyond your due. They recognize that you are trying to cut corners and they expect their pound of flesh. In that case you are no different from them. When a person offers an inducement, called 'speed money' without violating the law, he is probably a victim of the system. It is however bewildering to often encounter people who pay to flout and bend rules while at the same time pompously harangue about corruption in society! Such people are far more venal than corrupt bureaucrats or politicians. Arun Shourie once observed, 'The reason why the system does not work is because all of us have our little deals.' On the other hand, if you comply scrupulously with every rule in the book, adhere to every process that is legally necessary, and you invite the minister to inaugurate an event, the bureaucracy tends to bend backwards to see that all clearances are pushed through and the minister is saved from any potential embarrassment. Especially when one is not asking for something out of turn.

The security clearance process was exhaustive. All the directors required clearance from the point of view of drugs, terrorism, anti-national activities, criminal past, and on the like. It was time-consuming and exhausting. This meant that the CBI, Drug Enforcement Agency, the RAW (for intelligence clearance), Enforcement Directorate, and the police, among other agencies, would need to scan the present and the past of the directors. We soon discovered that we had come up against an obstacle and our files seemed to have disappeared into a 'black hole'. Gen. Narahari wrote a stern letter to the home secretary as chairman of Deccan Aviation. I was worried, if the letter would offend the officials, but the home secretary himself replied graciously and promptly. The clearance was granted within a week.

The only outstanding clearance were of a technical nature and largely from the DGCA. Even though others approached the DGCA with trepidation because it is known to exercise an iron grip over operators, I calculated that this should not take more than two or three days. The others rightly viewed this as reckless optimism because in practise it normally took two to three months for such clearances.

Our helicopter was owned by a Japanese company and had an American registration. It was to have been flown out of Nepal with an export certificate of air-worthiness from the US as it operated under the Federal Aviation Authority (FAA), the American counterpart to our DGCA. Before we could take possession of the helicopter, the aircraft needed various clearances for entering Indian airspace and release from the Indian customs. Finally, we needed a commercial charter licence from the DGCA to operate the helicopter.

I also invited the chief minister and other ministers to join the civil aviation minister for the inaugural flight. With immense confidence in my ability to pull it off, I placed an advertisement in the newspapers and sealed the future. I assumed that because their bosses would be the chief guests, the ministry and the DGCA would do their extra bit and oblige with the necessary clearances. We appointed Hindustan Thomson Associates as our agency. HTA was then the largest advertising agency in India, but our account was very small. The marketing manager and the accounts manager from HTA came to meet me. They were only interested in the size of the budget and realized we would try and pinch costs wherever possible. They wanted us to hire an event management company but I decided not to. HTA was clearly disappointed but did a good job. The invitation card said: 'A journey of a thousand miles begins with a single step.' There was a collective realization among all of us that Deccan Aviation was taking its first step towards a great future for the country.

All was in place, and we just waited for the helicopter to arrive. We were in for a minor shock a day before the helicopter was to take off from Nepal. The lease agreement bound us to make a six-month deposit before the helicopter physically took off. The funds were already in my bank account and could have been remitted, but there was a hitch.

If an aircraft was entering Indian airspace it needed both import permission and a YA number, which is valid for 24 hours only. A YA number is an international code issued by the DGCA of countries to a specific aircraft with a specific registration and serial number to enter a country's airspace. This is provided to the air-traffic control and the air force. These agencies recognize an aircraft with the flashing YA number as a legitimate flying object in the local air space. If it does not have a YA number it is turned back or the air force planes force the intruding aircraft to land.

We had the YA number and the import permit for the helicopter but faced some difficulty. In those days of tight foreign exchange control, the Reserve Bank of India controlled every dollar leaving the country. The reforms had begun but a comprehensive approach had not yet been evolved about foreign exchange remittances. Today, in many situations, you can transfer millions of dollars from any bank with a simple note from a chartered accountant. In those days, however, to transfer even one dollar you required RBI approval.

Mohan Kumar prepared the document for RBI's approval. The application that went with it said the company sought permission to transfer money abroad for the helicopter. We suddenly hit a roadblock. The RBI guidelines stated that the money could only be transferred after the goods, in this case the helicopter, landed in India.

The aircraft was actually outside the country and we had to send money to the Japanese leasing company to fly it in. The leasing company would not let us have the helicopter unless we paid a six-month advance on lease rental. The RBI regulations stated that if we did not have the aircraft in the country, as tangible proof of import, they would not permit the transfer of funds abroad. One way out was to get a bank guarantee from the leasing agency undertaking that the six-month lease rental advance would be returned to us if the company failed to send us the helicopter.

The RBI rules had been freshly formulated as a reaction to a fraud which came to be known as the notorious 'urea scam'. Following the urea scam, in which millions of dollars had been siphoned off without any urea actually being imported, the RBI had issued a rule that ensured receipt of the goods for which money was being transferred. This rule caught us off guard.

Members of the former prime minister Narasimha Rao's family were implicated in the scam. The opposition went for the jugular seeking to further embroil the ruling party. Its objective being to gain political mileage rather than unearth the perpetrators of the scandal. Political parties have alternated in power, and over the decades there has been a series of scandals and exposés. People related to the ruling party and the parties in the opposition have often found themselves implicated. However, the actual culprits have never been traced or convicted! Those implicated in the urea scam were also acquitted! And no one knows what happened to the money.

I knew that Doug would throw a fit if, at this last moment, I asked him for a bank guarantee. It would also appear to be ludicrous for someone who trusted us with a helicopter worth crores of rupees, to think of giving us a bank guarantee for the measly deposit, in relative terms, we were giving them. He would never understand the logic of the RBI which had its own legitimate concern going by the recent past record of importers. We had two days to go. Mohan Kumar said we should have placed this condition at the time when the lease contract was being prepared or opened a letter of credit. We failed to do either. It was a very embarrassing situation for me. It would appear to be an issue of lack of trust from our side or that we had been sloppy in our attention to details.

We were running out of time and I eventually overcame the embarrassment and called Doug. I explained to him that we had been caught off guard and that we were in a spot. I explained that it was a slip-up on our part and apologized, and added that it was the RBI that needed a bank guarantee and not us. 'Doug,' I pleaded, 'I have the money. You have to trust me. We've announced the inaugural event, printed the cards, and invited people. I will not betray your trust. You will be proud of this association. The money will be in your account within twenty-four hours of the helicopter landing in India.'

There was a long silence on the phone. I waited with a prayer in my heart. After what seemed an eternity, Doug replied. 'You will have the helicopter tomorrow. It will take off from Kathmandu. Don't let me down.' Then he hung up.

The helicopter took off on 30 August from Kathmandu and touched down at several towns for refuelling. It was to land at HAL airport on 1 September at 4 p.m. We were waiting at the airport with great excitement. Bhargavi and I, Ponnu and Jayanth Poovaiah, Maya and Sam, and Vidya Babu and his wife experiencing a sense of 'it's-too-good-to-be-true'! A dream was about to become tangible.

One or two incidents, however, occurred before the helicopter finally arrived. Vidya Babu suggested that I meet the local head of the DGCA who would be expecting me to call on him on a courtesy visit. I went over and gave him the invitation card. I said this was my aviation company and that it should make him proud that the company was based in Bengaluru and that the DGCA was part of the great new journey. 'You will be able to control a larger fleet if you facilitate the growth of this company,' I said, asking him to bless the launch.

K. Parameshwar, the local DGCA chief, was overwhelmed by my rhetoric but he recovered rapidly and, assuming the tone of one who is in control of the sector, said, rather coolly, 'Captain, that is all fine! But you should have consulted me on the inaugural date after the helicopter arrived in India and only then printed the card. You've gone and printed the card even before the helicopter has arrived. I am shocked.' He reminded me that even large corporate houses like the Tatas and the Mahindras put their helicopters into service two or three months after they were brought into the country. He was baffled that I had sent out invitations and prepared for the launch even before the helicopter had arrived. It was even more incomprehensible that I had decided to inaugurate the airline within four days of its arrival.

I explained to Mr Parameshwar the logic of my actions and saw that he was dumbfounded both by the tone and manner in which I spoke.

The YA number had been issued the day before and the aircraft had taken off from Kathmandu on schedule. We were in radio contact with the pilots throughout its journey. The helicopter had flown into Indian airspace the previous day and landed in Varanasi, the first port of entry. The customs wanted to do the clearance there. That would have meant a delay of two days. We wanted the customs clearance to take place in Bengaluru and requested the customs authorities in Bengaluru to call up Varanasi the previous day and ensure it did not get delayed.

The Varanasi customs authorities agreed to undertake 'rummaging' of the helicopter, a physical search for drugs, guns, and contraband. They would check the aircraft, the pilot, the cargo hold, and the belly to ensure that no contraband was being carried, but actual customs clearance of the machine would be undertaken in Bengaluru. The helicopter had taken off from Tirupati after refuelling and we now waited with bated breath and eyes glued to the north-east sky, the direction of the holy city of Tirupati. My feelings are difficult to describe, akin to those I experienced when the first inflorescence appeared on my first coconut tree after eight years of watering and tending. Now we could hear the unmistakable hum of a chopper somewhere in the distance. Blood raced through the veins and there was excitement all around me. Then we finally heard the unmistakable sound of the helicopter approaching and a barely perceptible dot appeared over the horizon.

Jayanth has the sharpest vision among us and was the first to spot the helicopter. He pointed it out to the rest of us. One small speck grew in size and became visible, its sound became increasingly distinct. The helicopter soon hovered above and landed right in front of us like a giant metallic bird. We had garlands ready. We gave the Nepalese pilots a hug and bouquets of flowers. Everybody went around the helicopter and touched it. We all shared a single, overwhelming emotion. The mix of quiet relief and joy soon however, gave way to crisp business as customs officials swooped down on the machine.

The customs officials asked us to stay away from the helicopter, undertook another 'rummaging', and sealed the helicopter. It was bonded and taken into their custody. We left the airport while the pilots secured the helicopter to anchor pins with weights to prevent its being blown away by a storm.

I had three days left. There were many tasks to be accomplished. Getting the customs clearance was the first. That would be a major hurdle. The customs still had a medieval ethos. In the early 1990s, if you landed at an airport, there would be more customs officials than passengers. Although the high-tariff regime was slowly being dismantled, a dichotomy of mechanisms had already been created, one dealing with the purveyors of contraband and the other with ordinary passengers. On the one hand, the regime encouraged big-time smuggling and let off those bringing in contraband for sale in the parallel market: the so-called Myanmar bazaars of the various large cities. Smugglers brought in contraband in boatloads, and no one could explain how with such a strong customs force there could still exist a thriving black market. The Myanmar bazaars featured an intricate labyrinth of shops that sold all kinds of imported goods that had by-passed customs. On the other hand, the same regime encouraged customs officers to pounce upon hapless passengers returning with little gifts: a digital watch, a cassette player, a bottle of whiskey, or a box of chocolates. In the eyes of the customs official, everyone was a smuggler: housewives, old people, tourists, even children. No one was spared scrutiny.

In such a scenario, something like a helicopter coming in would grab eyeballs. Fortunately for us, the government had a very liberal, prudent customs policy towards aircraft. So as long as an aircraft was brought in for public service, with a licence for charters, there was no customs duty but if you brought in a helicopter for private use, you paid it. In fact, the import permission by the DGCA was itself deemed to be a licence. A public notice had been issued to that effect by the Director General of Foreign Trade (DGFT).

There was no way the customs could stop it, but they could delay the helicopter's release. I decided to wait and watch. We appointed a customs agent for a legal fee to handle the release of the helicopter from customs. We were promised that the job would be completed by the evening. Life is however full of surprises: evening fell and the job had not been done. The agent assured us that it would be done the following day, but that didn't not happen either.

I began feeling nervous and decided to go to the airport myself. I went to meet the assistant commissioner of customs, waited for a couple of hours, and returned without having met him. Only one day remained before the launch. I had my back against the wall.

I was at the airport early next day, hoping to get the clearance before noon. I would then have the rest of the day with the DGCA. The inauguration was at ten the following morning. The morning wore on, it was close to mid-day and the agent kept assuring me that the file would be signed at any moment.

The DGCA office closed at 5.30 p.m. The pilot and engineer had to undertake a hover and ground run and certify it, and the DGCA had only to physically inspect the aircraft and stamp the logbook, certifying that this was a Deccan Aviation helicopter. All other documentation had been cleared. How was I to handle a situation like this? Even if the customs cleared the aircraft at 4.00 p.m., the DGCA would have very little time this evening.

I hovered outside the customs assistant commissioner's cabin and the officer eventually emerged at 4.30 p.m. He was casual and did not understand the gravity of my predicament. I walked along with him and introduced myself. He kept walking and did not acknowledge me. I repeatedly told him that I needed the customs to clear the aircraft. He responded brusquely and dismissively. He said, 'Yes, Captain, I've been informed of your requirement. But I have absolutely no time today. I have been asked to go over immediately to the central office and if I am back at this office before 6:00 p.m. this evening, I can take a look at your papers. If everything is in place, I promise to clear your aircraft first thing tomorrow morning.'

'I can't wait for tomorrow,' I said. 'Tomorrow is the inauguration. You must clear it today. I still have work with the DGCA.' I didn't want to antagonize the official but did not want to give him a feeling that he could take it easy. I said, 'Look, officer, this is extremely serious. It's a question of life and death for me. You have got to do it now.' He continued to walk towards his jeep and blurted out impatiently, 'Captain, I can't do it now. The commissioner of customs has summoned me. I'll come back and see it this evening. I'll give it to you first thing tomorrow morning. Nine o'clock!'

As I tried to plead with him, the officer got into his jeep and sped off, leaving a trail of dust and smoke in my face.

7

If I am unable to make the Gods above relent, I shall move Hell.

—Virgil

Preparing for the Launch

When the dust settled I looked at my watch. It was about 5 p.m. and I had eighteen hours for a reprieve. I was a desperate man. An advertisement had been inserted and would appear in the morning's paper. A teaser ad had already appeared a few days ago and there was no turning back.

I was livid with the customs agent and angry with myself for having trusted him. I resolved not to postpone the inauguration; I still had time. I contacted Reena Pandey at the PMO who, with her husband, had helped us get the licence from the aviation ministry. I explained to her that everything had been set, the inauguration was slated for the next day, all compliances had been met, the ministers had been invited, and the press had been informed but the customs had not cleared the aircraft. I gave her the name and telephone number of the additional customs commissioner, a phone call to whom would make all the difference. I impressed upon her that the lapse was not on our side: the helicopter had arrived three days ago and the customs had had enough time to scrutinize the documents. She now had all the information to equip her to request urgent action and tell the commissioner that there would be huge embarrassment for the government if the inauguration did not take place as a cabinet minister would be attending the event as chief guest. When there is no violation of rules and no special out-of-turn favours demanded, a call from the PMO usually sends a shiver down the spine of the bureaucrat concerned. To create additional pressure, I also requested a senior official in the chief minister's secretariat to give the commissioner a call.

Within half an hour of speaking to Reena, I got a call from T. Jayaraman, additional commissioner of customs. He was very pleasant over the phone, saying he had been briefed about the situation and asked me why I had not approached him earlier. I narrated my experience with the customs office during the past three days. 'Mr Jayaraman, I wish I had met you. I did not have any reason to doubt that your officer would clear the papers. There is no violation of customs regulations on our part. The authorized customs agent assured me that clearance is a matter of due process. I did not wish to antagonize your official who was on the job. The promised due process has not however taken place, as I should have received the clearance yesterday.' I did not fail to mention how the concerned officer had slammed the door on my face with rude indifference. Jayaraman was convinced and promised to call back, which he did after ten minutes, assuring me that the assistant commissioner of customs would call me shortly and clear my helicopter.

It was 11 p.m. The assistant commissioner of customs, the gentleman who had shut the door on my face, called me. He was ready to release the helicopter right away but the files were in the custody of a customs appraiser who was at a farewell party. If I could bring him over, he would sign the papers. He gave me the address of the venue of the party.

Without losing a minute, I drove in my jeep to trace the customs appraiser to the party which was being hosted at a resort on the outskirts of Bengaluru. As I entered the resort, I could hear loud music and sensed the party guests were in high spirits. It was a fairly large gathering with a lot of people milling around and I wondered how I could trace the person concerned. I asked around, praying that the appraiser had not left the party and gone home. Fortunately, someone pointed him out soon enough and I approached the young man.

I, introducing myself, took him aside, and explained why I had been looking for him. I said I had been asked by the assistant commissioner to bring him right away to the airport to clear the aircraft. The young man was having a good time at the party and looked annoyed that an official chore awaited him well after midnight. He was also surprised at the suddenness and the unusualness of the demand. However, recovering quickly he agreed to step out with me.

Located on the bottom rung of the hierarchy, the customs appraiser identifies a case as eligible or not for customs duty. He prepares documentation and sends it up to the assistant commissioner of customs. Providentially, it proved that the appraiser knew me and we shared a common past. 'I believe you were in NDA,' he began. 'So was I. But for some reason I discontinued. I spent three years there. It was the greatest experience of my life,' he said. 'Being ex-NDA and now in the customs, I will be very happy to help you,' he said. He made me privy to a little inside information. He had put up the documents to the assistant commissioner the previous day. Clearances should have been given yesterday. The assistant commissioner had not signed it for his own reasons. The young man smiled at me meaningfully.

The farmhouse resort was at the other end of Bengaluru, near Yelahanka. In those days, the countryside around Bengaluru was dotted with clubs and resorts where officials and corporate staff gathered for the odd official or semi-official celebration. It took us an hour to drive to HAL. The assistant commissioner was waiting for us. He looked sheepish and I made every effort to avoid appearing one-up on the officer. He however surprised me by saying, 'Captain, rather than putting pressure on us at two in the morning, you could have let me know you had an inauguration tomorrow. I would certainly have cleared it.' With that his sagging pride was salvaged and I played along. He finished his report at about 2 a.m.

Jayanth and Sam were waiting anxiously for the process to get through. The release papers were ready and all that the officer had to do was to physically see the helicopter and hand over the papers to us. There was yet another minor hitch. We were in the civilian enclave of the customs office and the helicopter was bonded in the defence hold-up area. We were running out of time. Jayanth quickly managed to secure special passes for all of us to enter the defence area inside the airport. During the next hour or so we had shown the customs officer the helicopter for physical verification and had finally got the aircraft in our possession.

We now had one major last hurdle to cross: DGCA clearance to fly the helicopter. We left the hangar and went home. Jayanth was to return at 6 a.m. for a ground test and a hover test, and complete other DGCA formalities. We however realized that there were many clearances to be obtained for the ultimate commercial operator's permit. We were faced with what seemed to be an insurmountable problem. We had brought the cup to the lip but there were still many a slip in between! At this most critical of all moments before the launch, N. Ramesh, head of air-worthiness of the DGCA in Delhi came to our rescue. He advised us that there was a provision in the rules that allowed a one-off ferry flight without passengers if the aircraft was air-worthy, and this would enable the authorities to use discretion and waive a number of formalities and requirements needed for full-fledged commercial operations. He also advised us to write a fresh letter asking the local DGCA to permit a one-off flight before the inauguration. We could obtain the commercial licence in the next couple of days. He promised to instruct his juniors in Bengaluru accordingly. I conveyed all this to Jayanth.

Jayanth and the local DGCA had reached the airport in time. Jayanth did the ground test and the hover test and helped the DGCA complete a series of statutory requirements. At nine I was supposed to reach the CM's office in Vidhana Soudha (the house of legislature) and bring him to the venue. I was still gripped by anxiety that some last minute hitch might prevent the helicopter from reaching the inaugural site in Jakkur airfield. Images of army life in remote border areas flitted past. During the wedding of an army officer or jawan posted at a remote location, the bridegroom gave the bride's party many anguishing moments. He had to negotiate extremely difficult terrain and use various modes of transport to reach the bride's home and the venue of the wedding. Occasionally he was stranded by a landslide or an avalanche along the way, missed a bus ride or a flight or ferry, and missed his own wedding. The wedding would however continue with the groom's framed photograph serving as surrogate!

I walked into the CM's office at 9 a.m. The inauguration was just half an hour ahead. The CM was ready to leave with me. Five minutes before I met him, Jayanth called. He said the officer was lukewarm about giving us the certificates. He was unhappy about the pressure that we had brought to bear on him from Delhi. He was picking out flaws in the documentation. He had never done such a thing in his entire professional life and was concerned that giving clearance might lose him his job. He spoke his mind. He thought we were crazy. At the end of the long message there was a ray of light: Jayanth felt that it seemed that in the end the officer would eventually give us what we needed.

Jayanth said: 'Gopi, the helicopter is perfect. I've done a ground test and a hover run. I'm all set and ready to take off. But our guy here has yet to give me thumbs up! We have just twenty minutes left. What am I to do if I don't get the go-ahead?' I was still on the phone with Jayanth when the CM came out. 'Captain, are you ready? Can we go?' 'Yes, sir,' I replied

I had a split second to decide. 'Take off!' I told Jayanth. 'We will face what comes. The future takes care of itself.' Once a resolution is made, whether for better or worse, the anxiety dissolves.

Only after I had spoken to Jayanth did I realize I had given an army command. What if Jayanth flew in violation of a DGCA order! I decided that my current worries concerned the inauguration alone. I would tackle the future when it came.

The CM and I now approached the airfield. I could see from a distance that the media had arrived. Reporters from newspapers and from a couple of TV channels which were broadcasting at the time were there. The venue bore a festive look. There were colourful festoons and confetti. People I could rely on had been entrusted with the responsibility of organizing the event. They had done a great job. They had set up shamianas and decorated the place. Everybody waited to give the CM a grand reception.

I kept glancing to the east from out of the window of the car in the direction of the HAL airport. The car stopped but I did not avert my gaze and there was the unmistakable speck of a helicopter approaching. Our car entered the special bay for the CM to alight. The car came to a measured halt and, as though specially choreographed to act in synchrony, the helicopter landed in a perfect touchdown. There was thunderous ovation in acknowledgement.

We led the CM to the stage. There were other ministers, dignitaries, and senior bureaucrats. I gave a short welcoming speech and thanked the CM for giving us the land in Jakkur and for agreeing to be our first customer. The CM lit a lamp and made a speech. He said, 'When I looked at this young captain, I was moved. How could I not but help him?' He wished us all the best and then inaugurated the first flight. The helicopter took off to booming applause from the guests and headed back to HAL.

I called and thanked Reena and all the others who had helped me. I also kept my promise to Doug and had the lease deposit money transferred the following day. I was leaving for Montreal that midnight for the second session of Henry Mintzberg's programme. I was concerned that I still needed the operational clearance for commercial flying—there is nothing more useless than a helicopter sitting on the ground! I called Sam and Jayanth and shared this anxiety with them before I flew out of Bengaluru. We knew it was a matter of a couple of days and they said they would take care of it.

Things worked out in the end and without much delay. Sam went and camped in Delhi. Together with our good old army friend, Col. D.V. Singh, Sam saw us through the bureaucratic maze. In a couple of days, we received a licence to operate non-scheduled charter flights. We were in business, as the saying goes. We only needed customers to fly. We shifted focus from the bureaucracy to marketing and sales.

There is a parallel between the mind of the entrepreneur and the mind of an artist. Camus described the artist's mind to be chaotic, but the practise of art requires enormous amounts of self-discipline. It requires the ability to choose from infinite possibilities. It requires the discipline to sit down and do things. The creative mind has a tendency to free itself from discipline. It tends towards chaos. Creative people, including entrepreneurs, need to inculcate the ability and the balance to tread this fine line between creativity and systems-and-processes. Being aware of my inadequacies as an entrepreneur, I forced myself to acquire a rudimentary knowledge of finance and accounting.

On the flight to Montreal, I tried to imagine who my first customer would be. I conjured up all kinds of potential clients. Who, however, would be the first to call? I experienced torment, anticipation, and elation. The truth had still not sunk in that I was now the CEO of a helicopter company. I had felt the same when I had decided to take to farming, and also the first night I had spent on the farm, in the open, gazing at the night sky.

I kept calling the office and I was told that the phones had been continually ringing but the first commercial flight had not materialized. All of them were in a state of expectant excitement.

Whenever I recognized a note of despondency I encouraged them and said it was just a question of time and things would definitely happen. I somehow possessed inextinguishable optimism which I shared with the others. I said the innumerable calls they were receiving were a pointer to future business.

I realized too how difficult it was to capture the country's imagination. Marketing and advertising continue to remain an open area of inquiry for me. Advertising is a necessary spend, but how much and how frequently? A helicopter sitting on the ground burns a big hole in the pocket. Advertising, when it is not effective, burns one more hole in the pocket. Effective advertising is a continuing dilemma. Advertising guru David Ogilvy is a man I admire greatly. Ogilvy once said, 'When I write an advertisement, I don't want you to tell me that you find it creative. I want you to find it so interesting that you *buy the product*. When Aeschines spoke, they said, "How well he speaks." But when Demosthenes spoke, they said, "Let us march against Philip."' The CEO of Ryan Air had said something similar: 'Forget all the ponytails that come and give you some creative nonsense. The only test of your advertisement: does it make the customer want to buy your product? Can your ad increase your revenues?'

We were novices in business and had no formal training in running it. In one way this helped because our minds were open to new ideas and innovations. We were based in Bengaluru but our customer could be from anywhere in India or the world. The investment climate was opening up and many foreign companies were looking for helicopters to help them undertake surveys of prospective sites. Customers with money wanted to pare off several days from travel time entailed in road or train journeys. It was a real challenge to catch the attention of the world with a limited budget. While Air Deccan was able to capture the people's imagination in a different way and is a household name, even to this day I encounter people who have never heard of Deccan Aviation although it began earlier and has existed far longer.

The highly differentiated media viewership—the vast number of television channels and newspapers—made it extremely difficult to choose where, when, and how many times to advertise. Market research companies came up with vast statistics and chart overlays to give you a choice of exposure but the budgets these entailed could simply wipe you out of business. This was therefore where my native intelligence came in handy. It told me to look for alternatives. I discovered that the best way to advertise on a shoestring budget is to get the media to talk about you. It takes an intuitive understanding to gauge what makes a good story. The reforms process had helped increase the competition among the media institutions. This was because there was a new newspaper or a new TV channel opening up every day. The reforms had helped break down the monopoly that existed and the media was now hungry for good stories because they were in competition with one another. He who lands the meaty story first gets a premium in the market which increases his circulation or viewership. That's how the media work.

Once we wanted to call a press conference. We got in touch with agencies that handled the media, which are typically PR agencies. They advise you on how to get good media coverage. They ask you to hire space in a five-star hotel and suggest that you invite journalists from leading media houses and treat them to food and liquor. They insist that the best way of making an impression on the media is through memorable gifts!

When I was running the micro-irrigation systems business, there were times when the business went through an almost hand-to-mouth existence. There was one occasion when I thought that attracting media attention to the business might lift it out of its perilous state. In the process I became a victim of one of these media relations agencies. The agency took responsibility for the press conference. It produced a formula for a successful media event: five-star hotel, drinks, dinner, and gifts. Reporters would not be interested in an event if it were not held in a five-star hotel. Drinks and dinner were to be a routine part of the event, and gifts would be useful mnemonics for the journalist.

I realized that if I followed the advice of the agency it would create a crater in my pocket. If, on the other hand, it guaranteed good press coverage then the money would be well-spent, so I agreed. The press conference was held. I hoped to see news splashes and bottom spreads in the news columns the following day, but in reality we had to pour over the papers with a magnifying glass to spot the news item about us. It struck me that reporters came, ate, and vanished. A phrase in Hindi describes this kind of a guest in colourful terms: 'Khaya, peeya aur khisak gaya.' In the newspapers there was only a small mention of us and that was tucked away in the inside pages. It was perhaps a four-or-five-line report, of column width about the size of a rupee coin. Some papers carried nothing.

I should have been outraged at the press, but looked at it from their point of view. What I had done really was to insult the press. I had thought journalists could be bought. They came, ate, and left because they did not want to insult us, the organizers. That was when I realized that to a considerable degree we have an honest press. There are of course some dishonest people in the media, as there are dishonest and corrupt people in other professions too. There are corrupt businessmen, corrupt and venal politicians. Similarly, there is the odd corrupt journalist who brings disgrace to the entire media circuit. If the journalist you invite for a drink is an honest reporter he or she might come but will go back with contempt. He will never respect you, and that actually works against you.

That was the last time I looked at the press in this manner. I gained intuitive understanding that the best way to advertise is to get a good press. Some things of course need paid advertising, but one inch of space in the columns of a reputable newspaper is worth a hundred inches of paid advertising. Any advertising professional worth his salt will agree to this. You of course know what creates a good news story, you must develop your own nose for news, to have the press hanging around you like the paparazzi. I had developed this insight long ago and, therefore, I was being covered by the press long before the helicopter company started and did not spend a single rupee for media coverage! I just spoke directly to the reporters with whom I had been interacting.

Media professionals are bound by a different logic. They see growth within the profession and the organization they work for in a different way than a salesperson would. The career growth of a sales executive is linked to one parameter: more sales. For the salesperson, sales is the reason for existence. For the reporter the only objective is to publish good exclusive stories every day. That is not easy: the competition is intense. The reporter has two reasons for existence (raison d'être). S/he has to ensure that the story is truly newsworthy and is able to catch the attention of the reader. This is of prime importance. Exclusivity of the news item or breaking the news first, for which the reporter has to strive to be the first to get the story and publish it before anyone else does, is also an important factor. A stale story, however well-written and researched, does not make news. Sometimes the press goes overboard. It looks at things not from the perspective you want them to look at but from an entirely different point of view. Will a particular published story help increase the circulation of the newspaper? Will it induce a rise in the readership of the paper and lend it an edge over the competitor's product?

I once heard a speech by N. Ram, editor of *The Hindu*. Ram said the editor in many cases is also the owner of the publication. The editor has to position the publication like a business venture. However, the editor has also to meet the social responsibility of the media, and this is huge: to balance between income (because the publisher has to pay his staff salaries and meet the costs of production) and reporting the truth for the benefit of society.

When the editor starts publishing merely sensational reports, the positioning of the newspaper is similar to that of a tabloid. It is a product positioning like Nirma or Surf. The product assures certain qualities and utility. The emphasis is on the sensational. There is crime and violence, photographs of celebrities, a gossip column. The language is racy, slang-ridden, and often salacious. If, however, you are positioning yourself as a serious paper then it is a challenge. It is difficult if you are the owner and the editor, but it is also difficult when you are the editor and you have a boss who is the owner. The editor has to serve his boss, on the one hand, and his profession on the other.

According to N. Ram, there is an increasingly blurring of vision between responsibility to society and responsibility to the owner or business. If you do not generate income you go bankrupt. You will not be able to serve society. That was why you became a journalist in the first place. This calls for a fine balance.

Good journalists have a nose for a good story. You can get a journalist interested in your business if you are able to tap that source of intuition. There could be one appealing aspect of your business, and if the reporter picks it up, you find yourself in the print and electronic media.

I was in the press almost every day after the launch of the helicopter company, but getting the press is not enough. You still need to advertise. The advertisement carries information to the public about the company, its contact details, telephone numbers, an idea of rates and reach, as well as an idea of what services you offer.

I used to call from Montreal, hoping for news of the first customer. For the company the first commercial flight would have been the most important because it would signal the beginning of commercial viability. Regardless of what you do, you must make a business profitable. Said Peter Drucker, 'Businesses have only one reason to exist—to make a profit'. It is only when businesses make a profit that they pay taxes. Making a profit ethically is the only reason for businesses to exist.

While what Drucker said is true for all times, the pressure of stock markets to put out quarterly profits, prompted Narayana Murthy of Infosys to observe, sympathetically but a little deprecatingly about the expectations: 'As the CEO, you are only as good as your last quarter.' You are there for the long-term and you have to pace your growth. Entrepreneurs face the challenge of how to build a business for the long-term without making losses in the short-term. However, companies that focus only on near-term profits and do not invest for the long-term build an edifice with a shallow foundation. They become vulnerable to even small economic crises. 'Greatness appeals to the future!'

The call came a week after the launch. It was from a corporate company seeking to hire our helicopter. We were also waiting for the chief minister. The first commercial flight caused great stir and excitement in the company. I was still in Montreal when I got a call. It was a great shriek from Sam. Sam said, 'Gopi, guess what! Tomorrow we are doing the first sortie. The money has come into the account.' We adopted this policy from the very first day. There would be no credit for anyone. This was not because we did not trust people but because we could not afford to give credit. I had learnt a lesson from my agriculture business. It was easy to sell on credit but an almost impossible task to recover dues from an amorphous group of farmers. You give a farmer an irrigation system. If the crop fails, he will not pay you. You give a helicopter for medical evacuation on credit; if the patient dies you will not receive your payment. We decided not to give credit under any circumstances to anyone. We did not want a system where you had to employ people to collect dues. We were a lean organization where the pilot was salesman, dinner companion, and helicopter cleaner all bundled into one high-profile executive. I helped with some of the tasks when I accompanied the pilot.

There is a reason for saying that my pilot was also my dinner companion! The managing director of the Bank of America once hired our helicopter. This was when we realized how important it was that we should build an impressive hangar. For about six months we had a tent for a front office. Then we built a hangar at a frenetic pace. I felt the need to create an image of a world-class and impeccable hangar; spotless in its upkeep, with a comfortable foyer for waiting passengers. I also wanted to build good maintenance facilities. It was a risk I took, because the investments were rather high. However, without such a facility we would have put off our customers and damaged the prospect of business growth right at the outset. We went ahead, built a great hangar, and set up excellent maintenance facilities.

The visit of the CEO of the Bank of America was an eye-opener for me. It gave me an idea of the scale and grand manner in which global CEOs operate, well beyond the imagination of ordinary people. The Delhi-based India head of the bank had read in the papers about Deccan's helicopter service. He called us to make enquiries and followed-up with several trips to Bengaluru. His first visit was a recce, an army term for reconnaissance, to explore the lie of the land. He wanted to see for himself what facilities we offered and told us the CEO would be busy at meetings in Bengaluru, in connection with investments the bank had made or planned to make. He was also looking for ways to keep the Global CEO's wife entertained during the visit. He observed that there was nothing much to see by way of tourist interest in the city. Was there something in the neighbourhood that would be of interest to a VIP tourist? We suggested a day-long programme. The lady takes off in the morning; she visits the royal palace in Mysore, a short haul by helicopter followed, by a lunche at the Lalit Mahal Palace Hotel and then flies to the game sanctuary in Nagarahole and watches animals in the wild; she enjoys a barbecue by the river, and then flies back to Bengaluru before dusk.

The India head was impressed, but he wanted an assurance from us that everything would work to clockwork precision; that there would be no glitches, and no faux pas. He warned us: the least cause for the lady's dissatisfaction would cause heads to roll, his included. We promised to do our best and he left.

The India head's report was appreciated and the office of the global CEO initiated the next steps. A team of aviation auditors flew in all the way from the US to do an audit of our operations. They checked our log books, our operations and maintenance books. They looked at our pilot records. They interviewed the pilot. They inspected our hangar. They looked at the remarks made by DGCA auditors. In short, they did what a DGCA auditor would properly do.

The chief of the auditing team then sent a fax to their office: there was no email in India yet. The fax read as follows: 'Guess what! I was expecting to find a banana republic kind of a shed but the Deccan Aviation facility is better than some of the best facilities in America.'

That assessment and the acknowledgement of our facility by the team made us feel really proud. We knew we were on to something really big.

Yet another team from Israel, an independent security auditing agency, visited our facilities for a security audit. We were amazed at the extent to which the corporate executives went to prepare ground for the visit of their global CEOs. They must have spent many times more on the visits by the aviation audit and security audit teams than what it eventually cost them to use our helicopter service. The elaborate preparations made by Intel executives just to get their global CEO to fly to Infosys campus from the centre of Bengaluru, a mere seven-minute ride in our helicopter, went even further. They insisted on a twin-engine helicopter which we had to fly in from Kolkata. It took the helicopter twenty-two hours to fly from Kolkata to Bengaluru and back, and the costs were borne by the company. Global CEOs of large corporations are surely a class by themselves!

The aviation audit team cleared us and the Bank of America's global CEO was the first of Deccan's many global CEO customers.

This was the kind of thing I had visualized. I was now exploring how to tap this great tourism potential for people who were hard pressed for time.

The reform measures had made it attractive for companies to explore the market in India. Many CEOs of overseas companies had begun, if warily, to come to India. The work of a CEO is never finished, as they say: 'Only Robinson Crusoe could get his work done by Friday!' If work does not get over by Friday, she or he stays back for the weekend. How does one spend the weekend? Visiting the restaurants and pubs at star hotels is one. A CEO from the Netherlands once told me that he had been to Bengaluru fourteen times but had never seen anything but his five-star hotel and the airport! I realized that such 'stranded' CEOs are like beached whales: they might want to get away and they would if they had handy and comfortable means of transport. I knew from my own assays into the countryside as a trekker and explorer that all the places worth visiting in Karnataka were a mere one to one-and-a-half hours' journey from Bengaluru by helicopter! These included the palaces of Mysore and Srirangapattanam; the historic ruins of the capital of Vijayanagara Empire at Hampi; the bird sanctuary at Ranganathittu; the wildlife sanctuaries in Bandipur and Nagarahole; the magnificent temples at Belur and Halebid; and the colossal monolithic statue of Gomata at Shravanabelagola. This was true also of the other places of tourist attraction elsewhere in the country: they were all within an hour or two from the nearest metro by helicopter. Many locations of tourist interest in Karnataka are not easily accessible by road and often there is no rail connection. There are no airports within hundreds of kilometres. How then do these senior executives reach those enchanting places? A heli-cab was the perfect answer!

We put out an advertisement with the bold caption Dial-a-Chopper. A customer could dial-up and hire a helicopter at the spur of the moment. The customer could fly to Belur and Halebid and see the temples there; visit the wildlife sanctuaries at Nagarahole, Bandipur, and Kabini; spend a night at a jungle resort on the banks of the Kabini River; and fly back by the end of the weekend. Before Deccan, this was impossible to do. A trip outside was planned at least fifteen days in advance. Travel agents offered inter-city packages but were not in a position to execute local visits and therefore all our great wildlife parks, forts, palaces, and temples were beyond the reach of people who had decided to fly.

We negotiated with property owners for landing pads. We asked them not to cut trees and leave the grass unmowed. Grass landings are good for a helicopter: it cushions the landings so that the helicopter gets more landings and a higher lifespan. Also there is no dust. By identifying designated pads, coordinates can be entered in the GPS systems aboard the helicopter and any pilot can land there. Without the GPS, an advance party would have to prepare a helipad and the pilot would have to look out for the landing spot.

We heeded Douglas Cavanaugh's suggestion and prepared a helipad directory of one-off landing pads that are not government helipads. The directory and a map would allow pilots to land without a problem.

We realized that there was a synergy between the owners of resorts and us. They needed guests to use their hospitality and we needed customers. They were however so difficult to access that the occupancy rates were low. For instance, Jungle Lodges and Resorts is a world famous wildlife resort in the Nagarahole forests. It also provides access to a fishing camp. The resort is five hours by road from Bengaluru. This resort was under-visited because of poor connectivity. I proposed a cooperative model to their management. We would print cards and publicize the resort with contact details and facilities offered. They would place tent display cards in bedrooms and prominent living areas and would also display posters providing details of Deccan Aviation charters. We did not ask for a commission on guest visits but asked for a room for our pilot and functional hospitality. We also asked for a place for landing and access to it. The resort had to ensure that the pad was free of trees or structures or other impediments such as power lines or telephone lines. The resort would receive both guests and the pilot at the helicopter pad, and transport them to the resort. They would also provide security for the helicopter. The resorts jumped at the opportunity.

Deccan pilots surveyed potential landing pads in major resorts and identified landing sites. Some were on farmlands; some were part of a school playground or police ground. They also located places where we could store fuel.

The comprehensive arrangements allowed us to serve customers at an hour's short notice. If a customer called at ten in the night, our pilot would be ready for take-off at six in the morning.

The global CEO of the Bank of America landed. It is an army joke that when the general comes you've got to take care of his wife. If she's upset, the general will skew your happiness. We had prepared an itinerary that included the Kaveri fishing camp, one of the best in the world, and one which sports and adventure magazines had ranked among the top ten angling camps in the world. The pilot would not simply ferry the VIP passenger. He would fly zigzag showing the lady interesting sidelights along the way: waterfalls, promontories, historical monuments, palaces, and temples. The journey would be as exciting as the destination because of the spectacularly close views it offered of scenic objects on the earth below.

After angling, the lady would be flown to Mysore for a visit to the palace and lunch at Lalit Mahal. Thereafter she would head for the banks of the Kabini. The evening would feature a campfire and barbecue. The next morning she would take in sights of the wildlife at the sanctuary and head back to Bengaluru in the afternoon.

We laid out the red carpet for the lady VIP. I remember the occasion. I asked Jayanth who would fly the lady, to ensure that the smallest detail was not overlooked. 'Jayanth, you are going to charm the lady. They are saying heads will roll if we don't keep them happy. Make sure yours does not,' I said. Jayanth is a great pilot and wonderful raconteur. He can tell stories till morning. Many of his stories are real and the rest he makes up. He would narrate stories from army days. He combined a great sense of humour with a poker face that make his most outrageous tales ring true!

Jayanth carried the day and no heads rolled. I asked the lady about the trip. She said, 'Jayanth is not only a great pilot. He is a great dinner companion too.' I knew which way to take the tourism mandate forward. This was the beginning of heli-tourism across the country. Today, in the tourist season, 30 to 40 per cent of our revenue comes from it.

All it needed was to identify the different nodes and players, and create smooth interfaces between them. We went about it in an unhurried and systematic manner so that the network fell into place. We coordinated with the police for security; got permissions from district authorities to land, and tied up with property owners for a landing patch. Looking back, these appear so easy that one wonders why it had not been done before us!

Heli-tourism was very niche, very upmarket. People who operated at those dizzy heights were ready to pay more. Pricing a product or service is always tricky. There was a suggestion that we price ourselves a little lower to increase volume. I had no clear-cut answers but I argued that if we priced lower than the Rs 35,000 per hour that we were charging the high-end customer, the customer who could afford to pay more would end up paying less. Also, as there was a huge hiatus between this category of customer and the next level, a discount of 20 per cent would not make it sufficiently cheap for other people not in this category to use our service. We would end up losing on both ends and realizing less revenue. For the high-end customer the pricing was ten times the price of a business class ticket. I drew an analogy with the price of a masala dosa at Oberoi's. It was priced about Rs 200 at the time. If you wanted to increase the dosa sales in the five-star chain, you might want to give a 20 per cent discount. That would bring the price of the dosa down to Rs 160. However, a masala dosa sold at an Udupi fast-food café costs Rs 10. A five-star hotel would never be able to match that level and pegging sales increase to such pricing would be disastrous for their business.

India had a measly two million tourists in 1995. Compared to that, Niagara Falls alone attracted twelve million tourists that year, and four million of those were foreign tourists. Singapore got six million tourists. I constantly worried about devising ways of getting more tourists to India. There was a single drone of thought, which rose above everything else. 'How do we crack this? How do we get more tourists into the country?' In other countries the entrepreneurs had to build tourist attractions such as a Disneyland or an Eiffel Tower, whereas our country already has the sights and we don't have to invest in creating the primary attractions. It requires infrastructure and policies that support the activity: this can be done by a single stroke of the pen!

One day, as I was driving to my sister's house for dinner with my wife and daughters, I got a call. It was about 8.30 in the evening. The caller asked if I was the MD of the helicopter charter company. The caller said she was British. She said her friends and she were on a Cochin–Goa Indian Airlines flight that had been cancelled midway and she and her friends were dumped. There were no onward flights to Goa in the next couple of days. The airline officials had told them to wait for two days. They would put the passengers on the next earliest flight to Cochin and from there fly them to Goa!

The airline's salvage plan for the passengers appeared to me like Tughlaq's travel plan. The caller said she seemed a little lost. She said, 'And, so we are stuck. We were planning to come to Bengaluru later. But now that we have two days at our disposal we were thinking maybe we could go to Srirangapattanam.'

I asked the lady what had brought her to India and what she did for a living. She replied in a matter-of-fact way, with some humour, 'Let's say I'm a lady of leisure. I would like to know from you whether you could arrange for a helicopter to take us to Srirangapattanam, the old capital city of Tipu Sultan more than 200 years ago.' I asked her where she was at the moment. She said she was in the bar at the Ashoka Hotel. The Ashoka was then operated by the Indian Tourism Development Corporation.

I always made it a point to ask a prospective customer how s/he heard about us. I had inculcated this habit in others too. Therefore, whenever they received a call from someone, they would ask how the caller had heard about us. I reckoned that was one way of understanding which channels to use to advertise the company. I wanted to know whether the prospective customer had read about us in the papers or heard about us from someone who had used our services. I asked the British lady and she replied that the barman serving beer at the counter had informed her about my company. She had asked the barman which was the quickest way to reach Srirangapattanam, and without further waste of time. The barman had advised her, 'Madam, why not take a helicopter ride?'

The barman illustrates a point I have often tried to make. When people call you, be good to them. People may not use your service or product, but they are calling because they nurture some form of goodwill for you. They mean well for you. They could be your sales front, unpaid and entirely voluntary, all because they are curious about you.

I understood how the barman had got this idea. The bug of heli-tourism had hit me and I had placed placards at the travel desks of five-star hotels in town. It was my idea, exaggerated at the time perhaps, that we would go around these hotels on Saturdays and Sundays in a bus and pick up visitors eager to patronize our service. It would be easier for a group of four tourists to pay Rs 25,000 each than for one to pay one lakh rupees, I figured. Guests forced to spend the weekend in Bengaluru would find comfort and pleasure in the quick getaway package we would offer them, and the resorts would welcome this bonanza. We were offering two or three combo packages. Going to Kaveri Fishing Camp and back the same day was one; Kaveri Fishing Camp, Mysore, and back the same day was package number two; Kaveri Fishing Camp, Kabini River Resort, night stopover and wildlife safari the next day and back was the third. Common to the packages was breakfast, lunch, and evening barbecue. The stopover package included dinner at a campfire. Pick-up and drop facilities were also a common feature; we would not allow our passengers to waste a drop of un-intended perspiration.

We added drama to the experience. We advertised in the local magazines and had write-ups published. We gave a lot of interviews. The sheer novelty of our venture had made it worthwhile for magazines to write about us. Magazines like *Bangalore this Fortnight* were given away with compliments at these hotels. They provided us the cheapest channel of advertising. The barman had seen these placards and magazine pullouts. The waiters at Ashoka knew about Deccan helicopters.

We were driving close to the hotel when the lady called. I told my wife that we would have to make a detour. I had become quite truant as far as family was concerned. I was a helicopter missionary at all hours of the day and all days of the week. I lived, breathed, ate, slept, and dreamt just one thing. I was unable to keep the word I had given my wife. I confessed to her that I smelt opportunity and did not want to lose it. I called the lady at the hotel and said, 'If you can buy me a chilled glass of beer, I will come and meet you rightaway. I'll help you make a plan.' She readily agreed.

The lady waited with two other men. She gave me her card. She said she had been commissioned by Macmillan to do a book on the East India Company. She had been in India for the last three months and was visiting all the historical places that had the faintest connection with the East India Company and British history in India. She had a writer and a photographer with her who wished to go to Srirangapattanam. I said that as they were going to Srirangapattanam anyway, they could include Kabini wildlife reserve, a ten-minute flight away, in their itinerary. She had however made up her mind. 'Everything else is secondary. Srirangapattanam is the most important.' 'We will take you to Srirangapattanam,' I assured her. 'It will be a thirty-minute ride. We will fly you early in the morning and give you packed breakfast. You take a look around. We'll get you a guide to show you the place. From there we'll fly you to Mysore. How does that sound?' I knew the topology of the land and quickly planned an itinerary that included, besides Srirangapattanam, the Mysore Palace, the tigers, elephants, and the game.

Even as we discussed her itinerary, I called Jayanth and asked him to send an engineer to identify a place for us to land in Srirangapattanam. He would send us coordinates of the landing spot, the pilot would key them into his GPS and home in on the pad. The lady was mulling over the prospect of seeing and experiencing Oriental exotica: the palace, tigers and elephants, campfire, barbecue, dinner by the lakeside, and boat ride.

After some serious cogitation, she asked, 'How much are you going to charge?' I said I would charge her Rs. 1.5 lakh. She said she could pay Rs 75,000. I suggested she skip Srirangapattanam and head straight for the wildlife sanctuary. Srirangapattanam, she insisted, was an absolute must. I yielded. I said she could do Srirangapattanam and back at one lakh rupees. That looked a bare offer and didn't have the bait I had earlier thrown. We threw the price back and forth and negotiated. She threw me her bait. 'I'm going to give you credits in my book. It will say, "Thanks to Deccan Aviation!" How much discount can you give me for that?' I committed five per cent. We settled on that.

India is the only country in the world to offer the entire spectrum of what the tourist finds irresistibly attractive. Not Africa, not Europe, not USA—but India! America has picturesque national parks but little wildlife and no heritage worth mentioning. Europe has heritage monuments but no wildlife. Sub-Saharan Africa has the big five of wildlife aplenty— hippos, giraffes, lions, rhinos and elephants—but no heritage in the form of temples, forts, or palaces of historic interest. The heritage of Africa is entirely concentrated in the awe-inspiring Egyptian pyramids. India has them all: temples, palaces, monuments, and forts; the majestic Himalayas, rivers, deserts, beaches, great forests, and the big five of wildlife: tigers, lions, elephants, rhinoceros, and leopards. Well-known travel writers Hugh and Colleen Gantzer came to interview me once. They prefaced their call by saying, 'Captain, we don't think anybody realizes that you have had the biggest impact on tourism in this country. We want to do a story on you.' The husband-and-wife team travels together for the first six months and stays put in Mussoorie for the next six, writing. They had been writing about India for thirty-five years. 'And after thirty-five years, we feel we have not even scratched the surface of India in terms of tourism,' they said.

The words of Hugh and Colleen echoed my continued bafflement at why, in spite of such an incredible gamut of offerings, the profile of Indian tourism remained abysmally low.

It was 10 p.m. when I shook hands with the guests after closing the deal. I suddenly remembered that my wife and daughters had been waiting in the hotel lobby for the past hour. I apologized to them and we drove to my sister's place. My sister offered us chilled beer, which thawed the cold strains in relations and I savoured it with the relish of a hunter who has just closed in on his quarry.

The lady and her team took off the next day on their trip. Time moved on and I forgot about them. One day, a year later, I received a parcel from London. I opened it and found a printed invitation card, a note, and a book. The card said: 'Macmillan invites you to the launch of their book: *East India Company*.' The credits included Deccan Aviation.

We soon began to undertake corporate and infrastructure sorties. We were hired by a British company to undertake a power line survey and by film companies for aerial filming. We were inundated with calls from the film industry in Bollywood and Sandalwood, the fledgling Kannada film industry, and occasionally also from Hollywood. We received calls from organizers who wanted flowers dropped from the air during an event. Those inaugurating a new temple wanted us to shower petals at the moment when the deity was being consecrated. We received enquiries from all manner of people. No market research analyst could have guessed that the helicopter had such diverse uses.

A very rich Kolkata-based businessman was celebrating his daughter's wedding in Goa. He wanted us to fly all the way from Bengaluru to Goa to drop flowers on the bride and the groom during the ceremony. The actual flower-dropping required only half an hour of local flying, but the flight from Bengaluru to Goa and back entailed several hours of flying and a huge cost. The customer was willing to pay the staggeringly huge cost of the operation. Many others, including Marwaris, Sindhis, and Rajputs, hired the helicopter in lieu of the white horse that the groom rides in the baraat to the bride's house, so frequently witnessed on the busy roads of Delhi and Mumbai. An ancient tradition acquired new-age colours with the helicopter.

Nikaah in the Helicopter

One day, late in the afternoon, a visitor called on me, wishing to hire a helicopter. He insisted on meeting me. I was curious and came down to the foyer. There were three people in suits and ties sitting in the reception area. They had come to sell a product or service and I dealt with them politely, turning to the security officer and asking him about the gentleman who wanted to hire the helicopter. The security officer pointed to a corner and said, 'Sir, it's him standing in the corner.'

There stood in the corner an unassuming, humble looking man simply attired in loose pyjamas and shirt with a collar and button-flap at the top. He sported a short goatee and appeared to be in his thirties, reminding me of the tonga driver who had taken me to the railway station in Hassan. He did not fit the profile of someone who would want to hire a helicopter, timid and reluctant to step forward. I asked the security officer if this was the man who wanted to hire the helicopter. 'It's him, Sir,' the officer said. I was very sceptical but said nothing, taking the man upstairs to my room.

The man spoke in Kannada with a whiff of accent. He told me his name. I put him at ease and asked him what had brought him here. What he said was touching in the extreme. He said he had all along wanted to make a memorable special gift to his sister who was soon to be married. Being the eldest in the family, he wanted his sister's nikaah, or wedding ceremony, to take place in a flying helicopter.

The man lived in a village, sixty-four kilometres from Bengaluru. He wanted us to fly the helicopter to his village, pick up the bride, bridegroom, and the priest, and take off for the ceremony. He said his grandfather's nickname was Aane Sahib (elephant landlord) because he had organized the nikaah ceremonies of all his seven children on elephant-back. The grandson wanted to do something to revive the family tradition. He was unable to arrange for elephants but a helicopter would do. He had often seen our helicopters take off and land from the gates of our heliport. Could I fulfil his dream for him?

I asked him what he did for a living. He was a small-time trader. He moved between weekly village bazars buying and selling chillies. He was not rich but doing well. He had decided to spend all his savings on his sister's wedding. I was touched by the strength of his resolve and by the brotherly devotion to his sister. I straightaway offered him a 50 per cent discount. Even making allowance for the discount, I had calculated that we would operationally break even.

He asked for the price. I said it would be Rs 75,000. He showed no emotion. He said he would get back in two hours. Quite frankly, I doubted his return and forgot all about him. At about 5 p.m., my security officer announced his arrival. He had returned with Rs 75,000 in cash. I called Jayanth and asked him to organize the sortie. I told the man that some preparations would have to be made. He would have to identify an open field for the helicopter to land and ensure that the soil was watered and dust-free. He would also need to throw a cordon to keep off jaywalkers from getting too close to the helicopter; an accident could occur if we didn't take precautions.

A great human impact story was about to unfold. A grandson's helicopter would stand in for a grandfather's elephant. I didn't lose time and called Maya Sharma of NDTV, the reporters for Star News, and a few newspaper correspondents. Our customer wanted us to do three rounds over the village mosque too and drop some flowers. He said we could expect 10,000 people to watch the helicopter wedding. I watched him in disbelief as he left the room.

On the appointed day, we carried two TV channel crew in the helicopter. It was a ten-minute helicopter ride from Jakkur to the village. A fire smoke signal had been set up. We spotted the landing area from the rising smoke but an ocean of humanity was milling around and we were unable to land. We failed once. People had overstepped the cordon and were rushing towards the helicopter. Jayanth was worried. The tail rotor was capable of hurting or even killing somebody. The police had underestimated the crowd. Jayanth tried a second landing but failed. I then asked Jayanth to manoeuvre a landing that allowed me to get off and control the crowds.

As soon as I was able to disembark, I walked over to the customer and told him I would give him his money back and the helicopter would leave if he was unable to control the crowd. He got the message and put his tough men on the job. They pushed people back using a strong rope. The patch was cleared and Jayanth landed safely.

It was an unforgettable experience. Two timid brides, two grooms, and a priest rode in the helicopter. There was nervous excitement: being aboard a helicopter, being married. The ceremony took place in the air. Once the marriage party got off, we circled the mosque and headed back.

By the time we returned, the Star News and NDTV crew were already broadcasting the unusual aerial wedding. The Deccan chopper flashed on screen every five minutes. News channels carried the report all day, and for several days at a stretch. It was an advertising blitzkrieg for Deccan.

I continued to grapple with the problem of how we could market and advertise our helicopter services across India. I sought national recognition for Deccan but it was too expensive to advertise. There were a hundred television channels but no single channel was capable of comprehensive national coverage. This was because of diverse demographics, diverse languages, diverse viewer choices, and a multiplicity of channels. NDTV 24 X 7 was the most widely watched, urban-oriented channel. Its national viewership however rated less than 5 per cent. If we chose television, we would have to advertise on ten or twelve channels to reach a respectable viewership, and a huge budget was required to create an impact. Regional channels also had limited reach. Tamil channels were not watched in Karnataka, Kannada channels had no viewership in Andhra, Malayalam channels were not popular in Maharashtra. It was necessary to advertise in all these states separately, not forgetting newspapers and magazines whose readership was equally fragmented.

We had to devise a method to increase advertisement exposure at optimal cost. Perhaps not many start-up entrepreneurs are aware that when they are chasing a dream with a shoestring budget, they need to aim for national exposure. The budget set aside for advertising might actually go to pay the retainer and service charges of the advertising agency they hire; they will have no money left to advertise their goods or services. Therefore, one cost-cutting avenue stood right before our eyes: change the advertising agency. Hindustan Thomson Associates (HTA), our agency, was part of Thompson Associates, which was in those days one of the largest global advertising giants. We were a tiny account for them. It would be better for us to associate with a smaller, quality-conscious agency with a large presence in India. Local agencies did not however have a national presence and did not have creative and administrative depth.

A solution soon surfaced. When I was on the look out for a new advertising partner, I happened to meet John Kuruvilla, who headed Orchard Advertising, a local, start-up company and a 100 per cent offshoot of international major Leo Burnett. John pitched for our account and I told him we could consider his agency if he gave us the quality of a national agency, the close attention that a small account needed, and zero retainer charge. Could they nurture us and hand-hold us for the long term? Our association would one day prove valuable, I said. Orchard needed to establish an identity of its own and this could be a good beginning. It proved to be a long-running and valuable relationship; as Deccan grew, so did Orchard.

While on the question of advertising, I recognized a pattern among fliers. All airline travellers might not use a helicopter but anybody who used a helicopter must fly airlines. People who could hire a helicopter flew business class in Jet Airways, Sahara, or Indian Airlines (IA). These airlines provided in-flight magazines for their passengers. I considered taking monthly advertising space in the in-flight magazines of three airlines operating in India and a few operating in international airspace like British Airways (BA) and Lufthansa. I saw that this advertising could give us access to target audiences across India for a fraction of the millions of dollars we would otherwise need to spend.

I never forgot the crucial role of the media: when they wrote about us or featured us in their channels, providing us with credible public attention at very little cost.

John Gray and Swami Kaleshwar

I received a call one day from a lady in California, US who said she represented Mr John Gray. I answered the call and asked how I could help Mr Gray. The lady realized that I had been unable to place John Gray and filled in the background. He was *the* Mr Gray, she said, who had made a name for himself with his book *Men Are from Mars and Women Are from Venus*. That was a famous work and I perked up because John had, and continues to enjoy, a huge fan following across the world. John got on the line. He said he needed a helicopter to fly to temples of active worship in South India and also to meet some swamijis, the ubiquitous Hindu godmen of India.

People from the West and other parts of the world have looked to India for 'instant nirvana'. India seems to have fulfilled that object for many through its towering Himalaya, its sacred rivers and temples, and its god-men and yogis. I could not however link down-to-earth John Gray and this cultism. I was surprised that he who had ventured to provide answers to important questions of life was himself seeking solace!

I put John in touch with Deccan's marketing department. Faxes were exchanged between John and the marketing executives but John kept changing his travel plans.

I stepped in and called John, suggesting that he keep the helicopter for ten days and fly it for three hours a day, using it like a taxi. We would charge him a flat fee of 5,000 USD per day. For 10 days that would be 50,000 USD. If he flew more than the designated 30 hours over ten days we would charge him extra on an hourly basis. The pilot would be with him and John could change the programme as it suited him so long as he gave the pilot sufficient notice for refuelling. Somewhat colourfully I added that the helicopter would serve as John's personal limousine in the sky. John liked the description and the proposal. He deposited the money through his American Express Platinum Card.

John wanted to visit temples in Tiruvannamalai, Srisailam, Puttaparthy, and Mantralaya. He also wanted to visit Penukonda, over 160 kilometres from Puttaparthy, where the internationally celebrated and revered Sai Baba lives. I expected he would want to visit the Baba at Puttaparthy but he had it in his mind to visit a relatively less-known swamiji in Penukonda called Swami Kaleshwar. This intrigued me!

John called up a few days later. He said he would be bringing Oprah Winfrey along and wanted me to keep this confidential. With Oprah in the picture, John wanted the logistics to dovetail to the last detail and the minutest schedules to be maintained. I reassured him. Personally, the news thrilled me. An Oprah visit would be a great story for the press. That she had visited India, keeping the news under wraps while she was here, and used a Deccan Aviation helicopter would be a wonderful piece of publicity.

How could I get this across to the media without breaking my promise to John and without discomfiting the visitors? One thing I definitely would do. Whether Oprah came on the visit or not, I would get the press to meet and interview John Gray. That would be equally exciting, if not as snazzy as it would be with Oprah.

I got in touch with my friends in the media. I knew the reporters on a first-name basis. Beat reporters called up once in a while, two or three times a week sometimes, depending on how hot the context was. One needed to be accessible to answer their calls. They love it when you are open, don't appreciate pompousness. They have professional pride, they compete fiercely with peers, and they want to be the first to get the story out.

Keeping John Gray's visit in perspective, I called up a couple of TV channels and one or two from the print media. I said John Gray was visiting India and would be using my helicopter. Would they like to interview him? They jumped at the idea. I did not have to tell them what to write about Deccan because the helicopter would anyway get featured alongside John.

John landed in Chennai. We picked him up and flew him to Tirupathy. Oprah had dropped out at the last minute. John spent the night there and the following day he flew to Srisailam and then on to Hampi. From Hampi he flew to Penukonda, to the ashram of Swami Kaleshwar. Together, John and the swamiji flew down to Bengaluru. Jayanth was the pilot flying him around. John was in control of his schedule; he could fly where his fancy took him.

I was inquisitive about John Gray. He is a celebrated author but I found his devotion to the swamiji a trifle baffling. I wanted to know from John how he straddled two extremes of imagery: a swamiji on the one hand and Oprah on the other. I had an image of a swamiji and tried to look for one who fitted it. I was reminded of the problem I had faced with the Muslim chilly trader who wanted to hire the helicopter for his sister's wedding.

I had expected the swami to have a flowing beard, imposing persona, luminous face, and a saffron robe. I had stereotyped a Swamiji after Bhagwan Rajneesh who was characterized by great charisma. When finally introduced to the swamiji, I saw nothing that matched the image I had conjured. He was introduced as Swami Kaleshwar. On closer inspection I realized he was young. He probably had something that had so enthralled John Gray but escaped people like me. My curiosity resurfaced and I persisted in questioning John about the reason that caused him to fly all the way from California to meet the Swamiji.

John had a story to tell about the Swami. The swamiji had asked John what he could do for him. Did he have a wish? If so, swamiji would pray that it was fulfilled. John had a career wish. He wanted Oprah Winfrey to invite him to the Oprah Winfrey Book Club. Oprah Winfrey is the most celebrated talk show host in the world. She came from a disadvantaged family background and was a victim of abuse as a child and in marriage. Oprah however showed the world what grit and determination could achieve. She changed her life, transformed the lives of millions of people, and she continues to exert enormous influence over millions around the world.

Oprah's talk-show features a 'Book Club'. In that programme, Oprah picks up a book she finds deeply interesting, not permitting anyone to influence her choice of book. She invites the author, if living, to the show and discusses the book with him/her. The very next day the book sales soar, topping the best-seller charts and the author becomes a millionaire.

We listened to John's story with rapt attention. As in a fairy-tale, we wanted to know what happened next. John continued, 'I told swamiji I wanted to be invited to Oprah's Book Club.' The swamiji blessed him and said, 'You will hear from Oprah.'

As though a magic wand had been waved, the very next day John got a call from Oprah inviting him to her Book Club. It was unbelievable. John was staggered by the swamiji's powers, convinced this was divine mediation on his behalf. John went to the Book Club and instantly won fame as one of the most celebrated authors in the US. He stayed on the *New York Times* bestsellers list for years.

The story does not end there. It is near impossible for an author to be invited to Oprah's Book Club a second time. John wanted this to happen. He approached the swamiji once again. Could Swami Kaleshwar do it a second time? The swami prayed for John and invoked his 'shakti' once again and simply said, 'Thy will be done!' Within 24 hours, John got a call from Oprah Winfrey inviting him to the Book Club to discuss his book a second time. John was dazed and dazzled.

John told Oprah the story of how Swami Kaleshwar had helped him. Oprah was keen to meet the godman and John took Swami Kaleshwar to the US to meet her. It was after this meeting that Oprah wanted to come and visit India.

The story of the Swamiji does not end here. We stood on the lawn, the four of us. John Gray, the Swamiji, Jayanth, and I. The helicopter was ready to take off. Just then Swami Kaleshwar turned to Jayanth and said, 'Captain, is there something you desire? Is there anything I can do for you?' Jayanth's character has an irrepressibly mischievous streak running through and through. His expression took on a shape that was halfway between a smirk and a smile, but merely suggestive. Jayanth then assumed his usual poker player's mien and said, 'Swamiji, there is only one thing that I really wish for. I have consulted many doctors but nothing has helped. Can you help me?'

The Swamiji said, 'Tell me, Captain what it is you wish. I shall pray and summon my shakti to bless you!' Jayanth bent down reverentially and, pointing at his completely bald pate, said, 'Swamiji I wish for some hair on my head!' I couldn't hold back, nor could Jayanth. The two of us burst out laughing. Jayanth is bald as an egg. The Swamiji was shocked but he rapidly regained his composure. He said, seriously, 'You mock me, Captain! But you just wait till we know each other better.' He was not offended but I did not want to lose a customer because of Jayanth's jest, and the two of them somehow patched up. The Swamiji and John Gray boarded the helicopter, Jayanth got into his cockpit and the chopper took off and dissolved in the sky as I stared vacantly and wondered.

After flying John all over south India for a week, Jayanth returned. He then confided to me that in Swami Kaleshwar's ashram in Penukonda he did not spot a single Indian devotee. It was a throng of foreigners there. I could not figure out what selective powers the Swamiji possessed that attracted foreign rather Indian devotees to his ashram.

Bhagwan Saibaba gives Darshan

Soon after this assignment with Swami Kaleshwar, we had a call from the Saibaba ashram. I knew of the humanitarian work that Saibaba had been engaged in. The hospital at Puttaparthy had conducted an operation on Raju's wife, i.e., the wife of my right hand man on my farm. The doctors had advised an open heart bypass and the surgery was performed absolutely free of cost. Saibaba is known to fly in the best doctors from Germany, UK, and France for some of the more complicated operations on his patients. These doctors flew down and camped at the Saibaba ashram. It is one of the best-managed hospitals in India, considering that it is located deep in the interior of rural Andhra Pradesh. In those days I could not afford to give Raju the kind of money necessary for an open heart bypass surgery. After the successful heart surgery, Raju's wife resumed normal life. This routine act of generosity on part of the Saibaba-led institution had increased my esteem for the seer.

Saibaba has a following whose number is hard to estimate. The charity work he undertakes is continually supported by donations from devotees across the world which continue to pour in. It might be a wild shot, but I think the Saibaba currently enjoys the largest following of devotees among all the spiritual leaders in the world. His followers range from the most influential to the lowliest; from scientists and film stars to ordinary middle-class city dwellers from across the world. His appeal is felt in dusty towns and in tiny village hamlets.

He has had his share of detractors. One such was the very well-known, highly respected educationist and rationalist, the late Dr H. Narasimhaiah. A doctorate in physics, Narasimhaiah led a life of simplicity guided by Gandhian principles. He was vice-chancellor of Bangalore University and was openly critical of the Saibaba. He once asked Saibaba to demonstrate his powers to create matter out of nothing before an independent panel of scientists and rationalists. The Baba often conjured up ash, a ring, or pendant out of nowhere for his devotees. Baba's devotees who look up to him with awe and reverence believe that he has divine powers. Many saw this as sleight of hand and accused the Baba of misleading people. Saibaba does not respond to his critics but his following continues to grow.

It did not matter to me that controversy surrounded the Saibaba. If he practised magic rather than the invocation of divine intervention, so be it. I did not believe in such things. If there were others who believed in it, so be it. I was willing to forget the accusations because of the exemplary charitable work the Baba does for people. Baba provides education, drinking water and medical facilities to thousands of people. His failings, if any, are perhaps small in comparison with the enormous good he is able to achieve. One day an ashram official called to say the Saibaba wanted to use our helicopter.

I couldn't help but think that while all Indian god-men preach simplicity, austerity, and relinquishment of material pleasures, the ashrams and life-styles of many god-men reflect opulence. They use the most expensive cars, fly helicopters, and their mundane routines are arranged with the fastidiousness of the world's most powerful and wealthy. The rich are taken in easily by their hypnotizing exhortation—that the way to happiness is freedom from desire, simplicity of life, and spiritual pursuit as opposed to material pursuit. I couldn't help seeing a mirror reflection between the guru and the devotee; one in the other.

The preparations that preceded Saibaba's take-offs and landings were very demanding and elaborate. A whole army of devotees attended on the Baba. They were highly educated people, and many held positions in the highest echelons of government and the private sector. Presidents, chief ministers, and powerful politicians were among the followers who sought his blessings. There were army generals, very senior bureaucrats, scientists, people of the arts and letters, and educationists and businessmen. Some had donated all they had to the ashram. Foremost among them were Dr V.K. Gokak, scholar, writer, and vice-chancellor and Dr Bhagavantham, scientific advisor to the ministry of defence.

The Swami's followers took charge of the arrangements. They did a recce and asked us where exactly the helicopter would land and on which side the door was, from which the Baba would ascend. They wanted to know where to bring the car and how many steps Baba would have to walk. They worked on the alignment of the helicopter embarkation ladder with the car's door. They measured the distance with a tape, placed a carpet along the stretch, and covered it with petals. The stepladder was not to have more than nine inches between steps. They therefore removed the default steps and got a carpenter to create fresh ones that would make it easier for the Baba to get on the helicopter. I was keen to meet the Baba and received him when he came to our hangar.

Baba's travel plans were fulfilled with clockwork precision. The take-off was at 8 a.m. A security jeep in his entourage was the first to arrive. The officers riding in it surveyed the preparations. A second security jeep followed. The site had been thoroughly checked and all loose ends had been secured. The Baba arrived in a limousine. The large limousine stopped 500 yards short of the helicopter on the western side escorted by a jeep. Another followed. Six armed guards jumped out of the jeep in front and took positions around the limo. They had their backs to the Baba's vehicle and kept a sharp eye on anything that might be lurking in the bush nearby. Their drill followed the security protocol observed for the American president. Another set of security guards threw a mobile cordon on either side of the Baba's limo and ran alongside as it came to a halt. There was such perfection in their coordination that the security preparations made ahead of the visit of a head of state would pale in comparison.

The Baba stepped out. He looked frail and gentle. He said a few words to me on his way to the helicopter. He then threw up his right hand in the air so that it was almost vertical. He proffered his palm to me, clenched to a pinch and dropped a few specks of sacred ash into my outstretched palm. He then moved towards Jayanth. I had warned Jayanth not to repeat any of the antics he had engaged in with Swami Kaleshwar. I had enjoined solemnity and a strict code of behaviour so as not to offend the Baba. I kept a sharp eye on Jayanth as the Baba stepped closer to him. Jayanth was as solemn as his physiognomy would allow him. The Baba asked him if there was something Jayanth wished the Baba could do for him. Maintaining his composure with great effort, Jayanth said, 'Nothing, Swamiji, I just want your blessings'. The Saibaba did the same for Jayanth. He threw up his hands in the air, swirled his fingers like a magician, and offered Jayanth a gold ring embedded with a precious stone. Jayanth has boxer's hands with thick, stocky fingers. The Baba seemed to have factored in the girth of his ring finger while conjuring the ornament from thin air. He himself put the ring on Jayanth's fingers and said, 'See how this fits you!' It was a perfect fit. I am not sure that Jayanth became a believer, but for once he was speechless. The glint of mischief that lurks viciously at the edge of his eyes had suddenly lost its sheen, misted over with astonishment.

The helicopter took off. I saw the Baba from amidst the select group of his devotees with expressions of utter reverence. They could have seen Indra (rain god) or Varuna (wind god) in the sky; were transfixed by awe as they stood there chanting, 'Bhagwan, Bhagwan' as the helicopter took off. They were lost in a trance for quite a while, as they stood rooted to the grassy patch until the helicopter became a speck on the horizon and to be seen no more.

Baba was for me was a great lesson in business. I had witnessed the protocol of faith in action.

8

Captivating Events at Deccan Aviation

Within two years the helicopter company was firmly established. We had built a diverse portfolio of contracts: aerial survey, aerial photography, support to oil rigs, geophysical survey for mining, logistics support, heli-tourism, and medical evacuation, among others. The intuitive feeling I had when I ideated the helicopter company, that the government would eventually open up many of the more protected sectors, was being borne out. The government, which had prohibited privatization of mining, comparing it to selling family silver, soon realized that software exports were more remunerative than mines and began hesitantly to award private mining contracts. These were, for the first time in the history of India, to be awarded to large multinational conglomerates. These companies used aerial surveys and aerial photography to prospect large swathes of land covering thousands of square kilometres.

The aerial surveys required specialized flying techniques because they involved carrying a heavy load of sensing instruments called 'electromagnetic birds'. One of the important components of these 'birds' was a metallic cylindrical object about 6 metres in length and about 50 centimetres in diameter that dangled about 30 metres below the helicopter. Cables from the object were connected to a computer on board and data were sensed and collected. The pilot needed to fly in accordance with precise straight-line coordinates and scan a large area of land sometimes covering 100 by 100 kilometres, flying 100 feet above the ground, all the while keeping the 'bird' in a steady horizontal orientation. We sent our pilots to Australia and got them trained to operate these special survey flights. Investment in the extra training paid off. International companies like De Beers, Phelps Dodge, Rio Tinto, and prestigious Indian remote-sensing organizations such as NGRI in Hyderabad gave us contracts. These contracts not only strengthened our bottom line but also brought us enormous professional prestige.

India was also opening up the oil sector, till then the preserve of government-owned public sector undertakings. Scottish company Cairn Energy in a joint venture with ONGC for exploration and production of crude oil, had sought bids from helicopter service operators for survey and logistics support for oil exploration in India. Helicopters are the lifeline of oil prospectors and miners, whether on land or at sea. Only those operators had a prospect of winning a contract who had had offshore experience in providing helicopter logistics support on the high seas. This demands very skilled technical engineering, and flying expertise which we did not possess. We sent in our bid but I had a feeling that we stood no chance unless we were able to tie up with the best helicopter operator, specializing in oil exploration and production in the world.

I called Barry Havery, an independent aviation auditor for Cairn Energy, who refused to speak because, in his perspective, I was a bidder and so there would be a conflict of interest. Not easy to shrug off once I have made up my mind, I made several calls and each time he disconnected. Then I decided to make one final attempt. When the auditor picked up the receiver on the other side I blurted out, 'Barry, don't put the receiver down! All I want to know is who in your opinion is the very best helicopter operator in the oil industry, with whom I can negotiate a joint venture to bid for the Cairn contract.' I said it would only help improve bidder quality and increase choice for cairn. Perhaps he was impressed by my logic, or, perhaps, simply wanted me off his back, but he muttered the name Bristow Helicopters, UK and slammed the phone down.

With the same sense of urgency that I had manifested over the Enfield Motorcycle dealership, I headed overnight for Chennai, and took the next flight to London. The following day I was at Bristow making out a case for collaboration. I met Chris Fry, the director for Asia and the Far East, and we struck a common chord. I convinced him that though I needed one helicopter to begin with, oil exploration in India just having opened up as a sunrise industry: there would be many more to come in the future. By the end of two days I had made a convincing case and planned out a joint-venture document for signature. Just as we were about to sign, a veteran of Bristow, looking after some other region of the world, walked in to consult Chris on some matter. On learning that I was from India and we were about to sign a collaboration deed, he cut in. 'What? ONGC? India? You must be mad!', he exclaimed, elaborating how Bristow had a frustrating experience with ONGC and that itself should act as sufficient forewarning not to commit the same mistake again. Bristow had made a bid for a helicopter contract with ONGC in the 1980s and blocked one to meet the terms of bidding. ONGC kept putting off a decision on the tender and did not decide for an entire year. The helicopter remained idle but ONGC had still not decided so Bristow pulled out. In addition to investment that had been sunk, the company had opened an account to run its India operations. Bristow's British pounds were in Indian rupees in an Indian bank according to rules but even after several years the company was not able to repatriate its own funds because of the foreign exchange regulations. Globally, helicopter contracts are closed within two months of the final date of bidding but the lack of a timely decision was frustrating for Bristow. The man was obviously bitter about the experience and did not believe a new engagement with India would make any sense. He held out an alarm for his colleague, and in the process came across as rather final and brusque as he breezed out after his work was done.

Chris looked at me and asked what was to be done. The incident was totally unexpected. I was completely taken aback by the way in which my country was shown in the poorest of light. The man was not wrong; but it was the sheer timing that seemed disastrous for my mission. How could I set things right? Not losing my composure, and also realizing that Indian bureaucracy was itself a British legacy, I said, hoping to sound convincing, 'Trust me. Things are different today and India is changing. Our bureaucracy is a British legacy and you have had it here too until recently when Margaret Thatcher dismantled it'. Chris smiled. We had spent two days together, toiling over the contract and had developed an implicit faith in the future of our relationship. He saw that India was changing: so much was happening in the country that had not happened in the past fifty years since independence. Again, Chris had put in two long days into the thinking process and had a hunch. He smiled and we signed the collaboration document.

The experience that Chris's colleague had narrated, made me uncomfortable about Indian bureaucracy. I asked myself if there was no way to make it mandatory for Indian companies in the public sector to decide bids within a specific time-frame without of course compromising on quality and the country's interests. It was obvious that they were being compromised when delays in decision-making discouraged and put off good companies wishing to do business with India. One recent example of the implications of bureaucratic delays is the debate over a new helicopter for the Indian Army. The government has been unable to decide which helicopter to choose for five years running. This illustrates the quintessential nature of political and bureaucratic dithering. There are obviously questions of what happens to current infrastructure for the manufacture of vintage helicopters. The consequences of such dithering could be serious, and serve as an example of what it means to compromise the country's interests.

After the collaboration agreement was signed I learnt that Bristow Helicopters had over 500 helicopters solely dedicated to offshore oil exploration. India had at the time about 100 helicopters deployed in multiple tasks. This gave me an idea of the future prospect for helicopters in India.

Allan Bristow, the founder of the company who passed away recently, put helicopters to unusual use. He was the first to use a helicopter for whale-sightings on the high seas, a precursor to its eventual application in offshore oil exploration. Bristow put his early helicopters, running wooden rotor blades, to help locate schools of whale. Whales are located by the spray they spout when they surface. The spray rises high above the water and is easily visible from far. The whale hunters in Hermann Melville's epic novel *Moby Dick* (1851) do the same. A sailor hoists himself to the top of the mast of the whaling ship and looks out for spouting spray through a telescope. When a whale is sighted, the sailor cries, 'Whale, ahoy! Whale, ahoy! There she blows! There she blows!' The entire ship is a-stir. Sea-hardened whale hunters descend in small boats, armed with harpoons and lances and rush headlong into the chase to row alongside, injure and weaken the whale, and then tow to the ship to extract whale oil. Bristow built an empire that is today the best and biggest in the oil industry. When, armed with the contract, I flew back I felt I had placed another brick on the edifice that we were painstakingly building. I recalled Napoleon Bonaparte words to the effect that it was a principle of war that it was not always canons but lightning speed that won battles.

Vijay Atre had joined us as marketing manager, and he and I handled most inquiries for chopper services. Vijay was a young graduate from the prestigious Faculty of Management Studies (FMS) Delhi. We both looked after marketing and sales as I wanted to be personally involved with everything in order to be able to take timely decisions.

Although I had given total freedom of initiative and action to all my colleagues, I was utterly impatient and unforgiving of people who delayed in the slightest in responding to customer calls and, wanted no gap between thought and action. Time was money, literally, to customers who hired our helicopters and slackness on our part could wholly undo their purpose and damage our business. In medical evacuation, time was the difference between life and death. I therefore laid down one cardinal rule in the company: no one would get off a call without resolution no matter when and where. The call had to lead to resolution, and everyone associated with operations had to move with lightning speed. I wanted them to shorten a straight line to reach their objective. Everyone had to carry their mobiles all day and all night, even when they went to bathe and, no alibi would be accepted.

I got a call, one day, sometime between two and three in the morning. A doctor from Manipal Hospital was on the line. He said he needed to mobilize a helicopter for an emergency medical evacuation. A friend had once told me that in accidents and trauma the first one or two hours are the 'Golden Hours'. Most patients died in the first hour or so of an accident if timely medical assistance did not reach them.

Helicopter sales people would of course have to work within certain restricting parameters but would need to think on the fly. They would need to rapidly identify and acquaint themselves with the geography and topography of the site of accident or where the patient had been brought; need to know what their pilots and helicopters could or could not do. They would have to mobilize and synchronize parallel rescue efforts too, bearing the golden hour in mind. They would have to coordinate activities to get doctors or paramedics on board; ensure that life-saving drugs were at hand, have ground ambulances waiting, secure various mandatory clearances, and organize the logistics of refuelling for the return trip.

The caller was neurosurgeon Dr N.K. Venkataramana, who had done commendable work in comprehensive trauma care across Karnataka. He said the wife of a colleague at the hospital had been seriously injured in a bus accident somewhere on the Bengaluru–Hyderabad highway. They did not know the precise location but it was about 200 km short of Hyderabad.

Could we evacuate the doctor's wife from the accident site? I agreed to dispatch our helicopter. 'But', I asked, 'Who will pay?' Dr Venkataramana said Manipal Hospital would bear the expenses. We got about setting up the operation.

Medical evacuation, unlike other forms of charter, pulled at your heart strings. It was undeniably a humanitarian effort that could and did save lives. The bitter truth was that running a charter like an ambulance service without proper accountability could send the company into bankruptcy. If the patient did not survive, nobody would have the heart to ask for money. The family could not be expected to have the willingness to pay. It was a poignant moment. Before all the moral issues were resolved within me, I felt that implementing the policy we followed with regard to other charters was the only way forward: advance payment. This conflict between heart and mind would persist. I called up Jayanth and asked him to take off at sunrise.

In India, then as now, there is no dedicated air ambulance service. All developed countries, even small ones, deploy customized and dedicated helicopters, planes, and ground ambulances for medical emergencies. The operation is end-to-end. A team, or several teams, of doctors, auxiliary medical staff, pilots, ground staff, biomedical engineering experts, and aviation authorities coordinate their efforts to enable speedy evacuation.

They stretch every sinew to save the patient, with stretchers fitted with ventilators and oxygen cylinders to provide medical care on the way to hospital. Specially trained evacuation units are assigned to these rescue missions. Doctors and nurses at hospitals are trained and equipped to take over immediately once the patient arrives.

The call from Dr Venkataramana had come even as I had been toying with the idea of specialized evacuation in India. Apart from infrastructural issues, it occurred to me, the major problem was people couldn't afford to pay huge sums on their own. There is an insurance cover for hospitalization and surgery but there is no insurance instrument that covers aerial evacuation of an injured patient. In developed countries insurance companies have evolved successful health insurance policies that encompass medical evacuation. In Europe and the US they sell premium policies that include medical evacuation. The policy buyer pays an annual $200 or $300 that entitles him/her medical coverage worth $5000. Medical evacuation is mobilized when a patient calls emergency, and the hospital and the helicopter service claim the costs from insurers.

Insurance companies could play a similar role in India. They need to undertake an actuarial audit of aerial medical evacuation and work out an affordable mass premium. An evacuation mission could cost anything between a lakh and ten lakh rupees, beyond the reach of most people. It is ironical that a patient who is covered for hospital expenses, is unable to reach the hospital. In a sense, insurance companies faced a catch-22 situation. If they offer coverage at a high premium, very few would opt for it; with a low premium they would have to spend a lot of money developing the business, and until the business is established their payout can be very high. This catch has been resolved in some countries, including New Zealand, where the government and the Red Cross buffer the initial phase. Once on rail, the model sustains itself. When more insurance companies offer coverage, more helicopter companies will offer medical emergency evacuation services. Together they will be able to put in place a much needed aspect of infrastructure.

Dr Venkataramana's call was our first for medical evacuation. As we were not a dedicated air ambulance service, we had to modify the helicopter to install basic rescue gear. It took our engineer just 20 minutes to remove the seats and make space for two stretchers in our six-seater passenger helicopter. The stretchers were fitted one above the other, bunker style. Three additional people could accompany the accident victims, possibly a doctor, a nurse, and a paramedic.

I told Jayanth he would have to fly along the highway and locate the accident location by sight. My confidence in Jayanth's ability to carry off the mission was natural. Jayanth, like many army pilots, had flown in war, in emergencies, and on rescue missions. He had flown over regions devastated by a natural calamity such as flood and earthquake. These pilots are agile, and intuitively aware of speed, improvisation, and safety—all necessary ingredients in such missions.

Jayanth and medical staff from Manipal Hospital were at the airfield before dawn. They took off with the sun and headed straight along the Hyderabad highway. Jayanth spotted the ill-fated bus and landed close to it in an open field. The injured had been moved to the nearest village hospital. Jayanth took off again and landed close to the hospital, picked up the doctor's wife, and flew straight back.

As soon as Jayanth landed in Jakkur airfield we rushed the patient to hospital in an ambulance. It took Jayanth an hour and a half to transport the patient over hundreds of miles. It was tragic and ironical that it would now take as much time to get her to the hospital on the other side of Bengaluru, driving through the city's chaotic traffic.

The thought kept recurring—of the innumerable seriously injured patients—we had been able to rescue just one. It was a sad reflection of our system that we had not been able to use the helicopter, a swift and highly versatile mode of transport, for such a useful purpose simply because of the question of viability, but that was the truth.

Unfortunately, even as the ambulance sped towards the hospital with a team of doctors and nurses attending, the patient breathed her last. We were deeply affected. If only there had been a helipad near the hospital, we might have been able to save her life. It was a gloomy day. Poor infrastructure had defeated all our efforts. I began thinking about ways of preventing something like this from happening again. Our team got together to ponder over this tragic end and brainstormed on how we could avoid such tragedy in the future. We were in the midst of the debate when the phone rang. It was Dr Venkataramana. He said in the light of the recent misfortune, doctors at the hospital had been discussing how to forestall such an eventuality in the future and the director of Manipal Hospital wanted to explore possible solutions with me. When could we meet? It was about eleven o'clock, and I said right away. We agreed to meet that afternoon.

The director, a number of senior doctors and members of the hospital board were at the meeting. I said we should identify a place near the hospital where a helicopter could land. A member of the board was quick to point out that the hospital owned an acre of land right next door. We had to examine the land and see if it suited our requirements. One of our pilots surveyed the land the very next day and declared that it was perfect.

We designed the work flow: names of people on either side to be called; numbers to be called; inter-agency communication protocols; and action prompts. We decided on a 24/7 emergency number and on the series of actions to be taken: by pilots on our side; by doctors, nurses, ambulance drivers, and emergency staff on theirs. We addressed issues regarding medicines, first-aid, briefings, billing, and other legal formalities.

We gave the medical evacuation operation a procedural structure that was dependable and fail-proof and undertook a dry run the very next day. We did a mock drill involving all the series of steps in the protocol decided and using a mock patient on a stretcher. The drill was successful and we called a press conference to announce the new medical evacuation service.

The drill had not come a day too early. That very day at midnight Jayanth received a call from Swami Kaleshwar. The Swami's mother had fallen, suffered serious head injuries, and was in a coma. By 6 a.m. the helicopter took off for Penukonda and brought her to the Manipal Hospital helipad which we had just created. Luck was with us this time and the old lady survived.

Medical evacuation using our helicopter caught the imagination of the middle-classes too. A fruit merchant from Belgaum hired our helicopter to save the life of a loved one. People who hired the helicopter were often not very rich, but faced with a life-threatening situation involving the near and dear ones. They cobbled together their meagre resources and hired the service.

There was a gentleman from Coorg who had a lung collapse and needed immediate specialist medical attention. Jayanth took off but found there was no place to land near the patient's residence and therefore landed at Tata's Gonikappa Golf Club not far away. Jayanth brought the patient to Manipal helipad and the latter survived.

In the years that have followed, Deccan has been involved in many rescue missions: in Kabul, Sri Lanka, Nepal, and in various states of south India. We have even airlifted patients from seafaring vessels on the high seas and enabled liver transplant by transporting liver from a brain dead donor from Bengaluru to Delhi. We have tie-ups, besides Manipal Hospital, with Apollo Hospitals, East-West Rescue, and Global International SOS based in Singapore.

Deccan Aviation today handles almost a case a day, and several other helicopter companies offer medical evacuation on a routine basis across India. However, even after twelve years since Deccan came into existence, only a miniscule proportion of the population is able to avail the service as insurance has still not stepped in. We have miles to go and many promises to keep!

We publicized many of these true stories of daring and human courage. The press lapped them up as the stories touched a sensitive chord and for the company it meant loads of free publicity.

As we went along, we discovered new uses for the helicopter. We got acquainted with its potential for innovative applications. One such use was suggested by an assignment we did for Discovery Channel. Discovery had commissioned a team to film the seven wonders of the world. They had covered the Pyramids and the Great Wall of China. For photography, the team had hired the services of the man who had filmed *Titanic* (1997) and *Out of Africa* (1985). The series director suggested to the channel that the meaning of the word 'wonder' be redefined to allow for a shift of focus from the Taj Mahal, without detracting from its magnificence, to a different India in the south, equally if not more wondrous, of which he was aware. South India, he said, featured temples of colossal size, scale, and grandeur that were of unsurpassed artistic brilliance. These temples were little known to the average tourist in the western world.

He spoke about the great temples built since ancient times, and continually added to or modified by the Pallava, the Chola, the Pandya, the Vijayanagara, and Nayaka rulers over hundreds of years, many built along the Kaveri river. He said they left the visitor with a sense of awe and wonder. The cultural significance of these temples, he felt, was quite unmatched by anything elsewhere in the world where the temples had thus far remained 'undiscovered'.

The channel concurred with the director's suggestion that they do a series in south India. Deccan Aviation was by this time well-established, so they wanted to use our helicopter. There were some technical challenges to be addressed by us. The Discovery team said they would be using a nose-mounted 'gyro-stabilized camera' which would be mounted outside the helicopter. The photographer would sit in the passenger compartment and control the camera using microwave actuated remote control device.

Gyro-stabilized cameras are designed to completely obviate vibrations and they cost almost as much as a small helicopter. The company involved with the project specialized in aerial filming, which is not the same as 3D aerial photography, and would be bringing special cameras from the UK. Aerial filming is done from hot air balloons, fixed winged aircraft, and helicopters.

I was greatly enthused by the idea of collaborating with such companies with whom we could share revenues. I discussed the idea with them and they were enthusiastic. We could also make the cameras available to Bollywood film-makers and television channels.

The greatest nightmare was government permissions for aerial filming. We still had archaic 1937 rules which banned aerial photography. Today's technology allows us to take high resolution pictures of a golf ball in action or the number-plate of a vehicle on the ground using cameras mounted on a satellite. Paradoxically, all the modern passenger aircraft flying into India have cameras fitted in the underbelly that continually display the terrain they overfly and the runway, especially, is visible with fine granularity including landing lights and the texture of the tarmac.

Aircrafts taking off anywhere in the world have to seek permission from the air traffic control and the defence ministry of the local government, and are obliged to submit flight plans to the authorities. This rule is intended to prevent spy-planes from operating in a country's airspace. However, aerial photography in India is regulated by rules published in 1937, since then technology has been revolutionized but the old rules continue to remain in force. Aerial filming needs clearances from the ministry of civil aviation, the DGCA, and the defence ministry. One old rule and three governmental agencies make for an immense tangle of red tape. Hollywood film-makers give India the go-by and go to Thailand, Malaysia, and Sri Lanka. India loses out on a vast stream of revenue.

The greatest challenge was to get permission from the defence ministry. The ministry said it would depute an IAF officer to accompany the filming crew on the flight and asked for the names of the crew who would fly that day, and the details of the locales they would overfly. A crew member whose name is once given cannot be replaced.

Approvals and permissions took six months. The filming was to take place over a period of six to seven days. The helicopter's flight path and filming locations were submitted to the ATC and the defence ministry.

The team had two photographers and a director, and the helicopters were fitted with nose-mounted cameras. All plans had been finalized and the final day arrived. Unfortunately, a UK-based cameraman who was to join the shoot on the designated day fell ill and could not join. We informed the defence authorities and asked them to allow us to bring on board a replacement. They however adhered rigidly to the rule-book and refused to allow a replacement. The Discovery team of historians, archaeologists, scriptwriters, and series directors had been camping in India for over a month. The channel had invested thousands of dollars in extensive research, filming, ground photography, people, and resources. Aerial filming was only one part of a mammoth exercise.

As the defence ministry remained unyielding there could be no filming on the scheduled day, for which preparations had been made over six months: all that effort went in vain. The defence authorities had lost track of the simple fact that what mattered was aerial photography and not who was in the helicopter. They said rules are rules and we said *the law is an ass*.

A few months later, I shared the dais at a function with Ramakrishna Hegde, former chief minister of Karnataka who was then union commerce

minister. I referred to the Discovery channel aerial filming incident and
said that the bureaucracy should stop riding on our backs. It was choking
initiative everywhere and throwing a spanner in all the works: be it a farmer
seeking a record of his tilling rights or a city dweller awaiting a relative's
death certificate; whether someone wanted a building plan approved or a
new venture licensed. I said the bureaucracy had inordinately increased
procedures and the length of red tape, and this in turn had led to greater
corruption. It was killing us.

Hegde listened to my comments with great indulgence. When his turn
came, he narrated his own experience of bureaucracy. A much-visited
temple had provided space and a rack for devotees to remove their shoes
before entering the temple. It had appointed an usher to receive the shoes,
hand out tokens, and collect a fee for each pair. A foreigner who knew that
Indian devotees took off their footwear before entering a temple found it
convenient to leave his shoes behind in his car. He had to pass the usher's
area to enter the temple. When he passed, the usher stopped him and asked
him to deposit his shoes in the designated area. The foreigner pointed to his
feet and said he had no shoes on. The man at the shoe-rack pointed to the
board put up by the temple administration that said, 'Remove shoes here!'
The temple usher told the foreigner that he had to remove and keep his
shoes in the specific storage area and not in the car.

Hegde said this was how bureaucrats interpreted rules. We would have
to live with that till we changed the rules, he said, to loud applause and
laughter.

Our contacts in the defence ministry helped us to get fresh clearances for
the filming. The series went on to become popular and re-runs continue to
be aired. Discovery paid us handsomely and gave us credits.

Closely following the Discovery project, we got many aerial photography
assignments, including one with National Geographic for their series *Ten
Biospheres of the World*. The channel had identified the Silent Valley in the
Western Ghats as an important and critical biosphere.

I cherished the calls I received. A call meant a new customer; a new insight
into human nature. One day a girl called Kaavya rang me. She was 21 or
22; no longer a teen, not yet a woman. She was very soft-spoken, very
gentle, and spoke haltingly. She had seen a Deccan advertisement and she
wanted to know how much a helicopter ride would cost. I said the cost
would depend on flight duration and waiting time. I said a three-hour trip
might cost anywhere between rupees one lakh and one and a half lakhs. She
seemed disappointed but she recovered her poise and asked if it was possible

to hire the helicopter just for half an hour in Coorg. I said we couldn't do that because the helicopter had to be blocked for the whole day. Besides, somebody would have to pay for the helicopter to fly to Coorg and back.

There was something about this young girl—woman; something puzzling. She did not disclose the reason why she wanted the helicopter. I asked some probing questions. Was she a student? Did she work somewhere? Why did she need a helicopter? How did she plan to pay for it? She told me her story. She wanted to surprise her father on his sixtieth birthday. She had been putting away her pocket money and cash presents she had received from visiting relatives and parents since she was a child. I, however, wondered how she had known all along that she wanted to give her father a helicopter ride.

They lived in Madikeri in Coorg. When she was six or seven, one evening her father returned home in a state of great excitement and exclaimed, 'Guess what everybody! I came home in a helicopter!' He had run into chief minister Gundu Rao at Kushalanagar and Rao had given her father a ride in his official helicopter. Her father and Gundu Rao were school chums.

Her father was absolutely thrilled, but once the excitement faded, he let out a sigh. That might be the only helicopter ride he would ever get to experience. 'I don't think I'll live to experience this again,' he had said. The words stuck indelibly in Kaavya's memory. She told herself she would save money to treat her father to a second helicopter ride.

He was close to his sixtieth birthday. She wanted to take him for a helicopter ride as a birthday gift. She seemed disappointed at the price but remained self-possessed and determined. She, said, calmly, 'I'll save money for another year and get back to you.'

It was only the second time I had experienced such a depth of feeling and intensity. This girl wanted to fly to Madikeri, give her father a surprise, pick him up from there, and bring him to Bengaluru. This was a business decision that pulled at the heart-strings. It was the previous Nikaah-kind of situation. I took a decision instantly. I told the young lady how much it costs per hour and how much time it takes to fly to Madikeri and back. I said, 'You decide your itinerary. Whether you give your father a joy ride or fly him down to Bengaluru, I will give you a 50 per cent discount on the actual fare.' She thanked me and hung up.

David Hooks, the well known Australian cricket commentator, called us one day to discuss an India–Australia cricket match. His fellow commentator was the cricketing master, Sunil Gavaskar. David said he wanted to hire a helicopter to show live images of the match on TV.

He said they would equip the helicopter for aerial filming. They would be inter-leaving the vision fields of the cameras on ground and on the helicopter. I agreed to loan them the helicopter and told him our charges. David Hooks got back soon. The principle organizers had said they could not afford to pay such high charges but were willing to give credits if we lowered the fee.

Sunil Gavaskar called to give us a clearer picture. He said, 'Captain, every time the camera focuses on your helicopter, we will say thanks to Deccan Aviation.' That would be at least a couple of crores of rupees worth of advertisement expenditure. I agreed, but insisted that they pay at least a third of the quoted amount, and also asked for camera to focus on the helicopter once every few minutes. The deal was settled.

On the day of the match, Steve Waugh and David Hooks got on board, I joined them in the passenger cabin, and Jayanth was at the controls. People in drawing rooms across the country watched the match covered by ground cameras. They had frequent bird's eye views of the stadium and the green vistas of Bengaluru. When these images appeared I could hear the emphatic voice of Gavaskar say, 'And these spectacular images from the sky are thanks to Deccan Aviation!' Then the helicopter loomed into sight with the Deccan logo clearly visible. The match organizers used the Deccan helicopter for about an hour and a half each day for three days. This exposure gave Deccan international visibility.

Sitaram Kesri, then Congress president, was on television one day making a statement to the media. He said he was not going to take any more nonsense from Deve Gowda, the prime minister. Congress with the largest contingent of 166 MPs was propping up, Gowda, who had 16 MPs, with outside support.

Sitaram Kesri's utterances were an indication that the government would be brought down. There would be an election soon, and I saw there would be need for helicopters, excellent campaign vehicles.

Our helicopter logged 25 hours of flying a month. With another helicopter, and intensive daily use, we could do six months' worth of business in one month. I reached for my mobile phone like a cowboy who goes for his gun in westerns. I left a voice message for Doug who was holidaying in a yacht, off the coast of Malaysia, and Doug called me back in less than five minutes, alerted by a paging system. It seemed almost miraculous to be able to reach someone far out at sea in an instant at a time when India was still far removed from the cellphone era.

I told Doug that the government was about to fall; that there would be an election. I had used the first helicopter for 150 hours during the previous poll campaign. I needed one more this time.

Doug called back half an hour later to say that he had a seven-seater Long Ranger available. I accepted it and planned to travel to Singapore with

Sam and our chief engineer Vidya Babu immediately, inspect the helicopter, sign the lease, and fly it home. It had taken me three years to get my first helicopter; it took me a mere three minutes to get my second. It showed me how important it is to build relationships.

At noon the following day, Sitaram Kesri was on television again. Congress had decided to withdraw support to Deve Gowda. TV channels flashed the news and I was tempted to think that Sitaram Kesri had taken his cue from me!

Three or four days before Christmas, we flew to Singapore. Doug received us and took us to the helicopter. It looked good. Doug introduced us to Mike McCormack, the engineer who would have the helicopter fixed and ready for air-worthiness certification. Vidya Babu would inspect the helicopter and Sam would test fly it. The helicopter was owned by a Japanese company operating in Singapore and had an American registration on which it would be flown to India.

I watched Mike at work, all on his own. He gave the helicopter a thorough cleaning, gathered wastes, carrying them on his shoulders, walked a hundred yards to dispose them of. He got back and did serious business with an FAA inspector.

The latter wanted Mike to complete the technical formalities in accordance with the regulations. Mike went about them unmindful of us with a focus that could only be termed religious. Viewed from this light, Deccan had a hierarchical work structure. It functioned like the mechanic shop I had in Hassan, in which the chief mechanic sat on a stool and shouted instructions while the 'grease monkeys' went about the chores. The Deccan engineer had a support team of ten people but he never got his hands dirty.

Mike, like his kind in the West, combined all roles in one: it was he who worked on the aircraft, he who checked off, cleaned up, and got the FAA auditor to initiate the final signoff. Indian work ethics encourage several people to hang around the engineer, with the engineer preferring to sit in his office; he is the 'sahib'.

Mike was a very experienced engineer. Babu recognized him as the boss in his previous company. Seeing Mike, I thought I must bring in his work ethics and the concept of metrics to our workplace.

Doug invited us home to dinner. We met his wife, Helen, a very gracious Chinese lady. As I have mentioned, Singapore has a large expatriate population, mainly of British and Dutch nationals, and there is also a large ethnic Indian population. The Chinese are in a majority (78 per cent), followed by ethnic Malays, besides the mixed Malay—Chinese, called the Peranakan Chinese migrations, began in the fifteenth century and gathered momentum in the nineteenth and twentieth centuries.

Now that we had a new helicopter we would have to transport it. Doug suggested that we hire professional pilots, who took a break from routine work for some adventurous cross-country flying, to India.

Elections were round the corner and we couldn't afford to lose time. Doug's mention of freelance pilots who flew for fun set me thinking about flying the helicopter and having some adventure ourselves. It would be faster, cheaper, and more exciting. Our plan was to take off from Singapore and fly overland via Malaysia to Thailand; cut across northern Thai territory and enter Myanmar; fly over the Arakan mountain range and land in Bangladesh; negotiate the arc from Chittagong via Dhaka to Kolkata, and finally hit the Kolkata–Bhubaneshwar–Vizag–Tirupati trail, heading for Bengaluru.

All we needed, to fly on our own, were clearances from the ministries of civil aviation and defence of countries on our flight path. On the helicopter side, we had submitted documents to be sent to the US for the export certificate of air-worthiness. The Singapore FAA cleared the helicopter on 22 December but, as Doug realized, everything in the US closed by 22 December. Ahead of Christmas, offices would remain closed till the first week of January, but we were stuck till New Year's Day!

On one occasion, Doug introduced me to a bunch of freelancing pilots. The conversation veered to our helicopter ferry plan. One of the pilots, someone like the old seafarers that hung around eighteenth century English colonial clubs, told us his story of Myanmar.

He said when he flew over Myanmar, his helicopter was targeted for attack by armed gangs, perhaps Myanmarese rebels waging a guerilla insurgency campaign against the Myanmar military junta on the Thai–Myanmar border, or perhaps it was the drug mafia operating in the nearby Golden Triangle. There was an avalanche of machine gun fire targeting his aircraft. The pilot was fortunate. He playfully warned us to be very careful: 'You fly Myanmar, fellows and you run the risk of being shot through your backside.'

We were unruffled. Sam is a decorated war veteran and I have seen action on the battlefield, but we didn't want to take any chances. We decided to fly a bit higher, above the usual 1000 ft above ground that helicopters fly, to keep beyond the range of small arms fire. We did our homework on rebel and mafia hideouts, not wishing them to take potshots at us.

Doug's networking helped and we were fortunate to have the export air-worthiness certificate cleared on 30 December. We left Singapore the following day. Babu flew back on a regular airline. Sam asked me to pack light so that we could carry more fuel and fly longer hours. I had bought a Panasonic video camera to capture sights on the way.

Sam and I went to the FAA, the US aviation regulator. Sam showed them his licence. We were anxious that the agency might raise objections because Sam had never flown an American registered aircraft and he did not have a US flying licence. We submitted our papers and waited. The FAA officer came up to Sam, asked him a few questions, stamped his licence, and handed it over. This lack of bureaucracy just astonished us!

We planned to take off at seven in the morning on the New Year eve. We had our backpacks and my camera ready. Sam had test flown the helicopter, checked everything, and signed the log-books. Doug briefed Sam on the flying time. That was done quickly. Sam started the rotors, and just then Doug called me a side and said, 'Gopi, you have not signed the lease agreement.'

We had spent ten days, Doug had spent a lot of money and done everything necessary to fly the helicopter out of Singapore, and now suddenly I realized that we had not signed the lease agreement!

This was evidence, if evidence was needed, that we trusted each other implicitly. I looked at the lease agreement. But the rentals were much higher than for the first helicopter. I said, 'Doug, the lease rentals are very high.' Doug was furious. His hands clutched at the lease agreement and were trembling. He looked at me fiercely, and snarled: 'Sign the f****** thing!'

A moment's stunned silence followed. 'You can't now get into an argument about the lease rental,' he said. Yes, that was true. I couldn't let Doug down, but at the same time I could not sign something that was ridiculously high. Also, as we had expended enormous physical and emotional effort in charting our business plans, pulling back now was not an option for either of us.

I told Doug, 'We should have sorted this out five days ago. But you've trusted me and I've trusted you. The British have been fair people. What I'm saying is simply this. I think the lease rentals are very high. If you charge me higher than the market price then you are actually shooting yourself in the foot. We are a start-up company. It's in your interest to keep me flying. This is only the second helicopter. I will lease a third, a fourth, a fifth ... If I go bankrupt because of a lease rental which is uneconomical then you will be responsible. You have to bring it down.'

I left it to his sense of judgment and fairness. We were running out of time. Sam, whose first flight it was across different countries, kept waving to me that a delay might cause us to miss our landing slot at Kuala Lumpur airport. We also ran the risk of losing entry slots to the other countries en route.

Doug returned with a revised document. I examined it and could hardly conceal my joy: the offer was better than that which might have suggested.

We signed the papers and Doug put them away in his briefcase. Doug joined Sam as co-pilot. The plan was for Doug to accompany us on two legs of the journey to help Sam familiarize himself with the local flying conditions. He hopped on to the flight deck into the rear seat.

Sam was initially a little uncomfortable flying in foreign skies. He was not conversant with handling the different ATCs (Air Traffic Controls), experienced difficulty in decoding the various accents. Doug was familiar with the different protocols and procedures, and he helped.

Our first halt was at Kuala Lumpur. Malaysia is a country of immense scenic beauty, but industrialization and development have taken a toll. Topsoil denudation and loss of forest cover are visible from the sky. Malaysia, Indonesia, and Brazil are home to the largest rain forests and serve as the lungs of the world. Indonesia had once preserved its rain forests better in its Sarawak and Borneo regions, but surveys have shown that these too are being denuded at an alarming rate. In South America however, and to a certain extent in Malaysia, the better part of the forest covers have been transformed into palm-oil plantations, rubber plantations, and mining and quarrying sites. My heart bled when I saw the price Malaysia has paid to be recognized as an Asian Tiger.

We approached the extremely busy Kuala Lumpur International Airport. Doug asked Sam to stay clear of marked areas which were defence zones. Doug sounded a little impatient but Sam is a fast learner and he soon got grip with things. We landed at KL and spent 20 minutes there: grabbed a coffee, refuelled, got back to the chopper, and took off to meet slot timings at various airports along the way.

We flew northwards towards Thailand, a breathtakingly beautiful country. We landed in Phuket at 5.30 p.m. and were dot on time. We planned to spend the night in Phuket. We found ourselves in an ocean of Caucasians: thousands of them thronged—all New Year revellers. They jostled with one another and did not mind where they went. They hungered for the sun and the pleasures and gratifications of Thailand.

Though Thailand is known as the Sin Capital of the East, one cannot help but fall in love with the land and its people: the beaches and mountains are enchanting and, the people are friendly and disarmingly affectionate.

Phuket airport was an ocean of tourists who shared a collective, impatient longing to soak in the sun and the waves on white sandy beaches, and indulge in the fiery gastronomics of Thai food. There were Europeans, Americans, and Asians waiting for tour operators to collect them. In Thailand, backpackers can holiday at $5 a day. I saw young couples, honeymooners from the subcontinent; families with children and old people in travel groups. The buzz was palpable. Thailand's controversial carnal offerings may be anathema to India's cultural milieu, but I couldn't help thinking about what could click for India, with so much to offer, to enable it become a tourist haven.

Doug called all the hotels in Phuket. He must have made hundreds of calls between 5.30 p.m. when we landed and 8.00 p.m. Hotels were full choc-a-bloc with year-end visitors—with not an inch of space to spare. I spotted poster advertisements of beach resorts on islands that seemed to form an emerald necklace. I found the islands irresistible and asked Sam if we could just take off and land on one of them and spend the night, as we did not seem to be finding a place at which to stay anywhere. Sam said the sun was setting and he needed landing coordinates for the islands and clearances.

We had resigned ourselves to spending the night at the airport when Doug found two rooms for the three of us at 8.30 p.m. Sam and I were scrounging every rupee so we decided to share a room, Doug taking the other. It was 10.00 p.m. by the time we reached the hotel. We were exhausted from the exertion and excitement of our first 'solo' cross-country flight. We needed to set off early the next day to ensure we did not miss the time-line for Myanmar, where the military government was extremely strict. Any deviation from schedule could mean spending an extra four to five days in Thailand.

Sam was a severe guy when it came to discipline. He ordered me to bed rightaway, adding that he must get a good night's sleep with a long day at the controls tomorrow. Having had his say, he headed for a cool shower.

An interesting thing happened after Sam got into the shower. I received a call from the reception. A lady said, 'Capt. Gopinath, are you comfortable?' I replied, 'Yes.' She asked if I needed a massage in the room. I said, 'Yes.' Then she asked if I needed a normal massage or a sandwich massage. I was flummoxed. She explained that sandwich massage is one in which two girls massage one man. I asked for a normal massage but two girls. I thought Sam could do with a massage too.

Sam was a severe, God-fearing puritan. I knew he would not want even a harmless, ordinary massage. I decided to enjoy a bit of harmless fun at Sam's expense. As soon as he got out of the shower, I rushed inside and left him to welcome the girls.

When I was in the bath, I heard the doorbell ring. Sam had no idea what I had done. I left the bathroom door a little ajar so I could hear him. He opened the door. The two girls walked in and closed the door behind them. Sam was taken aback. The girls spoke broken English. They repeated the word 'massage', 'massage'. Sam said he didn't ask for it. The girls insisted he had. Sam has this peculiar stock expression. When he is surprised, Sam's eyes nearly pop out of their sockets. He came charging towards the bathroom. I shut the door when I heard him coming. He knocked and ordered, 'Gopi, open up.' I opened the door a slit and peered out. Sam said, 'Did you ask for two girls for a massage?' I said 'Yeah, I thought we were tired and had had a long day. It would be good to have a good massage, otherwise, it would be like going to Scotland and not having whiskey.' He said, 'You can have a massage, I will not. On second thoughts, I will not let you have one either, because you'll not get up early and I can't sleep while you are having a massage. So I'm sending them back.' Without waiting for me to answer, he turned them back and closed the door. We had a good night's sleep.

We were at the airfield at 5.30 a.m. Doug said he would leave us at the end of the next leg of journey. By now Sam was comfortable handling the controls and the ATC. Before the Myanmar crossing we landed at Surat Thani airstrip in Thailand for refuelling and to grab a meal. Doug gave us a big hug and bade us farewell. We took off. Thence commenced our greatest adventure. Thenceforward, I became Sam's co-pilot. One of my duties as co-pilot was to read his map for him.

I was in the cockpit trying to make sense of completely unfamiliar territory and remembered the lines of Robert Frost's poem 'The Road Not Taken';

> I shall be telling this with a sigh
> Somewhere ages and ages hence:
> Two roads diverged in a wood, and I—
> I took the one less travelled by,
> And that has made all the difference.

We had another four days of travel and nearly 5,000 kms to cover. Sam focused on flying. I was like a little child savouring every new distraction that came my way. We flew over the Andaman Sea and then cut across the narrow strip to East on the South China Sea and flew straight North towards Myanmar. The sea was emerald blue; the beaches a soft white; the skies pure azure, and the green of the flora a deeply refreshing tint. The scene was of such exquisite beauty that 'to me it did seem apparelled in celestial light, the glory and the freshness of a dream'.

I kept urging Sam to descend slightly so that we could take a closer look at a lovely alcove or lagoon or bay or island. These design elements of sea and land appeared out of nowhere. Some of them looked like bizarre mishapen promontories ringed by fluorescent beaches, placed there for some strange creature to perch upon. They looked like a desolate retreat and I wished I were Robinson Crusoe shipwrecked on one of them. Along some beaches, men and women were sprawled naked in the sun. I frequently asked Sam for little detours and he, though severe of expression, never failed to oblige. We refuelled again at Hua Hin and like rally pilots raced towards the Thai border town by dusk and landed at Phitsanulok, South of Chiang Mai near the Myanmarese border.

We took off at the crack of dawn and entered Myanmarese airspace. As we flew over thick jungles, we kept higher altitude beyond reach of rebels' small arms fire. We did not want to take any chances with Myanmar and we were a touch nervous because aircraft had occasionally been turned back. Under military rule, Myanmar was paranoid of foreigners and very tightly controlled its airspace. There was very little civil aviation in the country. Even a minor problem or mess-up would be sufficient excuse for them to turn us back. When we were about 50 km from Myanmarese airspace, Sam flashed our YA number and radio ID. After a minute's pause someone at the other end asked Sam to repeat the YA number. Those moments, lasting a minute or two, were the longest I have experienced.

Sam received the clearance and gave the thumbs up sign. We were in Myanmar. Myanmar is politically, socially, and geographically a remote territory. We saw the thickest forest cover over Myanmar, which was at least a good thing for ecology. Spreading like an enormous umbrella, the forest glades prevented the sunlight from penetrating to the forest floor. One could imagine the dark, vegetated, musty, damp, and marshy undergrowth beneath. Large parts of Myanmar were like this. There were paddy-fields in the river valleys. The Irrawaddy is Myanmar's most famous river. According to Hindu mythology, Irrawaddy is the consort of the celestial elephant Airawatha.

When we saw the wilderness and inaccessibility of Myanmar, Sam and I felt we should have brought our engineer Babu with us. As he was our only engineer and had to attend to another aircraft quickly he had flown back directly from Singapore. Sam and I experienced a fleeting moment of fear: what if we have a technical glitch and were forced to land in this utter desolation? No one would know where to look for us. All the accounts I had read and heard suggested that Myanmar remained distant and sequestered from modern society.

Myanmar was, and because of its self-enforced insularity, perhaps still is, a country from another time, another world. It was beautiful, natural, untouched by modern technology. It lived in the past and far-flung settlements were perhaps 200 years behind the modern era. Its changelessness had a mystical aspect. Thinking of Myanmar as congealed history made me acutely aware of the loss of innocence. At the same time, I felt a longing to recover the loss of the primordial in me—in us. I also, however, imagined how difficult, dangerous, and life-threatening a trek it would be from any of these locations. One would have to walk for days in the marshy bogs, forests, and mountains before reaching civilization. I was struck by the dismal odds of being discovered and rescued if we got marooned. I made light of the fear and turned to Sam and said, 'If one is cast away in these jungles, one hopes to have someone like Brooke Shields for a companion, or a female pilot at least, so that we could spend the rest of our lives in the style of Tom Hanks, if it came to that!' Sam agreed. He was referring to the passenger and not the pilot this time. That somewhat lightened the moment for us.

We stopped to refuel well before sunset. As a rule we refuelled well before sunset or we would lose ourselves in the dark. As we approached Yangon, I could spot the golden domes of the pagodas. Yangon is known for its world famous Buddhist monasteries. Sam kept an eye for the airfield; I took pictures. My general knowledge often enabled me to identify which city it was that we were approaching or flying over, just by spotting some famous landmark or monument. I spotted the Shwe Dagon, the famous 2,500-year-old pagoda in the centre of the city. Sam had got his coordinates right. We landed at Rangoon for the last refuelling point in Myanmar.

I wished we could have spent a day or two in Myanmar. Along with Nepal, Myanmar too was part of the British Indian Empire. We share many common elements in our culture. I would have enjoyed exploring historic Yangon. We spent the night in a hotel. The food was much like ours. They served us rice and spicy curries. The pressure of flying ten to twelve hours a day, three days in a row, was telling on Sam. He was tired. He had to fly ten hours the next day. He insisted he was fine. He always wanted us to sleep on time and we did.

The next morning we were left with ten minutes at the airport before starting out. Myanmar is renowned for its precious stones, so I sneaked down and picked up some travel memorabilia for my wife and for Sam. I did not even ask how much they cost. Sam was livid with rage. He said we did not have time for shopping. As always, I convinced him that it was ten minutes well spent, and we took off on time.

As we took off from Yangon, the Irrawaddy valley suddenly opened out a vista before us. The celestial river shimmered in the horizon like an iridescent ribbon of suffused white light. After an hour of flying, we flew over the Arakan Yoma mountain ranges. My mind went back to the days at the IMA where I had studied the military campaign in Myanmar. Initially the British in Myanmar were relentlessly pushed towards the Indian borders by the advancing Japanese troops. The soldiers had to negotiate the thick impenetrable jungles of the Arakan mountains. The treacherous jungles claimed thousands of Indian, British and Japanese troops in addition to those who died fighting. The Japanese had surrounded the cities of Kohima and Imphal. I remembered that the Japanese had crossed these mountains to enter India during the Second World War and cut off the Myanmar–China road which was used to carry supplies. That is when the famous airlift of supplies over the Himalayas, crossing the 'hump' into China, one of the greatest and the longest-lasting airlifts in history, took place. The airlift kept China provisioned and prevented the diabolical plans of the Japanese to starve China to death. However, by the time the airlifts commenced, hundreds of thousands had already died of starvation. The 14th division of the Indian Army fought a campaign led by British General William Slim that drove the Japanese back from the current Indian border regions of Imphal and Kohima. The British prevailed and regained Myanmar. I thought aloud, addressing Sam as we overflew the ranges. 'Sam, I don't think anybody has set foot on these mountains in the six decades that have elapsed since the Second World War barring the local inhabitants!'

Reaching the Myanmarese border before dusk, we broke journey for the night at the last Myanmarese airfield in the historic town of Sittwe, or Akyab as it was known during the war. Myanmar and India shared cultural and culinary ties when they were part of that very British Empire. The affinity was greater at this border town and I longed for food cooked in the Indian style. We were fortunate to find an old-time gardener who seemed to emerge from Myanmar's British past who was familiar with our cuisine. We persuaded him to make us a simple meal of dal, chawal (lentil soup and rice) and spicy fish curry. The food was an excellent counterpoint to the rum I drank with the meal. Sam did not drink because he had to fly the following morning. As we slipped into slumber that night, we smelt the salty air of the Bay of Bengal which roared below the promontory of Akyab and a mélange of images of the sea, beaches, sand, and jungles dissolved into one another, transporting us to a dreamworld that seemed very real.

It was six in the morning by the time the helicopter was aloft. We headed for Bangladesh and drew up near Chittagong, landing there to refuel. Sam and I had been in Bangladesh three decades earlier during the war of liberation. Sam was in the Chittagong region, bordering Myanmar and I was in Dinajpur and Rangpur to the west, bordering India. We reminisced about those days. After a few more hops we reached Dhaka by the evening. In Bangladesh the people had hitherto been very helpful, warmly welcoming us, serving us food, treating us with respect, and engaging us in friendly banter. They took care of immigration formalities and wished us well when we took off.

Things were different when we landed at Dhaka airport this time. As soon as we landed, our aircraft was surrounded by what looked like a platoon of military and paramilitary armed soldiers. A jeep with blaring sirens raced towards us, flashing its emergency beacon lights and as if a hijacked aircraft was being cordoned off. When we disembarked, security personnel whisked us away to an isolated room for questioning. Sam and I looked at our 'interrogator' defiantly. I asked him, 'Are you a Major in the Bangladesh Army?' He replied 'Yes.' I said, 'Look, I am Capt. Gopi and this is Col. Sam, from the Indian Army. We were here during the Liberation War. We fought the Pakistan Army to help liberate Bangladesh. We have very fond memories of this great nation. So what is this fuss all about? Why are you treating us like criminals?'

Impressed by my defiant tone and what I had to say, the major was a changed man. He smartly saluted us and said apologetically, 'Sorry, sir. We never realized it.'

The major became friendly and began chatting with us. He took us to the cafeteria, bought us tea, saw to all our documentation. He told us that his father had fought the 1971 war. We eventually parted on very friendly terms.

There was one thing I noticed at Dhaka airport. Dozens of people sat around in the lounge areas, watching television. As with some Indian airports of the past, there were more government employees than passengers in the terminal, gossiping and whiling their time away, reading newspapers, watching television, and generally having a good time. Airline passengers were few and far between. Government servants lazed in the air-conditioned terminals. It was hot out there on the tarmac, and airport interiors provided the most luxurious way of escaping the scorching sun.

Bangladesh is an extremely fertile country; its people very talented. They have wonderful arts and crafts. It is a country known for its singers, poets, and writers. In physical features, the Bangladeshi most closely resembles his Indian counterpart in south and east India. It is difficult to tell him apart from people from those parts of India. I felt sad that the country, often rocked by violent upheavals, nurtured policies that did not allow for creativity, freedom of thought and speech. They did not seem to allow the creation of wealth, nor the growth of conditions conducive to enterprise.

Bangladesh is a country I knew as a young man and had played a bit role in its creation; as had Sam. This is where our adult life began. I gazed intently at the great expanse of poverty and saw excellent potential being wasted.

Our journey from Singapore had been along an inverted arc trajectory. As we moved north from the prosperous curve of Singapore–Malaysia–Thailand, the thriving economies and enlightened government policies yielded to tightly controlled bureaucracies and dictatorships that had stifled economic initiative from within.

We were brimming with excitement when we took off from Dhaka and headed towards India. We flew into Kolkata in the late afternoon, our joy unfettered as we had arrived at home turf. We heaved a sigh of triumphant relief, aware that should we face any technical glitch, help was just a phone-call away.

We had hoped to fly out of Kolkata to Bhubaneshwar that evening but were delayed by Kolkata customs. When we were eventually cleared for take-off, it was too late. Helicopters everywhere are given a separate flight corridor but India has antiquated rules that obliges helicopters follow the same tedious runway procedures and paperwork as fixed-wing aircraft. This delays both helicopters and aeroplanes. If a helicopter is landing or taking off an aircraft is made to wait, and vice-versa. Helicopters have limited fuel capacity. Once the engines are on and the rotors are running, if a helicopter is made to wait, its fuel is quickly depleted. If a helicopter that is capable of a two-hour flight is made to wait with its engines on, by the time it is cleared for take-off, it has used up much of its fuel and is not in a position to undertake a point-to-point flight. Successive DGCAs and airport authority officials who work in coordination have acknowledged this but have not implemented the necessary ameliorative measures. Also, as helicopters do not fly after dusk, if permission is not granted in time, it has to spend the night on ground in the hangar.

We were desperate to fly to Bhubaneshwar, but by the time we received clearance, Sam looked at his watch and made a quick calculation that we would not be able to reach there before sunset so he switched off the rotors and we stayed the night at the airport.

We took off at six in the morning and, crossing the Hooghly and the Gangetic delta, headed for Bhubaneshwar airport. It is impossible to miss the city because of the eye-catching cluster of the Lingaraj temple. At the risk of sounding repetitive, you can't help becoming ecstatic each time you view the magnificent temples all over India. Like an excited schoolboy, I kept prodding Sam to look at this temple or that waterfall. He sometimes chided me. 'Gopi,' he would say, 'enough of gazing at temples. Now focus on the map.' As we refuelled in Bhubaneshwar, Sam and I were determined to reach Bengaluru before sunset. We still had to touch down at Vizag, Vijayawada, and Tirupati to refuel and therefore had to keep a close eye on our watch. A few minutes after we took off from Bhubaneshwar we flew past the famous Chilka Lake. When we lifted off from Tirupati, on our last leg, we still had a little time. I asked Sam to do one perambulation around the sacred shrine of Balaji to pay obeisance. Sam glanced at his watch and headed straight for the seven sacred hills on which Lord Venkateshwara is perched. Then, after an aerial salutation to the deity we set course for Bengaluru which was now only an hour and a half away.

The sun was dipping in the west when Sam sighted the Jakkur airfield and informed the ATC. As we neared the helipad, I could see people next to our hangar waiting for and waving at us. We were overwhelmed by the joyous homecoming. Bhargavi, Sam's wife Maya, Jayanth and Ponnu, and Vidya Babu were there to receive us with cheers, flowers, and hugs. The exhilaration of being home more than compensated the five-day test of endurance and adventure.

My father at my school in Gorur

My (7th from left front row) passing out parade at the IMA on 12 June 1971

My wedding day

At my silkworm-rearing house with my brother Sampath

When my bullock-cart was my most trusted transport before my chopper!

Unique modes of advertising—anything to sell!

My silkworms and my family shared this house for many years

My first car—the Dodge Kingsway 1955—which the village boys prophetically
called the 'aeroplane car'!

In my political avatar—serving dinner to Atal Bihari Vajpayee at my house in Hassan

With Henry Mintzberg, the maverick management thinker

When there was time, it was family time—with Pallavi, Bhargavi and Krithika

The helicopter in my farm—from bullock-cart to the helicopter

With David Rockefeller and Capt. Valsaraj

John Gray, author of *Men are from Mars, Women are from Venus*, frequently used our helicopters visiting temples and holy shrines. Seen here with Swami Kaleshwar

With Capt. Samuel and my angel investor S.M. Ladhani

With my buddies Capt. Sam and Vishnu

With Warwick Brady and Mohan Kumar, the man who revolutionized and innovated aviation financing

Long queues for Air Deccan tickets

IF IT'S ON THE MAP,
WE'LL GET YOU THERE.

For exciting heli-tourism packages across India call any of the numbers given below.

DECCAN AVIATION
Your limousine in the sky

Corporate Office: Deccan Aviation Ltd., Jakkur Aerodrome, Bangalore - 560 064. Tel: 080-28567378/9. New Delhi: 011-32909542.
Mumbai: 022-26611601/2. Katra: 01991-234378/9. email: marketing@deccanair.com or raghuram@deccanair.com
Visit us at www.deccanair.com

One of my favourite advertisements from the marketing campaign
of Deccan Aviation

Air Deccan not only broke the cost barrier but the caste and
class barrier to flying

Snow-capped mountains at Dharamsala

I always made it a point to speak to the passengers

The Dalai Lama with Capt. Jayanth Poovaiah

The Air Deccan mascot—R.K. Laxman's the 'Common Man'

Air Deccan overtakes Indian Airlines!

A new revolution with Deccan 360

9

When we build, let us think that we build for ever.
—John Ruskin

Elections, Evangelism, Helicopters

The general elections had been announced. Indian elections were, and continue to be, a spectacle of colour and sound; of pomp, pageantry, and theatrics. Thousands of political hopefuls pit their fortunes. The competition today is fiercer than before with astronomical sums of money being spent by the parties and candidates. The hustle brings to mind the words of the bard of Avon: they are like the '[t]ale told by an idiot, full of sound and fury signifying nothing.'

Helicopters add a touch of drama to electoral grandeur, and serve as crowd-pullers. They are also practical, permitting politicians to change their schedules depending on the circumstances.

The helicopter company has to be adaptable and ready to accommodate new landing coordinates, move engineering and logistics support, and review security on the ground. It must never lose sight of the thumb-rule of the army: a helicopter service is only as good as its logistics' support.

Our pilots were equipped with Iridium satellite phones which allowed them to get in touch with the ATC and the company bases from anywhere at any time. The international phone service was offered by a consortium of companies that had invested billions of dollars in the technology and low earth-orbit satellites they had launched. Modern cellular mobile technology has made these phones unviable and now they are used only by the US defence forces.

People have been curious about how I managed to make politicians pay. Politicians consider the service provider's favour as an instrument of future exchange: licence, contracts, waivers. Large corporates that own helicopters lend them to politicians for use, free of cost, as indemnity for later use. Sometimes it could simply be a goodwill gesture.

It was the other way round with us. Helicopters are our bread and butter, and we had no other business to sustain us. We had already a reputation for reliable, prompt, and timely service, and political parties were aware that we did not offer our service free. They were apprehensive that they might not be able to hire our helicopter at a later date even if they paid for it because someone else would already have booked it. They fell over each other to pay in advance and by cheque. Nobody asked for a free ride.

We made good money during the elections, charging a higher rate because of the higher wear and tear and greater demand than supply. However, having paid in advance, no politician would tolerate a goof-up, even a minor one. We therefore stretched ourselves , working to our utmost capacity . Even so, notwithstanding the meticulous care we took,we could not completely escape the occasional glitch.

Once we had an incident with a UP-based politician, a former MP. He hired our helicopter to attend a string of election rallies, promising the pilot he would pay after landing. He failed to do so, flying from venue to venue, always surrounded by a posse of fully armed private security guards.

After one rally, when he was seated in the helicopter and the pilot asked for payment. The politician pulled out a gun and stuck it to his head. The pilot kept his cool and took off. As soon as the helicopter was airborne, and the politician out of earshot, the pilot called me up on the Iridium and described the situation: what was he to do? I asked him to keep going, and called up friends in political parties to check on the man's credentials. They said he was one of the biggest criminals with cases pending against him for murder and extortion; he would never pay and advised me to write off what he owed us. I called my pilot and told him to simply take off as soon as the candidate and his henchmen had got off at the next halt.

The pilot followed my advice. Once he had dropped off the thug-in-the-garb-of-politician and his entourage, he turned on full throttle and flew away. The court later found this very politician guilty of a criminal offence and sent him to jail.

There was another bizarre episode. We were flying former minister and veteran of Indian politics Sharad Yadav in the part of Bihar which has now become Jharkhand. During elections it was a lawless place. The helicopter was about to land when a huge crowd of supporters and onlookers closed in on the touchdown pad. As soon as the helicopter touched ground, someone began to pelt stones at the helicopter. Sharad Yadav and our flight engineer were hurt. The Perspex glass dome was damaged but the rotor blades were intact and still running so the pilot took off and escaped.

Another incident occured in Jharkhand. Our helicopter landed with BJP chief Venkaiah Naidu on board. A throng came forward to welcome Naidu when some miscreants threw a petrol bomb at the helicopter. The missile landed inside the helicopter just as Venkaiah Naidu, the pilot, and the engineer jumped out. The bomb exploded and the helicopter went up in flames. The three were whisked away to safety on motorcycle pillions. We sought the help of Laloo Prasad Yadav, who arranged for reserve police to escort the pilot and the engineer when they visited the accident site the following day to record details for insurance claims. The local police were simply unable to help us.

Deccan quickly became the helicopter service of choice for most politicians. We had a fairly ubiquitous presence. We were seen everywhere during the election jamboree. The money was good, but there was also the thrill and excitement of participating in the most spectacular democratic process in the world.

Many politicians feel uneasy and are intimidated by the presence of a helicopter. They look up to the pilot and obey his instructions. There are, however, others who are enthusiastic, and irritating, back-seat drivers. They know nothing about helicopters but they must issue instructions to the pilot. They are bullies who question the pilot's wisdom at every turn. Pilots are polite but they usually stand their ground. Some get bullied or intimidated, and occasionally come to grief. Jayanth once rebuffed Chagan Bhujbal, former Shiv Sena strongman and deputy chief minister of Maharashtra. Bhujbal was getting pushy and restless because he was desperate to make it to an election rally. On that occasion, it was nearing dusk and the weather was inclement. Bhujbal insisted that Jayanth fly him to his destination and began issuing instructions—a cloud here or a hilltop there. Jayanth humoured him for a while but found that he was unable to land because a detour under the prevalent conditions was impossible. Vexed by the politician's continuous meddling, Jayanth eventually turned to him and said, 'Would you like to take my place? If you can fly the plane, I'll be glad to cede my place to you.' Bhujbal spoke no more.

In the eventual count, pilots are only human, with foibles just like the rest of us. They are equally prone to placing excessive faith in their ability and judgment. Undue pressure exerted by a zealous politician or the urge to return home after a long break—sufficient to lead to an error of judgment which could end up in tragedy.

One of our finest pilots, Capt. G.V. Menon had previously flown in the army extensively, especially in the mountains of Kashmir and Ladakh. He was indefatigable and possessed an inexhaustible store of energy. He was a perfectionist in his line. Given that many of us once belonged to the army, we continued the tradition of socializing at a personal level. We visited one another's homes; got acquainted with the families. Many people in the company said we were too much like a defence organization.

Towards the turn of the 1990s, about eight or nine years ago, many evangelical organizations had begun hiring our helicopters to fly to the remote, tribal belts of Orissa, Andhra Pradesh, and West Bengal. They went there to preach the gospel, flying to a particular location and camping there, and preaching among the tribals and winning new converts to Christianity. The pilot stayed back in a small house for the next seven–eight days. It was apparent, from what my pilots told me, that the tribal populations, who are nature worshippers, were the principle targets of conversion. The attacks on churches in recent times are a reaction to the proselytization that began almost a decade ago. Such attacks create a chasm in society and do nothing to address the real underlying issues. Civic bodies and NGOs must examine the problem at its roots. They must realize that you cannot expect people not to convert when they are positioned in the lowest scale within their social milieu, are poor, and see no opportunities to make a decent living. Those who wish to remedy the situation must work with these communities to provide health-care, sanitation, education, and jobs. They must help these people find their voice and offer them the vehicles for expression in our democratic set-up, rather than focusing on preventing conversions.

One or two such evangelical groups frequently hired our helicopters to travel in the coastal areas in Andhra Pradesh and Orissa. On one occasion, one of these hired three helicopters on a fortnight's assignment. Three pilots, including Capt. Menon, formed part of the crew. Somewhere in the middle of these proselytizing and conversion missions, the organizers invited the then Lok Sabha speaker G.M.C. Balayogi, who belonged to that region, to attend a function which the evangelists had organized and be the chief guest. For the speaker too it made political sense because the meeting would strengthen his political bonds with the people.

Balayogi had a tight schedule. He had to be in Delhi to conduct the Lok Sabha session before ten the following morning. He would have to take an overnight train from Ongole, deep in Andhra Pradesh, to Hyderabad that evening and fly to Delhi the next morning. Balayogi was apprehensive that he might miss the connecting train and declined the invitation.

As the evangelists had three helicopters at their disposal, they requested Balayogi to stay back and attend their function and promised to fly him to Hyderabad in our helicopter in time for his flight to Delhi. The speaker agreed.

The evangelists asked Capt. Menon to fly to Hyderabad. Capt. Menon took off at six in the morning with Balayogi on board. It was a winter morning and there was a thick blanket of fog. Capt. Menon was probably under tremendous pressure from the evangelists and Balayogi to take off that morning, to enable the speaker to catch the Delhi flight in time.

One thought is a cause of perpetual concern to me. We are in the business of flying people and have to do what it takes to ensure that no accidents occur and no lives are lost. This is a fear I forever live with.

I was in Hong Kong at that time, having travelled to Macau on business and was in the middle of a meeting when I was called out: somebody from back home wanted to talk to me urgently. I was informed by our office in Bengaluru that one of our helicopters had been involved in a fatal crash, and that pilot Capt. Menon and speaker Balayogi had both died in the course of it. The news numbed me.

I cut short my trip and rushed back. Capt. Menon who was around forty years old at the time, had twenty years of flying experience. He had done duty in the Siachen glacier, the highest operational altitude anywhere in the world, and this under enemy sniper fire. He had negotiated the harshest weather conditions–rain and sleet, snow and fog. He had brought people and material to safety, flying over very inhospitable terrain among jagged peaks and had handled innumerable emergencies. That something like this could happen to someone of his spirit, caliber, and experience was totally unbelievable.

The report submitted by investigators suggests that he had taken off early, and soon thereafter found himself in the middle of dense fog. Most chartered helicopters around the world are flown visually, and are not equipped with an auto pilot and horizon stabilizer available to fixed-wing aircraft or specially equipped helicopters. When visibility drops in foggy weather, the pilot suffers severe disorientation and cannot easily determine his reference to the ground. In a fog, the pilot flies lower and lower till he can see better, bearing in mind all the while that he has to maintain a safe distance above ground. He can however fly only as low as his maps allow, i.e., above hilltops, high buildings, power lines, and the like. Over normal terrain, this level is 150 to 300 metres.

Capt. Menon had consulted his maps and found paddy-fields in the region over which he was flying at the time. As fate would have it, the paddy-fields had recently been converted into aqua-farms. These changes had not been made to the maps that were in circulation which the pilot had with him. A thick fog had settled over the surface of the aqua-farms. Hoping that the fog had a restricted spread, the pilot flew into it but was sucked into it. There was fog above, in front, and beneath. Eyewitnesses quoted in the report, said the pilot began descending for an emergency landing. This was because he hoped to be landing on a paddy-field which was inconvenient but not life-threatening. If indeed there had been the paddy- fields indicated in the maps, the pilot's decision would have been perfectly sound. That would have been the correct action to take at that moment.

When however he touched ground the pilot must have realized that the helicopter had landed on shallow aqua-pond water. Unaware of what kind of waterbody it was, whether a marsh or pond, the pilot must have panicked and pushed the throttle to the maximum for take-off. The tail rotor thus hit the surface of the water while in full throttle. The helicopter veered out of control and hit a coconut tree on the bund. There were three people on board, Capt. Menon, Balayogi, and his guard, none of whom survived the crash, all dying at the site.

We went to the scene of the accident and brought home the pilot's mortal remains. Capt. Menon was cremated in his home town. It was heart-wrenching. He had a wife and two young children. We took care of the family and gave compensation and insurance money. His wife joined our company. His son is now training to be a pilot in the US with Deccan's financial support and will soon join the company.

Not long afterwards, there was a call from a lady who gave her name as Beulah Bonugli. She was from South Africa and wanted to know whether I offered helicopters for sightseeing and charters. I said we did. She was surprised. 'Oh, I wish I had known. My tour operator never told me such service was available in India. Had I known, we would have hired your helicopter.'

As Beulah Bonugli was speaking, the thought recurred that advertising at reasonable cost remained our biggest challenge. How could you inform people around the world that a helicopter service was available? We often lose business as so many people are still not aware that we exist.

Vijay Amritraj, star of Indian tennis, is now on the board of directors of Deccan. At our first meeting, when I told Vijay that I ran a helicopter service, he was surprised that helicopters were available in India for private use. He told me a story about Bjorn Borg, considered one of the all-time greats of world tennis. Vijay showed Borg around during his visit to India the year before. Borg wanted to see the Taj Mahal. The first thing Borg had asked Vijay was whether they could hire a helicopter for the visit. Vijay made enquiries but the travel agents were not able to help him. They hired a taxi and drove to Agra. The journey took six hours one way and ruined the pleasure of seeing the Taj Mahal. Had Borg had more time, which a helicopter ride would have enabled, he could have seen two other wonders in addition, Fatehpur Sikri and Agra Fort.

I do not let go of a caller simply by providing information on rates and terms of hire. I will not put the receiver down until I know more about the caller. I am keen to know the purpose of their call, what they proposed to do with the helicopter, and itineraries, if any have been planned. I also wish to know how they obtained our contact information. It turned out that

Beulah Bonugli was on a fifteen-day trip to India. On the last leg of her tour, she and her husband had taken a train from Varanasi to Delhi. Somewhere along the way, they dozed off. When they woke up they found all their bags missing, including their passports and credit cards.

At the time of the call, Beulah Bonugli was staying in a Mumbai hotel, waiting for new passports, visas, and credit cards. She had seen the Deccan advertisement in the pages of *Mumbai this Fortnight*. She was in India for two more days. Was there something near Mumbai where they could go sightseeing? I suggested a half-day aerial sightseeing tour of Mumbai and a day trip to the caves of Ajanta and Ellora. I explained to her that the architecture of the painstakingly rock-hewn 2500-year old Buddhist caves would undoubtedly leave her spellbound and that she would not have seen their parallel anywhere in the world. She was happy with the fare and the deal.

We continued to talk. She asked all of a sudden, 'Why don't you have aeroplanes?' I replied, 'I am in the final stages of working out a deal. We should be inducting planes in the course of the next three or four months.' We had ten helicopters by then and were still small in corporate terms but had become the largest helicopter charter company in India. We were becoming well known among a niche clientele.

She asked me what plane I was planning to buy. 'A King Air–B200,' I replied. 'Why a King Air? Why not a Pilatus?' she responded. I had seen a Pilatus at an air show in Australia and knew something about it. The Pilatus was widely acknowledged as a good aircraft with greater seating capacity and longer range than the King Air which had become a standard warhorse for commercial charter operations. Pilatus had great avionics, a pressurized cabin, and flew at an altitude of around 9000 metres. The only cause for reluctance among operators was that it had a single engine and was, therefore, not allowed for commercial operations in India.

The aviation rules for aircraft meant for private use are a little less stringent than for commercial charters. They are far more meticulously applied when it comes to scheduled airlines because of concerns for passenger safety.

Beulah Bonugli knew a lot about the Pilatus. I asked, 'Beulah Bonugli, how do you know so much about the Pilatus?' What she told me in reply left me dumbfounded. She *owned* nine Pilatus aircrafts! And also owned a small bank in South Africa; she also ran a company which funded hire-purchase of white goods. It was of course not easy for me to believe her. She sensed it and said, 'Believe me, Captain! I'm serious. I think you should get a Pilatus. Are you sceptical about what I am saying simply because it comes from a woman?'

I recovered quickly and was willing to believe her, but had my doubts about the Pilatus's suitability for India and whether the DGCA would approve its use for commercial charters. According to Beulah Bonugli, the Pilatus was being extensively used in South Africa. She had leased aircrafts to Australia, Canada, and Kenya. 'Take my word for it! The aircraft is flawless. Why don't you come down to South Africa and see it for yourself?'

Without a moment's hesitation I said, 'Alright! I'll visit your place next week. Please send me a formal invitation.' That telephone conversation with Beulah Bonugli was to be a turning point for Deccan Aviation. I asked Vidya Babu to pack his bags. We were taking off for South Africa to check out the legendary Pilatus.

Vidya Babu, our chief engineer, and I flew to South Africa. My idea of Africa was shaped largely by *Hatari* and *Tarzan,* movies I had watched in childhood, and *Born Free,* which I had watched later. In those films small aircrafts flew in and out of airstrips in the middle of nowhere. I saw those aircraft as playing a major role in promoting tourism in India. Small aircrafts are convenient, eco-friendly and economical. All they require is a landing strip.

The American FAA, the British Civil Aviation Authority (CAA), and the European JAR had certified the new Pilatus which incorporated new technology and advanced safety standards. The US agency, known for its extremely stringent certification procedures, had allowed the new Pilatus for use in commercial charter operations. That alone, I realized, would help me push the case with the DGCA in India.

Beulah Bonugli had sent her representatives to receive us. She was an extraordinary woman. Her early life was a tough one but she overcame great odds to succeed. She looked young and attractive (I later learnt that she was sixty and a proud grandmother).

Bonugli had deployed four aircrafts, the balance belonging to other operators. I wanted to evaluate the Pilatus from a business perspective. Some still operated the vintage yet a modern, unpressurized Cessna Grand Caravan but Pilatus was the prime mode of transport between the game reserves. Beulah Bonugli suggested we begin by visiting the famous game parks.

We, therefore, boarded an aircraft. There were six of us: the pilot, Vidya Babu, Beulah Bonugli, her son and daughter, and I. The Kruger National Park was our first halt and Khagakama National Park our next. The Kruger, one of the largest on the continent, is in a fold deep within Africa. Kruger has the big five: the lion, rhino, elephant, giraffe, and the hippo. I sat next to the pilot and had a magnificent view of jungle and bush. The landscape was marked by grassy aircraft-landing strips every few miles. Aircraft charter operators here had tied-up with resorts and lodges, as I had in India on a much smaller scale. The tourist infrastructure, of aircraft and lodges, was enormous and catered to millions of tourists. The resorts were at the periphery of game reserves. Game reserves were a continuous unfenced expanse of grassland and forest. The national reserves were interspersed with large private game reserves. Although attending to such large numbers of tourists, the resorts kept the habitats clean, safe, and unpolluted for wildlife, and exemplifyng of how well-informed tourism, moderated by very heavy penalties for breach of game park regulations, can play a major part in preserving wildlife and natural habitats.

I thought about India and how we were choking tourism initiatives. Good tourism requires all those involved to observe the rules of the game. There is an ecosystem that begins in the country of origin of the prospective traveller. It comprises advertising and publicity, a traveller-friendly visa issuance system, reliable and easy ticket and travel arrangements, good transport, clean lodgings, and clean water and food. India lacks in one or more areas of the tourism ecosystem and it cuts both ways: there are no good resorts because there are no tourists; and there are no tourists because there are no good resorts. And the biggest deterrent—our places of tourist attraction are drowning in garbage and filth. We have high-end tourists and back packers. The high-end stay in five star hotels. The back packers pay two dollars and stay in basic shacks with a charpoy (cot) and a common toilet—a common sight in Goa and Hampi and such other places. The large overseas middleclass which is the mainstay of tourism, skip India. Could the Pilatus, I mused, propel Indian tourism as it did for Africa?

The grass strip at Kruger had a windsock for direction and there was no terminal building, not even a toilet. The fence erected to keep out wild animals was not effective. The more lissome among them like deer and zebras jumped over or breached it. The pilot said this was a common occurrence and did a well-practised low pass over the animals. It worked like magic, scattering the animals and leaving the landing strip clear.

There were three aprons (aircraft parking areas) on the strip. The pilot tethered the Pilatus to one of the stays on an apron like one would a cow to a stone mooring. He covered the aircraft Perspex with a tarpaulin shield. We got into a waiting jeep and drove off to the resort 9 kilometres away. The African resorts are very well managed; Indian tourism should take a leaf out of their book. They have almost entirely thatched roofs, beautifully done-up rooms, restaurants, and lounges under the thatch. All resorts harness traditional local expertise to build their structures.

We set off at five in the morning for the African safari. We saw giraffes, gazelles, elephants, and leopards. The jungle terrain in Africa differs from that in India. In India we have thick forests; the South African and Kenyan jungles comprise miles of grassland, the spectacular savannahs, which have virtually no trees apart from the occasional shrub and trees with a wide canopy but light foliage like the baobab and acacia. The big five in Africa prey on herbivores like zebras, various kinds of deer and gazelle. It is a revelation—realizing that grass plays perhaps the most important role in the food chain. The grassland extends northwards from South Africa right up to Kenya and Tanzania. The African forests are never littered with garbage and plastic like in most Indian forest trails.

At nine, we stopped for breakfast amidst surroundings that were as picturesque as could be wished, near a lake. One could watch from a raised platform the hippos splashing about and sporting in the water. We were told that more people die in Africa from being trampled or attacked by hippos than by lions. It was therefore a wise policy to keep safe distance. The breakfast featured a lavish smorgasbord of sandwiches and bacon and eggs prepared by local African guides. We throughout had the company of local African tribals who are excellent trackers and know the jungle like the back of their palms.

The trackers wanted to show us a lion's kill on our way back so the jeep veered from its prescribed trail. The adventure cost us quite a lot because, in no time, we were stopped by jungle rangers. They turned us back on to the permissible trail, but not before imposing a heavy fine of 500 US dollars. We returned to the base camp, heady with a surfeit of jungle smells, sights, and thrills. Lunch was an exotic experience. Africa permits the 'raising' of wild animals for the table and there were different types of exotic meat. As evening wore on, we realized we weren't through with the jungle yet. We set off on a night safari, and the jungle had more sights and sounds in store for us. We headed for Cape Town the following morning.

We were in the year 2002. Apartheid had officially ended in 1994. But in Zimbabwe, Robert Mugabe had unleashed a wave of persecution against the whites. Many had fled the country. In South Africa, there was no state-sponsored violence but the number of incidents of violence against the white minority was growing. African people now had equal opportunities but no education. Being marginalized for centuries, they did not have the skills and the training to qualify for jobs offered by modern-day industry and were therefore unable to participate in the economic process. Those few that had received education were locked away in prison.

The post-apartheid government was aware that if the whites were to leave, the economy would collapse. An entire generation of Africans would have to work their way in from the sidelines into the mainstream. Meanwhile, the government would create infrastructure, health and sanitation, and education facilities for them.

Crime had however definitely increased—muggings and robbery the most rampant forms. Crime flourished at traffic signals, at shopping mall entrances, and at public squares. There had even been carjacking, burglary, and arson. Beulah Bonugli's own house in Johannesberg was like Alcatraz, cordoned off with electric fencing. It had CCTV, guard dogs, and armed security. Her car, a Jaguar, had a flame-thrower to throw criminals off her scent. In her house, I saw photographs of her receiving awards from presidents and political leaders, and others of her with business people from around the world. She had posed for one with Richard Branson. I was curious to hear Beulah Bonugli's story.

It began over forty years ago. Bonugli was twenty at the time. She lived in Rhodesia with her husband, trapped in an abusive marriage. One night she decided she had had enough and would walk out. She took her belongings and her two children and fled to South Africa in a small battered car without telling her husband. Once there, she had no job, she had had no education, and absolutely no means of supporting herself. She took refuge in a church, she and her children living off the dole and eating at a soup kitchen. This continued for two years.

She was able to find a job as an assistant in a bank. From what she earned, Beulah Bonugli put herself through some formal education. With new skills and greater confidence in herself, she rose to become a secretary. One day, quite by chance, she found a business opportunity. She seized it and toiled day and night to make the business grow. It did, and Beulah Bonugli eventually created a business empire for herself, becoming one of the wealthiest women in South Africa.

She acquired qualities needed for a successful business entrepreneur, and ones I admired—was shrewd and astute. No lawyer was present at our meetings representing her or me. After dinner, we sat down to hammer out a lease deal for two Pilatus aircraft. I made two alternative proposals. It could be a fixed-lease charge or payment linked to each hour the aircraft flew. I asked for a three-year lease without any upfront deposit or minimum guaranteed monthly lease rentals. In return, I suggested revenue-sharing which suited us both. This arrangement would help me get off the ground without locking up huge capital. It was risky for her, but in return she would receive good compensation when the business took off.

Beulah agreed to the revenue-sharing arrangement, and before I knew it, the deal was done and she opened a bottle of Champagne. We celebrated.

We had two aircraft and eighteen empty seats. Why not a vacation with family and friends? We would fly the aircraft from Cape Town via Johannesburg to Nairobi in Kenya and head for Mumbai via Dar-es-Salaam, Djibouti, and Dubai. I calculated that the journey to India, with breaks along the way for local wildlife safaris, would cover about 10,000 km and take us a fortnight.

I told Beulah Bonugli we would go back, return with our families, and take a vacation ride back in the Pilatus. She offered to host us when we returned. Babu and I flew back to Bengaluru to complete formalities. We prepared a formal agreement for the aircraft lease and convinced the DGCA to let us import the aircraft and permit us to fly it as a commercial charter as was the case elsewhere in the world. We were now all set for the ferry.

The entourage—Bhargavi, Pallavi, Krithika, and I; Sam, his wife and three children; and Vishnu Rawal, his wife and his son – flew on a South African Airlines flight to Johannesburg.

We needed two more pilots to fly us back. I hired Sanjay Verma, a pilot who was flying for a local mining company in Orissa. In those days there were hundreds of pilots without jobs and therefore finding one was easy. Rahul Rawal, Vishnu's son, a qualified pilot, was twenty-one years old and looking for work. I asked Rahul, who was at the time away in the US training additionally as an engineer and freelancing as a flying instructor, to join us.

Beulah Bonugli lent us two pilots so that we had a pair each per aircraft. She also helped make local arrangements for our families. We visited game parks before embarking on the hopping haul back. We bid Beulah Bonugli a 'fare thee well' and took off from Cape Town.

We set off with a great sense of adventure on a journey that would take us across great landscapes: the hills of Zimbabwe, the great Nyasa and Victoria lakes, the savannahs of Kenya, Mount Kilimanjaro, the plains of Ethiopia, the Red Sea at Djibouti, the Gulf of Aden, a swathe of the southern Arabian Desert across Muscat and Dubai and the Arabian Sea, and coastal Pakistan into the Rann of Kutch and India.

Thinking of great adventure, I always recall Charles Lindbergh. Lindbergh was the last of the truly great aviation explorers of the twentieth century. His is a story of human courage and endurance of unimaginable proportions. He flew the *Spirit of St Louis,* a single-engine monoplane, solo, in an unpressurized cabin, strapped to the seat with eyes peeled for the entire duration of the flight which lasted thirty-three and a half hours. He took off at 10.20 p.m. from a field in New York and landed on a field at Le Bourget in Paris, 5800 km away across the Atlantic Ocean. He crossed the Atlantic at a time when nobody before had flown that far. Compared with what Lindbergh endured, our adventure was like a picnic to the city suburbia. We had a comfortably pressurized Pilatus cabin to fly us.

Lindbergh suffered a personal tragedy while in America and moved to Europe. There's a joke featuring Lindbergh and a lady. Years after the historic trans-atlantic flight, at a gala dinner at the Paris air show, Lindbergh found himself seated next to a society lady. The socialite itched to initiate a conversation, so she turned to Lindbergh and asked him in all innocence, 'So, Mr Lindbergh, have you ever been to Paris before?'

After enjoying the wildlife safaris in South Africa, we flew to Kenya. India has close ties with Kenya where a large number of Gujaratis have settled. The Kenyan economy is largely tourism-driven. There are two airports in Nairobi to handle the large number of arrivals. The Jomo Kenyatta International Airport is named after the first president of the country. Then there is the Williams International Airport, the smaller of the two, used almost exclusively for tourists arriving on charters and small aircraft. It is a point to ponder that while Nairobi, with an economy that is perhaps one-fourth that of Bengaluru, has two airports, Bengaluru chose to close one when it opened another!

We landed at Williams International and were piloted through a maze of aircraft parked cheek by jowl on the tarmac. There were hundreds of aircraft parked there and the pilots had a job carefully manoeuvering the plane in that aircraft parking lot.

The immigration check was quick and efficient. The next day, we flew to the famous Masai Mara Game Reserve. Some of the great Oscar-winning films like *Out of Africa* and *Born Free* were shot on location here. We were struck by the beauty of the African grasslands. The landing strip in Masai Mara was like that which we had seen at Kruger: no terminal building, no toilets, just a grass landing strip.

We landed there, and as our aircraft was being fastened to a stay on the apron, jeeps belonging to resorts in and around the game reserve had lined up. We got into one that would take us to our resort. Just as the jeep pulled out, we saw a fifty-seater DASH 8-200 Bombardier turboprop aeroplane landing on the airstrip. Passengers got off and boarded the other jeeps and left. Those who had arrived in the jeeps boarded the aircraft which took off without delay. There was a cyclical pattern: jeeps arriving, aircraft landing, offloading and loading, jeeps speeding off, and aircraft taking off. Everything was perfectly synchronized and that explained why there were no terminal buildings at the airstrips.

The safari began at five the following morning. We were eager to spot the big five of the Kenyan reserve. We had just missed the annual wildebeest crossing. The wildebeest or gnu are a kind of large antelope that are local to Africa. Millions of these very agile, large-horned, strong-necked, horse-tailed, sad-faced animals migrate over thousands of kilometres in search of grass pastures.

We flew the next day over Mount Kilimanjaro and the Horn of Africa to Djibouti, and on to Dubai via Aden, the capital of Yemen. At Dubai airport, close to where we landed, two Mercedes Benz cars were awaiting us. The airport authorities have deployed a fleet of Mercedes Benz cars to welcome charter aircraft passengers and take them to the facilitation centre. The facilitation centre was a mini-palace. Customs and immigration staff waited on arriving passengers, indulged them, and rapidly cleared their passport formalities. The Dubai government is evidently enlightened. It is aware that charter passengers are big spenders, and therefore it has made it easy and attractive for passengers to land, shop, and leave. It has also kept landing and parking charges low; and instituted fast-track immigration procedures. What the government spends on the indulgence showered on passengers, it makes up by the volumes of arrivals and the increased spending by these special passengers.

We took off from Dubai. As the Pakistan government had not given us permission to overfly or to refuel, we held a straight course for Mumbai, hugging the coastline without violating their airspace. We landed at Mumbai past midnight.

Mumbai was in stark, shameful contrast to Dubai. As our aircraft landed, we were surrounded by three jeeps. The one in front was the pilot and the two other brought up the rear, as if we were a renegade aircraft. There was neither a separate terminal for charters nor even a parking bay; we were herded to a remote area of the airport. The three jeeps threw a cordon around the aircraft. We were quarantined and we could not access airport facilities. Mumbai even today does not have a separate immigration facility for charters. We got off and were immediately surrounded by customs and airport officials. We had to pay landing, navigation, and parking charges.

We had informed the authorities that we would be completing immigration formalities in Bengaluru and were therefore not allowed to enter the terminal. We were in a remote and open part of the airfield with no restroom access. The Pilatus aircraft had no toilets. We had chosen ones that did not feature a toilet because we planned to use them for hardcore commercial flying. We had therefore to venture into the mosquito-infested bushes beyond the tarmac: the ladies, the foreign pilots, and the rest of us. This was nothing short of absolute and ridiculous indignity!

The pilot had to go to the other end of the airport to pay landing charges. The Airports Authority of India (AAI) did not accept credit cards so we had to pay cash but they did not accept dollar payments. The pilot did not have rupees. He trekked to the other end of the airport to the money- changers. The ATC was in another corner.

What most shocked us, after all the embarrassment, was being asked to pay customs duty on the residual fuel in the aircraft. We had 200-plus litres of fuel left over after flying in from Dubai in the tank. The customs officials asked us to pay duty of US$200 on that on the ground that residual fuel amounted to importing fuel into the country.

This is probably the single most ridiculous regulation I have ever come across. I was reminded of Ramakrishna Hegde's story about the temple usher and the shoes.

Putting up a mini-terminal or even creating a makeshift bay for charters involved neither high technology nor major investment. It required only imagination and a concern for human needs and also a realization that the entire bureaucratic infrastructure—the DGCA, the AAI and the customs department—existed simply because people flew in and flew out of airports and paid taxes and levies. This economic driver sustains the exchequer, the very bureaucracy, and the chain of economic activities creating a positive feedback loop. Even today, unless the charter is carrying a VVIP passenger, no airport in India extends basic courtesies: they are left in limbo and have to fend for themselves.

It was five in the morning by the time we took off for Bengaluru. We had been at the airport for over three hours, had had no sleep or rest, and were utterly exhausted. The welcoming first rays of the sun caressed and soothed us as we touched down. We alone knew how wonderful it felt to arrive home.

Prelude to the Pilatus

Jayanth and I were driving to Jakkur one day, discussing ways of expanding our helicopter business. We now had two helicopters in Bengaluru but there was insufficient business to keep them optimally engaged. There were two ways of expanding business. One: increase the number of flying hours. Two: induct more helicopters. Also, the future of the business depended on a national presence: we had to set up bases in other cities for comprehensive growth.

The complexion of politics was changing at the time. The common perception was that national parties had neglected regional development. This sentiment fed the soil on which regional parties had begun to grow. Chandrababu Naidu of the Telugu Desam Party had become chief minister of Andhra Pradesh, and he was the new kid on the block. S.M. Krishna was the chief minister of Karnataka. Although he belonged to the old guard and to the Congress, Krishna had initiated a number of measures to accelerate the development of the IT and biotechnology industries in the state. In spirit he was like Chandrababu Naidu. There was ferment of a similar kind in Tamil Nadu where new energies were being released, and also in Maharashtra and Gujarat. The reforms at the Centre had encouraged competition among the states to create the best climate for investment, by national and international business organizations. Infrastructure-creation was one of them and many projects had taken off.

Chandrababu Naidu depended heavily on IT and wanted to make Hyderabad the technology capital of the country, dispossessing Bengaluru of its lead. Naidu was an energetic driver of infrastructure projects and industrial development, and with a clear IT focus. He ran the state government on corporate lines and received the Best CEO Award instituted by the *Economic Times*.

Naidu was once in Bengaluru to address the Karnataka Chamber of Commerce. I attended the address and closely listened to his speech. Naidu said he wanted Karnataka entrepreneurs to come and invest in Andhra Pradesh. His government would lay out a red-carpet welcome. Naidu had his detractors and was criticized for his obsession with private sector participation in development. It is usual for the political opposition in India to take an adversarial position and oppose all that the ruling party does. The opposition derives its identity from opposing.

There is a joke about an opposition leader shipwrecked on an island. After several years of isolated existence, a ship strays close to the island's shoreline. The castaway screams for attention and the captain of the ship decides to rescue the man. The captain boards a rescue boat and paddles out to shore. The forsaken leader has been jabbering and gesticulating non-stop. As soon as the captain disembarks, the man accosts him, asking, 'Are you the government? Are *you* the government?' And without waiting for a reply, he provides answer. He says, 'If you are the government, then I am the opposition!'

Detractors spoke disparagingly of his heavy dependence on helicopters as a mode of transport, remarking that Naidu spent more time inside a helicopter than on the ground.

We were well on the way to Jakkur when I received a call from an acquaintance of mine. A former officer in the defence forces, he was now a pilot with the AP government. He said Chandrababu Naidu's helicopter had been grounded for major maintenance. The very next moment I thought aloud to Jayanth, 'If Naidu's helicopter has been grounded, he must surely require another. Why don't we station one helicopter in Hyderabad?'

Without waiting for a response, I asked Jayanth to turn back. I suggested we go pack some clothes and ride a helicopter out to Hyderabad. I asked A.

P. Singh, the pilot, to fly us out. Sugandha Raj of the marketing team joined us. We returned with bags packed and took off without further ado.

We landed at the Hyderabad airport and went straight to the secretariat. We did not have an appointment but did not wait to seek one. That would have taken us ten days to obtain. I confirmed with the pilot that Naidu was in the secretariat. I walked into the office of the CM's personal secretary, a senior IAS officer and introduced myself as an entrepreneur from Bengaluru. I said I had heard about Mr Naidu's address to the Karnataka Chamber of Commerce inviting businesses from Bengaluru to invest in Andhra Pradesh. I had also heard that the CM's helicopter had been grounded and had therefore come to offer my helicopter for his use.

I said I wanted to set up a helicopter base for Andhra Pradesh. I explained how the helicopter had become an important tool of development and was crucial for the reform and investment process under way in Andhra Pradesh. He understood me and I promised to have a helicopter ready in five minutes for the chief minister if he ordered one.

The secretary thought I was joking because it is common knowledge that to acquire a resource for government use involves a process, and a great deal of time: letters are written, bids are called for, tenders are opened and compared, till eventually the award is made. A company could be reasonably expected to take several days to provide a resource, and the helicopter was not a common resource. I convinced the secretary that I was extremely serious and said, 'I'm not joking. I've flown in a helicopter to your city. I'll leave it behind for the CM's use. I can take an Indian Airlines flight back to Bengaluru.'

The secretary did not look convinced and asked me to follow him. We went up a flight of stairs to the CM's office.

The CM was on a stroll down the corridor with his ministers. The personal secretary went up to him and whispered something in his ears. I heard Chandrababu Naidu asking the PS, 'Where is he? I will meet him immediately!' He left the ministers behind and took me inside. I told the chief minister that I heard his speech in Bengaluru and candidly added that we had finally chosen Hyderabad over Chennai for investment because we thought what he was doing in Andhra and in Hyderabad were great.

Chandrababu Naidu said, 'That's fantastic! Tell me what support you need from me.' 'Mr. Naidu,' I said, 'the first thing I want is a telephone.' The new millennium had just dawned but it still took a long while to get a landline connection. The intervention of a VIP alone could speed up the process. Besides, a telephone was an absolute necessity for our business. Cellphones had made an appearance but the networks were not yet India-wide and far from reliable. The chief minister called his personal secretary and asked him to have the telephone department give us three landline connections.

I also asked him for hangar space at Hyderabad Airport for parking, maintenance, storing tools and equipment. He gave instructions to that effect. This was great help because hangar space was not available at Hyderabad Airport unless you were Indian Airlines. To wrap up, I said he should use my helicopters and encourage me till the private sector demand for helicopters grew. Without a blink, he said that the government helicopter, now grounded for maintenance, would be given to the state police department to tackle the Naxal menace and that he would use my helicopter.

I invited Mr Naidu to inaugurate our helicopter base in Hyderabad. I said we would organize it on a day when he needed to travel the state. He willingly agreed.

We left the secretariat, thrilled to the core and decided not to check in to a hotel and found ourselves in an apartment instead. We bought mattresses to sleep on, drank rum and Coke, and feasted on Hyderabadi biryani in toast of our success. The Hyderabad base was set up.

Ten days later we returned to inaugurate our Hyderabad operations. Chandrababu Naidu flagged off the service and we received national and regional media coverage. Naidu was true to his word and was for three consecutive years our biggest customer, flying twenty hours or so a month. The corporate sector utilized the balance of flying hours, and we soon broke even. Chandrababu Naidu became a personal friend of mine. I admired his vision and determination to build a new Andhra Pradesh.

After setting up our Andhra Pradesh operations, we had opportunities to expand further northwards. The first call from the north, came from the secretariat of the governor of Jammu and Kashmir. The governor, had been a former inspector general of police in the state. The call was about a helicopter service to the holy shrine of Vaishno Devi, at about 2500 metres above the sea level. Vaishno Devi enjoys a vast devotee following as does Tirupati in the south.

Vaishno Devi, together with Amarnath and Mansarovar, is one of the most ancient centres of Hindu pilgrimage. Interestingly, a large part of the support infrastructure is provided by Muslims: transport (especially ponies and mules), food and accommodation, and accessories for the pilgrimage, including sacred offerings. Local Muslim families have set up shops where tourists can buy souvenirs, talismans, and other things. In commerce there is no religion. My involvement with the silk industry revealed this.

I would like to digress here to narrate a poignant story. At one point in time I used to rear silkworm cocoons and sell them in the market. Those were hard days. When the silkworms became cocoons we put them in lidded bamboo baskets and took them from Javagal to Ramanagaram in crowded buses.

On one occasion, the bus in which we were travelling arrived at the Bangalore bus station sometime after midnight. We wanted to reach Ramanagaram before dawn. So we took an auto-rickshaw to a private bus stand in Kalasipalyam near City Market. Private buses plied odd hours those days. We reached Ramanagaram at daybreak but found the entire town deserted and shops closed. It looked like a ghost town. We learnt that there had been communal disturbances in the town and a curfew had been imposed. We had no hope of finding a reeler to buy our cocoons. There were many like us who had arrived in buses with their cocoons. But without a buyer we were forced to dump the cocoons by the roadside. Yellow cocoons lay in piles upon piles along the road. It was a huge waste, a loss we would find very difficult to recoup. Thousands of farmers were in despair. With nowhere to go for succour, they faced ruin.

The silk supply chain comprises a frail ecology of mutual dependencies, a frail ecology of communal harmony. The supply chain is made up of players belonging to different communities. Harmony is therefore of essence for its survival. The farmer who rears silkworm cocoons is typically a Hindu. For the silk farmer the reeler is god. Without the reeler his cocoon has no value. And the reeler – the craftsman who draws the silk yarn – is typically a Muslim in this part of the country. For the reeler, the weaver is god. And the weaver, drawn from many weaver castes, is commonly a Hindu. For the weaver of the silken fabric, the wholesaler is god. The wholesaler is largely a Marwari, a Jain. The wholesaler sells the sari or fabric to his god, the retailer who is principally from the Vysya community – a Shetty, Chetty, Gupta and so on. The retailers depend on the ocean of humanity – a multitude of gods – for their livelihood: the consumers. The society is like the sari. Every thread represents a different community. The sari is metaphorically as rich in its texture and as delicate as the society that has produced it and will wear it.

Coming back to Vaishno Devi, the pilgrimage begins at a village called Katra, about 600 metres above sea level and 55 km from Jammu in the plains. It is a steep climb from there to Mata Vaishno Devi. Most pilgrims trek up the hill or get a pony or mule ride. The less able sit in palanquins and are carried up. Pawan Hans used to operate a helicopter service that picked up pilgrims from a helipad in Katra and dropped them at the foot of the shrine. Only those who were in a rush, or were very ill, or had a physical disadvantage, used this mode of transport. Most pilgrims, even those who would normally find it quite a task to climb a few steps at home, chose to walk all the way.

Pawan Hans had discontinued its helicopter service when I received the call. There had been an accident and the company had found it difficult to sustain the service. Regular users had felt let down by it and had exerted pressure on the governor to resume the service.

The caller was the governor's principle secretary, Arun Kumar, who was also secretary of the Shrine Board. He invited me for a meeting with the governor, which I accepted and went over to Jammu.

Six million pilgrims throng Vaishno Devi shrine every year. There is such a rush during peak season that pilgrims have to wait for a couple of days for their turn to trek up the mountain. People from all walks of life undertake the pilgrimage.

The governor came straight to the point. 'Captain, we would like you to take up this helicopter service!' My greatest concern was terrorism which was at its peak. Sensing my reluctance, the governor said the venture was a Hindu–Muslim one and would be free from terrorism. He would not take any chances however, and assured me complete security for the operations.

I needed some time to think it over. The opportunity was lucrative; would help build brand image; it was a service to the community and would be well received. I spoke to the pilots in the company, many of whom had flown in Jammu and Kashmir. There was no compulsion but would they be willing to fly to Vaishno Devi? The pilots were unanimous in their enthusiasm for the venture.

We signed the contract and the governor inaugurated the new service. The operation was a runaway success from the very outset. Soon we began carrying about a thousand pilgrims a day. Letters of appreciation and gratitude poured in from across the country.

Capt. Preetham Philip was a founding member of Deccan Aviation, and had set up our offshore operations. He had earlier been flying for Bristow Helicopters (later Malaysian Helicopters) in Malaysia and prepared a safety manual for one of their clients, which was adopted by Bristow Malaysia and Shell.

Preetham Philip camped at Vaishno Devi and set up standard operational procedure (SOP) for the operation of the flights. We positioned two helicopters at the Katra base camp and operated a shuttle from base camp to the shrine and back. Each shuttle flight carries four to five pilgrims. The success at Vaishno Devi led to a contract with the Amarnath Shrine to ferry pilgrims from the Baltal base camp, beyond Srinagar, to the caves at over 4500 metres up the mountain.

Deccan added new operational nodes as we went along. We set up base in Sri Lanka with local partners, our first overseas venture. It is a 52:48 split investment, featuring a helicopter and a small plane. The team members of Deccan—every one of them—have had a role in the success the company enjoys today. They scrounged every rupee, managed with frugal resources, kept expenses to the minimum, and worked zealously night and day and around the year for the company. Deccan became profitable within a year and remains profitable to this day.

In addition to operations in Bengaluru and Hyderabad, we added Mumbai, Delhi, and Bhubaneshwar where we offer regular services. From our bases in Surat and Rajahmundry we provide support for offshore oil exploration and production. The company has become synonymous with helicopter charters in India.

Kaavya Returns

In time I had become hostage to the cold logic of business. My natural urge for the aesthetic and the sentimental had become subject to the yen for profitability. Life has however its ways of making us listen to what lies hidden deep within each of us. It came in the form of a girl's voice. I could not recognize it initially, but there was a hint of persistence in her voice when she said 'Sir, I am Kaavya, the girl who wanted a helicopter for her father.'

Things had happened since we last spoke. Kaavya had married and her husband was lending her a hand. Together, the two would be able to gift a helicopter ride to her father. I assured her that the offer stood and scripted a drama for her. I told Kaavya, 'This is what we do. We fly you to Madikeri. You walk into the house. You ask your father to come out for a drive. When he agrees we will surprise him with our helicopter. In addition, we will fly you to the Kaveri river.' She loved the idea.

We took Kaavya's mother and sister into confidence. They had packed and kept her father's travel bags ready. The father was happily surprised by the daughter's sudden and unannounced visit. Kaavya and her husband followed the script. They invited the father outside and he saw the helicopter.

'He almost had a heart attack and I almost lost my father,' she said later, laughing. They cut cake in mid-flight. Her father had forgotten it was his birthday. We flew them to the Kaveri Fishing Camp. The Kaveri river is of special religious significance for the people of Coorg. From the fishing camp, the company flew to Bengaluru.

There was more food for the soul as we went along. A man called me who had a heavy Indian–American accent. He was calling from the US and his name was Manjunath. 'Did we hire out helicopters?' he asked. 'That is part of what we do,' I said. Manjunath wanted a helicopter to land right in front of his village house. He wanted us to pick up his parents and aunt and fly them to Chikmagalur and then fly them back.

Manjunath's village is close to Belur. We have a helipad near the temple in Belur. I said we would land the helicopter at the helipad. If Manjunath could fetch his parents and aunt to the helipad, we could take off from there. Making a landing in a village was cumbersome.

Manjunath was adamant. He did not care how much it cost. The helicopter would land in a paddy-field near his village house. He would meet all the costs. But why was he so insistent that we land in his village?

Manjunath comes from a small village in Hassan district. His father was a very poor farmer, but poverty did not stop his father from encouraging and supporting his son's education. A bright student, the son scored high marks throughout school and eventually got entrance in an engineering college. His father could not afford even the relatively small sum needed to pay for higher education in those days. He went around asking for a loan. He went to wealthy farmers and to money-lenders in the village but returned empty-handed. One day, Manjunath and his father walked into a gathering of the village elders around a pipal tree. A wag turned to Manjunath's father and said, 'Don't waste your money. Your son will be better off herding cattle,' and this led to general laughter. The sensitive youth felt deeply embarrassed by these flippant remarks.

He took a solemn oath never to set foot in the village until he had made something of his life and was determined to live his pledge. His father somehow scraped together resources by borrowing and mortgaging whatever he had and put him through engineering college. Manjunath went on to do his master's in the US, and then joined General Motors and rose to become head of the computer aided designs and systems lab for a division.

We flew Manjunath to his village and picked up his parents and aunt. They were visibly taken aback and were at a loss of words at the son's sudden visit and their tryst with the helicopter. The rest of the village looked on with wide-eyed astonishment. It was a sweet and very positive way of seeking revenge for the humiliation the boy had faced from the village elders, years earlier.

Stories like these were repeatedly lapped up by the media. As a result of the media coverage, Manjunath found himself a bride and took her with him on his journey back to the US.

10

It is not that I am a genius; I am infinitely more curious and I stay with the problem longer.

—Albert Einstein

Air Deccan: The Beginning of a Low-cost Airline

We inducted the Pilatus and busied ourselves building the helicopter service network. A wind of change had begun to waft across India, starting out as a gentle, subtle breeze and blowing with greater urgency as years passed. People expected change and novelty; they had begun to expect better standards of goods and services. They were seeing new possibilities. This applied to our helicopter business too. Customers wanted different; they wanted better and more. Chandrababu Naidu was quite succinct in his articulation of this altered consumer mindset. He posed this question to me: 'Why must a helicopter be a one-off service? Why not start a regular service to Vijayawada?'

Naidu had given the lead and other politicians took the cue. They began asking for regular helicopter flights to their constituencies, typically second- and third-tier cities like Hubli, Belgaum, Vijayawada, and Rajahmundry. It was not possible to accede to their requests because of the cost dynamics. Fare per seat, even at full occupancy, would be two to three times that for business class seats on an airline. That would not work out. It, however, got me thinking.

Things moved in a different direction when S.M. Krishna, chief minister of Karnataka, wanted to visit a temple near Palani but not in a helicopter. He said chopper journeys made him feel uncomfortable. Could I fly him by plane? I consulted my pilots. They said that they could fly him in the Pilatus to Madurai or Coimbatore. From there he would have to undertake a road journey to Palani. The road trip would take two or three hours, and that wouldn't solve the problem.

Rahul Singh Rawal, one of our young pilots, brought me an old Survey of India map. The map was drawn by British surveyors and is still used by the Indian Army and Air Force. Rahul identified a small airfield on the map located near Palani in a place called Dindigul. That came as a pleasant surprise! I asked Rahul to travel to the airfield marked on the map and undertake a ground recce.

Rahul hired a cab and drove to Dindigul armed with a GPS accompanied by a technician. Having arrived there he called me to report excitedly that the airfield actually existed. 'It looks fine to me,' he went on. 'There are one or two anthills on the field. I see some stray cattle grazing on the grass. Some cleaning up will make it perfect for landing.' That was great news for Deccan, and the chief minister. We already flew the Pilatus to Bellary and Mysore, landing on grass strips. We should now be able to fly the Pilatus to Dindigul and land it there. I asked Rahul to get in touch with the owner of the land.

The airstrip belonged to a man who owned a textile mill that had been set up by the British. Rahul asked the owner if he would help us land the chief minister on his airstrip. The owner said it would be a great pleasure and, as often happens in rural India, he went out of his way to help. He brought in workers to clean up the place and get the runway ready.

I called up S.M. Krishna and said we could now land him close to the temple.

Helicopters are best suited for short-haul flights over uncharted terrain. The Pilatus, on the other hand, is better suited for relatively longer routes provided there is a landing patch. The African experience had given me great confidence, having demonstrated that we could land a Pilatus on a grass strip.

Now that we had helicopters and the Pilatus, our operational reach had become extended. We wanted potential customers to know the travel options we could now offer them. We began an advertisement campaign. It was not a product advertisement but a tourism one, and featured a girl and a helicopter on an island, presumably a remote one. It showed the girl fishing on the island with the helicopter in the background. The copy simply said: 'If it's on the map, we'll get you there.'

The advertisement campaign brought us some unexpected results. People called up at any time of the day or night. Could we fly them, right away, to Jabalpur or Gwalior or Nashik or Nainital? They called us because no airline flew there. We quoted our price: two lakh rupees. When the caller heard the figure, there was the sound of a gasp on the other side, followed by long silence, a sigh, and the plonk of the receiver being placed in its cradle. I attended to some of these calls and recognized that the callers were middle-class people, one a bank official, another a teacher, and the third a government official. They had seen our advertisement which fired their imagination; they felt inspired to use our service. We were inundated with these inquiries, in the form of telephone calls and emails.

These were calls from people who were waking up to a new possibility. They were beginning to look at themselves differently. It was simply another matter that the helicopter pricing dynamics did not allow us to fly them, but they exuded a confidence towards things that once seemed the preserve of people belonging to well-to-do countries of the world. They represented the change that I had not thus far taken cognizance of both because I was preoccupied with work, but also because I failed to see it. I was like a father who suddenly realizes one day that his daughter has grown-up. My daughter does that to me sometimes. She turns to me and says: 'Papa, you forget I'm nineteen!'

These calls served as an eye-opener. I began to note the signs of change. I sensed the hope, optimism, energy of the newly emerging India. I saw on my road travels computer schools run within shacks and garages. I went into one such school in a remote taluq town which was run by a young man who had done some computer course or other and had decided to become an entrepreneur. It was a rickety, run-down building but the eyes of the young entrepreneur were bright and full of hope. I saw change in my own village. I saw a young woman farm worker, earning no more than Rs 40–50 a day, returning from a weekly village bazaar with a tube of Fair & Lovely face cream. The village people I had known used castor oil on their head and green gram paste as a skin-cleanser for the face. This new disposition—to buy what the TV advertised—was taking hold of rural India. Wanting to look lovely was good enough but *fair* as well seemed to me a reflection of our colonial mindset!

Village boys had now cast aside neem sticks for toothbrush and toothpaste. Friends who lived in district towns had refrigerators placed at the centre of the drawing room as an object of display. More people rode motorbikes in rural India. There were TVs everywhere. The well-to-do had at least a second-hand Maruti car. A newspaper article said that for companies such as Colgate, Unilever, and Hero Honda, villages were the new growth zones.

Jayanth and I were in the habit of arguing over the destiny of India. Jayanth would in exasperation sometimes say that there was something wrong with us Indians: we are an inferior race. He said we can't build a good road or produce electricity or clean water, and we can't keep our streets clean because we are inferior. I was tempted to agree, but then wondered if it was true that we are an inferior people. If we are, how was it that we built the Taj Mahal and the Madurai Meenakshi Temple, among others? How do we explain the musical genius of Bhimsen Joshi, Zakir Hussain, and M.S. Subbulakshmi?

I saw change on the ground through the worm's viewfinder. I saw it from air, from the bird's-eye view. I was curious about objects that glinted briefly and disappeared, the slimmest of slivers. They were however no chimera. Once flying from Goa to Bengaluru, I asked the pilot to fly lower over some gorgeously scenic hillside that hid a cluster of mud houses. From lower altitude, I discovered what the glistening objects were: they were large dish antennae for television. I counted one antenna to five or six villages. They represented the new landscape of the country.

India was once seen as a country with a billion hungry people to feed. The textbooks said: 'India is a poor country because it is overpopulated.' It was the staple image that politicians and economists alike manipulated for their plans and agenda. The image was of unappeasable hunger, of a bottomless gorge: no matter how much food the country produced or factories it set up, the majority would always be poor, unemployed, and backward.

This image of a population explosion allowed political parties to create maudlin poll campaigns. It allowed the government to launch family planning drives; to offer subsidies, dispense doles and charity.

I saw this image aslant, and with new eyes. India to me seemed not the beneficiary of a billion doles but a growing repository of a billion consumers. Notwithstanding the complexity of caste and community and the regional, ethnic, and religious pulls on the electorate, the forces of a new society were active. These were the forces of a new unifying caste, that of the consumer. When two billion hands produce and there are a billion mouths to consume, liability becomes the greatest asset!

I saw that people in rural India were playing an increasing role in the consumer space, to buy a range of consumer goods. What was remarkable, and this hid the seed of a future Deccan venture, was that people manifested an enthusiasm to buy everything except air tickets. This was the shock wave that hit me. India was on the march and a leap of faith was required. If India was to become a developed economy, its middle-classes should be able to travel by air between cities. I saw that there was no going back for India; it had launched itself on the high wave of consumerism and nothing would stop it from becoming an economic superpower in the next 20–30 years.

After we returned from South Africa, Sam had once suggested, 'Gopi, why don't we start a low-cost airline?' I said nothing at the time but his words set off a quiet buzz somewhere deep inside my brain. Sam repeated the same thing after a trip to the US at a later date. He had flown a low-fare airline and was excited about it. He thought that perhaps we should do this too.

The buzz in my head seemed somehow to connect with my intuition that development should enable the Indian middle-classes to buy an air ticket in the future. I had discovered, and brought out of obscurity, one air-strip near Dindigal. There must be many more on the map. Why not discover them?

I asked my pilots to mark all existing, used and unused, airports in India on a large map. What I saw, when the dotted map had been finally made, overwhelmed me. There were 500 airstrips and airfields across India but with no air connectivity. Some were large enough to accommodate a Boeing, some had gone to seed from disuse and inattention, some were politicians' gifts to their constituencies, some were Second World War airstrips, and some defence airstrips.

Not long thereafter, I attended an international helicopter convention in Florida, USA. I met a woman there who ran a helicopter tourism company at Grand Canyon. She invited me to visit her company office and I gladly accepted. Grand Canyon alone had twenty dedicated helicopters for tourists.

On the way to Grand Canyon I made a transit stop at the Phoenix airport. As I waited at the airport to be picked up by a helicopter my friend was to send, I strolled around the passenger lounge. A prominently displayed plaque there said that Phoenix airport handled 1000 flights and 1,00,000 passengers a day. I found it difficult to believe that this back-of-beyond airport, in the middle of a desert, handled more flights and passengers than all the forty airports in India put together. I rubbed my eyes in disbelief and went back to read the plaque once again!

I flew Southwest, the legendary mother of all low-cost airlines, to Phoenix. I was seated next to a carpenter, a regular American blue-collar worker. Big built, blue tattoo marks on forearm, and dressed in worker's overalls, the man was chomping on a large hamburger. I saw written on the napkin he held, Southwest's motto: '30 Years: One Mission: Low fares.'

Two ideas came together in my head and fused into one obsession: India needs an airline that goes everywhere, India needs an airline that will allow millions to fly. I didn't need a McKenzie to tell me it would work. I simply knew it. I remembered a Kannada proverb. 'Do you need a mirror to see an abscess on your palm?'

I saw it: you could call it a vision; I heard it: you could call it an oracle. The US operated 40,000 commercial flights a day, India operated 420. It was the middle of 2002 when I realized that at the current growth-rates, India would, in another thirty years, be in a position to fly approximately one billion passengers a year. These were a madman's numbers: a billion seats and 50,000 flights a day! Could it be possible? I continued the number-juggling. I said to myself that if only each of the 200 million middle-class people travels five times a year, a plausible figure, the magic figure of one billion a year seemed so palpably achievable. The gap was immense but it would still mean a hundred fold leap in the airline business at current rates.

The numbers were compelling. I wanted to get back right away so that I could direct my energies in this new direction of promise. The decision had been made as I stood there looking at the curious plaque. It was not a question of whether but how! I ended my trip to Grand Canyon on a buoyant note and headed straight back.

As soon as I landed at Bengaluru, I called up Girish Rao of the *Economic Times*. I did not pause to think of the pros and cons of what I would tell him. I announced with convincing finality that I was starting an airline for the common man. Girish flashed the news. It was in all the papers.

I pitched my idea to Mohan Kumar, pointing to the 500-plus mid-sized towns and cities in India. I said we needed to look beyond Delhi and Mumbai. A town like Bellary was a bustling industrial centre and export hub. It housed 15 per cent of the jeans manufacturing industry in the country, in addition to poultry, mining and textiles industries. Also, Bellary was handy to the illustrious historical ruins of Hampi. The town had three airstrips but no air connectivity. The first and the only flight, a hopping flight, had landed in Bellary in 1932 carrying mail.

I drew attention to many other great towns and cities with a rich past which were poised to make a big leap into the future. I mentioned Dehradun, the gateway to Haridwar and entry point to the Himalayas; Kanpur, with a population of four million (almost the size of Norway), and a city that used to be a manufacturing hub during the British times and had two airfields but no air connectivity; Kolhapur and Nashik in Maharashtra. Nashik had emerged as the wine capital of India and ABB and HAL had set up manufacturing facilities there, had two airfields but no air connectivity.

I reeled off statistics. Every day sixteen million Indians travelled by train and twelve million by bus. Together they made up nearly thirty million a day. Even if 5 per cent of this number travelled by air, that would be a whopping 530 million travellers a year. Even if this number looked huge, it did not mean 530 million different people travelling but 200 million middle-class people travelling two and half times a year, which was not an unimaginable prospect over the next thirty years. This was the writing on the wall and no market research was needed to interpret it for us. Mohan Kumar heard me. He said in his characteristically laconic manner, 'OK, let's do it.'

I did not think money, just as I did not think money before getting to the last point in my helicopter venture. I thought about the other nitty-gritty. The business model would have to be a profoundly, dyed-in-the-wool, Indian. It would have to factor in India's geography, culture, and heritage; incorporate the Indian genius; to be an airline for India's common man; for the masses. I only saw the beacon of light, passed over the shadows, and plunged head-on. However, challenges and stumbling blocks there were aplenty. Some glared one in the face, others lurked around the corner.

The entrepreneurial history of Indian aviation has its milestones, and its tombstones. The Tata-Singapore Airline venture, it was rumoured, had only recently been scuttled by the Indian Airlines and Jet Airways lobby. If I took that path, I could meet with a similar fate. I had however a measure of the power of the idea and was also aware of the politically correct populist appeal of mass air travel. It would have been difficult for a politician to reject a business proposal whose objective was to link rural India with urban India, and it would have been politically embarrassing for a politician to say no to a business proposal that would make it possible for the common man to fly. Such an idea could not fall on deaf ears, and that is precisely what happened.

I realized the idea needed political support and will of a different kind. I therefore began speaking to politicians whom I had met and knew. I met Venkaiah Naidu, Chandrababu Naidu, and S.M. Krishna. They showed unaffected enthusiasm. They realized connectivity would spur economic growth and that the airline would spur investments because if Toyota or Tata wanted to scout for a place to set up shop in Orissa, the first thing they would look for was air connectivity.

I was confident that if an airline model could work in the US and in Indonesia, economies at the two extreme ends of the spectrum, it should work in India, positioned somewhere in the middle. The most important thing for me now was to find the people who had intimate knowledge of low-cost airline management: the real people!

Planning an Airline

I did research and made enquiries with contacts about someone who had worked hands on in a low-cost carrier (LCC). I zeroed in on Connor McCarthy. Connor had been associated with Ryan Air for over a decade and worked directly under the legendary Michael O'Leary, CEO of Ryan Air. After leaving Ryan Air, Connor had helped set up Air Asia, a low-cost carrier in Malaysia. Connor's association with Ryan Air was crucial. Ryan was the most successful low-cost airline in Europe and had created aviation history by offering seats for one euro.

Ryan Air had achieved the apparently unachievable. It had the lowest revenue per passenger, the lowest operating cost, and the highest margin of profitability for an airline. It was the most ruthless cost-cutter of all times. Connor McCarthy had been deputy chief operating officer for Ryan for over a decade. He was the man I wanted to talk to. Few knew the nuts and bolts as he did.

Connor McCarthy dismissed the idea of a low-cost airline in India. India had made a mark in technology and software but its aviation was of medieval vintage and nobody took India seriously. Connor said a few conditions needed to be fulfilled for an LCC to exist: liberal rules and regulations and a conducive policy environment; high level of internet and credit card penetration, and a network of principle and alternative airports.

India did not fulfil these conditions: Indian aviation was tightly controlled by the government; Internet and credit card penetration was less than two per cent, and the number of serviceable airports was very small. I was not, however, prepared to listen to anyone who said LCC would not work in India. I was in love with the idea! I reminded myself of the saying: 'the heart has its reasons of which the head knows nothing.' I went ahead and called Connor McCarthy, saying that I wanted to come over along with my CFO and get his insights about LCC. Connor was abrasive. and said roughly, 'Well, I don't have time. And if I did, you couldn't afford me. I'm expensive.'

I was stupefied, but not put off, by his reaction. I decided to pursue him. I asked him, 'How costly are you? Connor said he charged 400 euros an hour. I said I would not haggle over the price. 'I'll fly in on Wednesday night. I want you to meet us on Thursday and Friday. I want you for eight hours each, those two days. Your fee would be 6400 euros. I shall pay you that. Friday night we'll go out for dinner. I'll pay for the dinner but not for what you say at the table.' Connor agreed.

I received a two-page contract the following day. He had billed us for 13,400 euros instead of 6400 and sent me an email explaining the reason for the inflation. He would have to prepare for two days to talk to us for two days. I called him up and said, 'Connor, you are trying to be smart by two and half measures. I am looking to establish a relationship on an ongoing basis. I'm not coming to you because you're a college professor but because you are a hands-on guy. I just want you to talk to me about what you did at Ryan Air. You worked with O'Leary for ten years. Tell me what you did there. I don't need a power-point presentation. In fact, if you need to prepare to talk to me, then I don't want you at all.'

Connor eventually agreed to my terms and we were soon in Dublin, the city of George Bernard Shaw, James Joyce, and the Kennedy clan. I wanted to see that beautiful city which is as famous for its legendary pubs as it is for its literary giants.

I booked twenty hours of Connor's time, sixteen hours of formally agreed talk and four hours over dinner. I got to see Dublin free of cost in the bargain. Meanwhile, I thought of making a radical departure from the cardinal principles of LCC. LCCs are advised to deploy a single aircraft family because that saves them money on training, spare parts, and maintenance. Now, however, I understood India from an aviation perspective and its ground realities were different. The 500 airstrips we had plotted on our map in small towns and cities could handle only small aircraft such as the ATR. The forty or so operational airports across India could handle both the larger Boeing and Airbus and the smaller aircraft. But Boeing and Airbus would restrict us to the metros and it made no sense to cannibalize the existing air traffic. Deccan's LCC would only make profit if it enlarged the pie and generated new passenger traffic. My idea was: tap the 'other' India.

For the LCC to succeed, I would have to bring in consumers from Dehradun and Dharmashala to fill the Delhi–Mumbai flight. We could fly the large aircraft between metros and feed these trips with passengers flying on our smaller ATRs from the small towns and cities. By marrying the two, I thought, we would be creating air traffic to and from India's tier II and III regions and the conditions for an implosion of air connectivity. I reckoned Indian aviation would benefit as more cities got air-linked.

I saw a parallel between this and the American experience with the railway, or railroad, as they call it. The American railroad was laid 150 years ago. It helped open up the vast American country and its economy. It linked up the coastal cities with the Midwest and the deep interiors. In the case of the American railroad, the pioneers had to contend with attacks by Red Indians. In my case, I believed I would have to contend with the proverbial red tape. Fortunately the idea of a common man's flight, not in fancy but in reality, so inspired the imagination of the bureaucrats that each of them laid out a red carpet for me along the corridors of bureaucratic maze! My idea of using two kinds of aircraft would also be in alignment with the policy of encouraging enterprises that helped rural India to progress. I thought the 'rural India progress' line might be a good pitch, coupled with the fact that all the government needed to do was simply spruce up and fill the potholes in existing airports and runways.

Aviation is not a key sector for governments in India. It is not considered integral to economic development. Politicians tend to be more sympathetic to what is perceived to be good than what is indeed good! They tend to look favourably at something that continues the parallelism in rural road development, rural electrification, rural agriculture, and rural health and education even if such projects do not actually lead to the desired noble aim of rural uplift. Political leaders who openly acknowledge the existence of corruption in these schemes have calculated that of every rupee earmarked for these projects only ten paise reaches the beneficiary. I had a vision for the country: I wanted the common man from the small town to be able to fly. I would do well to ride piggyback on the popular rural theme: rural is where I wanted to go, and the rural pitch would take me there!

I knew I would be mauled if I were to enter the aviation fray headlong. My competitors were powerful and would use every trick to finish me off. I also sensed that my competitors were happy flying the big city network and would not want to venture to tier II and III sectors in the interior. I, therefore, decided that a strategy of connecting non-metro urban centres would make them complacent about us and they would leave us alone. Even so, they could put spokes in the wheel and delay the project causing us to notch up cost overruns and impact our balance sheet.

Now that people knew I would be starting an airline, help was forthcoming. Politicians across India wanted to know when I would launch my airline. Did their town or city figure in the zigzag? Builders associations, chambers of commerce, and industry wanted to chip in.

By projecting relative cost, occupancy, and revenue per passenger, we decided that a forty-eight-seater ATR turboprop aircraft was best suited for the small-town interconnects. We would have two approaches for the business model. Number one: flights from small towns and cities would be feeders to flights between metros. Number two: the pricing would be different. It would be low fare and compete with the price point of AC first class of the railways. We calculated that a fare that is 25 to 30 per cent above AC first class and much above AC second class would make it a viable business model.

The Common Man Must Fly

The decision to launch a low-cost airline was actuated by an inner intuitive logic, but for me to realize the objective I needed a plan of action. The crucial thing about planning is timeliness of execution. The airlines business has three principle components: aircraft, pilots and technicians, and a hangar, maintenance facilities, and airport space. These three have to be mobilized and operationalized in optimal synchrony. Aircraft cost a lot but an aircraft has value only when it flies; it is worthless on the ground. I had to ensure that aircraft arrived when the other components were in place: not too early and not too late. Pilots and technicians had to be paid salaries, but they must be on board and must be aligned with the concept of LCC and Deccan's motto and vision before the aircraft arrived. Not too early, either. Hangar space attracted rent; spare parts and tooling are cold inventories if not put to use. They had to be ready but not too early.

However, before setting up the material basis of the airline, I needed to obtain a licence and official support. I set about it in full earnest. I knew Venkaiah Naidu, the BJP president and a sincere pro-reforms politician. I asked him to introduce me to Rajiv Pratap Rudy, the minister of civil aviation. Both politicians were known for their progressive attitude to development. Venkaiah Naidu was from Vijayawada and Rudy was from Bihar, representing regions that craved connectivity.

Venkaiah Naidu spoke favourably about me and my proposal to Rajiv Pratap Rudy, a young, energetic man with perceptible dynamism. I sold Rudy a vision: Deccan's proposal to launch an LCC. Rudy was doubtful about selling tickets at half the price of my competitors and making profits at the same time. He thought I would go bankrupt.

I explained the philosophy of LCC. I said it was not a new concept but a revival of an older culture of innovation and efficiency. It is an attitude to money and resources. It is a culture that does not allow you to spend on unnecessary things. It is home ecology conservation, about not wasting food, water, energy, materials, and labour; it is about frugality; about doing away with the redundant.

My father lived with this spirit of conservatism. We lived in separate houses in Bengaluru. I lived in the cantonment area while he lived in Basavanagudi, 6–7 km away. On weekends I sent my driver over to his residence to fetch him. My father steadfastly refused my offer. He said just because I could send a car did not mean he must use it. He took a bus to the nearest bus station, and walked. I used a different metaphor with well-known aviation journalist Cuckoo Paul, and said an LCC is like an Udupi hotel. She wrote in the next day's papers that I was launching an 'Udupi in the sky!'

An Udupi hotel, a fast-food restaurant, really, as I have explained earlier, is a low-cost affair. It is an excellent example of cost-cutting without sacrificing quality. It sets out its philosophy of business very clearly. People would have to serve themselves from the service counter and eat standing around a circular table on a fixed stand or at a sill along the wall. There is no opportunity, or tacit encouragement, to hang out, lounge around, smoke, read a book, or chat with friends. It is a zero frills area with no extras. The restaurant cuts down costs on several fronts. There are no waiters, real estate requirements are lower, maintenance costs are lower than in an AC deluxe restaurant, and there is less electricity consumed. These Udupi hotels across the city of Bengaluru are always crowded. The proprietors spend less and earn more; customers get to eat good and clean food served piping hot, at much cheaper prices, and they save time because the food is always served quickly.

The owner of an Udupi hotel makes it clear right at the outset that it is a place in which to eat and leave. When customers go to an Udupi hotel, they do not expect to sit around and be served. They expect no frills but get what they have really come looking for: good, inexpensively priced food served in a clean environment. That is what an LCC is all about.

An LCC is about inclusiveness, innovativeness and efficiency. It commits itself to fly the common man and prices the tickets so that a larger number of people at the lower end of the economic bracket can fly the airline. The rich and well-to-do are welcome but they must realize that they will not be pampered as they are on a legacy airline.

An LCC innovates. It flies point to point and saves time and cost on luggage transfers and dovetailed flight connections. Being a point-to-point airline means the contract with the passenger ends when he/she reaches the destination. Any further leg of the journey is a new contract. Onward travelling passengers will have to collect their baggage and stand in the next check-in line. In a full-service airline, a Delhi–Mumbai flight waits for a British Airways flight to land passengers travelling from London and Amsterdam. In such a hub-and-spokes model, onward flight schedules are made to dovetail with inward flight arrivals. Aircraft in such a model of operation are often on the ground for longer periods and this entails costs which passengers eventually have to bear in the form of higher fares.

LCC focuses on efficiency. It has more flying hours per aircraft per day and thus increases the operational efficiency per passenger. LCC aircraft take off early and finish late in the night. A prudent flier on a family visit or a small and medium entrepreneur on a business visit will want to stretch a rupee as far as he can and will be willing to fly out at 5 a.m. if a flight is available and the ticket costs half the usual fare. The CEO of a large corporate company will be willing to pay for the luxury of some extra sleep and will therefore choose a more expensive 8 a.m. flight.

Efficiencies are also possible when you don't serve food in flight. Cleaning is easier and time for loading and unloading food containers is reduced. The aircraft can take off almost immediately after the passengers have deplaned and new passengers have boarded. Fewer food containers on board brings down the weight and fuel consumption of the aircraft. When food is sold rather than served free the cost model becomes a revenue model; people are careful when they pay for food, there is less wastage, and less pilferage. What is a cost overhead for legacy airlines becomes a revenue source for LCC.

Prudent handling of water as a resource is a great cost-saver, and is an ecologically sensible thing to do. Not all the water that is served complimentary is consumed. There is plenty of wastage. Passengers are more careful with the water they purchase. Fewer water bottles on board mean lower weight and lower fuel burn. Free newspapers are another cost factor. You pay to buy a newspaper, and pay the staff that bring it on board and clear out old papers. At each transit, this process takes time, and eats into revenue.

Innovation can apply to cost-cutting and to creating positive revenue streams. We considered both. We would add on 23 per cent more passenger seats. We would do away with the business class and offer 180 seats rather than the 144 seats offered by legacy airlines. Besides, we would fly 25–30 per cent longer hours than other airlines. Another innovation concerned the distribution network. The LCC model eliminated brokers and agents which straightaway brought down costs by 15 to 20 per cent.

I explained to the civil aviation minister how our LCC would be able to offer the low fares through cost reductions per passenger as well as induct positive new revenue streams. I told Rudy that while the government was proactive about reforms, the reforms would not reach Kanpur or Ranchi without air connectivity. I spoke of the waste of time, and hence loss of revenue and productivity, when 200 million people travelled by road or railway. I said the economy would benefit when teachers and trainers, mechanics and plumbers were able to fly. I explained how investments would percolate to the interiors if air connectivity was ensured. Rudy asked me to address the civil aviation officials about low fare airlines. He himself was quite convinced.

I did, and explained at the meeting that Deccan would need only three airfields to get started: Vijayawada, Rajahmundry, and Hubli would do, and I sought a minuscule investment for each of these airports to be connected for the first time. These airstrips should be repaired and be able to handle take-off and landing of ATR aircraft. Just a shed where people could stand about and wait for their flight would be sufficient. My aircraft would land, pick-up passengers, and fly off within twenty minutes. All I required was a good runway with a thatched shed and a toilet!

Hubli, Vijayawada, and Rajahmundry were representative of the newly emergent economic centres of India that were growing fast and were straining for connectivity to help them sustain and further ramp up their growth-rates.

The deck was cleared after I cleared all doubts. The licences and permits for the airline would come in good time but what was of prime importance was the government's decision to allocate a few crore rupees to repair the runways in Hubli, Vijayawada, and Rajahmundry. The papers the following day reported that India's first low-cost airline would begin flights to Hubli and Vijayawada and link unconnected parts of India. It set the country aflame. This had a spin-off. I was flooded with calls from chief ministers' offices from all states wanting to know when I would start flights to their respective states. There was a frenzy of interest and no time to lose. We had to plan to be safe but move the project at lightning speed. After getting the go-ahead from Rudy, I went to Mohan Kumar to give him the news.

After meeting Connor McCarthy in Dublin in March 2003, I gave myself six months for the launch of the airline. I made a media announcement that Air Deccan would be launched in August. The die was now cast.

Mohan and I now had a very clear road map before us for the new venture. The decks had been cleared with the government, but we had no time to lose. We had to find the funding before the project lost steam or the government changed its mind.

Though all the economic sectors in India were booming—IT, biotechnology, cement, steel, automobile, and telecommunications— aviation was not. It was not looked upon as a sunrise sector. Wall Street analysts and financial experts were indifferent to it. Even the aircraft manufacturing industry was reluctant, although it was desperate for sales and was in the throes of a severe recession following the 9/11 massacre.

In the 1990s the government opened up the Indian skies to competition. A raft of airlines launched operations, each with the same business model and competing for the same pie. They did not look for ways of generating new passenger traffic. Competition was fierce and there was a shake-out, leaving most of them bankrupt, including East-West, NEPC, Modiluft, Damania, UB Air, and Gujarat Airways. This wholesale bankruptcy created a monopoly status for Indian Airlines, Jet Airways, and Sahara. Because the economy was stagnant at the time, no one thought of acquiring the bankrupt airlines. Now in the new vibrant economy, bankruptcy would bring in acquisitions and growth. At the time, in 2002, Indian Airlines, Jet Airways, and Sahara flew thirteen million passengers while Ryan Air alone was flying thirty million passengers in Europe. The timing looked ideal for the launch of a low-cost airline.

I decided to meet Ladhani in Delhi, when Mohan confirmed that we would be ready to launch with Rs 5 crore, to start off with. We travelled together in a Jet Airways flight from Delhi to Bengaluru, economy class. I explained my business plan to Ladhani. I said a traditional airline charged Rs 20,000 one way for business class and Rs 12,000 one way for economy.

My low-cost airline would allow you to fly this sector for Rs 4000 flat. Ladhani was a man who could afford to charter a plane from Delhi to Bengaluru but he flew economy class. He welcomed the prospect of flying cheaper even if it meant the seat would be slightly more cramped.

The licence stipulated that to start an airline we would need a minimum fleet of five aircrafts within twelve months of operations. We decided that we would launch with three aircrafts to achieve a minimum network scale and ramp up to five within six months.We decided to start with a forty-eight-seater turboprop and later upgrade it to seventy-two-seater. News reports that my airline intended to use turboprops led to an increased sales pitch from turboprop companies.

Another critical decision that I took, on which hinged the future of the airline, was that from the very first day we would distribute tickets only over the Internet and not print any. Passengers would pay upfront and book three months in advance. That would create a comfortable cash-flow for the airline. I told Mohan to go ahead and create the entire IT infrastructure to support the airline. The Internet distribution model would eliminate our dependency on travel agents.

Once the business model and processes were decided, I asked Ladhani for the money. He was aware that an airline enterprise would require an investment of anywhere between Rs 100 crore and Rs 200 crore. When I asked him for Rs 5 crore, he was quick to make his terms clear. He said I would have to return the money in six months failing which I would have to forfeit 50 per cent control of the helicopter company.

Ladhani knew instinctively that by committing myself I would never be complacent and I would go to any length, if necessary, to make the airline work. He also wanted an interest on the loan. Without batting an eyelid, I signed and we got the money. Thanks to Ladhani, Air Deccan was born.

If you are a corporate company seeking to diversify, you allocate funds for the company, find a CEO, and launch the project. If you are an entrepreneur with nothing but dreams, you start with what you have. Entrepreneurial soil is fertile. It sustains ideas and innovations. There is great energy in the entrepreneurial seed. It germinates in acute conditions of stress and nutrient deprivation. It pushes through the hardest of sod and shoots sprout. The belief in oneself and the will to succeed are not measureable in terms of money.

There was buzz about the airline much before it was launched. People felt aligned with it as though they were potential stakeholders. Everyone wanted the business to succeed: government departments, the DGCA, the ministry, and eventually aircraft and engine manufacturers. It was infectious.

We used three criteria in deciding between competing vendors and service providers: professionalism, quality, and what was best for the company.

There was no room for any personal agenda or predilections. This policy allowed us to learn a great deal about the business from competing vendors. They educated us about the advantages of using their company products and services and the disadvantages of using the offerings of the competition.

Before finalizing the aircraft manufacturer, we ran an intense competition between ATR and Bombardier. Turboprops were being phased out across Europe and the United States, with only the Bombardier and ATR remaining afloat. Their sales had plummeted so they were in dire straits and therefore desperate. Deccan was in a position to give them a new lease of life.

Vendors soon realized that we were obsessed about being low-cost and made their best offers. After an evaluation of the aircraft, we homed in on ATR. They were quick to respond. Their financial offer, apple for apple, was more competitive; and most importantly, they came not only with a financing solution for the aircraft lease, but they also structured an integrated maintenance, tooling, and logistics, and pilot/engineering training support which was so designed that it reduced our capital expenditure upfront and was a boon for a start-up company like ours.

I, however, thought that by visiting Toulouse I would get to know the management better, meet the CEO Jean Michel Leonard, and also get better terms. The long-term success of the airline was linked to how seamlessly we were able to work together on all these fronts. ATR was a collaboration of three European aerospace majors: Germany (EADS), France and Italy (Allenia).

When I went to Toulouse, I made a presentation to ATR officials. It was more about India than about Deccan Aviation. I spoke with passion and fervour about how India was going to be the future of the world, of India's ongoing economic reforms and progress; about how the country was poised for an aviation revolution. I said India would emerge as the largest generator of employment in the aviation field and spoke about why India needed a low-cost airline, emphasizing that the all-round growth of the economy would definitely make it possible for more people to fill the planes. I added that it was a symbiotic relationship.

I asked them to ensure they gave me five aircraft and extended all possible assistance, and I asked them to back me to the hilt. If I failed, they would fail too. We were partners in business. They must make money on me in the long-term. If they won in the short-term, and I lost, both of us would lose. If in the long-term I won, they would win too. The long-term perspective was a win-win. I spoke with a conviction about India in which I wholly believed.

I made it clear that ATR would also have to come up with a complete, comprehensive maintenance package. I would pay an hourly lease rental and they should maintain the aircraft end to end. They would bring in their engineers and take care of the entire logistics and inventory support. They would train our pilots and help my staff to undertake line maintenance. At the end of the presentation, they had bought the idea of India as a vibrant economy in the making and, from their business perspective, a potentially huge market for aviation products. The vibrancy of the Indian economy contrasted with the global slump at the time, and this captured their imagination. Without any cash flow upfront I had got a package from them.

Although aviation was in recession and there were fewer aircrafts being inducted in the skies, flying schools continued to train and turn out pilots. There were no flying jobs for fresh pilots. Some took up other jobs; some simply waited for things to improve. Most of them enrolled as unpaid freelance co-pilots. They flew for the experience and to log a larger number of flying hours.

I received calls from within the country and abroad. They were excited about the new project and wanted to contribute to the company's success. There were calls from senior and accomplished pilots as well. One such call was from Capt. Rajiv Kotiyal, chief test pilot with HAL.

Rajiv Kotiyal was one of the most distinguished Indian test pilots. He had followed in the footsteps of astronauts Neil Armstrong and John Glenn and trained as a test pilot for two years at the US Edwards Air Force Base. He tailed their career successes too. He was decorated with the Best Test Pilot in the World Award in 2001, an honour earlier bestowed to Armstrong and Glenn. Kotiyal had done a maiden test flight on the Light Combat Aircraft at HAL and had been involved with the design of the light combat jet along with the project director, Dr Kota Harinarayana.

Capt. Kotiyal was retiring as a test pilot and wanted to get into commercial aviation. He said he had read about my airline and wanted to work with us.

Capt. Kotiyal was seeking to broaden his work profile and willing to do more than just flying. I was looking for a chief pilot. If I were to attract talent from an existing airline, I would have to pay a quarter million dollars. I took Kotiyal into confidence. I said I would take care of his future if he shared in the common dream and made sacrifices. I asked if he would be willing to manage the entire flight operations.

Rajiv Kotiyal joined the airline on 1 April 2003 as Employee No.1.

I am grateful to the people who chose to join me early in the company's history. They were willing to join me on a great journey to the unknown. It was very important for me that those who joined at the top believed in the dream and in the revolution we were about to create. I made it clear that only those should come on board who shared the conviction that we would revolutionize Indian aviation.

Most of the people who wanted to join me had no background in commercial aviation. They were not fastidious about so-called best practises. They were ready to innovate, to challenge established norms—in sales, marketing, ticketing, flight operations, in IT and finance. Of course, in hardcore flying and engineering, experience and best practises are never tinkered with. It was, however, possible to do things upside down in the softer areas of finance, marketing, distribution, operations, and the management of engineering and flight operations. Every Deccan employee had the same kind of zeal and energy as I. They dared to ask 'Why?' to customary practice and 'Why not?' to innovation.

Not long after Capt. Kotiyal came on board, I received a letter from Vijaya Lucose. Vijaya had begun as an airhostess with Air India before moving on to Eastern Airlines in the US as head of training for cabin crew. Her software engineer husband had returned to India a few years ago and Vijaya had joined East-West Airlines as head of in-flight services. I needed someone to manage the cabin crew operations: induction, training, grooming, and on-board style and services. I found Vijaya Lucose very graceful, intelligent, and impeccably groomed. She had the perfect credentials but I told her at the time that we could not afford to pay her a fancy salary. Vijaya said money was not an issue and joined me.

R. Krishnaswamy was the next to join us. He wrote me a note to the effect he had just retired as a regional manager for Indian Airlines and was fully conversant with airline operations. I replied that I was not keen on taking people with an airline background and that I needed people who were innovative and flexible. Krishnaswamy asked me not to be too quick in judging him. He came over for a chat and I was deeply impressed by his commitment and dynamism. We decided he would head airport services for Deccan.

The heads were in place: head of pilots, head of cabin crew and in-flight department, and head of airport services. Mohan headed finance and revenue management and I initially headed sales and marketing. ATR for its part had promised to lend me the head of engineering. The only critical functional head yet to be filled was head of IT who would report to Mohan. Deccan became a functioning corporate body on 1 April 2003.

The IT system proved to be the biggest challenge. I was, and remain, computer illiterate. I cannot send email nor sit in front of a computer with any degree of patience. The Blackberry is as far as I have got. In the late

1990s, a new metric was evolved for deciding how advanced an economy is. According to it, the highest percentage of the gross domestic output of an advanced economy came from IT-enabled services. I did not like the logic of this new metric for the simple reason that we cannot eat information. We need people to grow our food, run our machines, and build our houses. We need people to keep our cities clean, to teach us, heal us, and care for us.

I recently read an article about a high-flying investment banker who became a monk. He quit everything because he realized that computers took us far away from the real world; computers don't give bread and milk. He wanted to recover his links with nature: feel the earth, get his hands dirty. He realized that man does not live by IT alone. Therefore, more urgently than ever before, the world needs a fine balance between the old economy and the new economy; between agriculture, industry, and manufacturing, on one hand, and software, IT, and other services on the other.

My general views on computers notwithstanding, IT was the single most important factor in ensuring the success of the airline. We needed an IT-enabled image that would trigger instant brand recognition in the consumer's mind. We needed the trigger to work as an unfailing stimulus–response mechanism: 'I want cheap ticket, I go Deccan.' Full stop! Media had been at work for us but we needed to get the nuts and bolts in place.

We needed all potential travellers to think Deccan, whether they were in Kottayam or Kolkata, Davanagere or Delhi, New York or Nagpur. However, once they thought Deccan we would have to make it possible for them to get the physical ticket. We had to create a ticketing distribution system that allowed the passenger to access the entire inventory of ticket availability on a particular flight on a particular date. The ticketing system was the cornerstone of the airline. Therefore, if the system could enable a passenger to respond in a tangible way with a physical or virtual trail, we would be hitting the bull's eye.

The answer was straightforward: only a sophisticated Internet-based reservation system could accomplish this. It would be a system capable of responding to a customer's query and transaction anywhere in the world. It would automatically update itself after each completed transaction. The data would simultaneously become available to all internal departments at Deccan. In addition to the interface it created with passengers, the system would be able to coordinate, and mutually assist, different departments. Flight operations, check-in and processing, HR processes and pilot and cabin crew roster, flight schedules, and other wings of the supply chain including food and beverages and fuel supply would all be dynamically linked so that all the nodes in the airline would always be transparent to operational heads and to decision-makers. It also would allow for some empowerment of the nodes at lower levels, where such empowerment is creative and useful.

The ticketing system would have to be linked to the bank's payment gateway, on one hand, and to the call centre and to thousands of new-age agents on the other. The system would be linked to the software system that decides the fare the passenger pays and also be linked to Deccan intranet linking departments within the airline, especially between airport counter and check-in and flight departure.

The software calculated the fare on the basis of simple rules. It assumed that tickets could be bought ninety days in advance. People buying earlier got them cheaper. The 180 seats on the plane were divided into buckets. Each bucket provided a certain number of fares that were much lower than the others. Bucket one would have, for example, two tickets at one rupee each if bought on ninety days prior to departure. If they were bought on that day, the fare scan moved to the next bucket where tickets were priced slightly higher, and so on. The fare structure was time-sensitive and automatically moved on to the higher bucket even if the tickets were not bought on the previous day. The number of lower fare tickets got smaller as the days passed until the day of travel. Even on the day of travel, the price of the ticket, while being much higher than that which was offered on the opening day, would still be significantly lower than that offered on legacy airlines justifying the overall philosophy of the LCC. Another crucial aspect of the system software was the fact that it had been programmed to bear in mind the profitability of the airline. It worked on the principle that the net average realization on an LCC would recover cost plus a profit, even though the net realization was still less than half that of a legacy carrier.

The fare-determining software was closely linked to whether I was an optimist or a pessimist. This was my simple insight. Mohan and I were discussing the relationship between the fare and occupancy rates of the aircraft. Mohan had calculated the fare basket on the basis of 75 per cent occupancy. Here I intervened as an optimist and reckoned 100 per cent occupancy. Assuming 100 per cent occupancy, the system would decide a fare that was half that at 50 per cent occupancy. The traveller would find it far more attractive to travel at such a fare and, as experience proved, this was self-fulfilling: fares were indeed decided in such a way that made this actually happen. This was how people responded to our faith in 100 per cent occupancy!

In addition to the major task of automating and regulating ticketing and distribution, the Internet-based system would also be able to coordinate the activities of different departments. Flight operations, check-in and baggage processing, HR processes such as, pilot and cabin crew roster, flight schedules, and the supply chain, including food and beverages and fuel supply. This would be transparent to operational heads and help in taking sound decisions.

We calculated that the system would lead to a cost saving of over 20 per cent from reduced ticket distribution costs on the Internet. Savings would also accrue by not having to print tickets. A standard legacy airline ticket is printed in the security press and uses special paper to avoid duplication. Savings would also accrue from transport and logistics of ticket delivery: from the company to travel agents to passengers.

Airlines are prisoners of three entities: travel agents, proprietary reservation systems (like Saber, Galileo, and Amadeus), and network service providers. All airline tickets must pass through the three systems. These entities control the airlines' inventory and cash flow.

The system works this way. There is a ticket consolidator who is a travel agent registered with International Air Transport Association (IATA). The travel agent is the only person with access to the airline inventory. Even the airline cannot sell a ticket at less than the travel agent's rate. Most airlines have a bonded agreement with the agents.

There are two kinds of travel agents. IATA travel agents are distinct from non-IATA agents. In India there are 2000 or so IATA travel agents and 8000 non-IATA travel agents or sub-agents. The latter do the bulk of the ticket bookings but it is the IATA agents who get a higher percentage of the commission: 7 to 10 per cent linked to productivity. The non-IATA sub-agents make about 2 per cent.

Deccan would straightaway save 10 per cent by avoiding IATA travel agents. There was another advantage to this. IATA travel agents were allowed to block and hold seats on different flights simultaneously. They offered these frills in tune with the legacy of full service airlines' philosophy of pampering passengers. If a passenger is uncertain of his date of travel, the travel agent can block seats on three different flights without paying for the tickets. There is no penalty if the booking does not convert into a ticket. Agents hold multiple tickets on different airlines. The airlines receive the passenger manifest at the last minute. They therefore resort to over-booking which leads to chaos if all the multiple cross-booked passengers for the same flight turn up. However, more frequently they fly with a lot of empty seats and therefore the passengers who fly have to bear the cost of the vacant seats which are always factored into the fare.

Airlines have to care for the extra passengers unable to board the flight, providing accommodation and meals leading to increased cost and wastage. The airlines are held to ransom by this system.

The system of travel agents is not a cartel but creates inefficiencies, wastages, and cost overheads. Deccan, by putting the inventory at the command of the passenger, would change all that. It would eliminate the 10 per cent agency commission to the travel agent and also eliminate charges paid for access to the proprietary reservation systems that controlled the airlines.

The purchase of a ticket to London and onward to Helsinki, for instance, attracts a $4 charge for the domestic segment and $8 for the international segment. This charge is paid to the reservation system. The connectivity between travel agents and the reservation system enables ticketing transactions. The reservation system is provided and controlled by network providers like SITA who charge another $2 per transaction.

Travel agents have formed associations and, as it often happens, the associations get together and control the airlines. The travel agents and network providers generally made money while the airlines generally made a loss or just managed to survive. The airlines get their money a fortnight or a month after the real time transaction. The delay hampers cash-flow. An airline like Indian Airlines or Jet Airways probably has up to Rs 1000 crore in receivables at any given point in time.

Other costs borne by airlines included bad debt insurance costs, working capital costs, costs on interest, costs incurred on clearing-house charges, and miscellaneous other costs. The assortment of cost types makes it necessary for airlines to hire an army of accountants whose only job is to reconcile receivables from travel agents and costs payable.

These processes, and the costs associated with each of them, were eliminated at one stroke by putting the ticketing inventory online. The airline could receive money upfront from the passenger when a seat was sold.

Sceptics said an Internet-based system for ticket distribution and for resource planning and operations might work in the US or Europe but might not be suitable for India. The LCC system along with the Internet-based reservation system was functioning in the US and Europe but my detractors doubted that Deccan could do this in the Indian context. Deccan however pioneered the creation of interfaces between customers and the payment gateway and brought in several other innovations in the concept of point of sale, cyber cafes and post-offices included, and broke the monopoly of the system of IATA travel agents. It helped a great deal that the Deccan team was mostly from a non-airlines background and were therefore open to new ideas. As for me, not being computer savvy, I wanted the system to be such that people who have no computer or can't use one can easily book tickets with us.

Just as the legacy airlines are in thrall to the monopoly of the legacy reservation systems like Amadeus, the LCCs are also captive to one major Internet reservation system, Navitaire. It was based in Denver, USA. Navitaire owned a software platform called Open Sky for use by LCCs. The company was subsequently acquired by Accenture. The company supplied Internet-based systems to some 30 airlines across the world. Though it was a form of monopoly, its charges per transaction were almost one-eighth of that charged by the reservation systems deployed by legacy airlines.

The company was rather cool to our enquiries, not regarding India as a very happening aviation market. Navitaire acknowledged India as a software superpower but did not think an LCC model would succeed there. India was a niche segment: only a small minority used credit cards and accessed the Internet. Navitaire at the time had enough business on its plate. I understood the tepid response to us and eventually fixed a video conference with the top man of the company.

We needed someone to head our IT department. I wanted someone who understood technology, not as an expert perhaps but in a savvy way; someone who understood how technology could be aligned with the direction of the business, and who was able to look at technology from the customer perspective. I wanted someone who could make technology work for the business rather than someone who would become obsessed with the technology for its own sake. At this juncture, I was introduced to Ajay Bhatkal.

Ajay Bhatkal was not a software engineer. He had spent a long time in IT companies and had the experience and the know-how to conceptualize products and services from the customer's point of view. He was down to earth and showed a depth of perspective and technical acumen. I told Ajay, 'E-ticketing should be our forte: I don't care what it takes, but we are not going to print tickets. You find a way, and only then can you join me.'

The conference call with Navitaire lasted four hours. I was prepared to hire a local company if the discussion with Navitaire fell through. It would be risky, perhaps suicidal. Local IT companies would not have had exposure to the airline reservation context and I did not want to be a guinea-pig for their experiments. However, without the online ticketing system the airline would not in any event take off. Better risk and die, rather than die without taking a risk.

Navitaire explained what the reservation platform would be able to do. The reservation system would connect to the call centre and to the airports. The virtual private network (VPN) backbone would be critical to the functioning of the reservation platform. It would provide robust and fail-proof connectivity.

VPN uses a combination of communication channels, including optical fibre cabling, the copper lines laid by the departments of post and telegraphs and cellular mobile phone infrastructure (base stations and cell transmitter networks). The VPN also uses VSAT or virtual satellite connectivity, a satellite-based transponder and receiver system. Specially designed software would control how the signals traverse the system comprising all these components. It would be a dedicated network with redundancy and back-up built into it.

We on our part were clear that we needed a system that allowed travel agent and passenger alike to be able to access the Internet interface and buy the tickets from the Deccan reservation inventory, the common ticketing resource for all.

We needed a reservation system that allowed the passenger, or travel agent, to pay by credit card. We needed software that interfaced our system and the bank. We also needed a bank that would handle the transaction authentication,and safe and secure VPN connectivity between the bank and the call centre. India in those days did not have call centres for Indians but only those operated by Indians for foreign countries as BPOs. Therefore, while ticket booking enquiry was logged here in Bengaluru for a Bengaluru–London or Frankfurt journey on a British Airways flight, the money-and-ticketing transaction took place abroad.

Navitaire said we would have to make an earnest deposit before they began to work on the system for us. From the day we deposited the money, they needed sixty clear days to customize the template that had been proven in operations in Europe, the US, and south-east Asia. The system would have to be married to our VPN interfaces and our software, and suitable handshakes created for the system to work seamlessly. Issues with credit card companies and banks would have to be addressed.

We only had six months to go for the launch. The meter was ticking with pilot salaries, aircraft maintenance, demurrage on real estate, cost of being on ground, and interest on borrowed money. We also needed to work with a bank to create a payment gateway and build software that talked to our software and securely handled transactions. We needed call centre software and needed to make all software mutually intelligible, mutually compatible, and speak the same idiom. We needed to create a system that was entirely safe, private, secure, and foolproof. We could not afford more than four months for systems and software development. We would then have two months for trials and fixing glitches and bugs.

I had made it amply clear to team members that they must bear two things in mind: they must create the lowest-cost airline and must create a supporting IT system that was robust, scalable, and easy for the passenger.

A passenger should be able to buy a ticket as easily as he bought a bottle of shampoo across the counter! They were free to explore ways and innovate but these two deliverables were paramount. This sense of freedom helped.

Everyone down the line, from senior management to new inductee, had to be given a sense that s/he had a domain of influence. Everyone must be made to feel that what s/he does in his or her area of influence can change the company's destiny. It is this conveyance and realization of a common dream that motivates people to raise the bar.

I often said to the head of sales and marketing that millions followed Mao because of an idea, a dream. Millions followed Gandhi, Hitler, and Nelson Mandela. The followers believed, and were given to believe, they could make a difference. This was happening at Deccan. I asked my team to find a way and to create one if none existed.

At Deccan every employee became an extension of the CEO. Every employee took a direct part in the adventure. It was a courageous leap taken collectively. The single decision taken, that we would not print tickets, uncovered new solutions.

Success in the case of the LCC depended on universal access, not just travel agents, across the world. Deccan was trying to create this new space by taking inventory out of the clutches of travel agents. It is sheer courage that opens up new vistas. The uncharted land is not accessible to those lacking the derring-do.

Home-grown IT companies also pitched their proposals to build an IT-based reservation system. None of them had a system up and running; it was still in their heads or on their laptops. We wanted software that had gone through the grime and the dust of robust use in real-life situations.

Navitaire had all that. Navitaire's system was being used by thirty airlines, was robust and scalable. They had made a name for themselves as the Rolls Royce of ticketing systems but were sitting on a high horse.

We had several rounds of Internet/video-conferencing with them before their team visited India. The team showed little enthusiasm for India, believing we were at least ten years behind time. However, as we had no alternatives I had almost decided to yield to them and make the huge deposit they had been demanding. There was no other alternative.

Navitaire made a presentation which my entire technology team attended. There were also a couple of representatives from Citibank. Citibank was the only bank that we were aware of at the time that had Internet banking.

Citibank was a global operation and would partner with us only if they saw potential for future growth. I called the local head of Citibank and asked whether the bank was willing to step in tandem with what could be India's largest airline. I said that if our model worked, the bank stood to gain and would also be able to attract other airline accounts.

I said the Citibank payment gateway software should be able to process all ticketing transactions issued by Master or Visa card globally. These transactions could be generated by individuals, booking agents, or call centres online. The software must be able to complete a transaction in seconds, because longer transaction time, or latency, would send up call centre communication bills. The software had to work at lightning speed and ensure end-to-end transaction, from first click to sale, in two or three minutes.

The transaction involved several steps: query, ticket inventory check, confirmation (whether available or not - if not, a new query is generated and it iterates), customer credit card detail input, credit card approval and acknowledgement, system confirmation and PNR issue, and print-out. The average time required to conclude each of these eight steps, provided there are no iterations, should not exceed fifteen seconds if the entire operation was to be completed within two to three minutes. These were intimate system requirements and it was very important for Deccan to work closely with a bank on this.

Meanwhile, IATA-registered travel agents attempted to exert oblique pressure and blackmail the airline, threatening to boycott my airline if I sold tickets through the Internet. I explained to their representative that I wanted to give the passengers a choice between booking directly online or through travel agents. Of course even travel agents would have to book online, and they could work out an arrangement of the service charges they would levy on their customers. I said that online booking was an idea whose time had arrived. If I did not adopt it, someone else would. I made it clear that I was not against travel agents but maintained that my airline would revolutionize flying in India and that the number of travellers increase many times over than they currently were. I said 100 million people would be flying in a few years when the LCC model stabilized. They therefore stood to gain more by controlling, for instance, 20 per cent of a larger pie when a billion people flew than by monopolizing the entire domain when thirteen million flew. The travel agents were not convinced, arguing that I must split the ticketing access between IATA travel agents and passengers, and not bring in sub-agents as we were doing at the time. I did not acquiesce to their request and they left in a huff.

The Navitaire presentation took all day. At the end of the sessions we decided to sign on for their reservation system by paying a million dollars as deposit, all the money that I had got from Ladhani as minimum income guarantee whether passengers flew the airline or not. Only minutes before signing the dotted line, the Citibank representative suddenly asked the Navitaire delegate what software they would be using to integrate with the bank payment gateway.

Navitaire cited the software system they were using whereupon the Citibank executive exclaimed and said the bank had already implemented an upgrade of the old software. He said he was concerned that the Navitaire software would not be able to talk to Citibank's upgraded software and that they had abandoned the legacy software two years earlier.

Four months of video-conferencing plus a couple of one-on-one meetings had yielded this conclusion. I suddenly saw that things don't happen because people don't communicate effectively. We don't sit across and talk person to person, hiding behind emails that are incapable of expressing the nuances of communication which only face-to-face interactions allow.

I was shocked. I turned to the Navitaire representative and said, 'I asked you to come to Bengaluru four months ago but you didn't. You were doing everything over the Internet and now you are discovering that your software is incompatible with Citibank's. You don't speak a common language. Forget software language, this is common sense!' We were now in a bind.

I asked the Navitaire team to call up and ask their superiors in the management whether the company would be willing to invest in the new software. The leader of the three-member Navitaire team said he would have to go back and confer with his team before deciding. I was, however, in a hurry. I could not delay the launch. The arrow had left the bow! I suggested they stay back for another day or two and sort out the matter with their colleagues but I must know whether or not they were going to do it.

The leader of the team went out and made a couple of calls. He came back and said, 'Captain, I don't think I'll be able to give you an answer. I have to go back to my head office and consult my colleagues.' I was blunt and said with finality, 'Look, if you walk out of this room without finalizing the agreement, I will cancel the MOU.' He looked at me in disbelief. I gave them two hours to give me their final decision, whereupon they went into a huddle.

The marketing people of an Indian company Interglobe Technologies (IGT) had been chasing me for this contract. I had not paid much attention to them, even though they seemed to be a smart bunch, because they did not have a system that was up and running. I knew that much of the Navitaire software was being developed in the back offices of Bengaluru, or Pune, or Delhi. I had told the Navitaire people right at the outset that I was considering them only because they already had a proven system.

When the Navitaire team went to confer with their colleagues, I went to meet the young team from IGT who had been anxiously awaiting the results of our negotiations with Navitaire. These software engineers had floated in on a wave of reverse 'brain drain' from the US to India. These IGT 'boys' had shown both energy and enthusiasm and had impressed me at earlier meetings, and wished I could have given them the contract but had been warned that it was suicidal to give it to a company with no experience with a functional system.

The IGT team exhibited the innate Indian trait of being able to deal with dilemmas and function in the midst of chaos. They seemed unfazed by the complexity of the IT infrastructure we would require. Our software and IT system logic was unique. We would be selling tickets at Internet cafes, petrol bunks, and post-offices. Passengers without a credit card could buy tickets at our call centre which would hold the ticket for a few hours until the passenger returned to make a cash deposit at Deccan's city or airport office. All these were very complex requirements, but the Indian techies from IGT were ready to come up with a solution. The problem with Indians, I have been told by foreigners, is that they don't know how to say 'No'.

After a while, the Navitaire representative called, but only to say he had been unable to contact his team back home. They would have to return to decide. I did not dither. I said, 'Let us kiss the contract goodbye.' The next morning I signed up with IGT. We had forty-five days to set up everything from scratch.

There were several other things we had to attend to. Most importantly, we had to get our own call centre up and running but also had to complete legal formalities with regard to purchase of aircraft, and organize engineering and maintenance support. We had besides to hire pilots and have them ATR-trained.

Qualified pilots certified to fly one type of aircraft, say a Boeing, cannot readily fly another aircraft such as ATR or Airbus because of the differences in instrumentation, process control, and performance, among others. In advanced countries, such pilots train on a simulator, a marvel of human inventiveness. It has been continually improved upon by manufacturers so that even conditions that a pilot does not normally encounter when flying are replicated. Manufacturers have realized that the simulator offers a fuller experience of reality than reality itself! A pilot who undertakes conversion training on a simulator is better prepared to fly the aircraft than training on the aircraft itself, which appears curious but is nonetheless true. After rigorous simulator training for about a month and a half, pilots elsewhere are able to straightaway fly the aircraft itself after one familiarization check.

In India, the DGCA, governed by rules formulated in 1937, required that a pilot who was qualified to fly one type of aircraft must fly 300 to 500 hours on the target aircraft type as a trainee for certification. This was the old practise and, after the arrival of the simulator, the DGCA asked pilots to do both: train on the simulator and also log 300 to 500 hours on the new aircraft for certification. For airlines, this is a huge additional cost, and for a start-up like ours it could be ruinous.

I pleaded with the DGCA to acknowledge present-day realities and bring their regulations on par with the US and European regulations. I was not in any way asking for a compromise on safety. The DGCA saw reason in my request and brought down the extra flying hours for captains from 500 to 300 hours in some cases and 300 to100 hours, in others.

Managing an airline demands that routines at every functional node are meticulously synchronized. This applies to the front-end of airline operations: bookings, check-in, and departure, and also to the back- end: flight operations, aircraft engineering and maintenance, and ground-handling. The chief engineer for maintenance would have to track the routine upkeep of aircraft, undertaken at night between midnight, i.e., after the last flight, and 4 a.m., i.e., before the first flight; track parts replacements, by calendar and by wear and tear; place orders with sufficient headway for the parts to be sourced and shipped in; and ensure the engineering inspection is meticulously undertaken every twenty-four hours.

We had to hire the line-maintenance engineers, rig up general and specialized tools and sheds, equip hangars, and acquire the requisite minimum inventory for DGCA approval. We could have tied up with Indian Airlines to provide aircraft maintenance services. The IA was willing, but that would add to our cost profile. Besides, being government-owned, IA were likely to be slow to respond to emergency requests we might occasionally make. Also, depending on IA would make us complacent about setting up our own maintenance and inventory management capabilities.

I had already included a clause in the agreement with ATR that they would provide the chief engineer, spare parts, and support for heavy engineering and major overhauls. I sensed some conflict of interest here. If there was a manufacturing problem it would not be as easy for us to complain to the

manufacturer than if there had been a third-party maintenance contract
or if we had decided to undertake it ourselves. However, that was just
the beginning of the venture and we needed ATR's support, and besides
it was in their interest to ensure that we succeeded. Our Indian engineers
would handle day-to-day maintenance under the supervision of the French
engineer from ATR, and the latter would also help us by providing some
pilot trainers to help us.

What remained were clearances from the DGCA, Bureau of Civil Aviation
Security (BCAS), AAI, and the Ministry of Civil Aviation (MCA). I fortunately
had the backing of Rajiv Pratap Rudy and so went ahead and fixed a date
for the launch. I decided to bill top political leaders on the programme note,
which would certainly help us attract media attention. There was however
one thing I religiously observed: I would not compromise on safety and
would be internally 100 per cent compliant with all mandatory stipulations.
That would give me the moral strength to pressurize the bureaucracy to
speed up documentation and clearances.

The bureaucracy reads between the lines. Once word gets around that
a project has the blessings of the minister, officials work doubly hard to
ensure permissions and licences become available in time. Rudy had made
an announcement in parliament, to thunderous applause from all the
benches, that Air Deccan would begin operations with the objective of
creating unprecedented connectivity. He was inundated with enquiries from
fellow ministers and MPs asking about the launch date and whether the
airline would be flying to Jabalpur, or Ranchi, or Tuticorin, or Nagpur.

Karnataka chief minister S.M. Krishna had agreed to be the chief guest.
Rajiv Pratap Rudy, Venkaiah Naidu, and defence minister George Fernandes
agreed to participate. Fernandes said he would get on board my inaugural
flight. The advance publicity, and the fact that nodal agencies, including
the DGCA, BCAS, AAI and the MCA had been very supportive, generated
expectancy, and the very idea that India would launch an airline for the
common man created quite a buzz.

We had also to attend to cabin crew and related matters. Vijaya Lucose
was on the job. We did not need to hire designers because Vijaya had an
excellent eye for sartorial propriety and aesthetics. I told her: 'Vijaya, you
have such impeccable sense of dress. Why don't you design the outfits
yourself?' There was therefore no splurging on expensive designer labels
or expensive fashion designers. We believed our air-hostesses should not
look flashy, flying as we were to semi-urban or rural areas with many of our
customers likely to be first-time fliers. We did not wish to embarrass them
or make them feel out of place.

We were lowering the social barrier to flying and felt that a passenger stepping into our aircraft for the first time should not be made to feel overawed. We must create the image of an airline dedicated to common people. We were breaking the cost barrier for airlines and, in a very important sense, I used to say, we were also breaking the caste barrier.

Vijaya recruited the cabin crew. I had shared my ideas of the profile of air-hostesses for the airline with her. I said there would be simple village folk, auto-rickshaw drivers, blue collar workers, people from the lower economic strata flying with us. I did not want our cabin crew to look down on the customer. I said, 'We do not want girls with city backgrounds and accents to look down upon first-time fliers from our rural areas.' I wanted well-groomed girls but not necessarily English-speaking ones. I mentioned the graceful air-hostesses of Thai Airways or Air China who did not speak fluent English. I told Vijaya to look for the qualities of a nurse in the cabin crew: they would have to help a passenger aboard/help them fasten a seat belt, overall they needed to make the guest feel comfortable.

I wanted an inclusive work force. I asked Vijaya Lucose to recruit people from small towns. I said, 'Don't take a Jet Airways air hostess as she will demand a high salary. Go to the smaller towns like Gwalior or Hubli. Girls there are looking for jobs. They will accept the job at lower salaries.' Incidentally, one year after I launched the airline, a minister put pressure on me to inaugurate a cabin crew training school in Rae Bareilly, a dusty rural town in Uttar Pradesh.

The uniforms we designed were modelled by children of the team: my daughter and Vijaya's daughter included who showed us how the different costumes would look. We debated the designs and finally settled on a blue-and-yellow dress that fell short of the ankle by ten inches.

Our entire effort was aimed at making the airline inclusive. The phrase 'inclusive business model' has become a cliché and people do not tire of talking about inclusive growth. For a business model to be inclusive in the case of an airline it must address a price point that generates a wider consumer base; it must have a larger footprint including the remote interiors. It must capture the imagination of the people, grab people's attention, and must differ in its image from that evoked by existing airlines. It must also be politically acceptable as a new idea. Lastly, and most importantly, it must make a difference to the country and people at large: I had no business to be here if I was not going to make a difference.

An entrepreneur must not only create a new product but fundamentally alter the very behaviour of consumers; create societal change. The entrepreneur must have a business model that is markedly different from the existing ones. However, the uniqueness of the business model must not be at the cost of viability.

Legacy players complained about losses because they were forced to fly to interior, non-lucrative sectors while I wanted to fly to these very areas. The angels feared, but I would willingly go there. The government wanted to bring more tier II and tier III cities on to the air map. I came along: it was what the doctor ordered.

Competition won't let you go ahead. In normal circumstances, but here competition would be complacent. I was flying to the 'other India' it did not care about. The thought of flying to small towns filled me with excitement. We would be welcomed there with open arms. That was the only way of challenging the existing players. Besides, there was no other way for a new airline to enter the airline industry but by creating a new market.

The small-city focus of the airline did not blind us to the fact that we must become a national presence. Mumbai–Delhi type of route was not ruled out. The small city connectivity would be in addition to the mainstream segment connectivity. This gave me the brand definition for my airline. We called ourselves *a national airline going to the regions*. We created very strong regional presence and linkages to the hinterland.

The competition would not be able to react as quickly on regional routes. Also, as there was only one licence applicable to feeder and trunk routes, once the airline had parking space, airport space, and a licence to operate, I could spring a surprise on competition by adding trunk routes to feeder routes.

To ensure viability, I would peg down costs everywhere in the company. I would be profitable. I would be *safe* and *profitable*, not one without the other. The safest place for an aircraft is in the hangar, but if it doesn't fly the airline doesn't exist. If an airline is unsafe people will not fly and the airline goes bankrupt. An airline has to be both *safe* and *profitable*.

Implicit in profitability was another element: *speed*. Speed to market, speed in technology deployment, speed in recruitment, resource acquisition, and raising finance; and speed in securing various government clearances. To be *safe, swift,* and *profitable* was the mantra. Low fares would stimulate the market. Existing passengers would fly four times rather than once. Train travellers would be tempted to fly instead of taking the railway. The airline for its part would enter uncharted territory, into the very bowels of India. This was our inner logic.

11

Lead, kindly light....
Keep thou my feet: I do not ask to see
The distant scene; one step enough for me.
—Church hymn

Taking-off

New technology causes a change in consumer behaviour. Marshall McLuhan aptly summed it up: The medium is the message. The invention of writing radically transformed human society. Printing took ideas beyond regional borders. Radio, TV, and now the Internet are all strides that humanity has taken in the creation of today's global village.

A new technology-based product or service offering alters the way things are done. For the offering to become useful, rules and regulations often need to change. It is the responsibility of the entrepreneur to work with the bureaucracy to bring about the changes. Some entrepreneurs bad-mouth the government in private but shy away from bringing the problems to the government's attention from fear of retribution. The entrepreneur has to have the courage to convey his criticism to the government but without causing offence. He has to be the active agent of change and work closely with officialdom.

We introduced the e-ticket system. The question was how to ensure that passengers with e-tickets were permitted to enter airports. I worked with the government and the law-making agencies to ensure favourable policies for e-ticket holders, carefully explained to the government that we were doing away with travel agents in favour of direct booking, adding that now even a travel agent would be issuing an e-ticket.

The government on its part facilitated airport entry to e-ticket holders. Deccan made it mandatory for such passengers to carry some personal identification. This was important too to prevent credit card fraud. As a consequence of the amended rule, a passenger could ring our call centre late in the night and book a ticket on an early morning flight. He was given a PNR number which s/he could exchange for a print-out from the Deccan ticket counter at the airport and check in.

Technology was a great enabler. Mobile phone service providers, first Airtel and later Reliance, made it possible for people to make a local call to to our call centre. We did not have a toll-free number. If a passenger called in from Delhi and spoke for an hour to buy a ticket and another bought a ticket taking one minute, then the excess cost of the former will have to be shared by the latter. That would not only have been unfair to the other passenger but negate the very philosophy of the LCC that you pay for what you use. We, therefore, decided that it would be a local call for the customer. Technology made this possible. Reliance later gave us a single number for the entire country. As we spread out to new states, we asked Reliance to increase the bandwidth. Reliance received its revenue from customers who made calls and we negotiated a fixed price regardless of the number or duration of the calls from across the country. This gave us a fix on our telecom costs.

We had multiple points of access for passengers. The call centre, Reliance cyber cafes, kiosks at petrol stations, bakeries and groceries, individual agents, and at airport terminals. Anyone with a computer at home and Internet access could of course book directly via the Web and obtain the cheapest possible ticket. Once the ticketing system had been integrated, the ticket counter outside airports and check-in counters within them had to be linked to our IT system. We outsourced this to HCL-Infosys. They maintained the computers and the VPNs and LANs across airports. Call centre activities were outsourced to Airtel and Reliance. This enabled us to ramp up operations across India at lightning speed.

We were hampered by shortage of hangar space. Most hangars were in a state of abandonment and disrepair, and the few usable ones were with Jet or Sahara or Indian Airlines. The AAI could not give us space for storage of essential equipment and spare-parts.

We entered into a time-share arrangement with the Indian Airlines: hangar space for a fee of Rs 50,000 a day. IA was paying the AAI a measly rent for the use of the hangar while we had to pay through our nose and were constantly threatened by the rider clause that hangar space could be ours subject to availability. Hangar space is so fundamental to running an airline, yet we had to depend on the competition for it.

In response to this crisis, I tied up with Taneja Aerospace, a private aircraft builder based at Hosur airport, 40 km from Bengaluru, for use of their hangar for heavy maintenance. This meant that we had to set up inventory, repair, and inspection infrastructure at a distance from our operational base, which for my aircraft entailed unproductive, empty-seat flights to and from HAL airport. At the HAL airport, and several others, aircrafts were, and still are, repaired and maintained on the tarmac, in sun and rain. This entailed additional costs. This was a huge handicap to begin with.

Even as I put together the airline, step by step, I had to contend with the scepticism of the LCC. Among them was industry veteran Naresh Goyal. Naresh ridiculed the idea and said low-cost airlines in India are a myth. He said LCC fare offerings would be impossible if other expenses like aircraft acquisition costs, pilot salaries, and infrastructure costs are the same as those for the traditional airlines. I countered with the example of successfully running an Udupi hotel in a country where the basic infrastructure cost is the same as that of the Taj or Oberoi groups. The cost of rice is fixed all over India and is standard for all hotels, I retorted, but did that in any way stop the Udupi hotel chain from functioning and catering to the low-budget needs of the common man ?

It is true that low-cost airlines contend with the same aircraft costs, the same lease rentals, and the same pilot salaries. However, an LCC differentiates itself from a legacy full carrier on several other counts. It saves huge costs by flying longer hours, accommodating more seats, distributing tickets on the Internet, and dispensing with frills. To clinch the argument, as I write this, Jet and Kingfisher, reeling under heavy losses, are busy converting almost 75 per cent of their fleet to the LCC model.

There is an interesting story about O'Leary of Ryan Air. During an inspection of his aircraft, O'Leary observed damaged aircraft seats. Most CEOs wouldn't have spared a second thought, but O'Leary sent for his engineering chief who identified the cause of the damage: large-bodied passengers trying to adjust their seats. O'Leary decided that Ryan Air did not require adjustable seats.

O'Leary once told me during a private conversation that he awoke every morning with a sword in hand. Which department do I target today for cost-cutting? This was his daily question. I took a Ryan Air flight from Toulouse in France to London, paying 59 euros for the passage: 29 euros was the ticket price including taxes; 15 euros per piece of baggage checked in; 15 euros for the one kilogram excess baggage. The logic was strange but simple. Use a service, pay for it. Passengers paid for every additional resource utilized. O'Leary was aware that smaller towns would welcome a flight landing and taking off from the local airport, benefiting from the spin-offs of air traffic.

He was, therefore, actually able to get the municipal council of many small airports, to pay his airline five to ten euros per passenger! The small cities realized intuitively air connectivity boosted tourism, trade and generated employment and decided to pay his airline five Euros per passenger who landed at their airport!

It is a paradox but true, the airline which offers the lowest fare is the most profitable of all. Ryan Air is in profit whereas legacy airlines such as British Airways, United Airlines, and Delta Airlines charge exorbitant fares and yet are losing money. A greater number of seats of course entails greater discomfort, and snobs are uncomfortable with the prospect of the the common man flying. Ryan Air garnered an array of uncharitable remarks. Some called it *cattle class*. If you are not a snob, you would recognize the beneficiaries, and the patrons, of LCCs as assorted, nameless, faceless, classless, working middle-class individuals who are in fact the real backbone of the economy.

I had to identify other ways of reducing the cost of operations. I visualized the aircraft as a shopping mall without footfalls but where merchandise went around. Meals from The Taj or the Oberoi were prohibitively expensive so we worked out a no-frills plan: no complimentary meals on board. Passengers would have to purchase what they wished to eat and drink including water. We were unable to identify a caterer who would help us customize food sales so I got an idea. I asked Bhargavi, who was running a bakery, whether she could take up the contract of selling food with longer shelf-life on the flights. She would pay us a fixed royalty on the sales every month on a turnkey basis. Our air hostesses would be the salesgirls and the passengers her captive customers. We told the cabin crew that they would receive a 15 per cent incentive on food sales. It was a happy arrangement: Bhargavi made a profit; we made a profit; and the cabin crew got a bonus. A cost stream had become a revenue stream.

We also saved on clean-up costs. We got the air-hostesses to do this and paid them a separate allowance. We appealed to passengers to avoid littering. We eliminated contract aircraft cleaners, saved on contractor fees, and saved on the time required for security screening and thereby also saved on aircraft turnaround time.

When the passenger numbers rose to several millions we decided to utilize Café Coffee Day to handle the on-board catering. They gave us a fixed percentage on their sales and this was linked to passenger numbers to keep the audit simple. Our revenue from Café Coffee Day was three to four crore rupees at eight million passengers. Every bit helped to either cut costs or add to the till.

We calculated that if we were to spend Rs 100 each on food for our eight million passengers, we would have to spend Rs 80 crore a year. With that money we could buy six Airbus aircraft on lease rentals! Air-hostess salaries were at a low base-line but with allowances: cleaning allowance, vehicle allowance, and an on-board sales allowance from Café Coffee Day, their salaries were higher than those offered by Jet Airways' cabin crew.

Pilot perquisites, especially pickup and drop and meals, also lent themselves to cost-cutting and rationalization. A helicopter pilot began his day in the morning and carried packed food from home. He flew to interior and far-flung areas where food could not be bought. In addition to this self-service, the pilot went to the Air Traffic Control to pay fees and cleaned up the helicopter. We thought that if a helicopter pilot could do that much, so should fixed-wing aircraft pilots.

The pilots were initially reluctant to accept the austerity measures but I reminded them that by keeping costs low, planes would always be full and no jobs would be lost; that the airline's sustainability depended on keeping costs low and that it was a socially laudable objective for the airline to fly common people, a feat nobody had hitherto attempted. They concurred with me and more than willingly accepted allowances in lieu of pick-up and meals.

I explained to them how an allowance of Rs 200 per day worked out to Rs 6000 per month and Rs 15 lakh which accrued interest in fifteen years, which could be saved for a child's education. I suggested they bring a sandwich or paratha from home, seeing no sense in paying money to The Taj or Oberoi. By doing away with the pick-up and drop schemes for pilots, we saved on vehicle purchase, fuel and maintenance costs; we also saved on driver and coordinator staff salaries and benefits, and above all, on office costs.

In 2003, HAL authorities opposed the launch of the new Bengaluru International Airport because they stood to lose revenue, yet at the same time they were not behaving like a commercial enterprise in refusing me parking and hangar space. As a service provider, HAL charged a fee and was behaving more like the PWD and electricity board.

I needed parking and hangar space for practical reasons and to fulfil conditions for taking delivery of aircraft. I was supposed to show DGCA that I had trained engineers and provided evidence that I had the capability to maintain aircraft. I had an arrangement with Indian Airlines for using their hangar space in Mumbai for day-to-day maintenance. For major maintenance I had tied up with Taneja Aerospace, but for day-to-day maintenance in Bengaluru I needed space as well as a simple open-air concrete space to park the aircraft overnight for morning flights to various destinations. The HAL was refused to give this.

HAL said they would undertake our ground-handling and asked for Rs 30,000 per ATR. This would amount to an additional burden of

Rs 1000 per passenger on a forty-eight-seater aircraft. Jet Airways was doing its own ground handling and I wanted to do the same. I had endless rounds of meetings and HAL proved to be one of the worst government departments in terms of bureaucratic red tape.

Furious, I rushed to Delhi to meet defence minister George Fernandes who I had come to know quite well by then and who had already agreed to inaugurate the launch. I said I had hit a stone wall with HAL. He immediately called the chairman of HAL, and said, 'This is an ex-army officer. I want you to go out of your way to ensure that he gets parking space, facilities to maintain his aircraft, and gets to do his own ground-handling. You should be welcoming him rather than adopting a hostile attitude.' For safety's sake I asked George Fernandes whether I could come back to him if things didn't work out. He said, with a twinkle in his eyes, 'I did not request him. I gave him orders.' The call had the desired effect because I got some twenty calls from the HAL chairman's office before reaching Bengaluru.

Our marketing department had innovated something new to add to the revenue channels. It struck a deal with Sun Microsystems to paint the exterior of the aircraft with their brand logo at a charge of Rs 20 lakh a month. It was a big coup as the amount came in handy to cover 50 per cent of my monthly lease rental on the aircraft. We had the aircraft exterior painted by Sun Microsystems, but when the marketing team went to the DGCA, the agency didn't approve this. I was not sure what the reason was, so we searched the archives and found the relevant rules governing external branding displays on aircraft. The Aircraft Rule 1937 said: 'No aircraft can be painted with any form of advertisement or slogan except the registration of the aircraft unless specifically permitted by the DGCA.'

The DGCA was headed by Satyender Singh. He was a good man but like all good bureaucrats he went by the book. I met him and said I needed permission for external branding. He was very quick to say 'No'; and that aircraft rules didn't permit it. Having read the rules I said I could perhaps do it with his permission. I handed him a letter. He asked his staff to find out why airlines were not permitted to carry advertisements. One of them said it was for reasons of safety. I said that as aircraft had their names painted on them, safety could have nothing to do with it. My engineers had told me that so long as the aircraft was painted in the colours and paint approved by the manufacturer and the paint did not peel off and enter the engine, there was no safety concern. I told the DGCA we would use paint recommended by the manufacturer and not use vinyl because vinyl tended to peel off at alternating high and low temperatures.

I also said low-cost airlines around the world painted their aircraft with brand names and made money and reduced fares. Satyender Singh, known to be a stickler for rules, was now in a tight corner, believing that if a rule had been imposed since 1937 there must, as with the scriptures, be a reason for it. He needed to be personally convinced, and till he was, he would not allow the aircraft to be painted. I brought this up when I went to meet Rudy. I said we had lucrative contracts from Sun Microsystems and NDTV but were being denied permission from the DGCA. The minister called up Satyender Singh and requested him to either clear the file or send it to him for approval. Satyender Singh dutifully sent the file across to the minister.

Readying for the Bengaluru–Hubli Launch Flight

The run-up to the launch was by no means easy. The same kind of problems kept arising till the last minute. Somewhat akin to what had preceded the launch of the helicopter operations. Initially, there were people in competition who did not relish our capturing the imagination of the country and winning the support of political leaders and bureaucrats. These cloak and dagger adversaries had MPs writing to the ministry of civil aviation, raising safety issues. One misinformed politician acting on behalf of an established airlines wrote that a low-cost airline would not have the resources to spend on the maintenance of aircraft. Our preparation in this direction was thorough. We had cast-iron answers to these feeble doubts about operational safety.

What was of greater concern to us was that we did not have trained Indian pilot captains to fly ATR aircraft and had to hire them from abroad. We had submitted a list of fifty names of foreign pilots to the Home Ministry and they would have to be screened by several agencies including the CBI, the police, the drug enforcement agency, the RAW, and the civil aviation ministry before approval.

The launch of Deccan was less than two years after the 9/11 terrorist attacks on New York. Security and intelligence agencies were naturally very wary about permissions to foreign pilots. I was cautious not to push too hard for permissions. Terrorists had earlier only hijacked aircraft and jeopardized the lives of passengers and crew but now they had begun to convert aircraft into missiles and had the capability to wreak destruction in the air and on the ground on a hitherto unimaginable scale.

It was not Rudy's turf and he rightly washed his hands off it. I used contacts in the defence and my point man, Col. D.V. Singh, single-handedly combed through the maze of sensitive ministries and agencies and was eventually able to obtain the requisite clearances. I suggested that while the agencies must take their own time about screening an applicant if they had even the slightest cause for suspicion, they should clear those with unblemished reputations. That would allow me to commence operations.

Just two days before the launch, the director general of air-worthiness, P. K. Chattopadhyay, a very good friend of mine and one of the most positive people I have known, called me. He was calling about our decision to have one air-hostess aboard a forty-eight-seater ATR. He said he did not want us to be grounded for flouting rules about the minimum number of cabin crew for each aircraft. The rules however stated that an aircraft must have one cabin crew for every fifty passengers and we had forty-eight seats so I felt we would certainly not be flouting them by having one air-hostess on the aircraft.

I rechecked after the DGCA's call. One of my team members said, 'Sir, the plane needs one air-hostess for fifty passengers. Another said, 'No, Captain, it's not about the number of passengers but about the number of exits in the aircraft. You must have one cabin crew to manage each exit.'

No-one had actually seen the rule book; just consulted the local DGCA official, and each had his own version of the rule. It was now necessary to see with our own eyes what the book said, which was that an aircraft must have one cabin crew for every fifty passengers. That settled the matter. This was a lesson I had learnt early in life. When people say it cannot be done, don't accept it easily but get into the habit of checking the rule book yourself.

Our next task was to get Hubli airport approved for commercial operations. Hubli airport did not have procedures for landing and therefore our chief pilot would not be able to undertake a trial landing. We needed to secure documents from the department of meteorology which was under the wings of the ministry of science and technology. The ATC and the meteorological representative had not yet been posted there, and without either we would not be able fly. The tarmac was not ready and baggage x-ray machines had not yet been installed.

Airport security is provided by BCAS which falls under the home ministry. The home ministry posts people to AAI on the basis of a requisition letter from that agency. These people look after various security positions. The AAI collects a passenger service fee through the airline, keeps a percentage of that fee and remits the balance to the home ministry.

It was the AAI's turn now to take us by surprise. The authority said I should get police and fire services support from the state government. The police commissioner in Hubli wanted to help but he needed to know who would pay for the services of police personnel. I told him the AAI would. He wanted a letter from the AAI to that effect, which the latter was reluctant to issue.

This problem was solved after I met the state home minister, Mallikarjun Kharge. I explained that the AAI was supposed to pay for police services from the passenger fee they charged for the service. It was simply a question of time and they would certainly pay, but waiting for a letter from them would unnecessarily hold up the launch. Kharge called the police commissioner and asked him to provide state police for airport duty within the venue, outside, and at security clearance posts.

At each step I had to innovate a solution for the ministry or the bureaucracy to act on without violating regulations. The goodwill I had succeeded in generating for the people's airline helped a great deal. The state government developed a sense of identity with the new airline. The first flight from Bengaluru to Hubli would make it appear that the airline was born in Karnataka. Hubli as choice for the inaugural flight sent out a message about the kind of people we were hoping to target. It was against this background that the drama about the police security for the airport took place. I liaised with the state government, the AAI, and the police department. The state government positioned its police at the airport security points and the problem seemed to have disappeared for good when I received a rude shock from another source, the BCAS this time. In a drama, the characters want to enact particular roles. Sometimes those enacting the lesser parts felt ignored and tried their best to be seen and heard on stage. It was now for the BCAS to demand more action and more dialogue in the play. The agency said we needed a certificate from the state government certifying that at least some of the police personnel being deployed for airport security were trained in anti-terrorism tactics.

The policemen and policewomen posted at Hubli airport were not trained to handle terrorism, not having undergone the three-day course the central government conducted for state police officers. We only had two days left, certainly quite inadequate for the course to be arranged. I asked my security chief P.N. Thimmaiah to follow-up with the police. The DGP moved heaven and earth to identify and deploy policemen who had undergone anti-terrorism training but the BCAS wanted a letter from the state government certifying that. I received that letter and alerted my own team and staff to scrupulously adhere to anti-terrorism measures. I instructed them to check every bag and every component till everyone and everything had been screened and found safe.

The ATR aircraft took off from Toulouse five days ahead of the launch after overcoming some minor hitches about export certificate of air-worthiness and import permission. The pilots we had deputed returned after training and received DGCA endorsement. We were the first airline to be using a large number of foreign pilots to fly in India. The DGCA wanted to conduct tests because there had been an accident long ago due to a misunderstanding between the pilot and the ATC and had caused the DGCA to become very strict about it. The pilots took an oral exam in English communication and Indian aerospace rules.

The state government was very helpful. It did not give us any subsidy but passed a rule enabling officials of lower rank to fly on duty. Only IAS officers had so far been allowed air travel; not assistant commissioners and tahsildars. S.M. Krishna passed gazette notifications putting this rule into effect on the eve of the launch. It was of direct benefit to us, enabling us to count on official patronage too.

Most vitally, IT had fallen into place. The software and networking had been implemented, and eight days before the launch, user-testing on the software was undertaken. We opened the booking counter online and launched teaser campaigns to support the bookings. The operations were on a massive scale and many things had to rapidly come together: the call centre, the bank, the anywhere-in-the-world travel agent, the communication service provider Airtel, and VPN and LAN service provider HCL-Infosys had to be integrated and made to work as a seamless web. Call centre operations continued to be given primary focus, and we recruited fifty people for the operations.

Our agency, Orchard Advertising, gave us a great advertising profile. The agency created the logo and tag line for the company, punning on the word 'Simplifly'. It implied that we were here to ease out and simplify air travel for everybody, who could now fly with Deccan without any concern. We chose blue and yellow as the official colours. Two upturned palms with fingers stretched up symbolizing dynamic lift and personal care was our logo. The two upturned palms were mutually positioned to symbolize a pair of wings. The aircraft was decked out in this manner.

On 22 September we had an evening concert at Jakkur. There was an audio-visual show on the airline, focusing on how it would change the economy of different regions of the country, create new jobs, bring the country closer, and transform the lives of millions. Dr L. Subramaniam gave an absolutely mesmerizing concert. The governor and the chief minister of Karnataka were special invitees to the programme. The first flight was scheduled for the next day at 10 a.m.

There is something last-minute about the last minute hitch. You cannot unravel it until the last minute. We still did not have the Air Transport Licence to operate the flight at 9.30 in the morning on the inaugural day. Rajiv Pratap Rudy, S. M. Krishna, George Fernandes, and Venkaiah Naidu were already at the venue when I received a message that the licence had not arrived.

We had been in total compliance and I knew it would come, but it was a cliffhanger. As in the case of the helicopter launch, the licence came barely twenty minutes before the flight. I had a back-up plan: I would do a one-time ferry flight to Hubli! But thankfully I did not need to resort to it.

The flight was flagged off by S. M. Krishna. For this we had two aircrafts ready. One took off for Hubli carrying the media and the passengers, the other flew to Mangalore with George Fernandes on board. As the flight took off the audience rose in applause. That single flight to Hubli, the rural dusty town in the middle of Karnataka, marked a historic moment that changed Indian aviation forever.

Beginning with the day of the launch, our flights had attracted a lot of attention. We flew the Mangalore–Bengaluru, Bengaluru–Chennai, and Bengaluru–Hyderabad routes at near 100 per cent occupancy. The planes were filling and the IT system ran perfectly. Our two aircrafts did ten flights a day each, and that was optimum asset utilization. People were booking tickets from everywhere in India and from around the world.

Two days later I was in for another rude shock when I received a call at 5 a.m. The local DGCA had turned up at the airport and stopped us from taking off with the Sun Microsystems logo and branding. He said he had still not received the letter from Delhi, allowing us to paint the Sun advertisement. It did not matter to him that the civil aviation minister had himself inaugurated the aircraft with the branding only two days earlier.

What happened was that Satyendra Singh had sent the file to the ministry for sanction. It had taken quite some time for the file to reach the minister's office and travel back down the line to Bengaluru. I was woken up at 5 a.m. by my people. I rushed to the airport and tried to reason with the DGCA official. He, however, did not budge because he had not received the letter. I was reminded of the story by A.G. Gardiner about the conductor and the lady with the dog, who forgot that rules were meant only for the comfort of customers. On a late wintry night in London, when there was a blizzard and it was biting cold, he kept driving a very, very old lady passenger, to the roof of the bus, even though she was the only passenger on the bus. He said, 'Mam, rules are rules. Dogs are not allowed in lower deck.' And nearly drove the old lady to death by freezing. We had no alternative but to camouflage the branding with water-based paint.

John Kuruvilla, who headed our ad agency Orchard, had quit and set up a property business on the Internet during the heady dotcom days. The bubble burst and the company folded up. He came over to our airline and I readily took him on as our marketing head. I really believe that most of the innovations that were made in the airline were authored by John. John showed great commitment and brought in loads of energy. He had a young team of innovative thinkers, one of whom had hit upon an idea that we should sell tickets through Reliance Web-world kiosks.

This solved a very tricky issue of refunds. How do you refund a passenger who bought a ticket from a travel agent in Delhi and cancelled it in Bengaluru? Our rules stated that the passenger had to go back to the travel agent from whom s/he had bought the ticket. The travel agent might have given the passenger credit, so if we paid out the refund in Bengaluru, the agent would be out of change. Our policy was to enable refund to the point of sale.

John suggested that we sell tickets at Reliance Internet cafes across the country, some 300 of which had just opened in large and small towns. Reliance was looking for additional sources of revenue, and received 5 per cent commission on the sale of a ticket just like any other travel agent. Selling our tickets would bring in one extra channel, and provide us with a national presence and free branding across their outlets.

John's team continued to be creative. They came up with the idea that we could sell tickets at petrol stations. We signed up with Hindustan Petroleum, asking them to offer tickets at 1000 petrol stations in different parts of the country. Petrol stations, unlike travel agents, work 24 hours a day and seven days of the week. These truly served as any-time ticketing points and John's initiative worked.

We took the innovation forward by introducing Internet-enabled mobile van ticketing, which worked on Internet-enabled mobile phone connectivity, and this created quite a buzz. The reservation system allowed access to these nodes anywhere in the country. The van moved about town making e-ticketing extremely easy and convenient, and also served as a mobile hoarding for the Deccan brand.

This idea succeeded at some places and failed at others, but it did create customer awareness about Deccan. John was adding agents every second day and we were in a position to scale up within the first fifty days. I realized that lack of imagination was perhaps the only limiting factor in any new enterprise or experiment.

One of the surprise discoveries of the channel exploration process was the Indian post and telegraph department. Perhaps the oldest colonial institution, the Indian P&T used to, till recently, have a very visible presence. I remember the red letter-boxes that hung from poles and pillars or stood at street-corners. All these boxes all had a little black window with space for three numbers and two letters to indicate the clearance time. I would never have considered the Indian post and telegraph as a potential channel for Deccan but for the post-master general of Karnataka, Meera Dutta.

I met Meera Dutta on a flight. She seemed to be an extremely innovative and energetic woman and very dedicated to her work. She told me that Indian P&T had plunged into a crisis with the arrival of the Internet and the mobile phone. The department initially had considered closing down many post-offices but decided against it when someone suggested that they could sell other instruments such as insurance and savings bonds, also make use of technology and re-train and infuse new blood into the organization. She told me a story that opened my eyes. She was travelling on a Deccan flight from Hubli to Bengaluru. Her neighbour was an ordinary village woman who no-one would ever have imagined, would fly in an aeroplane. Meera asked her where she was from and how she had bought her tickets. The woman told Meera that she lived in a village near Gadag, an hour by bus from Hubli. She asked her son to buy a ticket and he went to Hubli and bought the Air Deccan ticket. Meera said, 'Then it occurred to me that there are post offices even in small towns where people can buy your tickets. Some of these have now been Internet-enabled, so Deccan can definitely benefit from us.'

The Indian posts, as I discovered for myself, has 1,55,000 outlets across the country and 10,000 in Karnataka. Meera had told me that Karnataka would eventually have 1000 Internet-enabled post-offices: 500 were already in place. The P&T can actually reach out to one billion people in the country and is perhaps the greatest channel for any socially relevant government scheme or for any business that has the ambition to target the entire population. The discussion with Meera Dutta eventually led to an agreement with the Indian Posts to allow the sale of Deccan tickets at their outlets. We installed vinyl backlit displays saying 'Air Deccan tickets sold here'. Deccan now had visibility in the remotest corners of the state.

We had pioneered many routes and were the only ones flying to those cities and towns and enjoyed 100 per cent occupancy on those routes. On routes where we competed with the regulars, we managed a good 90 per cent occupancy. These were sectors like Bengaluru–Hyderabad, Bengaluru–Chennai, and Bengaluru–Mangalore. We were offering half the fare charged by Jet Airways and Indian Airlines. I never missed an opportunity to fly these aircraft and talk to passengers and acquire a feel of the pulse of people.

People liked the ATRs. The aircraft were small and check-in and boarding time was short. The aircraft had its own ladder and passengers did not have to wait for a step-ladder to arrive or a high-loader to load baggage. The plane had an informal ambience, which made the passengers feel comfortable and at home. At the point of arrival, passenger baggage was rapidly sent to the conveyer belts.

Competition had spread a rumour about the safety and reliability of our aircraft. People had gone about saying the aircraft we were using were old and unsafe, and this did serve to scare away some people who were new to air travel. People believed the rumours because, on the face of it, they thought that if you were running an airline at half the usual cost, surely there must have been compromises with safety. However, gradually the facts of our business model became well-known and we gained credibility as a safe and reliable airline.

A week after the inauguration, I received a call from the BBC in London who were excited by our emphasis on the 'unconnected parts of India'. The BBC producer said they wanted to interview me on board the Bengaluru–Hubli flight and also wanted to speak to passengers on board. They planned to spend the day in Hubli and visit the chamber of commerce. They were also keen to speak to small and medium entrepreneurs to find out what people thought about air connectivity and the impact they thought it would have on their businesses. There were other national and international media representatives who came and met me and wrote about the new airline.

We also had to dispel rumours about Deccan that our aircraft were noisy and shaky. That was not true, but it was true that our flights were getting delayed because we had a huge logistics problem. We were ramping up at the rate of an aircraft a month and had deployed seven aircraft in seven months, and at the end of six months we were operating sixty flights a day. Our original plan was to have seven aircraft in eighteen months, but having inducted seven aircraft we also needed seventy air-hostesses, seventy-five pilots, and thirty-five engineers. Some of the problems stemmed from managing growth but some came from poor access to airport infrastructure.

We had, however, to quash doubts about the safety of our aircraft immediately. Aircraft, new and old, are safe or unsafe depending on maintenance and observance of safety procedures. Flying discipline is another contributory factor. We were not compromising on any of these. Airlines like British Airways or Lufthansa fly aircraft that are ten, fifteen, or even twenty years old. It is only the low-cost airlines that have a fleet of relatively new aircraft. Being cash-strapped, we had begun with relatively older aircraft but would maintain them to perfection: this was our mantra.

The rumours were swirling around in my head. What if there was an ounce of truth in them? I spent a lot of time at the airport and in the workshops. I terrorized my people. I did not want them to cut corners, and wanting them to realize that low-cost did not mean low quality and low safety. We also put out an ad: 'We are cutting costs not corners!'

Water was the source of some initial dissatisfaction among passengers. Indians expect water to be served free and passengers asked us how we could sell water when it flowed freely. Our crew had to convince passengers why we could not serve water free. We ran advertisements in our in-flight magazine explaining why we don't provide complimentary water and catering on-board. Some showered compliments and some complained. Some told us what Deccan must and mustn't do. Deccan had become a people's airline.

I publicized that we could not give free water. I argued, 'You don't get free water on a KSRTC bus or in AC II Class train. You get free water in AC I Class.' Some suggested factoring in the price of a bottle of water in the ticket.

My energies were, however, focused on two fronts: engineering and flight safety. No compromise, no cutting corners. I told passengers we were committed to four principles of LCC: fly safe, be on time, deliver bags safely and quickly, and offer lowest fares. All these promises were measurable.

Regarding newspapers, I stuck to the original decision. We, however, allowed some publishers to place their issues on board; they paid us for it. We got a publisher to produce our in-flight magazine *Simplifly*. I used the magazine as a vehicle to explain the low-cost model to passengers and to convey messages. We also put our schedules, advertisements, and updates in it. Most importantly, it helped generate some revenue through the advertising.

Vijaya Menon, who joined me in Deccan Aviation, helped with media handling for Air Deccan, looked after the magazine, and handled customer relations. She did such an excellent job of the media relations that we were constantly in the news. People enquired about the PR agency they thought we had hired to manage our media relations, finding it impossible to believe that one woman was handling it all. It was truly a tribute to Vijaya Menon's acumen and ability.

Creating a brand image that has good recall is a tough task. How can one brand name stand out among thousands? Not more than twenty companies in India have that kind of evocative power. A company requires both media and marketing effort to achieve that. We wanted to achieve visibility and recall at the lowest cost. What we managed to do, with the help of the marketing team and Orchard, was to capture the imagination of the people. People recalled Deccan readily because they became brand owners and stakeholders. They identified with it as their own airline.

The reach of Deccan as a brand was phenomenal. Once, Renuka Ramanathan, CEO of ICICI Ventures, India's largest venture capital fund, who eventually invested in Deccan, told me a story about her son. Whilst she was at the dinner table, she asked her ten-year-old if he knew the meaning of low-cost airline, and before she could finish framing her question, he shot back, 'You mean Air Deccan, mamma?' On another occasion I received a very warm letter from one of our passengers who regularly flew my airline, a gynaecologist attached to the famous Manipal Hospital. She wanted to share an incident with me. 'I have a big fan of yours in my family,' she wrote. 'He is only nine years old.' She said she was tidying up her son's study table when among sheaves of paper and notebooks she chanced upon a cartoon about Deccan. Her son had drawn the cartoon with an aircraft in the centre and me beside it with the Deccan logo prominently displayed on it. She said nobody had ever asked the boy to do anything like that. It was indeed a tribute to the power of Deccan as a brand that had triggered the boy's imagination. She had enclosed the cartoon along with the letter.

Deccan's visibility as a brand and its widespread recall owed much to the creative inputs of Nitish Mukherjee, who took over as MD of Orchard Advertising when John left, Thomas, the creative director, and Nutan, accounts director. The three identified themselves deeply with Deccan.

The in-flight magazine served two purposes for Deccan. It allowed us to explain our low-cost carrier model to passengers and answer the questions that had been raised about safety. It also brought us regular revenue on the strength of passenger numbers. I asked the editor of the magazine to keep in view four quality parameters: layout, paper quality, style of cover design, and tenor and content of articles. I took an active part in the content design and outlined articles that I wanted featured in the magazine. I suggested they carry articles on tourism; on spectacular destinations; on the cultural labyrinth that made-up India, and on entrepreneurs. It was a simple deal. The publishers of the magazine would give us revenue based on the number of passengers flying Deccan. As numbers rose, the revenue also rose. The publishers' derived their revenue from advertisements.

We gave the publishing contract to Radhakrishna Nair, a former editor of *Business India* and an associate of the Anand Mahindra Group. He published and edited the *Man's World* magazine

We signed a separate in-flight shopping contract. We allowed the contractor to sell branded goods on our flights and received a fixed commission on the sales.

Our marketing team worked so hard, so creatively, and in such a focused manner that at the end of the first year we had 2000 points of sale across the country; at the end of three we had 7000 touch points. These were accredited and authorized sellers of Air Deccan tickets. In the first year we had one person handling these travel management accounts, and four at the end of three. We had managed to give the IATA travel agents a sense of confidence in our model and they began returning, realizing that the model was good for business and good for them. They all brought their boycott to an end and joined us.

When they heard of the successful launch of Deccan's regular flights to small cities and towns such as Hubli and Belgaum, chief ministers of various north Indian states began to call. Among them were Jharkhand chief minister Arjun Munda; Himachal chief minister Virbhadra Singh, and Uttaranchal chief minister Narayan Dutt Tiwari. They wanted to meet me on their next visit to Bengaluru. New states had been carved out from the old and large states of Uttar Pradesh (Uttaranchal), Madhya Pradesh (Chhattisgarh) and Bihar (Jharkhand). The political leaders were desperate for air connectivity to create conditions for economic growth. It was such a reversal of trend: political leaders were now wooing entrepreneurs because they saw the benefits that stemmed from creating new infrastructure. I was reminded of an incident in Bengaluru a few years ago when a chief minister and the chief secretary of Karnataka did not turn up for an appointed meeting with Ratan Tata for over an hour, compelling him to leave.

The calls from political leaders and the bureaucracy were unceasing. They were from principle secretaries of tourism and infrastructure development, who wanted me to meet their CMs. It was a refrain that they had met Azim Premji or Rahul Bajaj, or Narayana Murthy, and the industry leaders were willing to set up bases in their states only if the government could provide air links.

The enthusiasm of the political leadership for connectivity was both intense and widespread. At one point, I was often working simultaneously with twenty airports in unconnected interior regions of the country to have them ready for operations. I was coordinator between the different agencies and wanted to speed up official and statutory clearances.

I wanted to scale up operations quickly. By working with twenty airports at one time, and at an implementation ratio of one in four, I would accelerate the early completion of five. My team made trips to remote places where nobody wanted to go, travelling by train or bus. As a team leader I was tough. Between a tough leader and an easy one, one would prefer to work for an easy boss. But a leader who is not a taskmaster will cause the net energy of the organization to be negative and employees will not feel motivated.

This was my experience during the 1971 war. The Pakistani army deployed in East Pakistan was leaderless; their soldiers were degenerate, corrupt, and debauched. The Pakistani army on the western front was a fine fighting force, comparing well with the best in the world. That was because it was well led, disciplined, organized, and energized.

There was a reason why I worked really hard to get the airports ready. We had to take delivery of three more ATR aircrafts, and an expanding fleet needed greater airport space. If we did not get them ready in time

we would have to add flights on the Mumbai–Delhi or on the Bengaluru–
Chennai or Bengaluru–Hyderabad sectors which went against my strategy
and philosophy of opening new markets and creating customers rather than
take on established airlines like Jet and Indian Airlines by going to metros.
Someone gave me the analogy of a frog in water that was being slowly
heated. The frog would die when the water reached boiling point, but throw
the frog into boiling hot water and it will jump right out!

However, not withstanding above, Deccan's gradually increasing presence
roused the existing carriers from complacent slumber. Jet injected new
energies and initiated revenue management. It lowered its fares by 25 to 40
per cent and increased occupancy. The new growth was over an average base
line and not in absolute terms. It, however, looked promising nevertheless
because stagnation had overtaken the airline. Loads improved and it looked
a promising upswing, with Jet adding more flights and more aircraft. Indian
Airlines followed suit.

It seems intuitive to think that monopoly protects a business from
competition, but my experience is that it is competition that enlarges a
consumer base and protects the business and not the other way around.
I once holidayed at a seaside resort in an alcove along the Konkan coast
of Karnataka. That part of the shore attracted turtles. The waters were
pristine and the swimming experience perfect. It was a quiet and pleasant
retreat, but when I pondered the business aspect, it was disturbingly quiet:
a resort of that quality should have been busy with tourist arrivals. Why
otherwise did tourists prefer to head for Goa, slightly to the north, and not
come here?

People travel to Goa in large numbers because it caters to the entire
economic spectrum of tourism; it offers something worthwhile to everyone.
There is no competition in exclusion. I had another experience of a similar
kind in Hassan. I went to a pharmacy close to the district headquarters.
There were a dozen pharmacies in the neighbourhood. I once asked this
chemist, 'Your shop is located in a place where there are twenty other
pharmacies. Doesn't that affect your business?' What I heard from him is
an unforgettable lesson in customer psychology. He said, 'Sir, an isolated
chemist's shop in a residential area is far less frequented than twenty shops
in the bazaar area. You will ask me why. I say it is so because people come
there knowing that a cluster of shops together will have all the medicines
in the medical pharmacopoeia. Therefore someone looking for prescription
medicine would rather go to the cluster of shops. What the customer does
not find in one, s/he will find in another. Isn't that convenient?'

A similar principle operated in Hong Kong where the largest market for electronic goods used to be located in the cluster of by-lanes in Tsim Sha Tsui, on Kowloon Island; this is also true of Bengaluru's Chikpet or Delhi's Chandni Chowk.

Competition can only kill business when the business is inefficient. Competition helps to improve quality and brings down prices and is therefore good for the consumer. Monopoly, on the other hand, invariably stifles business. It is good neither for the consumer nor the business nor the industry.

꙳

I met Chandrababu Naidu once again to seek his help to start flights from Hyderabad to Vijayawada and Rajahmundry. Chandrababu Naidu was dynamic as a chief minister. Though not highly educated in the formal sense he was gifted with an intuitive understanding of the meaning of reform, technology, and infrastructure development. Politicians see that subsidies do not help the end user. They know that these are eaten up midway by agents and touts and the corrupt in the bureaucracy. Their populist plank does not however permit them to act to replace subsidies with core infrastructure creation. Chandrababu Naidu was different. He shrugged off populism and reformed the state at a frenetic pace. That alone did not help create jobs in small towns: he needed to build a business and economic ecosystem to do that.

Vijayawada and Rajahmundry were two airfields I was planning to make operational and had met Rudy and BJP supremo Venkaiah Naidu about it.

Although Chandrababu Naidu and Venkaiah Naidu were from different parties, they both realized the importance of air access to small towns and cities. Venkaiah Naidu spoke to Chandrababu Naidu and Rudy to expedite the repair of the airports at Vijayawada and Rajahmundry, and Chandrababu Naidu even gave a date when to launch the flight. This second launch was as important as the first launch for Deccan. It would reinforce the idea that Deccan was here to transform the country.

Launches from the hinterland were important to me. I flew personally to supervise the inaugural events at thirty unconnected airports out of sixty-seven, attending launches in Kolhapur, Agra, Pathankot, Kandla, Dehradun, and Shimla, among others. These high-profile events had the chief minister, the local MLA, the local MP, and the local film star in VIP attendance. Raj Babbar attended the Agra event and Vinod Khanna the one at Pathankot. The Buddhist spiritual leader, the Dalai Lama was present at the Dharmashala event.

We made elaborate preparations prior to each launch. Vijaya Menon and her PR team travelled to the site well in advance. They got the local media to create a buzz about air connectivity and Deccan's low-cost mission. John Kuruvilla and his team preceded Vijaya's trip to these places. They assessed the market and devised ways of driving up ticket sales. They named e-agents and identified sales outlets. These pre-launch visits gave us an idea of the other India: we saw a consumer enthusiasm in Tier II and III cities that was no less ebullient than that in the metros.

The launches had the support of local journalists, chambers of commerce, and small and medium enterprises. Political leaders saw in them an opportunity to add a new profile to their image. The ruling party claimed credit for the new facility and opposition parties were peeved.

I did get into one such political imbroglio, although a very minor one. One BJP MP from Jabalpur made persistent efforts to contact me. 'What can I do for you?' I asked him. He wanted my help to bring a flight to Jabalpur. I met him in Delhi over a cup of coffee and someone came and took a picture of both of us shaking hands. I explained to the MP that we had a resource constraint. Flights to Jabalpur and Bhopal were not immediately feasible, but these formed part of our flight map and would be instituted some time in the future. We parted on this note. It seemed a politically insignificant and innocent meeting.

A few days following this, I received a call from one of the ministers of Madhya Pradesh who asked me why he had not been taken into confidence about Deccan flights to Bhopal and Jabalpur. The MP, who belonged to the party in opposition, had printed the picture with me in a local newspaper and had a report published alongside which implied that it was he who was initiating Deccan flights to small towns in Madhya Pradesh. In doing so he sought to raise his political stock.

When chief ministers inaugurated our flights the state government bore the expenses for the event, we not having to spend more than Rs 40–50,000. All such cost-saving schemes helped bring down the fares and also ensured a relatively smooth programme. The events, however, were neither without incident nor without a touch of the comic for the detached third-party observer. Politicians are quite capable of bringing in an unintentional touch of the comic to an otherwise dry, humourless affair.

One such event featured Raj Babbar, sitting MP from Agra. We had invited Raj Babbar for the Delhi–Agra inaugural flight. A section of the audience began raising slogans against him, among who were former MLAs and MPs as well as opposition party politicians. As a policy we treated local MLAs, MPs, and ministers from the ruling party and important members of the opposition on par. We needed the goodwill of the ruling party and also wanted the good wishes of the opposition. Deccan sought to promote an inclusive business strategy. In many other functions the ruling party invariably stole the thunder and the opposition was largely ignored and left out in the cold, angry and disgruntled.

I sat next to Raj Babbar on the dais. The sloganeers demanded to know why they had not been invited to sit on the dais. We must be sensitive to rural political and cultural sensibilities. We should expect politicians to show off, be visible, and have their egos pampered. They also express petty jealousy without a thought for public sentiment. That is what happened in Agra. I asked for more chairs to be placed on the dais and invited senior opposition leaders to come and take a seat.

In Shimla, an ex-MLA stomped on to the stage, grabbed the mike, and demanded an apology from the chief minister for leaving him out of the VIP seating on dais because it was the state government and not the ruling party organizing the event. This resulted in a frightful melee.

Hyderabad Launch

The Hyderabad–Vijayawada flight was memorable for the right and wrong reasons. The future of Deccan hinged on it. I had asked Vijaya Menon to camp at Vijayawada and ensure that every local MLA, ex-MLA, MP, ex-MP, opposition leader, ex-opposition leader, and any leader with any pretence to political authority was invited. I included the name of Rajashekhar Reddy, Chandrababu Naidu's most vehement political opponent, who later succeeded Naidu as the chief minister.

Two ATR aircrafts had flown in from Toulouse for the second launch to be held on 23 August. In the aviation industry, the aircraft manufacturer plays an extremely critical role in the safety and air-worthiness processes. The ATR manufacturer had carried out the two most important examination protocols: C-checks and D-checks on the two aircraft. These checks are comprehensive, opening up the bowels of the aircraft and closely, inch by inch, inspecting them for the slightest traces of corrosion. They look into the avionics, the engines, and the fuselage. The C-check is the major inspection when an aircraft is new and the D-check for an older aircraft. The aircraft is almost ripped apart and re-assembled. These checks ensure that all the major components have a minimum half-life left. When the manufacturer performs these checks and passes an aircraft, they are almost as good as new. Our two aircrafts had passed these checks in Toulouse in time for the second launch.

We did not source our aircraft from a broker but from the manufacturer, and a manufacturer makes no compromises on the inspection procedure. In addition, we had had a third-party auditor to audit the ATRs for international standards before we took delivery. This move eliminated potential controversy over standards and helped us dispel rumour-mongering that our aircrafts were old and unsafe. The aircraft had flown 8000 kilometres from France and were obviously in excellent shape.

On 23 August a crowd of VVIPs milled around the Hyderabad airport tarmac. Almost the entire fleet of the state's political and bureaucratic top-brass was present. Chandrababu Naidu, Venkaiah Naidu, and Rajiv Pratap Rudy, the three stalwarts who had made this possible, were there. Both the local and national media were present in full strength. The television channels had set up their cameras and broadcasting vans at a convenient distance to capture the first moments of the flight.

An impressive function had been planned to receive the aircraft at Vijayawada airport. The local MP and MLA had planned a major reception. Speeches were made in Hyderabad. Rajiv Pratap Rudy spoke of how Air Deccan was poised to create Indian aviation history. He exhorted everyone to ensure the success of Deccan because Deccan's failure meant the failure of Indian aviation. After speeches and ribbon-cutting the guests boarded the aircraft. Venkaiah Naidu and Chandrababu Naidu came on board. I took a seat next to Rajiv Pratap Rudy across the aisle from them. The flight captain was our chief pilot Capt. Rajiv Kotiyal.

We fastened our seat-belts and were expectantly, if a little anxiously, awaiting the plane's take-off. The turboprops had been turned on; we could hear their whirring noise. Cabin crew had just closed the doors. There is usually a quiet moment before the aircraft actually starts taxiing: it lasts a few seconds and the aircraft moves. We had just begun to experience that trough of quietude when somebody shouted, 'Fire!' I looked beyond Rudy at the source of the alarm and beyond the window. I saw a blazing plume of fire trailing behind the turboprop engine. It must have been about 6 metres long and was blown outwards and backwards by the inrush of air as the engine was switched on. Within seconds I heard the sound of a fire-extinguisher squirting fluid and saw how the orange and yellow of the flame's plumage had now been smothered in the waving white cape of fire-dousing foam. It lasted a few seconds. The fire was completely extinguished, but meanwhile panic was writ large on the faces of passengers. Rudy had instinctively opened the emergency exit and passengers were rapidly alighting from the aircraft.

People and the media outside had seen the long tongue of flame as it spit outwards and also the response of the fire-extinguisher and the dousing of the flame. It had at most lasted a few seconds. As soon as the VIPs had recovered from the initial shock, Venkaiah Naidu, Rajiv Pratap Rudy, and

I drew up close. Venkaiah Naidu held my hand and Rudy's, and said, 'It's now very important that we speak the same language to the press.' Just as he left the tarmac, he told Rudy, 'Stay with Capt. Gopi. Deccan's success is important for the nation.'

My chief pilot Rajiv Kotiyal and the chief engineer told us it was not uncommon for aircraft engines to catch fire mid-flight. In that event, the pilot switches off the affected engine and lands with the help of the other engine. In the current case, they said, the fire was not inside the engine, but outside the engine and in all likelihood caused by some residual combustible fuel that had accumulated in a receptacle meant to hold trickles outside the turboprop. The fuel forms a film trapping readily combustible vapour. The heat generated by the propeller, the engine, and friction from passage of air at high velocity must have caused the vapour to ignite and burn. The flame would have died down in a few seconds and would not have even required a fire-extinguisher.

I had already begun to receive calls from home, colleagues, and business associates. The marketing team came up to me in confidence and suggested we suspend air operations for a month and resume them only after thorough third-party audit on our aircraft safety. They said that this would generate consumer confidence and we would also get a clean chit. They felt such a move would prove to the country that we made no compromises on safety. Just at that moment I had a call from Orchard in Bengaluru. They wanted to know whether they should go ahead with advertisement releases scheduled for the following day and had only 30 minutes left to catch the press deadline.

I put the call on hold and asked Capt. Kotiyal whether there was any safety issue. He said there was none, and that such incidents were not uncommon. He said he was willing to fly the aircraft to Vijayawada that very moment. I had to take a decision on the advertisement release and did not think for more than a split second after that. I resumed the call with Orchard and said we were going ahead as usual. If I had at that moment dithered and gone along with the suggestion to suspend operations for a month, Deccan would never have taken off again. The competition would have utilized this opportunity to bury me. The following day papers carried a report headlined something to this effect: 'Miraculous escape for Venkaiah Naidu and Chandrababu Naidu as Air Deccan flight catches fire.' Just next to that report, at the bottom, I saw our Deccan advertisement announcing the commencement of commercial flights between Hyderabad and Vijayawada.

The media were ready for the kill and surrounded me from every side. The incident had been captured in detail by TV channels. One of them asked

me bluntly, 'So, Capt. Gopinath, is this the end of your dream?' I gathered
my cool and presence of mind and said, 'Such things happen in aviation. He
who walks, stumbles. But Deccan is here to stay!' I said it was unfortunate
that this had happened, but something of the kind could have happened a few
months or a few years later. It was just bad luck. I said we were resolved to
carry on nevertheless. I said our aircrafts were perfectly safe and air-worthy,
and this very aircraft had come flying 8000 kilometres from Toulouse.

The media was not however convinced. They then pounced on Rudy
and asked, 'Mr Minister, are you going to allow Deccan to continue after
this? Are low-cost airlines safe?' Rudy said, 'I just checked with the DGCA.
There are no safety issues and this was only a freak incident. The country
needs a low-cost airline. Deccan will fly!' The press wouldn't let go and had
a field day. The image of our plane and the VIPs who had had a 'narrow
escape', my explanation and Rudy's reply were put on a loop and broadcast
throughout the day.

The media quizzed us for about two hours and continued the interviews.
I heard the revving up of the engine and Kotiyal was in his cockpit. He
gave the thumbs-up and took off for Vijayawada, which nobody reported.
Presumably, it did not have sufficient sensational value and the potential to
make good press copy!

The media exaggerated the incident. Some TV channels said Venkaiah
Naidu had jumped out of the plane and been hurt; others—that people
had suffered burn injuries. Of course all this was grossly untrue. There had
been no cause for panic because the flame had been extinguished within
seconds. The incident aroused nervousness amongst some individuals in the
company, especially my marketing team.

I returned to Bengaluru that evening and called a meeting to take stock.
The commercial launch was two days away and I needed confirmation from
my technical heads before launching commercial operations. I sent for Rajiv
Kotiyal who had weathered the crisis with poise and remained on top of the
situation.

We were all convinced that as the fire had been as recent as two days
ago, that would greatly dampen the enthusiasm of passengers and we could
expect very low occupancy for the first commercial launch. We were even
prepared for only two or three passengers turning up, but life is full of
surprises: the inaugural flight from Hyderabad to Vijayawada had 100 per
cent occupancy!

The country was with me in this decision. People commended me on my
resolve to carry on. They said, 'Do not give up. We are with you.' People
wrote letters and sent emails. One even said that symbolically, fire in the
course of a launch and a new venture, was auspicious according to Indian

traditions and beliefs. The fire had consumed and banished ill omens and taken the evil eye off the project. The Indian mind sometimes thinks in a bafflingly different way. The principles of Karma are entrenched and are a source of great strength during a crisis, if you perceive them in the right spirit.

We had acquired and deployed four aircrafts, four months down the line from the date of the launch, and were undertaking forty flights a day. We had flights to Belgaum, Hubli, Bengaluru, Mangalore, Coimbatore, Madurai, Chennai, Hyderabad, Vijayawada, Rajahmundry, and Cochin, among others. The most heartening result for business was that we soon achieved a positive cash flow situation. Deccan was charting a success graph, and seeing this steady growth, major investment advisory banks called us. They included, among many, Rothschild, ICICI, Citicorp, and Merrill Lynch.

I could not help recalling my early days of enterprise in Hassan. I had then done the rounds of the banks for a few thousand rupees initially, and here the biggest names in investment banking were pitching for my account. It felt good to be on the other side of the chase!

The Rothschild India team, headed by Munesh Khanna with Amitabh Malhotra as deputy, was the reason why I chose them. They were brilliant, extremely well-networked in global finance, and passionate about getting our account. They promised to hold our hands through the entire process, and the most appealing and convincing aspect of their pitch was their passion to become involved.

The team did all manner of number crunching exercises over the next six months, including sensitivity analysis and stress tests. They created information memoranda for potential equity partners, and our roadshows were based on these preparatory studies.

We chose Singapore for the Asia leg of the road-show and organized several more in Europe and in the US. The response was huge; many institutions wanted to invest. We identified a list of twenty potential partners and then short-listed four: Temasek, Indigo Partners, Capital International, and ICICI Capital.

Temasek was a large country fund while Indigo Partners had much aviation expertise and had earlier invested in Ryan Air. Capital International was also a big name while ICICI Capital was home-grown.

Temasek did not want to participate in a race. They straightaway offered to put in Rs 200 crore and said they would not go back on their word. Three others had however been selected by due process and we would have been unfair to them had we decided on one and foreclosed the deal.

Indigo Partners was the most respected investor for airlines. Their understanding of the low-cost airline business was unmatched. Friends from Rothschild advised me privately to go with Indigo. It may have been a good thing: they had the expertise, and would have seen me through the many unforeseen challenges and crises that Deccan would later face. I was, however, insecure that as a global investor they might interfere too much in the running of the company. ICICI chairperson Renuka Ramnathan is extremely knowledgeable and I knew her as a friend. As I knew no-one at Indigo Partners I decided to go with ICICI Capital and they agreed to invest about Rs180 crore.

We were examining the term-sheets submitted by prospective investors, when I received a call from the office of the chairman of Singapore Airlines inviting me for a meeting with the chairman and urging complete secrecy. I therefore flew to Singapore. SIA was still smarting over the Tata–Singapore Airline sabotage. Choon Chew Seng, the chairman, affectionately called CS, was looking for new opportunities to invest in Indian aviation. The Indian government was at the time considering allowing 49 per cent investment by foreign airlines in India.

SIA, the great Singapore icon, was initially set up by the Tatas and Air India. Choon Chew Seng's mentor was an Indian Singaporean, the first chairman of SIA. He told me during my visit to the island country that if the Indian government legislated in favour of investments by foreign airlines, SIA would like to invest in Deccan.

Singapore Airlines is a great airline with excellent operational and engineering efficiencies. It is known for its service standards and customer care. SIA would benefit Air Deccan very substantially. I invited Choon Chew Seng, and his deputy Liam Song, to visit us at Bengaluru. They came over and took a closer look at the working and fundamentals of my airline. I also took them out to Belur and Halebid, Kabini Game Reserve, and Jungle Lodges and Resorts.

They went back and sent a large team comprising investment bankers UBS, lawyers from Amarchand Mangaldas Jain, and heads of flight operations, marketing, IT, and engineering. They did due diligence and agreed to invest in the airline if legislation was favourable and we shook hands. Unfortunately, the political weather changed and elections were announced. The BJP-led government was in a rush to pass several bills, including that permitting foreign airlines to participate in Indian airlines. The cabinet is believed to have decided that more discussion was needed on the legislation. The BJP did not return to power and the bill remained on the back burner, and the Congress-led government rejected it. Our hopes of a partnership with Singapore Airlines were therefore dashed, and the law also precluded another potential partnership for Deccan–with the legendary Richard Branson.

Interaction with Sir Richard Branson

Our quest for investment partners continued. After SIA, I got a call from Richard Branson's office. Branson is a celebrity in more than one sense. He is a much loved entrepreneur with many facets to his character who has done myriad things. He has an abiding passion to push himself to the limits of the human, physical, and mental endurance. He has attempted a great many feats from the glossary of adventure sports. He attempted to cross the Atlantic, the Pacific, and the world at various times in various kinds of contraptions, including a hot air balloon, sail-boat, and speed-boat. He created a record for the fastest crossing of the English Channel in an amphibious vehicle. He has also acted in television serials and in films. He combines the persona of daring adventurer with a keen nose for pioneering businesses, that together form his eclectic character. He attracts the youth of the world with his charisma, aura, aplomb, and an irresistibly endearing manner.

Branson's secretary said they would like to arrange a meeting for me. He owns a full-service airline, Virgin Atlantic, which he holds very dear, and which is one of the most successful in the world. Branson had however also set up low-cost carriers like Virgin Express and Virgin Blue before setting up Virgin Atlantic.

It was decided we would meet in Oxford where Branson lived. I asked my daughter Pallavi, who was studying in Liverpool at the time, to join me. I knew Richard Branson was easy on the dress code so I had decided to wear semi-formals but without a tie. Pallavi, however, insisted that I at-least wear a jacket.

Richard Branson was unstuffy, informal, wearing a white linen shirt and slacks. I was glad I had not put on a tie! We had hoped to see him at his Oxford house and chat over a drink before heading out to a restaurant. The London traffic however got the better of us and we called to say we would arrive late. Richard suggested we head straight for the restaurant. He was there to greet us; warm and affable.

Once seated, we got talking. Branson took out his famous black leather diary and began jotting down notes. His autobiography said he never used laptops or computers but relied entirely on his traditional paper notebook. He came across as a man brimming with ideas, ever-ready to seize upon any new idea that excites him and to take up a challenge.

Branson told me he had set up Virgin Express as a low-cost carrier in Brussels but the airline failed. His CEO from the airline, Bret Godfrey moved to Australia. Godfrey suggested that Branson should start a low-cost airline down under and Godfrey would manage it for him. Branson asked Singapore Airlines, which had a 49 per cent stake in Virgin Atlantic, to invest $10 million dollars in his new venture. SIA refused. It said that associating with a low-cost carrier would dilute their brand. Choon Chew Seng confessed to me later that it had been a big mistake. Virgin Blue in Australia eventually became very successful, and Singapore Airlines for its part launched its own LCC, Tiger Airways.

Virgin Blue did not initially make money but held out. When things seemed really bad and bankruptcy stared in the face, Anisette, Australia's major LCC collapsed. Overnight, the passenger traffic shifted to Virgin Blue. Within two years, Virgin Blue became profitable and became a huge stock market success earning millions for investors, including Branson.

Branson wanted to hear the Deccan story. I told him about my dream to empower every Indian to fly and about the need to connect the interiors of the country. Branson said he would like to invest in Deccan. That was very good news for me but there was a catch. There was no legal provision allowing foreign airlines to directly or indirectly invest in Indian airlines.

Across the street from the restaurant was a students' hostel, with boys and girls lounging around. As soon as they saw Richard emerging from the restaurant, they came running towards him, screaming 'Richard, Richard!' Richard said, 'I must run for it now. Good to have met. Bye!' and made a dash for his car. The girls caught up with him and were tugging at his sleeve. Richard's trailing voice uttered something to the effect that 'My wife will divorce me if you don't let me go ....' He managed to shrug the girls off his sleeve, got into the car, and sped away.

Richard Branson later sent across a team to do due diligence on Deccan. Everything was studied and they found good levels of synergy with us. However, as was the case with SIA, we were unable to shake hands with Richard Branson because the law did not permit us. That was indeed an acute disappointment for both of us.

Incident with Citibank

All the systems at the airline had gradually begun to fall into place. Our IT system was basic and had been a source of concern but soon we were able to resolve most issues. Money came in from customer to the bank and from there got credited to the company account. There was, however, a small problem.

The transaction of money—transfer of money from customer account to ours—was taking a certain amount of time. Citibank was managing the payment gateway. The transaction began when the call centre operator swiped a card or entered a number. The payment gateway took time to acknowledge the transaction, leading to a delay in issuing the PNR number. Rather than the three minutes we had specified, it was taking seven to ten. This was too long. Data showed that latency was high and customers were dropping off. People do not like to hold on for an extended period. Also, critical to our cash flow, Citibank was taking five to six days to transfer our money to us.

This was not acceptable. I called Citibank and demanded that their transaction time be reduced to two-and-a-half-minutes as I would be flying several million passengers a year. I reminded them that if any customer of their's delayed credit card payment by even a day, they charged 2 per cent interest per month. So a similar rule should apply in this case as well. I said, 'You are sitting on my money for eight days. I don't care how long you sit on the money, but for each day I'm going to charge you interest at the same rate that you charge credit card defaulters.'

The Citibank team leader said the delay was due to reconciliation of accounts. I refused to buy the argument. It was their responsibility to devise a way out. I was angry but still had not considered any alternative arrangements. However, a remark of his infuriated me. He said, 'Captain, we'll try to do this, but you must know that only Citibank has this capability in India. Nobody else can do it for you.'

Very angry, I warned them that I would get somebody else. I said, 'Whatever software it is, it is being devised in some back-office in Bengaluru or Pune or Hyderabad. You had better start working or I'll get somebody else.'

He did not believe me. I called Ajay Bhatkal right away and said Citibank was not the right partner for us and that he should begin discussions with someone else. ICICI at the time was into retail banking. I liked their philosophy of going to small towns. I told Ajay Bhatkal to talk to them. Let us give customers the option of booking tickets with either ICICI or Citibank. I did not wish to be blackmailed; did not wish to do business with someone who was both complacent and arrogant. Ajay got ICICI working on the project and they had it up in 45 days. At midnight, on the forty-fifth day we switched to the new system that gave customers a choice between the ICICI and Citibank gateways. The transaction with ICICI took two-and-a-half-minutes, raising the energy levels at the call centre and enabling them to close calls sooner.

With ICICI our money was transferred online so there was no question of any delay. The system worked perfectly for the fifteen-day trial period agreed upon so we put ICICI as the first option and Citibank as the next.

We positioned it in such a way that 90 per cent of the business went to ICICI and 10 per cent to Citibank.

People at the Citibank woke up. Top management called to ask what had gone wrong. I said, 'You guys were smug. What I did was my only recourse.' It was again a lesson for me. If Citibank could lose business with us, we would lose our business with a client if we were not sufficiently committed or not quick enough to respond to customer needs.

12

If a man does not know to which port he is steering no wind is
favourable to him.

—Seneca

The Growth, the Challenges, the Changes

Although we were low-cost and were offering low fares, we had among our passengers many high-profile individuals. Some of them were flying us because of Deccan's novelty: new, different. Some used our services because we were flying to rural and small-town destinations where others didn't venture. The great sarod maestro Amjad Ali Khan once tearfully acknowledged his sense of gratitude to us for flying to Gwalior, his home town. Among the other celebrity fliers were Azim Premji, Sunil Dutt, Vinod Khanna, and Raj Babbar. Someone in my team suggested that we could get one of them to endorse our brand. I however thought differently. We were aiming to fly the common man. The image of the star flier who flew occasionally was not the image I wanted to create. Secondly, a celebrity-branding exercise would add to the cost. Our cost-cutting had always been ruthless, and this new cost would have been incongruous. We would also have to raise fares. Fare calculations had been based on certain parameters, and changing one parameter would require us to rework the entire process. It did not seem advisable. I wanted the common man to identify himself with the brand.

A chance glance at a newspaper helped me decide what image to choose. It was a cartoon by R.K. Laxman, the creator of the ubiquitous Common Man. R.K. Laxman is one of India's greatest cartoonists. In his early years, this Common Man was urban, male, and had all the qualities of being 'common'. Laxman defined him through the logic of absences: he is not plebian, not philistine, not the element in the rabble, not a member of the Spanish philosopher Ortega Gasset's 'mass', and not 'working class' as Lenin would have seen him. He is aware, alert, perspicacious, sensitive, able to discern hidden personal agendas in political rhetoric, possesses opinions of his own and is able to reason 'why', 'what', or 'how', and has an immense store of empathy for others of his kind. There is a cheerful resilience about the character. This Common Man has one major deficit: he has no voice: it is lost in the cacophony of the powerful. He, nonetheless, has one source of illimitable strength. Using it he can shake governments and move the earth. It is the power of silent comment. Laxman seems to be subtly autobiographical in acknowledging the helplessness of speechlessness of the Common Man while at the same time celebrating the power of silent comment in his own recreation. Over the years, the Common Man has gone beyond urban geography and shed his implicit gender bias. His constituency now encompasses the rural as well as the feminine. One might even read him as a metaphor of all things Indian!

I was reminded of the power of this silent comment when I saw a cartoon in the *Times of India*. It was a telling comment about what it means to be a common Indian and the snobbery of the not so common. Both had been juxtaposed as metaphors, and as people in flesh and blood, seated next to each other in an Air Deccan flight. Perched in the aisle seat, his one unshod foot pulled up and placed on the seat, the rustic traveller sits back expansively with arms thrown about in imperial abandon. A staff in hand, and like others in his rural fraternity, he is wearing a turban, a jubba, and dhoti. Placed next to his seat in the aisle and impeding the movement of people, there is a rail water jug with a lid that can be screwed on. Called 'rail chombu' in the south, this water jug was used by passengers everywhere before packaged water became ubiquitous. His bed-roll has been placed in the cabin baggage bay, but it shows.

Occupying the window seat is the self-effacing Common Man, wearing his characteristic chequered and dog-eared tweed coat and dhoti, and a bewildered expression on his face. He has his old-fashioned long umbrella hanging by the armrest. The Common Man is balding, avuncular, and amiable in a way that is both endearing and exhibits an eager willingness to please: if only you are willing to listen! The Common Man has his face turned towards his well-dressed, upwardly mobile fellow passenger. The passenger in the middle seat is sandwiched between the rustic and the Common Man. He sits plaintively, uncomfortably, arms folded, and wearing the exaggerated air of social claustrophobia. He makes it obvious he is not used to social milieus of the kind that Deccan is encouraging to fly. He desires exclusive company but does not wish to be seen as a snob. He says: 'I am not really a snob, but if these airlines bring down the fares any further, I will start travelling by a train or bus!'

Having seen this cartoon, I thought that I must ask Laxman to let us use his cartoon as our brand metaphor. I knew the people we intended to attract as passengers would identify themselves with it. Deccan's philosophy could have no better mnemonic and psychic association to equal the Common Man. When I suggested that we approach Laxman, I was dissuaded. The advertisement agency people said when they had tried to get him to agree to their using his cartoon character as a logo for a previous account; he had bluntly refused. I had better abandon the idea, they said. I, however, wanted to give it a try and therefore wrote to Laxman and he readily agreed to give me an appointment.

Laxman lived in a flat in Mumbai's Worli suburb. There was something reassuringly old-world Mysore and middle-class about the flat. The furniture, the décor, the library and study where Laxman sat each day to draw his daily cartoon—he has done so without a break for over fifty years—and the uppittu that was served reflected comfort and quiet industry.

Hanging on the wall I saw a large framed cartoon by the artist—of a young boy who is surrounded by a plethora of all variety of calculating gadgets and mathematical formulae, and looking quite lost in their midst. It was a cartoon inspired by his son. I asked Laxman whether his son also drew. Laxman was quick to reply. With a stolid, deadpan expression on his face, he said, 'Yes ... he draws [long pause]. He draws money from the bank.'

Laxman and I talked about a variety of things: about my airline, my philosophy, and my dream to make the common man fly. Then I told him about the cartoon he had drawn and asked whether we could use his Common Man as Deccan's mascot. Laxman was amused at the idea and without a moment's hesitation he said 'Yes'. I said we would paint our craft with the motif of the Common Man. Deccan would be known as the common man's airline and would immortalize Laxman's inspiration. Laxman agreed and we got to use Common Man as our mascot.

I returned from Mumbai armed with the mascot. We now had the mascot and the metaphor, but we needed to get in place the things they evoked. The power of the metaphor is that in a single flash the entire idea is revealed. Working systems are however made up of components, and to see the whole, one must make an effort to imagine and perceive the larger picture.

Our pilots, engineers, and managers were great at their jobs but they worked in isolation and were in their own individual silos. For a company to deliver its product or service, all departments must work individually, in tandem, as well as together. This requires cross-departmental dialogue and collaboration. On one occassion two departments whose heads had sent each other emails but had never sat across the table and spoken to each other even though their cabins were alongside had completely misread each other, and in consequence of this incomplete communication we nearly came to grief.

After the near-disaster, we decided that every Monday the department heads would meet. They spoke their views, shared their concerns, and made efforts to understand one another. We had a similar meeting of managers from across the country once a month.

I took upon myself the task of ensuring that communication channels were open and people understood one another's requirements. In the execution of this task I travelled to our eight bases: at Thiruvananthapuram, Delhi, Bengaluru, Mumbai, Ahmedabad, Kolkata, Chennai and Hyderabad. I undertook a tour of each of these bases once every two or three months. I spoke to people on the ground and at airports; to technicians and engineers, sometimes hearing appalling stories. Accompanying me on these trips were the head of operations, the CFO, and head of HR. I asked the heads to try and understand grassroot realities; to walk across to an engineer working all by himself at night or visit a logistics centre and speak to technicians about their difficulties.

I realized that no management meeting was complete without visiting and understanding the nitty-gritty at first hand and at ground level. The visits encouraged employees and raise their morale. I always returned from these visits with the feeling that we were not doing enough for employee welfare.

There were problems with infrastructure because of pressure exerted by the existing monopoly players on the AAI. While Indian Airlines and Jet Airways had multiple parking slots in Mumbai and Delhi, which allowed them to locate routine repair and maintenance facilities in two places and bring down their operational costs, we were given only one parking slot at an airport, so that we had to invest in the same kind of facility at each of these centres. This completely stretched my finances and managerial abilities, and resulted in my having eight operational bases across the country for sixteen aircraft.

Multiple slots at one airport base for five aircrafts would have been very useful. The number of staff and resources you require to maintain five aircrafts at one base is far less than for five aircrafts in five different bases. The number grew to sixteen aircrafts based in eight different locations and it became a nightmare. However, employee dedication and management commitment helped us overcome the problem. A year down the line it worked to our advantage because overnight we became a national presence and we were able to continually absorb and deploy aircraft coming in over the next forty-five months, one a month, at different location in the country.

We had five years to go public, one of the conditions that had enabled us to raise institutional equity finance from ICICI and Capital International. There was renewed enthusiasm in the aviation sector and the market was getting hotter. The deployment of an aircraft a month was good for the growth of the company as a long-term investment, but it also meant we were front-loading the finances for the particular year and we constantly needed money to ensure we had the resources to sustain the rapid growth.

Acquiring new aircraft meant cash-flow problems. Not acquiring aircraft, and thereby not expanding, meant we would not be top of the line and competition would erode our flanks. The only way out was to expand operations at breakneck speed. It was a deliberate decision that we would deploy fifty to sixty aircraft and then take stock of growth. We would reposition the routes later to enhance the cash flow and make it sustainable over the long run.

Tickets @ Re 1...

We had sufficient cash-flow initially, but competition awoke to our presence when we hit major trunk routes like the Delhi–Mumbai thoroughfare. Jet and Indian Airlines were operating 350-plus flights daily on these trunk routes, as opposed to our fifty flights a day, and began offering lower fares. Indian Airlines, for instance, came up with its 'Check Fare' scheme of low fares. The two had worked out a deal to position a flight just half an hour before the Deccan flight, largely Indian Airlines. Jet seemed to have persuaded the national carrier to offer itself as a sacrificial goat if it came to losing. Their campaign asked customers to compare fares with competition, us, that is, and then buy their tickets. The airlines were deliberately offering lower fares to undercut us, known as predatory pricing; it is a practice that well-entrenched airlines utilize to kill competition and is unlawful in the US.

India had no such legal provision and the monopoly cartel tried to defeat us with predatory pricing. It works in the same way as when private buses in Karnataka try and upstage government-run buses on rural routes. A private bus arrives at a stop only a minute ahead and picks up passengers. It also offers a fare that is a rupee or so lower. It goes full while the government buses run empty. The private bus-operators are known to bribe the drivers and conductors on government buses to allow them to do this.

We wanted to shoo off Jet and Indian Airlines and so we reinforced our dynamic pricing with an offer inspired by Laxman's cartoon. We introduced a small number of early-bird tickets at one rupee, hoping to create an unprecedented explosion in the number of people taking to air travel. Laxman's Common Man had become a brand to which most people could easily relate. On a Bengaluru–Delhi flight, the cartel of Indian Airlines and Jet Airways was offering an average price of Rs 12,000 one way. We offered fares starting at one rupee for early birds, with an upward ceiling of Rs 7000 for last-minute fliers. We had a system of dynamic pricing that varied inversely with countdown to the date of flight: the closer to the departure date, the higher the fare.

What IA and Jet lost because of the Check Fare scheme, they made-up by marginally increasing the fares charged to passengers travelling in other sectors where we were not operating. They initially made gains because the number of flights we operated was small so they could gain leverage quite easily. I saw that if we ramped up our operations rapidly and deployed more flights across the country, the leverage would be gone and it would prove self-defeating for the cartel to use predatory pricing. This is exactly what happened. After Deccan got more routes and flights going, they abandoned the Check Fare scheme. Meanwhile, passengers on our flights were checking among themselves the fares they had paid and realized the advantage of early-bird tickets. The result was higher occupancy on our flights and lowered the occupancy on Jet and IA flights. The other carriers did not have more than 60–65 per cent occupancy. One-rupee tickets fired the imagination of the people and very rapidly became a buzzword.

Critics of this dynamic pricing system arrived and described me as being out to wreck the industry. I countered by saying that I was not an evangelist but that I had evangelical zeal, and that helped my business because low fares and low-costs were growth engines for the company and the country.

People from all walks of life thronged the city booking offices to buy the one-rupee tickets. Most were middle-class but there were some from the upper social bracket too. Office-going white-collar workers or blue-collar factory workers formed the majority. Among them were rickshaw-drivers too.

I soon realized that continued front-loading of the finances would, sooner rather than later, make it imperative for us to go public. I made this clear at the very first board meeting after ICICI and Capital International brought in equity. KV. Kamath, executive chairman of ICICI and one of the legendary bankers in the private sector, advised me not to lose time. He said it was better to do so when things were hot. 'Don't try to time the market. Take the money when you need it if the market is buoyant. Don't keep waiting. If you need the money now, take it now,' he said. We appointed two companies to manage the IPO exercise.

One of them was ENAM, the company led by Vallabh Bhansali, a very highly regarded investment banker and an astute reader of market sentiment. He had built an excellent network and was very knowledgeable about Indian market conditions. Any offering backed by Bhansali came with the assurance that it was a reliable offer. I decided to appoint ENAM as the lead banker and ICICI Securities as the other banker.

The economy was buoyant and the investment climate in India very encouraging. When, therefore, Deccan announced its public issue, it caught the imagination of the media, which gave extensive and positive coverage to our road-shows in India and across the world. There was a unanimous belief that our stock would be oversubscribed by ten times or more at a time when market sentiment was generally responsive to new offerings. Many companies had been heavily over-subscribed. Reliance for instance was over-subscribed by sixty times. Institutional investors were more than willing to pitch in substantial amounts of money running into millions. We wanted to raise $75–$100 million on the market for dilution of up to 26 per cent equity. I was inundated with calls requesting private placement. SEBI rules required that we apply for permission when filing the nomination papers for the public issue. The rules also required that as Deccan had not as yet broken even, 50 per cent equity should first be subscribed by institutions before the balance was allotted to retail investors.

Although the overall investment climate was affirmative and many issues were oversubscribed, some stocks that had traded just ahead of our IPO had not fared well. Bhansali advised me not to overprice the issue. The Jet Airways shares were issued at Rs 1200 but were trading well below that. I took his advice and we priced our Rs 10 share issues in the range of Rs 148 to Rs 155.

On the actual day of trading we were in for a rude shock: a huge tidal wave hit the market. God knows what went wrong, for within the first hour, the market crashed by 1000 points from its 13,000 mark and was described as the worst market crash in 150 years. Within a few hours it had crashed by 2000 points. Brokers and investment managers for mutual funds, rather than deciding how much of their funds to allocate for the Deccan issue were busy deciding which stocks to dump. They set up a trend by dumping stocks: as more brokers dumped, yet more followed suit. The market index which initially slid, had soon begun to tumble. It had a cascading effect and the market was shellshocked.

Circuit-breakers had been applied automatically at two points when the rate of fall had been too rapid. Trading was suspended twice, but when nothing seemed to work, Finance Minister Chidambaram intervened to restore confidence.

There are two kinds of investors: short- to medium-term and long-term. Most IPO investors are mutual funds that make money for their investors in the short- to medium-term. On that fateful day, nobody was buying. The mutual funds, many of them foreign institutional investors or FIIs, were scurrying for cover. They were considering only two options: sell or hold on. They were in no position to invest in our IPO. No financial analyst had the vision to forecast this mayhem on the market. Number-crunching analysts have little foothold in reality. In fact, the crash came at a time when newspaper reports had predicted further surges beyond the 13,000 mark. The reports speculated about the possibility that the index would touch 16,000. The economy was doing so well that it had to happen, they argued.

The post-mortem analyses were prompt: analysts glibly concluded that the Indian market had overheated and a correction had been a systemic necessity. No-one was however any better for this hindsight. In fact, their forecasting models had gone so awry that it made astrology seem almost respectable!

Institutions called and asked me to withdraw the IPO, on the ground that an under-subscribed initial offer was a humiliation. I remembered former British Prime Minister Winston Churchill's very forceful exhortation to his people during the war. 'If you are going through hell, just keep going.' It was a wry comment about the need to weather a prolonged phase of adversity during the war. I thought of the African proverb: 'The only way out of a desert is through it.' I said I was not going to withdraw.

I conferred with Mohan, Vallabh Bhansali, Renuka Ramanathan, head of ICICI Ventures, and Bala Deshpande, who also represented ICICI Ventures and was on our board. They were the sheet-anchors that held the Deccan ship together during the worst storm it had ever weathered.

I called up MD of SBI, MD of New India Assurance Company, and the chairman of LIC. I asked them not to judge Deccan on the basis of one incident. I said these were temporary speed-breakers and said that Deccan and the India growth-story were here to stay. They reposed faith in the Indian dream and stood by me like a rock. While the much-hyped fancy FIIs and mutual funds panicked and tucked tail, the staid and oft-ridiculed public sector funds bailed us out.

Retail investments in Deccan had already been over-subscribed but SEBI guidelines, which specified that institutional investors had to first pick up 50 per cent equity, prevented us from collecting the money. Vallabh Bhansali advised me to lower the issue price, which was the only way of ensuring that there would be some money on the table for the institutions that had invested. We offered a price at the lower band of Rs 148 and waited with our fingers crossed. The wait was interminably long, lasting all of five days.

I had felt it deep within me that I should not withdraw. This faith was borne out by many who called. The financial institutions developed cold feet but retail investors showed great faith. When the financial institutions recovered their breath and mustered the courage to pick up our stock, Deccan was marginally over-subscribed. We raised about $75 million in that IPO, which was akin to oxygen on Mount Everest.

Some companies withdrew their IPOs but Deccan stayed the course: we had to protect our brand value and justify people's faith in it. It was after all a peoples' carrier.

Things were brightening up on the financial front and I was now confident we would be able to sustain the airline in the near term but I needed to take decisions for the long-term; to understand the logic of the market-place and the logic of growth. I saw a compelling lesson in the predatory games played on Deccan by Indian Airlines and Jet Airways. If our growth was slow-paced and cautious, we would never gain the momentum we required to keep afloat: they would surely underprice us and cut us out of the competition. My growth plan had therefore to be fast-paced, or at least sufficiently swift to ensure that their check-fare and other underpricing measures did not affect us.

I had two options. First was to work out a conservative growth plan that would prevent us from falling prey. And the second was to chart out a course so furiously fast-paced that the competition became irrelevant. Indian Airlines had at the time not been adding any new aircraft for several years and Jet Airways too was stagnant. I decided that the only way out was to expand operations at breakneck speed and relentlessly acquire, absorb, and deploy fifty to sixty aircraft and exponentially grow the airline. That would be a blitzkrieg no competitor could ever imagine, let alone anticipate and prepare for.

Global circumstances too favoured such a course. Post 9/11 the aviation sector was facing the worst ever recession in its history. About 3000 aircrafts had been grounded in the US and were parked in open parking lots at an airport in the Nevada desert. Desert air has the least humidity and causes the least damage to aircraft. It was an innovative solution to keep maintenance costs low. Airlines across the world had reduced the numbers of flights. Aircraft manufacturers with excess capacity and inventory, were desperate to find customers and were willing to allow quite substantial paring from the list price. The two major manufacturers of large aircraft, Boeing and Airbus, had no orders on hand.

Memories of the big shake-out in Indian aviation were still fresh and the mood was low. As usual, where others saw gloom I saw light or lit a candle. The dream still remained: I would sell a billion tickets a year some time in the future. The potential travellers had not gone vanished, the market remained and only needed someone to give it a booster dose. As I was mulling various possibilities, I had a visitor from one of the airlines that had folded up during the big aviation shake-out. The visitor had been at the helm of operations of Gujarat Airways. He said he wanted to come and congratulate me and doff his hat. 'You have the guts, Captain! Hats off to you!' he said when he met me. I asked him about his airline and why it had to close. He said it had been a small operation largely within Gujarat and Maharashtra, flying to smaller destinations. The airline had a small fleet of turbo-props with a seating capacity of ten to twenty.

Pilots are an airline's most critical asset. If you have no pilots; you don't operate. Within the community of pilots there exists a social hierarchy. The smaller the aircraft, the lower the prestige the pilot commands, besides a relatively lower salary. Career pilots are continually seeking to fly bigger planes because this enhances their image in the drawing room and brings in greater monetary returns and professional advancement.

My visitor said that underlying the failure of his airline was the lure of a better career for pilots. Fifteen pilots, all that the company employed, came to his office one morning and said they were resigning their jobs en masse. Jet Airways had poached them.

The ability to sense danger is a positive spur. It pumps up the adrenalin and impels you to act. If it could happen to Gujarat it could happen to Deccan. I realized that I must act without losing a single moment, and did.

I decided to order fifty or sixty aircrafts, thereby resolving two problems in one go. I would stave off competition and create that kind of confidence in the future of the airline that the competition could not dream of creating; they were not equipped for such an attack from the flanks. By taking this course of action I would not only retain pilot resources but attract fresh talent, and experienced talent, from the competition; would be the predator rather than the prey. I felt a rush of adrenalin.

Ramp up? Yes, I had decided that. But, how was I to do it?

I sat with Mohan to do some homework. An aircraft from Airbus Industrie had a listed price of roughly $55million. We would have to muster $3.3 billion to order 60, a staggering figure.

Mohan has the unusual ability to make the most impossible task seem within reach. He is able to intuitively break down a huge problem into smaller, do-able sub-problems. He never lets the enormity of a problem overwhelm him, breaking it down, into components that come tagged with a timeline. In this way, you don't take the problem head-on but in parts, and in the language of the EMI with which most people are familiar, Mohan is able to see further. He comes up with a revenue stream in cases in which the lay person sees a humongous cost overhang.

With regard to the task of buying sixty aircrafts, Mohan reasoned as follows. Aircraft manufacturers ask for an upfront payment from the buyer of 15 per cent of the sale value of the aircraft payable over a period of twelve to twenty-four months. Banks are willing to finance the entire cost in tranches. Mohan worked on the assumption that although we would be ordering for the serial manufacture of sixty aircrafts, they would be delivered to us at the rate of ten aircrafts a year. He saw a possible way of cycling the finance on an annual basis: when the commitments were met for the first year we would roll it on for the next year, and so on.

He hit upon a brilliant idea. He suggested that we pay a deposit of one per cent upfront for the entire sixty aircrafts. He then figured a staggered payment schedule. We would first pay a 15 per cent deposit on the first ten aircrafts. This schedule would be accomplished over a gradually deferred span, beginning with twelve months for the first, fourteen months for the second, and so on. Once the deposit requirement for the first ten aircrafts had been addressed, it would be possible to recycle the deposit successively for the eleventh, twelfth and so on. For example, the deposit paid on the first aircraft would go to pay to the eleventh aircraft. He worked out a way of directly operating a lien between the bank and the manufacturer. We would service the interest on the deposit but if for some reason we defaulted, the manufacturer would return the money to the bank when he had sold the aircraft to some other buyer.

Mohan saw the possibility of creating these kinds of financial linkages that benefit all parties, with the least risk to any. The aircraft maker sells and makes money; the bank receives its interest and its lien is secured, and we get the aircraft at our terms. It was a coup in financial thinking: the 15 per cent deposit and recycling it in the Indian context. He spoke to bankers of SBI, and they were agreeable to this kind of arrangement.

We now had three sources of funds: the IPO, equity partners, and the bank lien. I decided to go ahead. I called Kiran Rao, global head for pricing and Asia head for sales at Airbus, and said Deccan wanted to place orders for sixty Airbus-320 aircrafts. He must have had a heart attack! He said he would fly down to Bengaluru with his boss and chief commercial officer, John Leahy.

Kiran Rao, and John Leahy and his wife, were in Bengaluru soon after. I organized an outing for all of us at Kabini Game Reserve. I wanted a break from the hectic routine, and here was an excellent opportunity to blend business with leisure. Bhargavi joined us on that trip. Nature is a good primer before embarking on serious business, softening and mellowing us. We become more willing to give and also more amenable to concluding a deal.

We flew by Deccan helicopters to Kabini where we did the safari, followed the elephant trail for some distance, and relaxed on the riverbank. We lit a campfire in the evening. After two days spent on the banks of the Kabini River, we flew to Hampi. I believe that Hampi has the most variegated rock formations in the world. Its landscape is far more differentiated with far more distinctive features than the landscape at Grand Canyon. The ruins of Hampi are spread over around 20,000 hectares of hilly terrain with rock, boulder, and ridge. The Tungabhadra River meanders through this scattered topography, forming little pools here and turning into sharp eddies there. Many of these riverine alcoves are completely surrounded by boulder formations that simply astonish the visitor.

The land there is parched and dry except along the course of the river where trees shoot through nooks between the rocks. The pools in the niches are sacred, and legend has it that ancient sages chose those locations as meditative retreats. At sunrise and sunset Hampi is suffused with the mud-orange colour of the rock and the earth. A miasma of dust hangs over the landscape as day dawns. The light is a dull burnished copper. Historians have wondered how the rulers of Hampi were able to attain the near-perfect north–south alignment of the important architectural features of the once resplendent city.

We chose a resort that was neatly tucked into the boulders on the hillside. We went around and saw the ruins: the palaces, the temples, the musical pillars, and the huge apron of the durbar hall.

On the evening before our departure, John, Kiran, and I sat on the balcony overlooking the Tungabhadra where I offered them whiskey. I had so far avoided discussing business. After we were through with the first drink, John, unable to contain himself any longer, said, 'Gopi, I thought you invited us to discuss the purchase of Airbus aircraft. We are leaving tomorrow and you have not even broached the subject.' I said, 'John, I deliberately did not broach the subject in Bengaluru or until now. There are two possibilities. I order sixty aircrafts and we finalize a deal in one hour; alternatively I could appoint a purchase committee and run an elaborate techno-economic comparison between Boeing and Airbus to choose the best which could drag on for six to nine months as you bid against each other. I have done my homework and I have met CEOs of international airlines. I know the price. If you make an offer I can't refuse, we can choose the first option and close it in the next hour and toast the deal on the banks of the holy Tungabhadra and in the midst of this historic city.' John stared in disbelief. He said, 'What is your asking price?'

I said, 'I am willing to buy sixty no-frills Airbus-320 aircraft from you at the rate $28.5 million apiece. If you say $29 million then we will have to go through the due bidding and evaluation process between Airbus and Boeing. The decision is yours.'

John and Kiran looked lost at the suddenness of this quote. They left their whiskey glasses on the table and went indoors to consult the management of Airbus Industrie in France. They returned after an hour and said, 'Give us twenty-nine.' I said that would not be possible. Once the equity investment came in investors would want stringent audits of all major decisions Deccan made. My prerogative would then be curtailed. I asked them to think about all these factors and gave them till the next day to decide. 'If you agree, we can be in Bengaluru by 10 a.m. and sign the purchase contract by 1 p.m. I will call a press conference at 4 p.m.,' I said. Kiran Rao, whom I had known earlier, tried to reason with me in confidence after dinner that evening. I however reiterated what I had already said, and refused to budge.

I was already seated at the breakfast table when John came in, and as he took his seat, proffered his hand and said, 'Captain, Congratulations! Let us shake hands. You have the deal at 28.5! but we have to rush to Bengaluru as we have a lot of documents to prepare to seal the deal.' I straightaway called Mohan and conveyed the good news. I told him that we would be landing by 10 a.m. and we had three to four hours to get the documents finalized. We would meet the press at 4 p.m.

We took off in our choppers, did a perambulation of the Virupaksha temple, got an aerial view of the magnificence of Hampi, and flew straight to Bengaluru. Both teams got together to work out the nitty-gritty of the MOU. I had called and asked Vijaya Menon to organize the press meet at 4 p.m. The document was signed before the well attended media conference. The following day we made the headlines in all the leading newspapers. They screamed: 'Deccan places order for sixty aircrafts with Airbus Industrie.'

John and Kiran were happy that the deal had come through. John said he would give Deccan an extra $15 million to fund combined marketing, recruiting training captains, and to hire the best consultants in the world for systems and processes. In addition to this $15 million, Deccan got $10 million as part of the purchase for pilot training and engineer training, thus saving us $25 million in cash expenditure that we would have had to incur had we gone in for the purchase of second-hand aircraft. The celebrations had begun.

It was unbelievable that with less than a crore of rupees in our bank account we had ordered aircraft worth 12,000 crore. This changed Deccan and Indian aviation forever.

When I ordered my fleet of 60 airbuses strange reactions came from different people. Minister Praful Patel was one of the first to call me. He asked, 'Gopi, is this some kind of a joke? I hear that you have ordered 60 airbuses?' There was huge uproar in the parliament—members asked questions as to how come an upstart startup like Air Deccan could order 60 airbuses while Indian Airlines after being in the business for 55 years still struggled to order a handful!

Around the same time I got a call from a former member of the parliament. I thought it was one of the routine calls that I used to get from politicians requesting for tickets to the smaller cities—since it was only Deccan that flew to destinations like Rajamundhry, Jamshedpur, Gwalior etc. But I soon realized that the call was for a reason far more important than I ever would have thought. So we decided to meet and discuss the issue.

When we met he said he was in Delhi a few days back and was taking a walk in the parliament and met a prominent politician. The politician asked him if he knew me well and what he thought of Air Deccan. He then said that the file for leasing 60 airbuses had reached his desk and he had to clear it before it reached P.Chidambaram. The subtext here was that I needed to pay up—'donate' to his party fund, as was euphemistically put—to get him to clear the file. I was both angry and surprised to hear this—on one hand hung the fate of my company, on the other the very principles I run the company on!

I barely could sleep that night and after much deliberation I decided I would not pay the bribe. Next morning I called up cabinet minister Chidambaram's secretary and asked for an appointment.

P. Chidambaram is known for his razor sharp mind and no non-sense attitude. He never has the time to suffer fools. When I met him, after a brief chit-chat he asked me the real reason why I wanted to see him. I said that I wanted him to change a certain rule in his ministry. I said while I can transfer any amount of money to any account across the world, when I am buying aircrafts, without any government approval, when I am leasing aircrafts and transferring much lesser sums, I need a formal clearance from the finance ministry. I insisted that this resulted in loss of time, energy and business. On hearing me out the minister said that I should not try to teach him how to run his ministry but yes, if there was any specific problem that I encountered he will certainly help me. So reluctantly I told him about the incident. He asked for names and I had no option but to divulge them too. The minister then said that if I pay a single penny my file will not be cleared but yes, if the papers are in place, then my file will be cleared soon. On hearing this I left, still unsure about my fleet of airbuses and the future of Air Deccan. Just as I landed in Bengaluru, I got a call from my secretary and she said the file had been cleared!

⤙

Deccan's fortunes were looking up, as testified by the turn of events. At about the time we signed the Airbus contract, ATR had got a new CEO, Filippo Bagnato. Filippo Bagnato, an Italian by birth, is one of those rare people you only encounter in life if you are very fortunate. He is a very affectionate person, and is also endowed with an intellect of a very high order. He is a great leader of people. He is an aircraft design engineer who had worked on projects for the Euro-Fighter, Ferrari, and Boeing. When he took over ATR, according to the rule that the CEO would be French and Italian alternately, the aircraft manufacturer was facing the same kind of problems as Deccan: managing explosive growth. I called him to say that Deccan was interested in buying thirty ATRs. When he came to India, I took him to Bellary and Hubli, and other small cities and told him that Deccan planned to fly to these Tier II and Tier III cities in the country. I said I wanted to lease ten ATRs and buy thirty.

Mohan and I flew to Paris to finalize the deal with ATR. In exactly the same way as I pursued the deal with Airbus, I asked him to give me the aircraft at a specified rate and I would sign. Filippo agreed and voluntarily offered us support to strengthen our engineering operations. Filippo, since then, became a good friend and I have frequently consulted him on many issues. Once when I was having problems with some of my board members who were interfering and meddling in my functioning as a CEO, I went to Filippo and asked him for advice as to how he as a CEO dealt with his board members. He said to stand firm at all costs and never to let the board undermine my decisions as a CEO. He finally said that the board must concern itself with strategy, vision, corporate governance and overall performance of the company at the end of the day—but not in the 'Kamasutra' of management.

⤙

Mohan Kumar was doing something akin to creating the *perpetuum mobile* of finance. He teamed up with Ramki Sundaram, London-based finance executive with a South African bank called Investec. Ramki, who has an engineering degree from one of the IITs, is endowed with a razor-sharp mind and an excellent temperament. Mohan discussed this fantastic modus operandi with Ramki Sundaram. This was the idea: Investec would take the sixty Airbus aircraft we had ordered on assignment from us and give us $100 million upfront in tranches. Deccan had negotiated a price for each Airbus aircraft we were buying from the manufacturer. The aircraft price appreciates with time so we would agree to sell the aircraft just ahead of delivery to a leasing company for a profit of $5–8 million. Deccan and Investec would split the profit between ourselves in such a manner that Investec got its $100 million back and a return on the investment. The assignment to Investec of the 60 aircrafts was without prejudice to Deccan, losing its first right to buy or undertake sale and lease-back so that flight operations would escalate as planned. If Deccan defaulted for any reason, there would be no recourse, i.e., Deccan assets would not be touched. Investec for its part would however have the assigned 60 aircrafts, or what remained of the number at the time of default, and actually stood to make more money.

Investec agreed to this deal but wanted a consent letter from Airbus. Initially, Airbus was reluctant to issue the letter, but I drew their attention to a clause in our agreement that allowed us to assign aircraft to whomsoever we chose. Deccan had agreed to take the downside if it came to the crunch, arguing that Deccan had the right to benefit from the upside too. Airbus eventually agreed. This piece of wizardry was acknowledged: Deccan and Investec were chosen for Euromoney's Most Innovative Financial Deal of the Year Award that year. Euromoney is a well-known publisher and events organizer related to aviation finance.

Mohan Kumar's ingenuity flowed on. He next came up with the idea of e-Coupons for frequent travellers. Deccan sold these e-Coupons for an advance payment of one lakh rupees on the Airbus sector and 50,000 rupees on the ATR sector. The subscriber to these e-Coupons would get thirty-five tickets which he or she could use for one year, at one e-Coupon exchanged for a one way journey. Many passengers travelling regularly on long-distance flights subscribed to these tickets. We made these coupons blackmarket-proof by requiring that those who bought them would have to list the names of the people who would use them in the course of the year. Deccan checked passengers by their ID cards so no impostor could use them and no agent could misuse them. E-Coupons brought the airline committed, sums of money in advance and ensured higher occupancy. It was hugely popular with the frequent flyers.

Each time a new process of transaction was added, the software had to be tweaked too. The software was tinkered to allow e-Coupon transactions to take place outside the dynamic pricing loop. Each transaction was noted and the next time the subscriber booked a ticket, the system discounted the previous instance of use. This worked smoothly.

Deccan's Rupee 1 and Rupee 500—book early pay less philosophy filled the planes and brought in large cash-flows. The tickets were valid for purchase three months ahead of travel. The tech savvy, among others, managed to get the best deals. On the day that rupee and other early-bird offers were announced, there was such a rush on our IT system that it slowed down. The techies worked in the 24-hour cycle and often booked it at the dot of midnight and were, therefore, the first to register for the tickets. There was a fair degree of suspicion in the public mind that perhaps our one-rupee tickets were a sham. Nobody had met those who bought such tickets and travelled. We gave journalists names and contact details of these. Journalists got in touch with the passengers to ensure we weren't lying. It actually happened that these one-rupee fliers were people with an address: a software engineer from Infosys or a retired government official. The word spread and it proved to be a really worthwhile strategy that drew more people to us.

Whenever I travelled I made it a point to ask the air-hostess to announce that I was on board and that I would go around meeting passengers. I was interested in first time travellers and those who held one-rupee and 500-rupee tickets. I told the air-hostess to hand them the public address system and ask them to say a few words about where and how they had got the tickets. There was one man who was travelling to Jammu with his wife. He came on the address system and said that earlier he used to go on a trip with his wife by Rajdhani Express once a month; he now travelled by air on Air Deccan. He continued to talk, and caused much merriment. People clapped and cheered him while his shy wife shrank into the depths of her seat and covered her face with her pallu to avoid the gaze of the amused passengers.

Among the people who called and gave me valuable, and encouraging, feedback was C.K. Prahalad. When my secretary got me on the phone I did not know it was *the* C.K. Prahalad, one of the most internationally respected management visionaries. He said, 'Captain Gopi, I am calling from Delhi airport. I am boarding a flight to Jaipur. Right in front are three lambani tribal women who are about to board with all their gypsy belongings. I wanted to congratulate you. You have really made the common people fly. Hats off to you! I am coming to Bengaluru next week. I have a few things to discuss. Could I come over and meet you?'

He came over the following week and we had dinner together. Prahalad has an arresting way of speaking. He can make very complex concepts seem simple. On the other hand, if you explain to him the way you are doing something, he quickly draws a pattern out of it and enunciates a little law that has a much wider appeal than that, its specific use enunciated. He is a true model builder; a theory builder, a perceptive thinker and has a very mesmeric presence. We spent about three–four hours together.

Prahalad said he had just published a book, *Fortune at the Bottom of the Pyramid*. It warns us not to treat people who are economically disadvantaged as poor people but rather as customers. It is they who sustain the pyramid of fortune at the top. He also said he was spearheading a seminar at the Infosys campus, and wanted me to address it, to which I readily agreed. There was another project on hand. He had been commissioned to make a half-hour documentary on thirty entrepreneurs around the world who had changed businesses by including the bottom of the pyramid. I was one of the thirty and he wanted to make a film on Deccan and me.

The Air Deccan website became the largest commercial one in India. Our revenue rose steadily initially and then suddenly surged. By the end of three years we were garnering $1.5 million to $2 million a day. This cash-flow kept the company going, but after a year and a half, certain events occurred that began to trouble the company.

The Challenges

Growth brought me a fan following. People thronged dinners, talks, and events I attended and said they admired the company. Village elders showered their blessings on me.

However, amidst all this admiration, as time passed, people began approaching me and very gently and hesitantly, began complaining about frequent delays. I was extremely embarrassed by such negative feedback. I immediately sought explanations and dealt toughly with the issue. People had missed a wedding, got late for an exam, cancelled a meeting. It was a nightmare and gave Deccan a bad name. Journalists were among my frequent fliers, many of whom had never flown earlier but were now flying regularly. There was always one on board a Deccan flight. Each time a flight got delayed a reporter was at hand to relay bad coverage.

There were reasons for delay or cancellations: lack of communication or cohesion, of leadership and planning. We had been in some difficulty because of the rapid growth. In three years, Deccan had grown from one aircraft to thirty-six; in three and a half years, Deccan had grown at a blistering pace from two aircraft to forty-five aircrafts and from 2000 passengers to 25,000 passengers a day and ramped up from flying daily two airports to sixty-seven airports and 380 flight everyday across the country. This process of growth was continuing. One of the major problems was lack of right people in the right places to manage things. Besides, the IT system which was good initially began to show weakness and was unable to handle the surge in numbers.

I hired Spencer Stuart, a reputed global headhunting company, to source the best people in the industry for us. They put Belgium-based Thierry Lindenau, who specialized in senior-level placements in aviation, on the job. I told Thierry to find someone solid to head our operations either from Ryan Air or Easyjet or Southwest. Thierry got Warwick Brady from Ryan Air for me, who joined us as the chief operations officer. Brady and I sourced the head of heavy engineering from British Airways, the head of line maintenance from Ryan Air, and head of flight training from KLM.

Ryan Air had overcome the many problems we were now facing. It had reached a point of no return until strict measures were introduced to turn it around. Brady introduced a policy stating that if a flight was cancelled, it stood cancelled and passengers would receive a refund according to the contract. Period. I felt terribly guilty about this because we still had an ethical responsibility to the stranded passenger. Brady said the problem would be fixed in five to six months. And that was the only way to focus on fixing the problem rather than attending to stranded passengers and taking care of them like full service airlines.

With growth came both good and bad publicity. We were regularly on TV for the right reasons: for opening a new route or for having achieved a new landmark; and also for the wrong ones: for neglecting passengers and for giving them a raw deal. Passengers were seen on TV losing their cool and venting their ire, manhandling our ground staff; seen attacking our points of sale. We were the unwitting suppliers to the media of juicy bits of news.

It was at this juncture that we took a decision to invest in upgrading our engineering, flight operations, and logistics abilities. Deccan's unprecedented success had had positive spin-offs for the aircraft-manufacturing companies. ATR's manufacturing inventories revived. However, the resurgence of Indian aviation also came as a challenge to both ATR and Airbus. Both were forced to stretch their production capabilities. Both had major supply chain issues because their suppliers had not been geared up to dovetail supplies to match the order books. ATR slipped up on spares' supply and we suffered. ATR made things worse for us by sometimes supplying spare parts and components that did not match specifications. This led to a blame-game between our engineers and theirs. It was akin to a tennis rally. I frequently intervened to find workable solutions.

The other source of problems for us was the emergence of new airlines like Spicejet, Kingfisher, Go Air, Paramount, and Indigo. The new airlines needed planes and ordered tens of aircrafts to be built. This put pressure on aircraft manufacture and delivery schedules. The daily flight density at airports rose. There was pressure on airport space and ground-handling facilities. The new airlines were offering competitive fares resulting in a flood of seats in the market and affecting our yield and profitability. We raised prices somewhat to help the bottom line, but that alienated customers.

Meeting Vijay Mallya

A few months before he launched Kingfisher Airlines, Vijay Mallya wanted to meet me. Kiran Rao of Airbus facilitated our meeting. Kiran hinted that Vijay Mallya was probably seeking to invest in my airline. I went to meet him.

I then lived in a modest apartment block located on the same road as Vijay Mallya's imposing mansion. I used to walk to office or drive a small car, travelled economy class, stayed in my guest-houses and very rarely in five-star hotels. I had read about the man from the time I was in my late twenties and was aware of his glamorous lifestyle.

Everything about Vijay Mallya is grand and larger-than-life. The driveway to his bungalow is lined on either side by eye-catching grottos, fountains, cascades, and majestic figures in stone. There is a regular boulevard with ornamental palms, creepers, and well-manicured flower beds. As I walked towards his palatial old-world mansion, I was attracted to the figure of a rider on a prancing horse.

I wondered what it was that this man wanted to say to me. Was it perhaps a desire to meet a fellow entrepreneur? Mallya had launched UB Air in the early 1990s. That was when East West, Damania, Modi Luft, and Gujarat Air had emerged and folded up as rapidly as they had arrived. A UB Air aircraft had met with an accident but there were no casualties. The airline however closed down soon thereafter, sharing the fate of six other airlines of its vintage. Might this be a prelude to a second attempt at starting an airline?

It had been rumoured that Vijay Mallya was planning a brand new airline. The name of Kingfisher Airlines had been suggested. It derived itself from the 'King of Good Times', a catch-phrase that has attached itself to Vijay Mallya. Kiran Rao was certain that Mallya would relaunch his airline, and assuming he did, I urged Airbus and Kiran Rao to incorporate a six-month gap between deliveries to us and to Kingfisher. Kiran would not listen, and with the unimpeachable logic of the salesman said if they didn't sell to Mallya, Boeing surely would. I had warned aircraft-makers that it would be counter productive for them to sell to everyone before the market matured, arguing that it would only trigger a new aviation shake-out and no-one would survive except the monopolies. I sensed a hint of prophecy about my own words. A CEO has to show sales, and stock-markets pressurize CEOs to deliver for the short-term. Airbus wanted to deliver for the short-term as did Deccan.

The Mallya bungalow is surrounded by well-maintained lawns and an adjoining patio. Giving access to the house is a wide portico. There is an enormous garage at some distance from the portico where the Mallya family has a museum of antique cars. About thirty or forty of them, their metal exteriors gleaming, were parked cheek by jowl. At the front porch was a Bentley. Down the cobble-and-grass pathway to the side stood a gleaming new Mercedes and a brand new sports car.

Inside the house, on one side, is a temple that is as impressive as the rest of the ambience. Vijay Mallya sat on a swing on a raised deck in the veranda. Mallya is a good model for a modern maharaja. The raised platform looked on to a large and impressive swimming pool. Seated a little distance away from Vijay Mallya was Ravi Nedungadi, his group CFO, cigar in mouth, a flute of smoke rising from it. Ravi sat there calmly like the Buddha, a figure of utmost composure. The cigar was his logo. Some homes are marked by a strong smell of burning incense, some by the sound of wind chimes, some invoke a visual motif (a mandala or chakra or some geometric shape to haunt you while you are there), some home interiors resonate to a painting as the centrepiece. In the opulent interiors of the Mallya residence, the cigar was the central motif, both visual and olfactory.

When I drew closer, I saw that the swing on which Vijay Mallya was seated was made of solid silver, his feet rested on a silver stool. Silver was the counterpoint: the foil. Solid antique gray silver!

Vijay Mallya noticed my wide-eyed amazement. I was like a village boy in a big city for the first time; like a village boy who is completely in the thrall of the sights and the sounds. I gave it away; felt no embarrassment at being in awe; had no inhibition in manifesting it. What really bamboozled me were two tall columns of silver placed symmetrically a few feet away from the ensemble of the silver furniture. They had limbs that forked upwards like the fronds of some artificially selected palms; simply stood there. I asked Ravi Nedungadi what these were. He said calmly, as though any rapid movements would offend the choreography of the occasion, 'Gopi, they are candlesticks.' I imagined large candles in the holders, lighted and burning forever. I had never seen anything like them, not even in the celebrated Salar Jung Museum in Hyderabad.

Vijay Mallya welcomed me and straightaway offered me a drink. I settled for a beer, which was promptly served. Vijay Mallya is an affable and very hospitable person. He uses his carefully engineered pug image as a front. He came straight to the point with no preliminaries. He said, 'Gopi, you are from Bengaluru. I am from Bengaluru. Why do we need two airlines?' I promptly replied, 'Vijay, we are very different as individuals. We have different philosophies, outlooks on life, and styles of functioning. How would it help to erase our individual borderlines and identities?' He suggested working together as one airline so as to avoid eating into each other's market share. He said he would like to invest in my airline. No word-mincer, Vijay spoke as if he wanted to buy me out. He would call the new airline Kingfisher Airlines.

I said, 'Yes, it's not a bad idea, but I need to think about it. If we can't make a single airline through your investment in Deccan, I am sure we could collaborate. We could share our engineering and other resources.'

We chatted aimlessly and shot the breeze. I kind of liked him. He was friendly and jovial; had a twinkle in his eyes. I hung about for two hours. When I came out, Kiran Rao asked me, 'What do you make of it?' I said, 'I don't think it's going to work. We are two very different people.' I left it at that. My whole dream was to build this airline and not to make money for myself. I could have sold the business and retired on a fat compensation, and had that happened the entire history of Indian aviation might then have been different, as would the course of my life.

Once the mist of Vijay Mallya's charisma and opulence lifted, I returned to my own real world and was seized with the faith reposed in me as chief executive of the company. I recalled my mandate: that the challenge of creating something is worth striving for, living for, and dying for. It had been my dream to achieve that, and I had sold the dream to a team of people. It did not take me long to say 'No' to the overture. Kingfisher Airlines was born in its avatar because I said no. Otherwise, within six months Deccan would have been reborn as Kingfisher Airlines.

At around the same time there were developments that had an impact on the future of Deccan. Deccan was losing money, flights were being cancelled, flights were being delayed. By the time we got one problem fixed, another raised its head. Popular sentiment was no longer in our favour. Part of the problem was of our making, part that circumstances were ranged against us.

The new airlines needed skilled people to run their operations. They poached and there was attrition. We faced an acute HR shortage. We lost pilots and engineers to competition. One morning I received the news that our Ahmedabad–Bengaluru flight had to be cancelled because the pilot and engineer had left and joined Kingfisher Airlines. On another day, fifteen co-pilots resigned en-masse and joined Indian Airlines.

The regulations did not allow airlines to employ foreign nationals as co-pilots, and the latter joined the exodus. We were in for a serious crisis. I had to get something done. I persuaded the government to change the rules to enable foreigners to operate as co-pilots in India. The problem with captains was far worse. Other airlines, particularly Kingfisher, offered inordinately high salaries to our captains in a bid to attract them. I had recruited them from non-aviation sector companies and assignments, paying them 20 per cent less than Jet Airways. Our employees however, including pilots, earned more through allowances. We had worked out a load factor index as a performance parameter. All employees, regardless of rank and function, got a load factor allowance every month. If they pushed up the load factor, they would get a higher allowance.

Pilots were given a sector allowance in addition to the load factor allowance. The more they flew, the more they earned. Their basic pay plus various allowances put together worked out to an emolument higher than that offered by Jet Airways.

Other HR functions also suffered. While the core team and those who had joined the company early stayed, the newcomers began to leave. I had not had the opportunity to interact with the new recruits. Kingfisher Airlines and the other airlines were brazen about their poaching exercise: they openly set up recruitment bazaars at airports. Our airport handling was outsourced; airport cadres were working for us through an agent. The Kingfisher bazaars attracted the agents' staff and many quit service with the agents without as much as a day's notice. We faced a similar crisis with engineers. Vijay Mallya had clearly mandated to his recruiters: 'Get the best from Deccan,' and they did.

IT and Fund-raising

We hired quality trainers like Hero Mindmine to train our front line customer service executives, but the best of them left after training, to join the competition because of higher salaries and the attraction of working for a principle rather than an agent. The attrition was unabated. There was a hole in the bucket which we were unable to fix. Let me give a few instances of how the bucket leaked. There was an airport manager with us who received a salary of Rs 35,000 a month. He left overnight to join SpiceJet who had offered him Rs 1,50,000. After we had inducted the Airbus, we recruited another chief pilot on a salary of Rs 2 lakh. Kingfisher offered him Rs 3,50,000, a car and a house so he moved over. It was like the nightmare—the director of Gujarat Airways had described to me earlier.

One day the crisis deepened: twelve engineers resigned and went over to Kingfisher Airlines. I was furious with Vijay Mallya and publicized his unethical practises in the media. Mallya used the media to get back at me.

We went to and fro. When the steam cooled the two of us met. I said, 'What you are doing will prove to be counter-productive and bite you back in the long run. Once you increase pilots' salaries you can't bring them down, and their numbers are limited. Why don't you import them? But don't touch my pilots and engineers.' He seemed to see the truth of my logic and we signed a no-poaching agreement.

That agreement did not deter Mallya's HR which continued to poach in my backyard. Mallya is an extraordinarily busy person and I was willing to believe that he might not have known. I called him and gave vent to my ire. He got back. We exchanged a volley of incendiary words. The no-poaching agreement proved a non-starter.

The spurt in airline numbers had caused a huge rush at the airports. The infrastructure was woefully inadequate to cope with the vast numbers. This was particularly bad in Delhi, Mumbai, Kolkata, Chennai, Bengaluru, and Hyderabad. It was so bad in Delhi, Mumbai, and Bengaluru that it became routine for aircraft to circle over the airport for an hour before being permitted to land. One minute of flying drains Rs 1300 of fuel on an ATR and Rs 2200 on an Airbus. It made for huge losses and hurt us most severely further delaying our flight operations. While other airlines had aircraft to spare in the event of flight delays, we had none. Even after we managed to fix many of our engineering problems, the reputation had stuck.

As a low-cost airline, we were flying to smaller airports, which was a source of a new problem. Some of these were under the defence ministry and closed at a particular hour, by 4 or 5 p.m. If we were delayed elsewhere we could not land at these airports and this added to our un-intended truancy. Jammu and Gwalior, for instance, were IAF airports while Vizag was a naval airport. If an aircraft headed for Gwalior was delayed at Delhi and could not land there because of the time bar, it had to return to Delhi. Many small airports did not have night-landing facilities. At others, government airport staff worked only till 6 p.m. The AAI had not recruited additional staff even after so many new airlines had commenced operations.

The problems piled up one on top of another. After we fixed most operational glitches, we were short on break-even by Rs 300 to Rs 500 on an average per passenger. We had very little debt, our turnover having crossed Rs 2000 crores. We only needed to stay the course some time longer. However, while we waited for airport infrastructure to improve, a terrible misfortune befell us: our IT system collapsed.

It was a huge disaster. We had outsourced the reservation system operations to Interglobe Technologies (IGT), a company promoted and headed by

Mr Rahul Bhatia. I had reposed deep and implicit trust in the company not because of Bhatia, whom I met much later, but because of the young, enthusiastic, and hard-working bunch of software engineers who provided me with a good alternative to Navitaire. I had begun hearing rumours that Bhatia was going about the business of setting up his own airline. I called Bhatia and said that if what I had heard was true then there was conflict of interest. I pointed out that he would become my competitor and he would have access to all my data. He denied the rumour, but when I asked him to commit his denial in writing, he dithered.

With all its problems, Deccan had become big and was a force to reckon with. Had Bhatia spent more time on Deccan's IT system and made it more robust and versatile, the system would have catapulted him to the global stage and put him in the league of Navitaire and Saber.

Bhatia's IGT had signed a contract with us to provide us all the features that Navitaire was offering, at contract cost; plus add-on features as and when necessary, for which a separate fee was to be negotiated and paid by us. IGT was required to create a full-feature, robust system within a ninety-day period from our signing the contract. However, even a year and a half later the revenue-management system with dynamic pricing and the basic essentials had not been developed. IGT had given us the Internet-based reservation system, the second of the two-component software, in its simplest configuration: it was to be made robust to be able to handle large passenger hits which required much attention and a fresh injection of investment. Bhatia had done neither. Apparently, IGT had failed to invest in upgrading the system to handle the increasing customer volumes. I was told by my marketing executives and investors that Bhatia was setting up his own airline. I did not believe them but gradually the lack of investment by IGT to support Air Deccan was evident as the system was not able to handle ever-increasing passenger volumes and traffic to our website.

My team warned me many times. They said, 'Captain, the writing on the wall is clear. Please see it. Don't close your eyes.' They identified three areas of conflict of interest between Deccan and IGT. By then Bhatia had already launched his Indigo in partnership with Rakesh Gangwal from the US a well known aviation professional who had stepped down from the post of president of US Airways. My marketing executives said the first conflict of interest lay in the fact that our IT system, was experiencing problems, slowing down and causing much inconvenience to passengers, and was not being restored or upgraded. Each time our system collapsed, operations went caput. Travel agents could not book tickets, change the status, cancel reservations, or get refunds. Passengers had no way of accessing the system. Each time the system collapsed, Indigo, and the other low-cost airlines, benefited.

My executive identified a second conflict of interest with Bhatia's IGT. For the new airline he had launched, Bhatia did not use his own IGT-made system but implemented Navitaire. His choice of Navitaire indicated clearly that he had little faith in his own system.

Third, Bhatia's IGT had my airline's data which he could use in planning his routes and pricing which could trigger the collapse of my airline. Mohan and I listened with disbelief. And to our horror we realized we were, to use a slang, 'made suckers'. We decided to tackle Rahul head on and told him that we wanted to migrate. After a series of meetings between our teams, Rahul eventually offered to sell us the system. He had developed Version 2, and we agreed to buy the upgrade for $7 million. This however involved migration to the new system and required the active collaboration of Bhatia and his team. He for his part seemed to be in no hurry to take the transition forward and each day's delay meant much anguish and loss of business to Deccan. It also meant that as he had all our data he knew which of the sectors were the most profitable. The combination of our data in his hand and delayed migration to the new IT system was proving to be a boon for him and a disaster for us. It was a straight case of unresolved conflict of interest.

I once asked Azim Premji of Wipro why Indian IT companies, known for their software programming wizardry the world over, had no presence in the aviation reservation systems although it was a multi-billion-dollar business. It was Galileo, Amadeus, and Saber for full-service airlines and Navitaire for low-cost airlines. Why hadn't Indian IT companies like Wipro and Infosys joined the race?

Azim Premji said, 'Captain, mission-critical IT requires huge investments. You have to build and test the system. No airline uses a new IT vendor to provide critical services to the company because of the danger of glitches. If you want to avoid glitches you need to invest huge amounts of money, time, and resources. That is because you have to run your IT software on a platform where it works. IT people who have worked with airlines for fifteen to twenty years have a great advantage. They have developed and tested the system on a live platform; are familiar with it. Yours has been an enormous platform for IGT. You have provided them the opportunity to build and test their system live on your platform.'

A cold shudder ran down my spine when I realized my vulnerability and that the very survival of Deccan was at stake. Mohan and I were acutely aware of how dire and urgent the situation was. We had to move quickly but cautiously to extricate ourselves from the insidious enemy. We approached Navitaire and asked them to sell us their system, they wanted a no-objection note from Bhatia. We asked Bhatia and he served a legal notice on Navitaire, requiring them not to deal with Deccan until the IGT contract with Deccan had run its course. That road for us came to a dead end. We looked out for other possible software partners and discovered Radix, a US-based IT company.

We began working with Radix to customize the system to handle larger passenger numbers and capable of accommodating growth. We worked quietly with Radix who brought it into their own system and customized it for us. In three months we migrated to the new Radix system. The switch happened at midnight. At 5 p.m. on the previous day, just as courts were closing, we filed a caveat in all the high courts concerned that we would be switching to a new IT system as the existing system was jeopardizing the interest of passengers and the airline's business. We stated that it was a mission-critical switch and that the court must not grant a stay to IGT, should that company approach the courts, without giving Deccan an opportunity to represent itself. We also filed for damages.

We switched systems and waited with deep anxiety to see how the new system worked. The worry was well founded: the following day there was chaos at many airports and hundreds of passengers' names did not figure in the manifest although they had obtained e-tickets in the IGT system. By evening we realized we had lost passenger data and didn't know how much. Assuming the seats were empty, the new Radix software had automatically sold tickets. We were, however, surprised when passengers with tickets already issued to them by the IGT system turned up. The uncertainty would persist for three months, the advance period over which bookings had been made consequent to the data mayhem. We had to ride the storm and had no alternative but to compensate the passengers.

The media had a field day. They accused Deccan of over-booking the flights to speed up its cash flow. Those three months were the worst in Deccan's history. We lost bookings data and passenger contact records. Our cash flow suffered immensely. We were compelled to put the travelling public through much inconvenience and our public image took a beating. We had been brought almost to our knees.

This was ironic because we collected Rs 7 crores a day when we needed about Rs 8 crores to break even, the loss amounting to one crore a day. It simply incinerated all the capital we had raised. That other airlines also were losing money was no consolation. The aviation scene was again in a tight spot. Jet Airways could not raise a single dollar in the public market; Kingfisher was unable find any equity in the open market; Indigo too failed to raise money. It took three months for Deccan to fix its IT problems and plug the loopholes. It stabilized time-bound flight schedules, cut down delays, and ironed out engineering issues.

It appeared that Deccan could make it; it had begun to reacquire its original public image. The public once again began placing faith in us; gone was the hidden snigger. I received letters and email from passengers acknowledging the transformation. There were very few cancellations and for on-time departures and arrivals we were the best. I had asked the DGCA to publish every month the on-time performance of all airlines. Deccan beat the rest.

Deccan had regained its position on other parameters too. In network spread it was the largest with sixty-seven cities to Jet Airways' and Indian Airlines' forty-three cities. In passenger share percentages, Jet was 22.6 to Deccan's 22, and Indian Airlines 19 per cent. In less than four years Deccan had become the largest airline, replacing Indian Airlines as the nation's carrier. The political leadership had begun to look to Deccan rather than Indian Airlines to connect to remote parts of India.

Given a little more time, Deccan could have weathered the storm and overcome the cash crunch but time was running out. I might have pulled it off had my IT system not collapsed. We had to bear in mind the welfare of four thousand employees; the public insurance funds and retail investors we had to answer to. We had people in secondary employment; a stake in regional economies.

When I thought about it, it no longer mattered to me whether I remained at the helm or not. External funding would erode my control and I would no longer have a say in the day-to-day running of the company, but bringing in outside capital would protect Deccan. The dream must live on, I thought to myself.

I named Edelweiss, a Mumbai-based boutique investment advisory firm, to raise equity in the market.

Vijay Mallya kept persuading me to merge our two airlines. I resisted his proposition and maintained that the marriage would not work. The analogy of marriage was a powerful one. I frequently used it to show how diverse our interests and goals were. I remarked to the press one day that Vijay Mallya was from Venus and I was from Mars. How could the two meet? We differed radically, and irreconcilably, in our thinking, lifestyle, and business philosophy. A merger could not be the solution for Deccan's growth. Deccan was a phenomenal brand; a great investment. The company's debt was negligible when compared to its revenue.

Reliance Overtures

Any new investor in Deccan would begin with a fantastic advantage. They had readymade infrastructure, fleet, routes, manpower, and expertise. We had our own hangar in Chennai, eight bases across India (Delhi, Mumbai,

Kolkata, Thiruvananthapuram, Bengaluru, Hyderabad, Ahmedabad, and Chennai). With about 500 pilots and 500 trained engineers, we had engineering and operational capabilities across India. We were in everybody's hearts and Deccan's name was on everybody's lips, from the president to the peon. We had a low-cost culture with the lowest cost per kilometre, which was the envy of any investor. Also, in addition to solid material assets, our work ethics was all about maintaining clockwork precision in all matters.

I had to choose a partner who would take a larger stake in the airline than I; was on the look-out for deep pockets. I wasn't certain how long it would take for us to break-even, though we needed only about Rs 600 per passenger. This uncertainty stemmed from runaway oil prices, congestion at airports, and unrelenting induction of aircraft by all airlines including Deccan. I sensed that because of the brand and size of Deccan and because of the strong stock market sentiment, the time was ripe to dilute holding and sell equity to fuel growth. If by chance we did not break-even going forward and the market collapsed, it would be a huge calamity—for employees, vendors, investors and customers, and I would be responsible. I resolved 'I won't let my ego to decide the future of the airline.' I felt intuitively, as I had on previous occasions, that I had to move fast and close the funding if I were to keep alive the low-fare model and the common man's flying dream.

Madhu Kela, head of Reliance Mutual Funds, was among the first to call. 'Capt. Gopi, why don't you give us a stake?' he asked. I went over and met Amitabh Jhunjhunwala, Anil Ambani's right-hand man. Then I met Anil Ambani himself. He had just come out of a very bruising, public battle with his brother Mukesh Ambani and emerged unscathed, proving his mettle. The war of words traded between the brothers had evoked much interest in corporate, bureaucratic, and political circles.

The Ambani brothers presided over India's largest business empires. People wondered whether Anil Ambani would have the ability to execute business plans without his brother's help. The unexpected result was that rather than halving, the company became two businesses. One brother became Number One, the other, Number Two.

Anil Ambani was also very aggressive in all his ventures. His mutual fund became the largest MF, his infocom business wiped out previous losses and began registering profits, racing ahead at the heels of Airtel.

I met Anil Ambani at his office; in awe a second time. The Ambanis have a mental and genetic make-up that inspires you to work twenty-four hours a day to the exclusion of all else. They demonstrate to their investors and shareholders that they will go to any extremes and do whatever it takes to succeed; that they will not let them down.

We met over lunch. He served me the food himself and proved to be an extraordinarily gracious host. He was not in the least pompous but exuded a quiet acknowledgement of his own sense of power. There is a magnetic field to power of all kinds. Sitting before him, I felt the aura of the power of colossal wealth and far-reaching influence. The lunch meeting lasted three and half hours. I spoke for half an hour about my dreams. Anil Ambani spoke non-stop for the next three hours. He said nothing about Reliance, said nothing about investing in Deccan. He told me the story of how his father had built Reliance. His father, Dhirubhai Ambani, had started out as a petrol station attendant and ridden to school on a cycle. He had worked hard and built wealth for the people who had trusted him. He was trying to convey that should he decide to associate with me, he would be lending us a name that was very precious to him; was trying to tell me that he would not share the name unless he was confident that the name would not be sullied. I got the message.

When we took leave, Anil Ambani complimented me, referring to a quote of mine in the newspapers when I asked Naresh Goyal to fight me in the market rather than hide behind politicians. Anil said he admired my guts. He was keen in investing but his finance people would work out the numbers.

I asked K.V. Kamath, by now a friend and advisor, to check with Anil Ambani if he was serious about the investment. I didn't want to waste my time and his. Kamath called back to say Anil Ambani was indeed keen to go ahead, 'But', he said 'the rest is for you two, to decide.'

I met Anil Ambani a couple of times after that. The finance teams of both companies did due diligence over the next two or three months. They validated our numbers, undertook a sanity check on our business model, and subjected it to stress tests. Amitabh Jhunjhunwala was attending to the entire process. We eventually shook hands and signed a preliminary term-sheet and decided on a date when the final term-sheet would be signed. The media had learnt through the grapevine that Reliance was likely to invest in Deccan, and this made for a lead story. Such is the power of the Reliance brand that a mere hint of its associating with Deccan sent the stock prices up. It is not such a good thing for the prospective investor because when stock prices shoot up, he ends up paying a higher price for the stock. We had agreed that Anil Ambani would take a 26 per cent stake in the company, and according to SEBI guidelines, he would be obliged to make an open offer to the public of 20 per cent. He would be required to acquire the public shares at a minimum price that matched the price of investing directly in the company.

There are some people with an intuitive understanding of business; have a nose for money. I don't think any MBA programme can teach this. They *simply* know what makes a business tick, *simply* know what needs to be done to scale-up a business. They are *naturals* when it comes to managing the environment. I felt tying up with Reliance would be in the best interests of the company and investors. Anil Ambani said they were aware that the cash burn was likely to continue for some more time but would do whatever it took to continue the growth. Their single concern was to ensure returns to investors. Anil Ambani said just as Deccan had made it possible for the common man to fly, Reliance had made it possible for the average man to invest in public shares and get a good return on investment. It meant that if the losses continued, I would not be able to prevent them from taking charge of the company through majority investment. This would of course jeopardize my own position, but I was game because the company and its employees and investors mattered most.

We agreed that Reliance could invest more money even if it meant their assuming a 51 per cent share in the company. We sat down and worked out a draft—legal document deciding on the share price, the initial deposit, the structure and roles of various parties in the new board, and their functions and prerogatives. We also fixed a date for signing the final term-sheet: exactly fifteen days after we had signed the preliminary document. We shook hands affirming our total commitment to the deal.

Although we had arrived at an in-principle arrangement between Reliance and Deccan, we had not legalized the relationship. I was aware of many possible last-minute changes of heart and remained open-ended about the deal. I continued to respond to inquiries from investors. There was one from Texas Specific Group headed by David Bonderman who had invested in various American aviation companies. He had also been the chairman of Ryan Air. He had used our helicopters once or twice and I knew his team in Mumbai.

I was still dogged by one concern: what would I do if the Reliance deal fell through at the last moment? This was improbable, but surely not impossible. I still retained a healthy scepticism about the world.

News got around that Reliance had decided to invest in Deccan. Vijay Mallya resumed his overtures but I avoided taking his calls. Others therefore called on his behalf: senior politicians, senior executives, and Mallya well-wishers. Even Kiran Rao of Airbus pitched in. They asked me to reconsider Mallya's offer: he was willing to accommodate my demands. They seemed to visualize a Deccan–Kingfisher alliance as a beacon on the Indian aviation map. They realized that a tie-up between us would help stabilize the markets—saw synergies: resources, expertise, flight and engineering operations, logistics, maintenance and inventory. They said that operationally speaking, there was a perfect fit: Kingfisher Airline had Airbus and ATRs, so had Deccan. The only difference, they agreed, was that Mallya's was a full-feature service; ours was an LCC. They saw commonality; I saw the difference in our philosophies and work-styles. I was from Mars and Mallya was from Venus.

The fifteenth day arrived: the day on which Reliance and Deccan were to sign the final deed. They were supposed to give us the deposit money. Amitabh Jhunjhunwala called to say that Reliance was also in discussion with another airline and that it would like to close the two deals together. Could I give them another fifteen days? I said I was like an unmarried bride and could wait for another fifteen days, pointing out however that I was not morally bound, and might not refuse—should another suitor propose.

I had no particular reason to suspect Reliance's good faith. We had gone through a series of painstaking negotiations, audits, and documentation processes, but the world of business is not a charity fair. People did not pick up the fallen simply to help them up; there are no good samaritans. More than anything, however, I was aware of the dynamics of the stock-markets; aware of Deccan's strong brand equity. A collapse of this would mean downgrading of brand equity; abdication of positions of advantage and vulnerability at the negotiating table. I did bother about what I would do if Reliance did not keep their word and pulled out.

Amitabh Jhunjhunwala had reassured me that things would be fine. Bulo Konsagra, a London-based NRI who was promoting Spicejet, had called to say Reliance was seeking investment in their airline so there was nothing dubious in the wings. What worried and bothered me was 'The deal is not done till it is done—with money in my bank'. Can I take a chance? What if....

The day I received the call from Amitabh I was heading back to Bengaluru from Mumbai by the evening flight. I received a call from R. V. Deshpande, a senior member of the Congress party in Karnataka and a former minister who wanted to meet me. I was at home by 9.30 p.m. and Deshpande dropped in.

Inking the Deccan–Kingfisher Alliance

Deshpande broached the subject. He said it would be a good thing for Karnataka if Mallya and I joined hands and worked together. He said there were many things common between the two of us and we should take advantage of that in order to give the people the best deal in aviation. I patiently repeated the same words that I had been using to describe our mutually disparate characters. Deshpande finally said the least I could do was to take a call that Mallya would be making that night. I said I would certainly do that.

Vijay Mallya called me a little after ten that night. He spoke endearingly and in a spirit of camaraderie. He said, 'I know you've shaken hands with Reliance. It does not matter what they have offered you. I am willing to better every term in the deal. You quote the price. I will not negotiate. Let us do the deal.'

Mallya was calling from Monte Carlo where his $100-million personal yacht, the *Indian Empress,* was berthed, and hosting his famed annual party on the eve of the Formula One race. He said, 'I am calling from Monte Carlo. I am at the dinner table with a host of VVIPs. The Prince of Monaco is here, the stars of Formula One are here. I am calling you in the midst of all this because it is very important to me. Please make a note of all the major terms of the deal. I will call later.'

Before retiring to bed that night, I sat down and jotted down the non-negotiable terms I wanted Mallya to meet in the unlikely event that he would go all the way and actually offer to meet them. I was disappointed with Reliance's wanting a deferment; but surprised by Mallya's persistence. The day had been a long one and I slipped into deep slumber.

The phone rang at about 4 a.m. when I was fast asleep. I think he called a second and a third time. I woke up and received his call, stepping out to the balcony to avoid disturbing my wife. I said, 'Vijay, I want you to know this is serious. I've already shaken hands with Anil Ambani but they need another 5–6 days more. However, I've already got a preliminary term-sheet from them so let's not discuss this unless you are going to meet some major points. Point number one is that you will not dilute this business model.'

Mallya spoke to me in Kannada. He was disarming in his tone and began on an elaborate pitch. He sounded urgent but winsome. He said it was his philosophy to address all the segments of the market: low, middle, and high. He had done this with whiskey and beer. He said he was aware of my commitment to a low-cost airline and he respected that. Together we would be good for the industry. However, with Reliance's entry into the fray, the bloodbath would continue. Our coming together would altogether transform the scene.

Vijay Mallya asked me if I had the list ready. I read out my list which included conditions that would deter Mallya. I said, 'If you are serious about investing in Deccan, you will have to make a deposit of Rs 200 crore immediately. Then you will have to take a 26 per cent stake in the company through direct investment and another 20 per cent through open offer from the public shareholders. You must be prepared to make a total investment of about Rs 1000 crores. You will have three directors on the board and I will have three. There will be another six independent directors jointly selected by us. I will be the chairman.' Vijay interjected at this point to say, 'Can I be vice chairman?' I said, 'Fine. We will have six independent directors who will be truly independent. We will have a CEO who will not report to me but to the Board. Ramki Sundaram, our CFO, will be the officiating CEO till we find an alternative. Most importantly, I can only believe that you are interested in carrying this deal further if you make the deposit in three days; otherwise the deal is off.'

Any sane investor would take three months to bring in investments that run into hundreds of crores. Reliance sat on thousands of crores but took three months to decide. I was not at all certain whether Mallya had that kind of money and whether he could raise it at such short notice.

Mallya agreed to all the conditions, but requested that the 200 crore deposit was too high and was ready to deposit 100 instead. I said, 'Won't do'. He said, 'Let us agree on 150.' I said, 'Fine, and I also want you to give me Rs 160 per share.' He haggled and suggested 'Rs 155?' I agreed, but he would have to pay the balance of Rs 410 crore within four weeks or he would have to forfeit the Rs 150 crore. He agreed.

It appeared surreal. He was in his yacht in Monte Carlo, I was thousands of miles away. The deal was concluded in forty-five minutes. It was perhaps the shortest time ever taken to negotiate a deal of that dimension.

Vijay Mallya concluded the conversation by saying, 'Gopi, Thursday afternoon you will have the DD by 2 p.m. Friday we meet the press in Mumbai.' I told him I would hold the board meeting at 4 p.m. on Thursday. I would call it off if I did not receive the DD by 2 p.m., insisting that I was dead serious.

I slept fitfully after this telephonic haggling with Mallya, half from the fatigue of disturbed sleep and half from excitement. I woke up just before noon when Ravi Nedungadi called. We decided to meet at the Oberoi at 2 p.m. Ravi was there, a glowering cigar in mouth. We discussed the documents that needed to be prepared. Auditors and lawyers on both sides sat together all of Tuesday and Wednesday to hammer out the details of the agreement. They looked at SEBI guidelines and compliance issues and had the term-sheets ready by 4 a.m. on Thursday morning and called me over to the hotel. It was a very large document running into a very large number of pages. I checked the key details and signed a preliminary agreement with Ravi Nedungadi representing Mallya. I, however, made it clear to Ravi that this term-sheet will become null and void if the demand draft did not reach me by 2 p.m. in the afternoon and also that this money will get forfeited if the balance money did not come within four weeks. The Kingfisher representative agreed.

The deal was done. I don't know whether what I did was right or wrong: the jury is still out on that. Many were of the opinion that I should have joined hands with Reliance, but the deal with Mallya seemed the best course at the time.

I called the board for a meeting. Deccan shares were priced at Rs 125 and I was going to sell them at Rs 155. I was getting Rs 560 crores injected into equity. No one could decry that. I was confident, as always, that I could take a decision and the Board would support me. They were well aware that I did only what was in the best interest of the company and stakeholders.

The board met on Thursday. The media had got wind of the deal, and by the time I went to office at 1 p.m. Deccan's office was like a fortress. The press had besieged it and was camping outside. They had set up OB vans all around the office. The media wanted to cover the entire event live. I allowed them entry, so they set up cameras inside the board room. I thought it would be good publicity for the company and was still wondering if the money would actually reach us in time. It was like playing flush.

My respect for Vijay Mallya grew. He had not discussed anything with me face-to-face; had not seen our balance sheets; had not done due diligence. He wanted Deccan very badly and had moved swiftly. He wanted the kill. It did not mean much to him whether I was chairman. He would inch his way in and own 46 per cent of the company. If Reliance had taken over the business, it would have been almost impossible for him to recoup his own losses. Reliance would have presented a formidable challenge.

He also realized he would be creating the largest airline in India. Deccan was twice the size of Kingfisher. Our revenues were greater, we had more aircrafts, and we ran more routes. Without Deccan, he would probably have had to spend three times the agreed amount, Rs 3000 crores, to achieve Deccan's scale.

The DD had not arrived by 1.30 p.m. when I got a call. The caller said the DD had been purchased and the courier was on his way. Kingfisher was worried too that I might decide to cancel the deal if the draft did not reach before 2 p.m.; it was delivered a few minutes short of that deadline.

The board meeting lasted an hour and half, and was perhaps the first time in India that a board meeting was broadcast live. Reporters asked us leading questions. Cartoons appeared in the newspapers the next day and the following days, lampooning the 'marriage of two airlines'. The captions said it signalled the end of the era of low-cost air travel for the country. Be prepared, they said, to pay higher fares.

Vijay Mallya kept his word. He sent us the remaining Rs 400 crore over the next four weeks; and made a public offering and invested a total amount of Rs 1000 crores. The next day I flew to Mumbai, Vijay came in from Paris and we met at the Oberoi and addressed a press conference in a hall that was bursting at its seams. Vijay Mallya was at his charming best and successfully parried all uncomfortable questions but said he was committed to keeping Deccan as a low-cost carrier.

Although it would take three more months for Vijay Mallya to join the board, I invited him to attend the management meetings. I wanted to win his confidence and familiarize him with the way we were running the airline. I told him that putting together a professional management structure would allow us both to withdraw from day-to-day management functions. He spent two hours at the first meeting. The public image of Vijay Mallya is that of an extremely rich man who is forever partying; who loves to be seen in the company of glamorous women; and, who loves to splurge on expensive cars, yachts, jets, villas, and islands around the world. I, however, realized after the first two meetings that he is also a workaholic. Though he comes across as pompous on screen and on media, face to face he has a disarming charm, is endearing, courteous to a fault and a generous host. He also exudes immense charisma. I realized soon that he is extremely shrewd, razor sharp and a brilliant marketeer. His only foible is that he is late for meetings—very, very late. Unlike common belief, he does not party all the time; has a hundred things on his plate. He is forever in the midst of meetings and always at work. The venues are different and glamorous: his home or yacht or on an island he owns, or on his business jet. He seems, however, not to draw a distinction between work and personal life. He did not plan meetings in a way that made sense to those waiting for him. His sense of planning is utterly bizarre.

As chairman, I told him as politely as I could that if he did not turn up for my meetings in time, I would start the meeting without him. I had to show regard for the other directors, including a general on the board. He made an effort and was only one-and-a-half to two hours late. This, I was told, was an extraordinary improvement by his standards of punctuality. He rose in my esteem just by the sheer effort he had put in.

Rebranding and the Merger

Vijay Mallya came for the next management meeting having done some really intensive research. He had hired marketing agencies for some field-work, having got them to undertake some dipstick research about how the combined brand was being perceived. Mallya combined brand power with value and priced his product on the basis of both. He said, 'I can spend Rs 500 and make it look like Rs 5000, so I can charge more. I generally agreed with him, but for the low-cost model, every rupee is vital. Five hundred rupees is a lot of money. And I, therefore, stressed that we needed to control costs. This was a fundamental disconnect between us.

Mallya made a presentation, encapsulating his market research findings. He wanted us to rebrand Deccan and suggested ways of locating and driving synergies. Deccan and Kingfisher would share material and human resources, equipment and facilities. I said we could do that only if we made employees feel part of the same airline combine. He, however, came up with an idea that continually pushed the costs up as we went along.

Deccan and Kingfisher engaged independent teams to undertake market research. Both teams were unanimous about Deccan: that it had excellent brand recall and was the most preferred brand across the board. On the negative side, it was perceived as prone to delays and did not evoke high quality. Based on these findings, the management decided to reposition the Deccan brand and bring the company under the umbrella of Kingfisher Airlines.

I had occasion to talk to retail legend Kishore Biyani on this rebranding exercise. Kishore runs the Big Bazaar retail chain that has a nationwide presence. He did not endorse the positioning of Deccan, saying, 'Keep the two as distinct as possible. Deccan is a great brand. Kingfisher is a great brand. By repositioning you will be blurring distinctions and diluting the brand value of both. You should be deriving all the synergies only in the back-end.'

Prof. Thirunarayana, independent director on the board of Deccan and professor of marketing at IIM-B, pointed out the danger of 'getting stuck in the middle', citing Michael Porter who had said that a brand loses its distinctiveness and positioning by doing so.

Vijay Mallya made a presentation to both our teams. In it he depicted *Deccan* in big red font. He said we should have a common colour: red. He proposed renaming *Air Deccan* as *Simplifly Deccan*. *Simplifly* was what the airline stood for. He said the Kingfisher bird mascot would appear on the tail of all aircraft and on buses to the airport. It would, he said, make it easier to drive synergies.

During the break, I asked my team to consider the suggestions and come up with their own assessment. I wanted not servile agreement but rational deliberation; a meaningful, well-reasoned decision.

The teams met separately and deliberated. Most new entrants to my marketing team said they liked the new look. They felt that by 'sexing' it up we would be able to get a customer shift and re-woo those we had lost because of our 'shoddy' appearance. They believed that the refurbished image would allow us to charge a little more. This came as a surprise to me, but the discussions took place in a spirit of openness, and based on them

I agreed to rebrand. But in hindsight now, I think I probably should not have agreed.

I asked myself what it would cost to re-brand the airline; was it affordable on such a large scale? We were losing money; Mallya was losing money. The re-branding was estimated to cost the company upward of Rs 70 crores. It involved refurbishing points of sale and customer relations in sixty-five airports; the creation of new signage, new uniforms, and new airport counters, and repainting aircraft in third-country destinations and the concomitant loss of revenue. It was a huge cost. We had not done any financial analysis to determine the affordability of the exercise. Wasn't there a cheaper way of re-branding?

Vijay Mallya was confident it would be good for Deccan and good for Kingfisher. He asked me not to worry about the money; he would pump it in. Eventually however the money spent was not Kingfisher's but came from the Deccan account—not from the cash flow but from the precious equity Mallya had injected. This aggravated Deccan's losses.

There was another development that was eroding Deccan's character: One-rupee tickets had been stopped. Kingfisher had directed the revenue management team to maintain the minimum fare at a level higher than Rs 500.

I learnt that all the airlines had come together and marked up the minimum fare on all flights, and the fare distinction between them and Deccan had blurred. This was cartel price-fixing which I had opposed earlier. The association of Indian airlines had earlier met to discuss a minimum price structure for all airlines. I was the target of the entire discussion agenda because Deccan had dynamic pricing. I opposed the minimum price-fixing because it did not reflect the costs of individual airlines. I said that if a full-legacy service airline fixed its bottom price at the same level as an LCC, passengers would migrate to the FSA. I also pointed out that it represented cartelization of the industry. There was no legal bind in India, with the exception of the somewhat mild one relating to the MRTP Act. I had stormed out of that meeting. Now all the airlines had got together and fixed a minimum entry level fare and called it fuel surcharge to avoid being accused of price-fixing, which was what it was.

Now that the new revenue management team had agreed to fare-fixing, the entry level fare became Rs 2900, reducing the difference between a low-cost carrier airline and a full-service one to about Rs 400 to Rs 500. If an LCC and FSA have the same entry level fares, the occupancy or load factor tilts in favour of the full-service carriers. The low-cost carriers succumbed to the pressure tactics of full-service airlines and raised the fare hoping to cut their losses. They cut down loss-making routes but did not redeploy the aircraft to maintain utilization. Reduced asset-utilization of aircraft meant the cost per kilometre rose, and this had to be recovered from the fewer numbers of passengers flying the airlines. That meant higher fares. When you fly a larger number of hours, the aircraft is more useful, as are HR, management, airport services and space, fixed costs, insurance, and pilots with fuller utilization. An airline achieves a multiplier effect through cost savings.

I had bitter arguments with Vijay Mallya, describing this was hara-kiri. If we did not cut costs things would billow out of control.

The Kingfisher management thought they could attract more customers by adding frills. They decided to give free water on board Deccan and free newspapers. I opposed these moves. I said Kingfisher must be a better airline than Jet at a *lower* cost and that Deccan must be a better airline than other LCCs at a *lower* cost. My advice fell on deaf ears.

Almost a year down the line, when the Kingfisher management was rooting for additional frills and the Deccan management felt bulldozed and losses were mounting, Vijay Mallya came up and did a conjuring trick and plucked a rabbit out of a hat. He said he had yet another market research exercise and said the results showed that he was losing money because of the Deccan brand.

Mallya's market research had put the blame for his losses on Deccan, but that very month CNBC gave Deccan a consumer award based on a survey by an independent agency across sixty-five airports. Deccan received the award for its on-time performance, connectivity, and routing network. This was not a rigged award. They had hired a third-party consumer research and survey company which had interviewed consumers and judged the airlines on a variety of parameters.

Vijay Mallya sought to convince me and the board of directors that his survey results correlated losses and the Deccan brand and, by implication the low fares. The results suggested that the Deccan image did not allow us to raise fares so we were losing money. In reality the contrary was actually true, and this had become quite patent: when you increase costs and fares while promoting a low-cost model, losses increase due to falling occupancy. Vijay Mallya leveraged the results of the market research to suggest that we should re-brand again to evoke a closer association with Kingfisher, akin to Kingfisher Lite or Kingfisher Red.

I was opposed to this move and thought Vijay Mallya was behaving like Tughlak who changed his capital twice. I reminded him about his earlier mindset. 'We have just changed the brand once spending seventy crores,' I reminded him. 'You had wanted to use the Kingfisher bird logo on Deccan aircraft. You had then said that *Simplifly* is the best possible brand name and that everyone you spoke to said Deccan was the most vibrant brand.'

He said, addressing me, 'You know Gopi, when I get off my private jet the first thing I do is take a look at the garbage bin at the airports. You know what I find there? Torn and discarded Deccan baggage tags. It is clear that passengers are ashamed of travelling on Deccan.' I got back on that, saying, 'Vijay, people shopping at Wal Mart do not display their shopping as if displaying a Louis Vuitton. Wal Mart is nonetheless the largest retailer and the biggest brand in the world. A passenger on Ryan Air might throw away his baggage tag too, but Ryan Air is in profit.'

Vijay Amritraj was sitting on the board meeting that day. Pointing to Vijay Amritraj, I said, 'If Vijay Amritraj here lost his Wimbledon matches, he should improve his game by training and by working hard. He has to change his game and not his name to win the match. I also had this friend of mine who went through a bad financial patch. An astrologer told him to change his name because the numerology of his current name did not augur well. Instead of working out a solution for his financial woes, my friend changed his name. He had to make out affidavits, intimate various agencies, change his ID card, passport and bank particulars. My friend went about wasting time and money on a name change and went bankrupt.'

Vijay Mallya, however, sincerely believed the brand was preventing him from making money. His way out of the crisis was that he would spend Rs 500; make it look like Rs 5000, and charge more. However, the actual way out for LCCs, as Ryan Air had demonstrated, was to innovate; to use and leverage technology to bring about higher asset utilization. Airlines have negotiated crises by the deployment of technology. Airlines have used innovation, staying power, resilience, and courage. I argued with Vijay Mallya that as oil prices and airport handling prices had risen and average flight occupancy was 50 per cent, we had to do hawkish cost-cutting. He did not however listen.

I then realized that it was better for one man to run the company, and that anything was better for the company than conflict. Besides, the thought crossed my mind that he had put in a 1000 crores and that had to be respected. This coincided with the time that Vijay Mallya requested me to tell the heads of engineering, revenue management, and airport services to report to him directly. That would allow him to coordinate with them and accrue higher revenues. I agreed and picked up the phone to tell my management team what Vijay Mallya wanted them to do and asked them to report to him.

This was a moment of trauma for my team. Senior management like Reshma, head of logistics, Vijaya Lucose, head of in-flight, Capt. Preetham Philip and Capt. Sam came over to my office. They had tears in their eyes.

They were attached to Deccan and hurt by the way Kingfisher was operating which had very little of Deccan's core values.

Vijay Mallya rapidly implemented his new strategy, entirely altering the pricing philosophy. A lower bound for fares was implemented and early-bird fares ended. Occupancy was no longer as important as it had hitherto been. Unviable routes were cancelled but the aircraft were not redeployed to maintain the old utilization levels. Kingfisher flights were rescheduled to precede Deccan flight departures. On many routes the Deccan flights were completely stopped. This caused migration from Deccan to other LCCs such as Spicejet or Indigo rather than Deccan to Kingfisher which had been hoped for. On routes flying both Deccan and Kingfisher, passengers who did not need the frills moved to Deccan.

There were other unintended consequences of subsuming Deccan under the Kingfisher brand. A repainting and brand-changing exercise began a second time, and in full earnest. The blue and yellow logo and name of Air Deccan were repainted red. The name on some was changed to Kingfisher Red. This was an expensive affair.

I worried that changing the name of Deccan to Kingfisher Lite or Kingfisher Red would cause brand blurring. Not finding much distinction, passengers travelling Kingfisher Economy would fly Kingfisher Red or Lite. A similar appearance and feel would create cannibalistic competition for the mother brand. Mallya was creating trouble for himself. I told him that this was exactly what happened when British Airways set up Go and KLM set up Buzz. Both airlines eventually killed their low-cost subsidiaries. People stopped using the parent brand as there were cheaper fares on the subsidiary. Singapore Airlines set up Tiger Airways bearing in mind the need to maintain a distinction from the parent brand. Qantas has a similar approach: its Jetstar is a very distinct brand.

Vijay Mallya and I were heading for a major conflict. I told him as gently as I could, but without mincing my words. 'Vijay,' I told him, 'whatever happens there is something I must say to you. It is about the people who surround you, the majority of whom, with the exception of one or two, are sycophants. This could prove to be a major weakness in the future.'

I said nothing after that, but we remained good friends. He was likeable on a personal level. He argued his case very strongly, I mine. One day he said that if this was where we were headed, it would be best to merge the two companies.

I believed a merger would lead to a loss of shareholder value and an erosion of the Deccan brand. He, however, insisted that it was the best way forward, and the decision to merge became a foregone conclusion.

Vijay Mallya made it clear he wanted to run the company the way he thought fit. He changed its name and the business model. The merger had to be fair to both sides, I said that if Deccan suffered, he would suffer too. I had not sold my stocks but the grapevine had got it wrong and it was rumoured that it was a sell-off. It was as though Deccan's life system was being extinguished.

I agreed to the merger. He would have bulldozed his way to that had I not, having consolidated his holding to 51per cent. I could have dug in my feet and created a rift. That would have damaged the company irrevocably. It was with deep pain and sorrow that I agreed to the merger.

The merger had to be approved by the board, the shareholders, the banks, suppliers, and lessors who were creditors, and the Karnataka High Court. We needed to figure out the holding structure in the helicopter company, Deccan Aviation, the parent company which I had first founded. Mallya said he would hive off the helicopter company into a separate company, which I could run independently. He would not stand in the way. We made a deal. He would have a minority shareholding in the helicopter company and I could have the majority shareholding. He would be chairman and I would be the vice chairman of the merged airline entity to be called Kingfisher Airlines.

We held several board meetings before we took the decision to merge the two companies. There was a real danger that the low-cost model would die. I received thousands of mails from people. Passengers across the country wrote to me; MPs and ministers, journalists, to some of whom I had become quite close, wrote personal notes to me, about how they felt. They all said they had come to identify with Deccan as an airline that was their own. They said they felt sorry for the passengers who had patronized Deccan and that though they were not sure, the merger would probably put an end to the old dream.

As a first-generation entrepreneur, I had developed a strong sense of identification with Deccan. Obsessive attachment makes it difficult for the entrepreneur to allow his enterprise to develop along professional lines. Equity can also be an obsession and can shackle the entrepreneur. It is better to have a small stake in a multi-billion-dollar company than have big stake in a small company. There is always the danger, when one clings to a small company, that a bigger player will come along, introduce better technology, and wipe you out of the market space. On one hand, my heart bled for Deccan which was slipping out of my hands; on the other, I felt an irrepressible urge to build a very large company on the lines of Infosys or Larsen & Toubro. That dormant desire was now awakening.

Before I could begin to dream anew, I had to resolve one nagging thought: the future of the retail shareholders in the company owning 200, 500, or 1000 shares. At shareholder meetings in the initial stages, they used to ask me: 'Captain, we admire you and will follow you as a messiah, but enlighten us about one matter: when will the stock appreciate? When will we make money?' I used to say: 'I cannot say when, but we definitely will. You have to believe in me.'

The growth of Deccan was indeed inspirational, but not being able to give a clear answer to the shareholders made me feel guilty. Beyond a point one gives oneself over to the tide of destiny. Some shareholders were unhappy about Deccan's low-fares policy. Happily, notwithstanding all the turmoil within the Kingfisher–Deccan combine, the wheel of fortune halted at a favourable destination. The promise I had made to shareholders was not belied. Just ahead of the Deccan–Kingfisher merger, Deccan stocks peaked at Rs 330 per share and the Deccan market cap reached a dizzying, bizarre 1.1 billion US dollars. Though I knew the market capital of the company may not be the true worth of the company, I felt redeemed that investors who had reposed faith got good returns. And many original investors including Ladhani, institutional investors and retail investors exited and reaped rich returns.

My own shares, because I had never sold them, and Capt. Sam's shares amounted to quite substantial a sum. I decided to channel the proceeds into a new company which I was incubating and begin all over again. Sam came over and said 'Gopi, you can use my stock in the way you consider fit.' When I had nothing, I built Deccan. What I had in hand now, a princely sum, would allow me to begin all over again. I thought of Kipling's poem 'If' kept on my desk in NDA and decided to pitch everything on a new venture I was incubating.

> If you can keep your head when all about you
> Are losing theirs and blaming it on you;
> If you can trust yourself when all men doubt you,
> But make allowance for their doubting too;
> If you can wait and not be tired by waiting,
> Or, being lied about, don't deal in lies,
> Or, being hated, don't give way to hating,
> And yet don't look too good, nor talk too wise;
> If you can dream—and not make dreams your master;
> If you can think—and not make thoughts your aim;

If you can meet with triumph and disaster
And treat those two imposters just the same;
If you can bear to hear the truth you've spoken
Twisted by knaves to make a trap for fools,
Or watch the things you gave your life to broken,
And stoop and build 'em up with worn-out tools;
If you can make one heap of all your winnings
And risk it on one turn of pitch-and-toss,
And lose, and start again at your beginnings
And never breathe a word about your loss;
If you can force your heart and nerve and sinew
To serve your turn long after they are gone,
And so hold on when there is nothing in you
Except the Will which says to them: 'Hold on';
If you can talk with crowds and keep your virtue,
Or walk with kings—nor lose the common touch;
If neither foes nor loving friends can hurt you;
If all men count with you, but none too much;
If you can fill the unforgiving minute
With sixty seconds' worth of distance run—
Yours is the Earth and everything that's in it,
And—which is more—you'll be a Man my son!

—Rudyard Kipling

[Poem framed and placed on every cadet's writing desk at the NDA]

13

Fortune favours the brave.

—Virgil

A New Adventure Beckons

During the trying last months before the merger I had begun to incubate a company. It was a logistics company, floated in response to harrowing experiences we had in the early days of Air Deccan. The source of these experiences was spare parts. For want of a spare part, even something as small as a propeller blade, flights were delayed, even grounded. We had these parts airlifted from foreign suppliers. Parts from anywhere in world arrive in Mumbai within twenty-four hours, but from Mumbai, if you committed the package to the logistics system operational in India, it took from two to twenty days for it to reach a small city such as Guwahati or Jabalpur or Jammu. This bothered me and I felt a buzz like that which I had felt when I thought of starting Deccan. I realized there was no cargo airline flying to small cities.

One day, a flight from Delhi to Kolkata was hit by a foreign object. The pilot lost use of an engine in mid-flight. Losing use of an engine in this way is not uncommon for pilots. Bird or debris hits or, fire or malfunction can disable an engine, whereupon the pilot switches to the second one. On that occasion, however, I was on edge when I heard the news and remained very nervous till it landed safely. Once the aircraft landed in Kolkata, the pilot and the engineer took a walk around. They noticed that one engine was completely damaged by a bird hit. Deccan had high asset utilization in those days. The moment a plane landed one set of passengers disembarked and another set embarked. On rare occasions passengers were made to wait because some problem had arisen. In the Kolkata incident, 180 passengers were ready to board. As they were getting into the coach, the engineer called to say the flight had been cancelled.

There was a near riot at the airport. Passengers broke our airport counters and manhandled our staff. Television crew covered this ugly incident. We had no spare aircraft and it could take up to twenty-four hours to change the engine. We had a spare engine each in Delhi and in Bengaluru but not in Kolkata. A brand new engine costs about $15 million. We would find it prohibitively costly to locate a spare engine in all the fifty cities to which we were flying. This is a problem for logistics and inventory management.

Efficient and express logistics support is usually provided by a company that has integrated air-cargo and ground-cargo facilities. An engine cannot be sent by road. It would have taken seven days to reach the destination, and because the road conditions are poor, one loses the warranty on the engine, if it is sent by road. If for any reason you decide to send it by road, the part has to be placed on air-cushioning and transported very slowly. On that occasion we decided to send the engine by air. It took us an entire day to figure out how to send it by air. My team could not find an operator to fly it to Kolkata because none of the aircrafts available in India had the capability to lift an engine.

Blue Dart is the only cargo-cum-logistics company in India but it did not have an aircraft which could accommodate the engine. FedEx came only to Mumbai and Delhi, and were not permitted to operate anywhere else in India. We were in a bind. Someone suggested the Russian Antonov. We contacted an agent in Dubai but the agent asked for a quarter of a million dollars to be deposited in advance. It would take three days to get an aircraft from Russia. It was frustrating.

Eventually a solution was found and we sent the engine from Delhi to Kolkata. How did we accomplish this? We sent the engine from Delhi to Singapore and from Singapore to Kolkata via Singapore Airlines Cargo. It took all of six days!

For six whole days we had lost revenue on the grounded aircraft, an Airbus-320 which undertook 6–7 flights a day. It was traumatic. We cancelled the flights, faced irate passengers, and refunded their money. In the process it tarnished our reputation.

I saw that there was no end-to-end logistics company operating to the smaller cities in India. What logistics support we had in the country served only the metro circuit and ignored the smaller cities. I saw this as a great opportunity. Once I began thinking in this direction, I realized that the world's largest airlines are not passenger carriers but logistics companies. It was not Lufthansa, not Air France, but FedEx and UPS. These logistics companies together own about 1600 aircrafts. FedEx and UPS together earn revenues of over $90 billion a year, and operate in 200 countries. I had read about how Fred Smith built this great company, FedEx.

Fred Smith first wrote about the hub-and-spokes model of logistics in his MBA dissertation. There is a story about the source of the basic idea but it could be apocryphal. Fred Smith, as this story goes, had heard about the Indian Posts using Nagpur as a hub for sorting and redistributing mail.

Nagpur is at the geographical centre of India. The Survey of India has a pillar marking this crossing of latitude and meridian. Indian Airlines flights emanating from different destinations used to halt there briefly at night before undertaking the onward journeys. These flights, it is said, used to carry mail emanating from different centres, presumably from Chennai, Thiruvananthapuram, Hyderabad, Mumbai, Kolkata, Jaipur, and Delhi. The planes were parked next to one another in a row. From their cargo holds, ground-handlers would remove large bags of mail and deliver them to the postal hub at the terminal. There, postmen sorted the mail, placed them in new bags, and had them reloaded into the cargo holds of the destination carriers. This is the experience from which Fred Smith is said to have drawn his blueprint for FedEx. Fred Smith got a C Grade for his MBA dissertation but he went on to build the largest integrated logistics carrier in the world and changed the way the world does business.

The bank, the Internet and the mobile phone all operate in a similar fashion. Tokens were sent from source points to a central hub, sorted there, and re-sent to target points. In the case of a bank, if you issue a local cheque of your bank to a service-provider in your neighbourhood who uses a different bank, his bank branch sends the cheque to a common centre called the clearing house. At this common point representatives of different banks come to match and reconcile cheques issued with the relevant accounts, and send or take away mutual advices to honour or dishonor cheques drawn on their banks. On the Internet, if you are sending email to a friend or colleague in the office, the electronic stream of bits is first sent to a server that could be anywhere in the world. The server acts as the central hub where your email addressee is located and the mail is sent out to him/ her. In offices, emails are often sent between colleagues sitting across the aisle from each other. On the mobile phone, too, your signal is sent to a common point in the neighbourhood and forwarded to the receiver, who could actually be in another part of the same house!

The philosophy of logistics companies like Blue Dart Express, an Indian cargo company that has now been acquired by German cargo company DHL, and FedEx and UPS, has been to link India with the rest of the world. Their focus was import and export and their mandate was not integrating India. There was not a single air cargo carrier going to Jamshedpur or Coimbatore; the six metros were their destination, and that was it.

The idea of a cargo carrier aimed at the small Indian cities—got into my head some time during those five days spent waiting for the engine to be airlifted to Kolkata from Delhi via Singapore.

The transport of the engine from Delhi to Kolkata via Singapore, which had given us all a nightmare, had nothing to do with the customs but the officials had got involved. They asked us why we were sending out an engine to Singapore and bringing it back to India without any repair work being done on it. The customs authorities refused to believe that in India we did not have the capacity to send the engine safely and without damage from Delhi to Kolkata. It took a lot of painstaking and patient convincing.

It was another eureka moment. Without another thought I reached for the phone and called a Belgium-based friend of mine, Thierry Lindenau of Spencer Stuart, who had helped me source my COO Warwick Brady for Air Deccan. I said: 'Thierry find a CEO for me, either from FedEx or UPS or DHL.'

It took me just an instant to decide that I would start a complete end-to-end logistics company. I was not keen to set up an air-cargo company. Air-cargo is different. I had no idea then that Deccan would be merged and was confident that Deccan would stabilize in the course of two or three years. Once it had grown big, there would be no challenge for me so I would set up another company. The idea had been conceived; it took hold of me and took on a life of its own.

It was six months before Thierry and I could find a CEO. I interviewed people from across the world and selected Jude Fonseka who had been with FedEx for over twenty years. I told Jude that this time around I wanted to do things differently. There were huge lessons to be drawn from Deccan. There had been mistakes. Here was an opportunity for us to build a new company with the right DNA. I was going to be its chairman and play the role of investor and incubator. I would obtain the licences and the seed money. Jude wouldn't have to waste his time with ministers and the bureaucracy. He had a clear mandate. He would bring in a team, he had two years to build it up, and I would monitor and guide him. I said I wanted to build a company with good corporate governance and build a solid infrastructure for India.

Immediately after deciding on Jude as CEO, I made a call to Mohan Kumar and asked him to take charge of the new company and guide and show Jude the way.

I told Jude that our factories and industries were deep in the interiors; that farmers had apple farms in Jammu, reared fish in Gujarat and Kerala, and grew rice in Punjab. Large parts of India were languishing for want of logistics connectivity. Industries and agriculture ran sub-optimally and were desperate for logistics support. The new company would integrate the country into a seamless technology platform ranging from—transport and delivery to warehousing. India needed it more than ever. India was over a trillion-dollar economy and its GDP was growing at a frenetic pace but we had only five dedicated cargo aircrafts, all with Blue Dart Express, while China had a hundred.

This was also a time when the major cities had grown hugely and it had become difficult to find space for expansion of manufacturing facilities or service hubs. Existing manufacturers and service-providers were moving out of cities and towns to relocate in rural centres. This was profitable too for many major companies, because it meant the release of a lot of expensive real estate in the urban centres, for more profitable use. They were attracted to the new special economic zones (SEZ) being set up everywhere, to which the government was offering tax holidays and other subsidies such as land at inexpensive prices or free.

When I was incubating the new company, I told Vijay Mallya that I was stepping out to take charge of my new company, Deccan Cargo and Logistics. Vijay Mallya said, 'Why do you want to do that? Why don't you go and retire to your farm?' I said, 'Vijay, that is like asking Subbulakshmi not to sing or Ravi Shankar not to play the sitar.'

Vijay Mallya offered to pay compensation if I signed a no-competition agreement undertaking not to start anything in the aviation sector because Kingfisher would be in cargo, in MRO, and other such areas. I said, 'Yes, I will sign a no-competition agreement undertaking not to set up an airline, but as I said I'm an entrepreneur and will do that which gives me the adrenalin rush; what gives meaning to life. I will build and create; I will start all over again.'

Under the no-competition contract, I agreed not to start another airline but I would not be restricted in spaces in which he was not operating. I told him I should be free to use the Deccan name because he was in any case extinguishing it.

I also told Vijay Mallya that Kingfisher would need Deccan to survive because the consumer before migrating to Deccan was travelling by train. It was a natural progression from a train to a low-cost airline, and from a LCC to a full-service airline. I cited C.K. Prahalad, 'Wealth in India gets created at the top. But the top of the pyramid cannot survive unless the middle and the bottom of the pyramid are thriving.' For Rahul Bajaj, for example, to be able to buy a Mercedes Benz and dine at the Oberoi and fly his own business jet, he would have to sell motorcycles and scooters to millions and millions of common middle-class individuals. Unless you have a huge ecosystem where there is a vibrant middle-class with disposable income, wealth does not get created at the top.

I realize that the task ahead is daunting: the venture is huge. On the day we launch, we will be twice the size of our nearest competitor. We will have greater cargo capacity and twice the reach. We will integrate large parts of India to the metros. We will go where the industry is going, we will go where the SEZs are going, we will go to states like Chhattisgarh and Uttarakhand. Hero Honda is setting up industry in Himachal and Bajaj in Uttarakhand. These states are offering incentives. We will go to ports like Kandla and Tuticorin which are desperate for connectivity. This venture will be larger than Deccan ever was.

I have acquired 50 acres in Nagpur to set up a cargo hub. I chose Nagpur over Hyderabad because we got resources and land from the government of Maharashtra on easy terms. Nobody wanted to go to Nagpur so the government gave us a special package. Nagpur is in the heart of underdeveloped Vidarbha. It is underdeveloped because there is no connectivity and no infrastructure there. I have decided to be at the forefront of creating infrastructure there and with infrastructure will come investment. Nagpur will become India's central warehousing hub.

I have plunged headlong and invested all I had. Many of my friends remarked that I must be crazy, and advised that I should simply return to my farm and settle down. They want me to go and play golf, perhaps buy an island. The challenge for me is in building; in creating wealth. It is a criminal waste to keep money idle. It is not in my blood or heart to put money in stocks.

Successful business people became successful because they took risks. The biggest risk is that once successful, they stop taking risks. I become insecure if I cannot take risks. Without risks life becomes meaningless, and would imply that I had courage when I built up Deccan, but that now have become timid because I wish to protect my wealth. I find any such thought disturbing and I say to myself: 'It's a criminal waste of money to lock it up. Like Ulysses, I must start all over again.'

With Jude and a large number of people from the aviation side of Deccan who joined me with Capt. Preetham as their head, and a bunch of very bright kids who have joined me in the new venture, I repeat to myself the words: 'The journey of a thousand miles begins with a single step.'

The exhilaration lies in building and creating. I am embarking all over again on another great journey. With my old buddy Sam, ever in the background, and Jayanth and Vishnu, taking over the reins of Deccan, the future beckons. There is great adventure in store for the future.

> I cannot rest from travel; I will drink
> Life to the lees: All times I have enjoy'd
> Greatly, have suffer'd greatly, both with those
> That loved me, and alone...
> To strive, to seek, to find, and not to yield.
>
> —Lord Alfred Tennyson

GOPI'S FARM

GOPI'S FARM

Henry Mintzberg

Gopi grins a lot. So I didn't take him seriously when I met him. That was my first mistake.

Gopi lives in the city, where he does his deals, and escapes to his farm, where he grows coconuts. So I took him to be a gentleman farmer. That was my second mistake.

The city is Bengaluru, in southern India. Bustling Bengaluru, where Gopi bustles. Now it's helicopters. And bread. Before that irrigation systems. Honda dealerships before that. And lots more before that.

Deccan Aviation, 'Your limousine in the sky,'—will do almost anything its helicopters can do. Like just getting to Bengaluru the first time, from Singapore. Gopi signed the contract ten minutes before the helicopter had to take off. He and his partner pilot flew it over Malaysia, then Thailand, then Myanmar, then Bangladesh, and finally down the Indian subcontinent, stopping every few hundred kilometres—twenty times in five days—for liquid refreshments. A very thirsty helicopter indeed. 'No destination is impossible. No boundaries exist,' Deccan's promotion claims, with some authority. They have six helicopters now, or at least they did when I wrote this, only to get an e-mail that Gopi was expecting three more.

Bread was in the family, at least in K.T.'s family (a famous old bakery in Bengaluru). K.T. married Gopi's sister. Franchising is the thing—Gopi decided—so now he takes care of that. He would like to open one in London. You have to call it 'Gopi's Bakery,' I kid him, and be sure to put underneath, 'Let them eat bread.'

Bhargavi is Gopi's wife. She runs production. Ye Gods, I thought before I met Bhargavi, he's married to a bakery boss. Poor Gopi. That was another mistake. Bhargavi is small and adorable. You would never guess that she runs a bakery, let alone is the mother of Pallavi, aged 17, whose soft, shy look could stop a helicopter, and Krithika, 11, who dances around the house like a little lady Gopi.

The Gopi family is urban. So I was surprised when, shortly after meeting Bhargavi on our way to buy a couple of bicycles said, 'I miss the farm so much.' There were almost tears in her eyes.

It's four hours to the farm by car, and with the kids in school (which is why they moved to Bengaluru) Bhargavi rarely gets back there for more than a few days at a time. You will understand her feelings when you find out how Bhargavi came to the farm.

Captain Gorur R. Iyengar Gopinath left the Indian Army at the age of 27, thanks to a signature he wrangled out of some high official. He returned home to find his native village in crisis. A dam had been built that flooded the ancestral lands. The government paid compensation, but that was only money and quickly being used-up. Other land was offered, but at some distance, and suspected by everyone. Except Gopi. He decided to go have a look. So he hopped on a motorcycle, and when the road ended, he walked the last four kilometres through the bush. He came back and offered to buy everyone's land for deferred payment in five years. Better than nothing, they agreed.

Gopi was determined to grow coconuts on that land. So he took a kid named Raju from the village, pitched an army tent, and they began to plant little coconut trees. Then the rains came, and carried the little coconut trees away. So they began again, planting them earlier and more solidly. In the dry season, with no sign of the promised electricity, Gopi and Raju carried water to the trees by hand, one pail on each side. A thousand little trees each thirsty for about four pitchers of water a week.

Almost a year of that and Gopi began to dream of donkeys. So he found a deal—four donkeys for ninety rupees each (about $7 in those days). He got his money's worth: they were even less enthusiastic about carrying water than Gopi, and, tired of grazing, they insisted on eating the beans Gopi had grown to sell. The local farmers come to look and laugh. Mercifully the electricity arrived soon after.

When the time came to get Gopi married, a match was proposed, in proper Indian fashion. Bhargavi and her mother and sisters set out in a bullock-cart to visit the farm. Gopi loves to tell that story. (Actually Gopi loves to tell all his stories.) Bullock-carts have two huge wooden wheels that rock back and forth through the ruts. So it's a good idea to put in the little pins that keep the wheels in place. Otherwise a proposed marriage could end up in the mud. Well, on arrival, after an hour of this rocking, it was discovered that someone forgot to put in the pins. Someone else, apparently, was looking after Gopi and Bhargavi.

But they were not out of the mud yet. Bhargavi's mother took one look at the scene and warned her daughter off this crazy marriage. Coconut trees take ten years to mature; what would they eat in the meantime, and in a tent at that? But proper Indian marriage or not, Bhargavi had made up her mind. So Gopi got a wife as determined as he.

They planted coconut trees together, Gopi and Bhargavi, and gradually earned their farm. In the meantime, they lived off silk cocoons, and in a mud house with a thatched roof that Gopi was able to build in place of the tent. After Pallavi came along, and had to go to school, the family moved to Hassan, near Bhargavi's village, where Gopi started to do his deals. Later they moved to Bengaluru, a bigger city with better schools and bigger deals, while they continued to tend the land they love.

Like lots of people who do deals, Gopi wears a Rolex watch. Like them, he's proud of his watch. But they bought their watches. Gopi earned his.

On the back is inscribed 'The Rolex Award for Enterprise,' with Gopi's name. But not for the kind of enterprise you might imagine. This international award was in recognition of Gopi's contribution to organic farming. The fancy book that accompanied the watch cites his work to 'expand ecological silk-farming to improve living standards.' It explains that, after failing with various crops, followed by dismal results with silkworm-rearing, Gopi 'switched his approach radically'.

There followed a string of innovations. To grow mulberry berries to feed the silk worms, 'Gopinath ... does not plough the land. Instead he covers it with a thick carpeting of mulch ...' (One newspaper wrote that the Rolodex Awards are given to people who 'break new ground'.) Moreover, 'Gopinath protects his silkworms without powdered disinfectants or fungicides .... To keep out rats, he instilled a low electrified fence outside. Mosquito nets guard access to the rearing houses. Water channels prevent ants from invading the premises.'

Gopi sent me a big pile of articles on his organic farming, some written by him, others about him. There are technical papers presented at conferences and practical papers published in farmers' magazines. A comment Gopi made to a national newspaper, The *Hindu*, shows how he thinks.

> Farmers and people from the agricultural department advised me to keep the soil 'clean' and use chemicals to prevent termite attack. I posed the question: If termites are indeed so lethal how could forests have survived over thousands of years? Termites ought to have slowly assaulted and reduced them to dust. But forests have survived. So have termites .... I supposed the termites must have lived off the litter and the debris that you find on the floor of the forests. I sought to create a similar environment here on the farm ... I dumped the debris closely around the trunk of the trees as mulch, hoping that the termites would find it as rewarding to

feed off the debris as off the trees. And, I discovered to my surprise that instead of attacking the trunk, the termites attacked the mulch and found it delicious. They left the trees alone.

Another article, in a magazine called The *March of Karnataka,* from his home state, tells about the water.

He noticed the depletion of ground water and the stream running along the farm going dry soon after rainy season. He had read about 'zero cultivation' resulting in increase of water table. A thirty feet width of land along the stream was left uncultivated. Soon shrubs began to grow ... and trees began to emerge. The weeds were left free. Soon the erosion was stopped. Water holding capacity increased. The microhabitat was revitalised. Insects, birds and earthworm population increased. Deposition of humus increased leading to increase in soil fertility. Water table shot up.

Anything but donkeys!

Gopi is a big fan of weeds and pests. Some weeds should be kept and recycled, he told a reporter. They 'indicate a healthy soil ...' And farmers should 'budget a portion of the harvest for insects and for rodents.' They 'aerate and enrich the soil with their droppings and carcasses. You can't kill the pests without killing the rest' he said, so 'we will not fret or get desperate at the sight of a rat nibbling a coconut, for instance, if we understand the intricate, benign workings of nature.' To Gopi the soil is not inanimate: 'agriculture,' he told another newspaper reporter, 'is not a physical science, but a life science.'

Back when I still knew Gopi as a gentleman farmer, he invited me to his farm. Actually, he lured me there with a proposal that we go bicycling, a deal he knew I couldn't refuse. He hadn't been on a bike since his army days, when one was issued to all the junior officers to get them around the base.

That is how I came to accompany Bhargavi to the bicycle store in Bengaluru. Better not an ordinary bike, I thought, for the likes of this Gopi I did not know. So we got two snazzy ones: semi-mountain bikes with five gears and flat handlebars. Next day, off we went, the bikes tucked into the back of a little van Gopi rented.

'It must have been quite a mess,' someone remarked later when I said I had been to an organic farm. Images of debris rotting naturally everywhere, not to mention all those weeds and pests. Another mistake.

We arrive at this lovely place—secluded, perfectly neat, beautifully cared for. Tall palm trees loaded with coconuts grace the entire area, the leaves crinkling gently in the wind. Another world. No wonder Bhargavi loves this place. We are greeted by a tall, handsome man (Raju is his name), still here, now looking after the whole operation. Various small buildings appear, including a proper Indian house now. You squat over the toilet, pour water on yourself for a shower, sleep on a hard bed, and have dinner outdoors by an open fire, under the palm trees, after a drink of sweet coconut juice with rum, Gopi's favourite. There are no deals here, and the mobile phone, like the worries, stopped working on the road from Bengaluru. (Gopi is a terror back in Bengaluru on his mobile phone.)

There is peace among the palm trees as we walk along at sunset, Gopi telling me stories non-stop, a farmful of stories. I hear about the leopard who came in at night and dragged off the dogs, one by one. (Sounds like the pest has become a pet.) He's still out here somewhere, Gopi assures me, like the cobras.

Most of the stories concern Gopi's experiments. He points to a ring around a tree, where the mess is ordered into that 'delicious' mulch for the insects. At one end of the farm, near the building where the silkworms are reared, Gopi shows me a structure with walls of plastic sheeting that can be rolled up and down, and the roof retracted. For years Gopi wanted to get his silkworms into an outdoor atmosphere, where they could be ventilated naturally. On television, he had seen the new dome stadiums with retractable roofs in America. But that was a little costly—even for Gopi. Then he came across these structures in Holland, where they are used for growing tulips. So he brought in a Dutch guy to build one here, to see if he could adapt it to his silkworms. Back at the house, sitting on the veranda, Gopi points to a lump of leaf hanging over us. It's a tree ant colony, he explains, and pokes a hole in it, lifting up a bit of the leaf to show me the activity inside. We watch in fascination as the ants pull back the bit and knit the tear closed in a few minutes.

Gopi takes special pride in picking up ideas from other farmers and feeding back what he finds out. 'Farmers from every nook and corner of the state visit his farm regularly,' wrote the *March of Karnataka* 'and he is always willing to give tips to modify their methods.' (I'll bet.) They still come to look, but no longer to laugh. Nonetheless Gopi is concerned that any talk of 'farming with nature' can make a person seem like a 'Luddite', on the 'fringe community of farmers'. Not that it stops him: you can't be 'a natural farmer in isolation when farmers all around you are spraying poison,' Gopi has written.

The next day we are off cycling. Can we find a quiet road, with not too much traffic, I had asked. You could say that Gopi has complied. Until mid afternoon, every vehicle we see is capable of running on grain: all three or four bullock-carts and bicycles.

'I'll bet he stopped and had to explain every tree to you,' his sister said to me, laughing, a few days later in Bengaluru. No, not *every* tree, I replied, not quite, although Gopi did explain every single mango tree in bloom (his special favourite). Actually Gopi has all sorts of favourites, so we were off the bikes more than on. When we stopped at an exquisite tree flowered with 'Flames of the Forest', Gopi said, 'I wish I were a bee Henry!' Helicopters with honey! I think he was serious.

Eventually we reach a small town where we visit a temple and get red dots on our foreheads from the Hindu priest, a friend of Gopi who invites us home for tea. After that, a brief stop for adjustments at a local bike shop brings out a crowd of kids; even the owner has never seen a bicycle with gears before. Then it's on to paved roads back to the farm, with the occasional bus and truck going by.

A kid follows us on his bike. What a pest. Go away kid, I think to myself. Then I hear an enthusiastic 'This is much better!' and I turn around to see a grinning Gopi on the kid's bike, a temporary deal having been struck to the delight of both parties.

Next day Gopi has arranged to visit his friend Sunil, who runs his family's coffee plantation a couple of hours farther west. So it's back in the van. The road is beautiful, surrounded by coconut farms (lots of coconut farms). This is a pretty competitive business, I think to myself. Not like helicopters.

When we arrive in mountainous country, with stunning scenery, I muse about cycling it. In no time it's decided. Next year we shall do just that, from Sunil's coffee plantation back to Gopi's farm. As we drive along, Gopi keeps upping the ante. We'll camp along the way, he says. Hey, how about if Raju drives ahead and sets up a tent at night. He can prepare dinner for our arrival (not to mention sweet coconut juice with rum). Maybe the family would like to come too. How about eight days? Mercifully the drive ends before he has us biking to Srinagar in the Himalayas.

Sunil has built himself a new house near the top of the mountain plantation. What a house! Marble everywhere, incredibly appointed, impeccably clean. We walk down to the valley where the coffee beans are being husked and washed. Sunil explains that chemicals are added to the residue for treatment before it is released into the river. I can hear Gopi's mind start up, like one of his helicopters. 'Why don't you just pump it back up the hill?' You are not allowed to do that, Sunil explains. There are rules about these things. Gopi is gazing off; 'rules' don't figure in his scheme of things.

The next day we walk through the plantation. The land is as clean as the house. But Gopi is looking beyond the cleanliness. His mind is on high gear, spinning off one suggestion after another.

He looks at the leaves, which are covered with white spots, and tells me that these are the most oversprayed places on earth. ('Coffee-growers drench their plantations with pesticides and fungicides … and saturate their crops with chemical fertilizer,' he had written in a newspaper.) 'Why don't you isolate one section and try different things?' Gopi says to Sunil, who replies, 'I should do that.'

Wait a minute, I think to myself. If this is a 'plantation', why is Gopi's place a 'farm'? On farms, you reap what you sow. On plantations, you reap some by-product of what you sow. If Gopi plants palm trees to harvest coconuts, what does he farm?

Then I remember yesterday, all those 'farms' along the road: coconuts are a competitive business. In Bengaluru, I can buy one—a big heavy coconut—for eight rupees.

And the guy cuts it open for me and throws in a straw. He will even carve a section out after I am done drinking to fashion a spoon so that I can scoop out the white stuff. All that, shipped all the way from these 'farms,' for eight rupees. Do you know how many coconuts it takes to get what Gopi gets for an hour in one of those limousines in the sky: ten thousand! No, Gopi can't be in it for the coconuts. The deal is just not sustainable. Yet Gopi is most determinedly in it. So what's the deal?

Then it hits me: Gopi *is* a farmer after all. His is not a plantation to grown coconuts; it's a farm to grow ideas. Conventional farmers exploit; Gopi explores. He plants experiments, fertilizes them with imagination, and harvests the ideas that take root. These he offers on the open market for the price of our attention.

If you think that's cheap, then you are making what could be our final mistake. For these ideas takes a great deal of human determination to exploit. It is so much easier to keep the environment clean by the application of chemicals. That is why the world is such a mess. And that is why I have written Gopi's story.

ACKNOWLEDGEMENTS

While many helped write this story, I must especially thank Pratyasha Singh, my colleague, who spent days and months transcribing 260 hours of recorded ramblings—seemingly an impossible task!

It is M.K. Shankar, a 'man of many parts' to whom I am indebted who edited the transcript and sat with me patiently for almost six months and rewrote it again and again with infinite patience and brought out a lucid account of the haphazard narrative. I cannot thank him enough—especially as he had to put up with my hectic and erratic schedule.

And my other dear colleague, Cecilia who has the patience of an angel, who must have typed all of 600 pages a million times for my proof reading again and again and again—as I still don't sit in front of a computer. Where would I be without her in today's hi-tech world.

And also Vijaya Menon, who assisted in all the publishing work, collecting and collating data and pictures and help keep the timeline.

INDEX

used 185000 fixed
term - 5 Yrs.

New 270000 fixed
term - 5 Yrs.

B7.